Institutional Change and Economic Development

The UNU World Institute for Development Economics Research (UNU-WIDER) was established by the United Nations University as its first research and training centre and started work in Helsinki, Finland, in 1985. The purpose of the institute is to undertake applied research and policy analysis on structural changes affecting developing and transitional economies, to provide a forum for the advocacy of policies leading to robust, equitable and environmentally sustainable growth and to promote capacity-strengthening and training in the field of economic and social policy-making. Its work is carried out by staff researchers and visiting scholars in Helsinki and via networks of collaborating scholars and institutions around the world.

World Institute for Development Economics Research (UNU-WIDER)
Katajanokanlaituri 6 B, FIN-00160 Helsinki, Finland
www.wider.unu.edu

UNITED NATIONS
UNIVERSITY

UNU-WIDER
World Institute for Development
Economics Research

Institutional Change and Economic Development

Edited by
HA-JOON CHANG
Faculty of Economics, University of Cambridge

United Nations University Press

TOKYO • NEW YORK • PARIS

ANTHEM PRESS
LONDON · NEW YORK · DELHI

HD
73
I568
2007

NORTH AMERICA AND GENEVA EDITION

This edition first published in the USA by
UNITED NATIONS UNIVERSITY PRESS, 2007
United Nations University Office at the United Nations, New York
2 United Nations Plaza, Room DC2-2062, New York, NY 10017, USA
Tel: +1-212-963-6387 Fax: +1-212-371-9454 E-mail: unuona@ony.unu.edu

United Nations University Press is the publishing division of the United Nations University.
United Nations University Press
United Nations University, 53-70, Jingumae 5-chome,
Shibuya-ku, Tokyo 150-8925, Japan
Tel: +81-3-3499-2811 Fax: +81-3-3406-7345 E-mail: sales@hq.unu.edu
General enquiries: press@hq.unu.edu • Web: http://www.unu.edu/unupress

Library of Congress Cataloging-in-Publication Data
Institutional change and economic development / edited by Ha-Joon Chang.
p. cm. "The chapters in the volume were all prepared for the UNU-WIDER project on
'Institutions and Economic Development:
Theory, History, and Contemporary Experiences.' An initial project planning meeting was
held in Oxford in March 2004. ...
The project meeting was held in April 2005 at WIDER in Helsinki"--P.
Includes bibliographical references and index.
ISBN-13: 978-9280811438 (pbk.)
1. Economic development--Congresses. 2. Institutional economics--Congresses. 3.
Economic policy--Congresses. I. Chang, Ha-Joon.
HD73.I568 2007
338.9--dc22
2007020214

ISBN: 978-92-808-1143-8 (North America and Geneva edition - Pbk)

UK / EUROPE / SOUTH ASIAN EDITION

Anthem Press
An imprint of Wimbledon Publishing Company
www.anthempress.com
This edition first published in UK, 2007
by ANTHEM PRESS
All rights reserved.

75–76 Blackfriars Road, London SE1 8HA, UK
or PO Box 9779, London SW19 7ZG, UK

A catalogue record for this book is available from the British Library.

ISBN: 978-1-84331-281-9 (UK edition – Pbk)

Cover illustration: Detail from 'Preparation of War to Defend Commerce'
by William Russell Birch, 1799. Courtesy of the Naval Historical Foundation.

1 3 5 7 9 10 8 6 4 2

Printed in the United States of America

Advance Reviews

"Just when the institutionalist approach to economic development is at risk of seeming like a 'black box' for tautological non-explanations, this volume of richly historically informed and nuanced studies will restore confidence in the value, if not superiority of this approach to the political economy of development."

Jomo K.S.,
Assistant Secretary-General for Economic Development, United Nations

"Much has been said about institutions in development, but this book takes us to a new level of analysis, with a very thorough understanding of the history and political economy of institution-building. Along the way it demolishes much of the conventional wisdom, and sets a new standard that all future research on institutions must match."

Tony Addison,
Executive Director of the Brooks World Poverty Institute, University of Manchester

"A thought-provoking and challenging analysis of the role of institutions in economic development. It is a necessary antidote to the orthodox writings on this subject. A must read."

Ajit Singh,
Professor of Economics, University of Cambridge

"There is a growing confluence of economic opinion on the centrality of institutions in the development process but few detailed comparative historical studies of the interface between their form, function and context. Ha-Joon Chang, under the sponsorship of WIDER, has assembled a cogent set of essays richly presenting a tapestry of institutional experiences from virtually every region of the world. The volume will prove to be an important resource to counter the latest institutional orthodoxies on governance and property rights coming from the World Bank and IMF as countries look beyond the latest fashions from the Bretton Woods organizations."

Howard Stein,
University of Michigan

CONTENTS

FIGURES

TABLES

CONTRIBUTORS

Nelson Henrique Barbosa-Filho, PhD, economist, is currently Deputy Secretary for Macroeconomic Policy at the Finance Ministry, Brazil, on leave from the Institute of Economics, UFRJ Federal University, Rio de Janeiro. His main research interests are macroeconomic policy, econometric modelling, and financial development.

Leonardo Burlamaqui, PhD, economist, is currently working with the Ford Foundation, New York, as Programme Officer (Governance and Civil Society; Global Economic Governance) on leave from UERJ State University, Rio de Janeiro. His main research interests are evolutionary economics, global economic governance, patterns of economic development, competition, innovation, and economic regulation.

Ha-Joon Chang is the Reader in the Political Economy of Development at the Faculty of Economics, University of Cambridge, UK.

Thomas David is Assistant Professor at the Institute of Economic and Social History, University of Lausanne, Switzerland, and previously a visiting scholar at the Center for European and Russian Studies, University of California (UCLA). With André Mach, and financed by the Swiss National Science Foundation, he co-directs a project on the Swiss elites during the twentieth century. His publications include a volume about the participation of Switzerland in the Atlantic Slave trade (*La Suisse et l'esclavage des Noirs*, Lausanne, 2005, with Bouda Etemad and Janick Marina Schaufelbuehl), and forthcoming, a book on the history of corporate governance in Switzerland (with Martin Lüpold, André Mach, and Gerhard Schnyder).

José Antonio Pereira de Souza, PhD, economist, is currently working as Economic Advisor to the Board of Directors at BNDES (National Bank for Economic and Social Development), and is Assistant Professor at Candido Mendes University, Rio de Janeiro. His research interests include financial development, technology, and the economic regulation of business.

Jonathan di John is a lecturer of Political Economy of Development in the Department of Development Studies at the School of Oriental and African Studies (SOAS), University of London. He is also a research fellow on the

Crisis States Research Programme at the London School of Economics. Dr di John's research focuses on the political economy of industrial policy and economic growth in Latin America, and the political economy of taxation and tax reform in less developed countries.

Gerald Epstein is Professor of Economics and founding Co-Director of the Political Economy Research Institute (PERI) at the University of Massachusetts, Amherst. His major areas of research are Macroeconomics and International Economics and his recent publications include two edited volumes (both Edward Elgar, 2005), *Financialization and the World Economy* and *Capital Flight and Capital Controls in Developing Countries.*

Peter B. Evans holds the Eliaser Chair of International Studies and is Professor of Sociology in at the University of California, Berkeley. He has worked for many years on the role of the state in promoting development, an interest reflected in his 1995 book *Embedded Autonomy: States and Industrial Transformation.* His current projects include a manuscript in progress on 'counter-hegemonic globalization' that focuses on the role of transnational social movements.

Julius Kiiza teaches the Political Economy of Development in the Department of Political Science and Public Administration at Makerere University. After his doctoral studies at the University of Sydney, Dr Kiiza won a prestigious fellowship to pursue postdoctoral studies at the University of Cambridge. He was recently a Visiting Professor (Dickinson College, USA) of the US Summer Institute working on the 'US Political Economy and the Global Economic System'. He has implemented several research projects financed by UNU-WIDER, DFID, the Global Development Network, and other agencies, and publishes in the areas of economic governance, institutional reform, and the political economy of development.

William Lazonick is Professor at the University of Massachusetts Lowell and Distinguished Research Professor at INSEAD (European Institute of Business Administration). He specializes in the study of industrial development and international competition. Currently he is writing a book on the implications of the 'new economy business model' for the evolution of high-tech employment opportunities in the United States. Many of his papers are available electronically at http://faculty.insead.edu/Lazonick/.

André Mach is Senior Lecturer in Comparative Political Economy at the Institute of Political and International Studies, University of Lausanne, Switzerland. His research areas include organized interests and business elites, Swiss corporate governance, industrial relations, competition policy, and more generally the impact of globalization on national policies.

Patrick Karl O'Brien, former Director of the Institute of Historical Research at the University of London and past president of the British Economic History Society, is now a Centennial Professor of Economic History at the London School of Economics where he acts as Convenor of GEHN (global economic history network) and teaches on the masters programme in global economic history. His publications in European, Egyptian, and global economic history are on his website. His current book is about regimes for the production of useful and reliable knowledge in Europe and China, 1368–1842.

Eric Rauchway is Professor of History at the University of California, Davis, and the author most recently of *Blessed Among Nations: How the World Made America (Hill and Wang, 2006), and Murdering McKinley: The Making of Theodore Roosevelt's America (Hill and Wang, 2003)*.

Erik S. Reinert is Professor of Technology Governance and Development Strategies at Tallinn University of Technology, Estonia, and heads The Other Canon Foundation, Norway (www.othercanon.org). His main research area is the theory of uneven development. His books include *How Rich Countries Got Rich and Why Poor Countries Stay Poor* (Constable, 2007) and *The Origins of Development Economics: How Schools of Economic Thought Have Addressed Development* (Zed, 2005, edited with Jomo K.S.).

John Toye has been successively a Professor of Development Economics at the universities of Wales, Sussex, and Oxford. He has also worked for the United Nations, as Director of the Globalization Division of UNCTAD Secretariat 1998–2000. He has written seven books, his first being *Public Expenditure and Development Policy in India* (Cambridge University Press, 1981) and his most recent being *The UN and Global Political Economy* (Indiana University Press, 2004, with Richard Toye).

Meredith Jung-En Woo is Professor of Political Science at the University of Michigan, USA. Her publications include *Race to the Swift* (Colombia University Press) and *The Developmental State* (Cornell University Press 1999).

Tianbiao Zhu is Associate Professor, Chair of the Department of Political Economy and Associate Dean of the School of Government, Peking University. He received his degrees from University of Sydney, Cambridge University, and Cornell University. His research focuses on political economy of development.

FOREWORD

Until not so long ago, the understanding of institutions in the profession of economics was, to say the least, limited. Economists treated institutions as a black box, in much the same way that they treated technology for some time. Yet orthodox prescriptions, advocated by multilateral institutions and bilateral donors, sought to harmonize the role and also the form of institutions across developing countries irrespective of space or time. The underlying presumption that one-size-fits-all was wrong. There are specificities in space: institutions are local and cannot be transplanted out of context. There are specificities in time: institutions need time to evolve and cannot be created by a magic wand. But this was not quite recognized.

There has been a discernible change in the situation since the 1990s as the role of institutions in economic development received increasing attention in the literature. This emerging interest is perhaps attributable to experience. Economic reforms that sought to focus on policies but neglected institutions met with failure. Economic liberalization that moved from over-regulated to under-governed systems led to financial crises. Economic conditionalities of lenders or donors who attempted to harmonize institutions across countries ran into difficulties. This experience coincided with developments in institutional economics, both orthodox and heterodox, which contributed to an understanding of institutions.

The recent recognition of the significance of institutions, even if late, is welcome. But there are unanswered questions. First, we do not know exactly what institutions in exactly what forms are necessary, or at least useful, for economic development in what contexts. Second, even where we understand what role particular institutions can play in economic development, we often do not know how to build such institutions. Indeed, much remains to be done, in theory and policy, to improve our understanding of the creation and evolution of institutions. This book endeavours to fill these intellectual gaps. In doing so, it makes a valuable contribution to our knowledge and understanding of the subject.

The structure of the volume is unusual. Its contents are new. The approach is different. The first part, which provides a theoretical overview, translates the abstract theoretical notions that underlie the present discussions on the role of institutions in economic development into more concrete terms that are relevant for policymakers. The second part, which considers the evolution of particular institutions, such as the bureaucracy, central banks, corporate governance, taxation systems, and legal traditions, with reference to a large number of countries over time and across space, enriches theoretical understanding by revealing aspects of real-life institutions that are unrecognized or neglected. The third part, which examines experiences that range from Britain, Switzerland and the United States in the industrialized world to Botswana, Mauritius, Uganda, Brazil, China, and Taiwan in the developing world, studies institutions in their national historical context to extract stylized facts and draw lessons from experience. Some other country experiences are also discussed in the theoretical and the thematic chapters, although not in as much depth as in the case-study chapters. These include Colombia, Costa Rica, El Salvador, Guatemala, Japan, Korea, Malaysia, and South Africa. Given the diversity and complexity of the subject, the study of institutions requires a multi-disciplinary if not inter-disciplinary approach. Thus, the contributors to the volume are drawn from a wide range of disciplines: economics, political science, history, sociology, public administration, and business management.

The findings that emerge from the study are valuable. Some deserve mention. Institutions can, and do, serve multiple functions, so that there is no simple relationship between a desired function and an institutional form. Appearances are deceptive, so that informal institutions based on local values and norms may be far more important than formal institutions. Institution building is not a technocratic exercise but an integral part of political processes. The human factor, actors and ideas, is critical in institutional change, so much so that institutions are often shaped by someone somewhere who made choices that were not obvious or expected. Institutional change is characterized by unintended consequences, positive or negative, and by intended perversions, for better or for worse. In spite of the differences, there are similarities between countries, so that there are lessons for building institutions: for instance, it may be more effective to start with desirable activities rather than with desirable institutions, the utility of institutions may change over time as catalysts may turn into road-blocks, and there are dangers implicit in an institutional over-dose as too much could be counter-productive.

The essential conclusion to emerge is that there is no simple formula for institutional development that countries can import or replicate. Different countries find different solutions at different times for similar problems. In fact, the study shows that real-life experiences of institutional development have been achieved through a mixture of deliberate imitation, or adaptation, of foreign institutions and local institutional innovations, sometimes deliberate and sometimes accidental. Even so, there is much that developing countries can learn, as latecomers, from what went wrong and what turned out right elsewhere in the past. It is also important to recognize that, in many ways, institutional development is a consequence rather than a cause of economic development. Yet, there is some interdependence between institutions and development that could, if concurrently pursued, make for a virtuous circle of cumulative causation.

This volume provides a sensible blend of high-brow theoretical constructs and down-to-earth empirical work to coax stylized facts and draw robust conclusions. It shows that, even in this inherently complex area, it is possible to extract some general principles that enrich our understanding, especially if we are willing to beyond the rather narrow theoretical and empirical confines of the orthodox discourse on institutions. By doing so, it injects some new ideas and fresh thinking into the study of institutional change and economic development.

Deepak Nayyar
Chair of the Board, UNU-WIDER, Helsinki
and
Professor of Economics, Jawaharlal Nehru University, New Delhi

ACKNOWLEDGEMENTS

The chapters in this volume were all prepared for the UNU-WIDER project on 'Institutions and Economic Development – Theory, History, and Contemporary Experiences'. An initial project planning meeting was held in Oxford in March 2004, between myself as the project director, and the three most senior authors, Peter Evans, Patrick O'Brien, and John Toye. Deepak Nayyar, the Chair of the WIDER Board (then the Vice-Chancellor of Delhi University, currently back to his old job as a professor of economics in Jawaharlal Nehru University) also took part in the meeting and provided very helpful inputs. The project meeting was held in April 2005 at WIDER in Helsinki. In addition to the authors of the chapters, Deepak Nayyar, Jomo K.S. (Assistant Secretary-General, Department of Economic and Social Affairs, United Nations), Thandika Mkandawire (Director, United Nations Research Institute for Social Development), Ajit Singh (University of Cambridge), and Howard Stein (University of Michigan) participated as discussants and provided very helpful comments.

The subsequent process of revision and editing benefited greatly from the support of WIDER staff. Tony Shorrocks, the director of WIDER, and the members of the Board of WIDER, to whom I reported the progress of the project in their June 2005 meeting, provided encouragement and extremely useful critical reflections on the project. Tony Addison, the Deputy Director of WIDER (and now Professor of Development Studies at the Institute for Development Policy and Management, University of Manchester), not only provided the administrative oversight but also critical intellectual inputs to the project. Adam Swallow, the Publications Assistant, gave the project team very helpful advice on the organization of the volume and oversaw the editing process. The project staff, Barbara Fagerman, Tuuli Levit, and Janis Vehmaan-Kreula provided efficient and kind support.

Ha-Joon Chang
Faculty of Economics, University of Cambridge

UNU-WIDER gratefully acknowledges the financial contributions to the research programme by the governments of Denmark (Royal Ministry of Foreign Affairs), Finland (Ministry for Foreign Affairs), Norway (Royal Ministry of Foreign Affairs), Sweden (Swedish International Development Cooperation Agency – SIDA), and the United Kingdom (Department for International Development).

CHAPTER 1
INSTITUTIONAL CHANGE AND ECONOMIC DEVELOPMENT: AN INTRODUCTION

HA-JOON CHANG[1]

1. The rising interest in the role of institutions in economic development

The issue of institutional development, or 'governance reform', has come to prominence during the last decade or so. During this period, even the IMF and the World Bank, which used to treat institutions as mere 'details', have come around to emphasizing the role of institutions in economic development and tried to improve the institutions of developing countries as a way of promoting their economic development. For example, the IMF put great emphasis on reforming corporate governance institutions and bankruptcy laws during the 1997 Asian crisis, while the World Bank's 2002 annual report (*Building Institutions for Markets*) focused on institutional development, although from a rather narrow point of view, as indicated by its title. There are a few reasons behind this rather dramatic change in the intellectual atmosphere.

First, the institution-free technocratic reform programmes promoted by the IMF and the World Bank and by many donor governments since the 1980s have almost universally failed. Many of these reform programmes blatantly ignored institutional differences across countries, thereby recommending identikit policies, in what has come to be known as the 'one-size-fits-all' approach to economic policy. Today, it is widely accepted even by many orthodox economists that policies directly derived from the experiences of the developed countries – or, even worse, from economic textbooks – are likely to fail in developing countries, where certain institutions whose existence these policies take for granted (e.g., well-defined private property rights, a developed government bond market) simply do not exist.

Second, a number of devastating large-scale financial crises in developing countries around the turn of the century (Mexico in 1995, Asia in 1997, Russia in 1998, Brazil in 1999, and Argentina in 2002) have prompted debates on the need for reforming a range of institutions in order to prevent and deal with such crises. Emphasis has been placed not only on financial institutions and corporate governance institutions, which determine the likelihood of the crisis and its immediate consequences, but also on labour market institutions and social welfare institutions (and the fiscal institutions that underpin them), which affect the way in which the social impacts of the crisis are managed.

Third, the increasing attempts by the developed countries to 'harmonize' institutions across countries have prompted debates on the suitability of so-called 'global-standard' institutions for developing countries (see Chang, 2005, for a critical discussion of the global-standard argument in institutional development). The most obvious sources of such pressure have been the IMF and the World Bank, which have increasingly attached 'governance-related conditionalities' to their loans (Kapur and Webber, 2000). Developed country governments have strengthened such conditionalities by making their aids conditional on countries passing the 'health test' by the IMF and the World Bank. In addition, the WTO's unique sanctioning power has made the adoption of institutions mandated by it (e.g., strong patent law) unavoidable. Of course, many critics point out that not only are many of the 'global-standard' institutions inappropriate for developing countries but they are also unlikely to take root within the 5–10 years' 'transition period' that is typically granted by international agreements that mandate the institutional change. However, despite such criticisms the pressure on the developing countries to adopt the global-standard institutions has been increasing enormously.

Added to this increasing awareness of the importance of institutions from the policy-oriented point of view have been the recent theoretical developments in institutional economics. The last couple of decades have witnessed the rise not only of the orthodox (neoclassical) New Institutional Economics but also of a variety of heterodox institutional theories. As a result, we now have much deeper understanding on issues like the emergence and the role of institutions, compared to even a decade ago.

However, there are still some important gaps that need to be filled before we can say that we have a good grip on the issue of institutions and economic development, both theoretically and at the policy level.

First of all, we are still some way away from knowing exactly which institutions in exactly which forms are necessary, or at least useful, for economic development in which contexts. For example, everyone may agree that a 'good' property rights system is essential for economic development. However, what is in fact a 'good' property rights system? That it is not necessarily Western-style private property rights system is clear from the excellent economic performance of China over the last two decades, where such a system simply does not exist. To focus on a more concrete aspect, should this 'good' property rights system include strong intellectual property rights? That this may not be the case for developing countries was revealed in the debate surrounding the TRIPS (trade-related aspects of intellectual property rights) agreement in the WTO (see Chang, 2001, for further details). These kinds of questions can be asked in relation to just about all the major institutions, but the point is that there is a large variety of institutional forms that work. And if this is the case, it becomes even more important that we are able to identify the exact conditions under which particular institutions (and the exact forms they take) help economic development or otherwise.

Second, even when we understand what role a particular institution can play in economic development, we often do not know how we can build such institution. The few guidelines that exist in relation to institution building tend to assume that the best way to improve institutional quality is to import 'best practice' institutions wholesale, as suggested by the so-called 'global standards' argument. Yet, as many of the chapters in this volume show, real life success stories of institution building are typically a mixture of country-specific innovation and chance developments as well as deliberate learning from the more advanced countries. If so, we need to better understand the process of institutional change.

Filling these intellectual gaps calls for new approaches to the study of the role of institutions in economic development.

First of all, we need to translate the abstract theoretical notions that underlie many discussions on the role of institutions in economic development into more practical terms. In particular, we need to develop new discourses on what may be called the 'technology of institution building'. For example, having agreed that a developing country needs to build better fiscal institutions in order to enlarge its fiscal base, we still need to decide: How much of this will come from tax and how much from government borrowing (taking into account the fact that often the latter can be increased only when the former is expanded, as higher tax revenue acts as an implicit collateral for the lenders to the government); which forms of taxes are more appropriate in which economic and political contexts and for what social purposes; how different forms of political resistance to different taxes may be overcome; and how best an effective tax collection machinery can be built; and so on. The existing literature on institutions and development do not adequately address such questions.

Second, in order to improve our understanding of the process of institutional change, we need more case studies on actual experiences of institution building – both from the history of today's developed countries and from the recent experiences of developing countries themselves. Real life experiences of institution building are often more imaginative than what theoreticians have suggested on the basis of broad generalization and abstract reasoning. This means that learning more about real life experiences of institutional change will not only help us develop better strategies of institution building but also enrich our theoretical understanding by revealing aspects of reality that theoreticians have neglected or failed to grasp due to the inherent limits of their theories.

The present volume is the result of an attempt to fill these gaps. In doing so, it was felt that, given the complexity of the issues involved, we needed to gather a team that spans the conventional disciplinary divides and make them look at a wide range of cases, both in terms of the country, the time period, and the topics. The team thus assembled comprises scholars working in economics, history, political science, sociology, public administration, and business administration. Given the multiplicity of the approaches taken by the team members, no attempt was made to impose a single theoretical template.

Nor is there a single topical focus. Given the overwhelming importance of state-sanctioned institutions in modern economic life, there is a natural focus on those institutions. But a conscious effort has been made not to work with the broad category of 'the state'. The state is de-composed into many of its constituent institutions – the political system, the bureaucracy, the fiscal system, the welfare state, the institutions for industrial policy, and so on. A conscious attempt was made to look at a very wide range of countries, rather than focusing on a narrow set. Numerous countries get mentioned, but there are more than a dozen countries that get substantial attention. They include, in alphabetical order, those in Africa (Botswana, Mauritius, South Africa, and Uganda), the Americas (Brazil, Colombia, Costa Rica, El Salvador, Guatemala, and the USA), Asia (China, Japan, Korea, Malaysia, and Taiwan), and Europe (Britain and Switzerland).

2. Key findings from the chapters

2.1. *Functional multiplicity of institutions*

Institutions can, and do, serve multiple functions. As pointed out in the chapter by Chang (chapter 2), for example, budgetary institutions serve functions such as investment in productive assets (e.g., physical infrastructure, R&D facilities), provision of social protection (the welfare state), and increasing macroeconomic stability (e.g., through its 'automatic stabilizer' function). At the same time, the same function can be served by different institutions in different societies (or in the same society at different times). For example, social welfare is typically taken care of by the welfare state in most European countries. The same is provided by a combination of a (weaker) welfare state, company welfare schemes, family provision, and other means in East Asia. If we looked only at the welfare state, we may misleadingly believe that the level of social welfare provision in East Asia is much lower than what it actually is.

The functional multiplicity of institutions makes the task of institution building most difficult, as there is no inevitable and simple relationship between a desired function and an institutional form.

Unfortunately, this point has been rather neglected in the mainstream discourse on institutions and development. As a result, there has been a tendency to assign a single function to each institutional form – the central bank should focus on inflation control, corporate governance institutions should serve the interest of the shareholders only, etc. This tendency, which Thandika Mkandawire referred in the project meeting to as 'institutional mono-tasking' is highly problematic not simply for esoteric theoretical reasons but because it has serious implications for the way in which we design and implement institutional reform.

First of all, institutional mono-tasking makes us fail to fully exploit the potential of an institution, as best exemplified in Epstein's chapter (chapter 6) on the central bank. Epstein shows that there are many 'developmental' functions that the central bank can play and has historically played, including the support for government-targeted manufacturing industries and the promotion of the financial industry, but that they have become increasingly neglected because of the currently dominant view that the sole function of the central bank is to guarantee price stability.

Second, institutional mono-tasking also makes it easier for particular interest groups to hijack certain institutions and make them work mainly to their advantages, when those institutions can, and should, serve other interests too. Lazonick's chapter (chapter 7) shows how shareholder-oriented institutions of corporate governance have allowed shareholders (and the professional managers who have bought into the doctrine) to assert their interests over those of other stakeholders in the firm and of the broader society, when 'governing' the corporations.

Third, institutional mono-tasking increases the danger that countries import certain institutions for one function and do not carefully think about their 'other' functions. For example, if a developing country imported a set of shareholder-oriented corporate governance institutions thinking that the only role of corporate governance institutions is to control managerial excesses and to prevent expropriation of minority shareholders by dominant shareholders, they may end up importing a set that is very poor in serving other functions, including the management of other types of conflicts surrounding the corporation (e.g., labour-capital conflict, conflict with environmental groups, etc.).

2.2.   'Appearances can be deceptive' – formal and informal institutions

The absence of one-to-one mapping between forms and functions of institutions is one reason why 'appearances can be deceptive' when we try to understand the role of institutions in a society.

Institutions do not function in a vacuum but interact with other institutions. If a country tries to change its institutions by importing new forms of them (or even import the kinds of institution that are currently absent), they may not function well if they are incompatible with local institutions; perhaps because they are founded upon moral values that are incompatible with local moral values, perhaps because they assume the existence of certain other institutions that are missing in the local context.

The problem of compatibility will be more severe in relation to informal (that is, non-codified) institutions that interact with the institution in question. When introducing a new institution, it may be possible to change all the 'surrounding' *formal* institutions by rewriting all the relevant laws, but it is impossible to change the informal institutions (e.g., customs, business practices) in a short span of time. This means that the institutions of a country as defined in the laws may be very different from what they actually are.

Using the example of Malaysia, whose common-law tradition was compromised by the all-powerful prime minister's desire to use East Asian-style administrative guidance arising out of the civil law tradition, Woo shows in her chapter (chapter 9) that the formal legal system cannot determine how decisions are made and conflicts resolved. Zhu's chapter

(chapter 14) also clearly demonstrates that, despite the apparent differences in their formal institutional forms, how the actual institutional matrixes that have supported rapid economic transformations in China and Taiwan are remarkably similar to each other.

2.3. *Politics of institution building*

All the chapters in the volume reveal that institution building cannot simply be a technocratic exercise. All institutions, including the market (which is often assumed by mainstream economists not to be an institution) are defined in relation to the structure of the rights and obligations of the relevant actors. And as the definition of those rights and obligations is ultimately a political act, no institution, including the market, can be seen as being free from politics (Chang, 2002b, elaborates this point).

Di John's discussion of the tax system in different developing countries (chapter 8) reminds us that beneath all aspects of state capacity, including its ability to create and change institutions, lies its ability to tax, which ultimately rests on its political legitimacy.

The chapter by Burlamaqui, Pereira de Souza, and Barbosa Filho on Brazil (chapter 13) shows that many instances of institutional reform in the country were motivated by the desire to solve distributional struggles between different groups and how the political compromises made in one era critically affected the way the economy evolved later – the effect of wage indexation on subsequent episodes of inflation being the best example.

David and Mach show in their chapter (chapter 12) how the establishment of key economic institutions in Switzerland in the late nineteenth and the early twentieth century required various political compromises. To take just one example, they show how the Swiss central bank was deliberately created as a mixed (part public and part private) company with majority shares owned by the Cantons, in order to allay the fears by the private sector and the Cantons of dominance by a centralized public institution.

What also emerges from the chapters in the volume is that the politics involved in the institution-building process can be often very unpleasant. The efficient tax institutions of Britain fuelled its imperialist expansion and repression of lower classes at home in the name of protecting private property (O'Brien, chapter 10). The American federal system, while allowing the 'losers' of the nineteenth-century globalization to partially protect themselves, also preserved institutions that persecuted the blacks and the poor in the Southern states (Rauchway, chapter 11). The South African tax system's exceptional ability (among developing countries) to tax the rich ultimately originated from the country's shameful history of apartheid (di John, chapter 8). And so on.

At one level, these 'dark' origins of certain institutions limit their applicability. For example, few would want to recommend (at least openly) that developing countries create institutions that repress the poor to emulate the British economic success in the eighteenth century. Nor would anyone argue that the South African experiences show us that we need exclusionary politics in order to build a good tax base. However, as we shall see later, institutions can be used for purposes that were not originally intended, and therefore the 'darkness' of their origins need not keep us from imitating and improving upon them.

Having emphasized the importance of politics in making institutional changes, it has to be pointed out that political compromise alone is not enough in making positive and durable institutional changes. The chapters by Epstein on the central bank (chapter 6) and Toye on the modern bureaucracy (chapter 5) show particularly well that 'technical' details matter in determining the benefits and the sustainability of certain institutions.

The analogy will be a family having an internal feud over what kind of house they will build in their plot of land. Deciding the kind of house they want to build is arguably the most important first step that may require a lot of fights and compromises ('politics'). However, even if the family was able to forge a durable consensus on the kind of house to build, without skilled architect and builders ('technocracy'), it may not be able to build a good house that will last.

In other words, the emphasis on politics should not be misinterpreted as a denunciation of technocratic expertise in the Maoist fashion. While there can be no institutional solution that is purely 'technical', poor 'technical' design of an institution may ultimately undermine its political legitimacy by creating discontent even among its main beneficiaries (e.g., the poor design of a state pension system ultimately discrediting state pension itself).

2.4. *Structure and human agency in institutional change*

As the theoretical chapter by Chang (chapter 2) emphasizes, in the mainstream theory of institutional change, there is no 'real' human agency. In the mainstream theory, material interests that motivate people to change institutions (e.g., pressure for democracy from small independent farmers) are pre-determined by 'objective' economic (or even natural) conditions, and therefore what a 'rational' actor will choose is already structurally determined. In other words, there is no meaningful choice (Chang and Evans, 2005). Many chapters in the volume show that history has developed the way it has because someone somewhere made choices that were *not* 'obvious' according to the structural parameters.

For example, as Kiiza's chapter (chapter 15) shows, Botswana could overcome landlockedness and 'resource curse', two conditions widely (if contentiously) believed to be a main obstacle to development in sub-Saharan Africa, and has developed a prosperous economy because its political leaders made certain deliberate political decisions about the appropriation of diamond rent and its use.

The chapter by Woo (chapter 9) shows that Malaysia has its current form of administration because Mr Mahathir decided to weaken the common law system inherited from British colonial rule in favour of an East Asian administrative guidance system based in the civil law tradition.

In discussing the Central American countries, Evans (chapter 3) points out that, despite similar economic and social conditions, the political elites of Guatemala in the nineteenth century decided to concentrate property in a small class of landlords while their counterparts in Costa Rica opted for a more broad-based property ownership, with very different results in terms of growth, income distribution, and social peace in the twentieth century.

The emphasis on the role of human agency brings us to the issue of the role of 'ideas' in institutional change. If human actors are not automata responding to structurally-determined incentives, their ideas − how they perceive their interests, what their moral values are, how they think the world works, what actions they think are possible and impossible, and so on − matter a great deal.

Sometimes ideas can be used as tools by human agents in their attempt to change institutions in the way that they prefer. While ideas cannot be seen as being totally independent of the 'structural' conditions surrounding the human agents holding them, human agents are certainly capable of developing ideational discourses that are not totally 'structurally' determined and use them to advance their interests in particular directions.

Lazonick (chapter 7) shows how the American professional managerial class has been able to use the shareholder-value ideology, which identifies them as main targets of restraint, in a way that allowed it to build institutions that enrich itself (e.g., stock options). For another example, Kiiza (chapter 15) shows that the influence or otherwise of developmental nationalism was the key variable explaining why some sub-Saharan African countries were more successful in building institutions like developmentalist bureaucracy than others.

However, ideas are not merely tools that human actors cynically manipulate in order to make the institutional changes that they prefer. Institutions affect the ideas that human actors hold, and therefore shape the human actors (Chang, 2002b and Chang and Evans, 2005, call it the constitutive nature of institutions). In other words, ideas may not be totally manipulable by human actors.

Zhu's chapter (chapter 14) shows how the 'socialist' institutions of Taiwan and China have subsequently affected the way their policy-makers behaved, while Woo's chapter (chapter 9) shows how the centralized political and bureaucratic institutions made the Korean policy-makers liberalize the economy after the 1997 crisis often through centralized and illiberal means.

2.5.   *Unintended consequences and intended 'perversions'*

Emphasizing human agency in the process of institutional change does not imply that those who plan and implement such changes can be certain about the consequences of their actions. This is because there are unintended consequences of institutional change.

The unintended consequences may be positive or negative. Toye (chapter 5) shows that the US Tenure of Office Act (1820) gave the President and the Senate the power to reappoint every office in the government, with the laudable intention of preventing 'the emergence of an official aristocracy able to pass office on to its children', which was a serious problem in many European countries at the time. However, he points out that it 'also stopped dead the emergence of a class of professional public servants', thereby producing a negative unintended consequence of harming the development of modern bureaucracy in the country. Conversely, Rauchway (chapter 11) shows that the inability (and unwillingness) of the US federal government to impose fiscal discipline on the state governments unexpectedly produced positive consequences by encouraging the development of investment banking much earlier than in other countries with similar conditions (e.g., Canada, Argentina).

Institutions may serve functions that were not originally intended not because their original inventors did not think through their consequences (as seen in the above examples of 'unintended consequences') but because some actors deliberately chose to use them for purposes other than the ones that had originally been intended.

When discussing how patents may be turned into vehicles of rent-seeking (as in the case of Britain at the time of Adam Smith) or even into an obstacle, rather than a stimulus, to innovation (as in the current case of the recent extension of patents to the genetic level), Reinert (chapter 4) shows how there can be 'institutional perversion'.

However, 'institutional perversion' need not be a negative thing. If we use the term to simply mean that the institution in question is used for something other than the original purpose(s), without necessarily implying that the original purpose was good and the subsequent change in the purpose is bad, we begin to see some interesting possibilities of institutional change.

For example, the chapter by Woo (chapter 9) shows that the Korean administrative guidance system, which was a main institutional vehicle through which the Korean state exercised its influence, was used by the Kim Dae-Jung government as a means to reduce the role of the state. This is a 'perversion' that may or may not be considered positive, depending on what one believes about the appropriate role of the state and the legitimacy of the administrative guidance system.

For another example, the chapter by di John (chapter 8) shows that the effective institutions of taxation of South Africa were built as an integral part of the detestable apartheid system. However, despite their 'dark' origin, such institutions may be used for redistributive purposes, as it is slowly happening. Such 'perversion' may be considered positive by many people.

Thus seen, the possibility of 'institutional perversion' has positive and negative implications. On the negative side, it shows that there is a definite danger of a beneficial institution being turned into a harmful one by deliberate actions by certain individuals or groups. On the positive side, it suggests that an institution need not have a 'noble' pedigree in order to be utilized for good purposes.

2.6. *The 'technology' of institution building*

The chapters in the volume clearly show that there is no 'one-size-fits-all' model for successful institutional development. Different countries found different solutions to the same problem. For example, in the late nineteenth century, the USA tried to deal with distributional conflicts through regulating banking and suppressing cartels (Rauchway, chapter 11), while Switzerland responded to the same problem by allowing cartels in certain industries and providing protection to less productive sectors like agriculture (David and Mach, chapter 12).

Emphasizing the diversity of institutions across time and place, however, should not be interpreted as saying that there are no common principles in the 'technology of institution building' that can be applied across countries. The chapters in the book suggest some of them.

One relatively well-known such principle confirmed by the chapters in the volume is that 'institutions that at one point were beneficial can ... with passage of time become roadblocks for development', in Reinert's words (chapter 4). Institutions that had worked well for a long time may suddenly become obsolete because of some new challenges arise that they cannot meet. Evans (chapter 3) shows this while discussing the case of Botswana, where the lack of mobilization mechanisms in the old institutional arrangement proved to be the major obstacle to the country's ineffectual management of AIDS/HIV crisis, which is now threatening the very viability of its once-successful economy. Therefore, policy-makers should never rest on their laurels and be ready to reform institutions when the need arises.

A less obvious principle in the technology of institution building that the volume suggests is that it is often more effective to start the process of institutional reform by introducing desired economic activities than by introducing the desired institutions. This is a point made most explicitly by Reinert in his chapter (chapter 4). Reinert argues that 'an institutional system is mainly moulded around the needs determined by the mode of production, not the other way around' and therefore that policy-makers should target 'the kind of activities that would bring the right kinds of institutions, not the other way around'. This is an extremely important antidote to the currently prevalent thinking that development can be promoted by introducing the 'right' kind of institutions. It is also in line with many case studies in the volume (especially the chapters on Brazil and Taiwan/China) and with the extensive historical examples provided by Chang (2002a), which shows that most of the 'good' institutions that exist in today's developed countries are products, rather than causes, of economic development.

A more unusual insight on the technology of institution building that emerges from the volume is that, even when we agree that some institution is likely to be 'good' for almost all countries at least for some purpose, there is always a danger of what Reinert calls 'institutional overdose'. Nowhere is the potential for 'institutional overdose' great as in the mainstream discourse on private property rights, as shown by Chang's chapter (chapter 2). Chang theoretically points out and gives some historical examples which show that, even if some protection of private property is absolutely necessary, it is wrong to infer from that the stronger the protection is the better it is, as the conventional wisdom goes. In the same way life-saving or health-giving drugs can turn into poisons if taken in too large quantities, an 'overdose' of an institution that may be beneficial at some level may be harmful for economic development.

3. Concluding remarks

The chapters in the volume show that there is no simple formula for institutional development that countries can import and neatly apply in order to promote their economic development. Functional multiplicity, the importance of informal institutions, the existence of unintended consequences and intended 'perversion' of institutions all imply that importation of 'best practice' formal institutions does not guarantee any particular positive outcome, even assuming that the imported institution can actually take root in the importing country. This is why real life experiences of institutional development have been achieved through a mixture of deliberate imitation and adaptation of foreign institutions, on the one hand, and local innovations (sometimes deliberate, sometimes accidental), on the other hand. Consequently, the process has been a long drawn-out one with diversity across countries.

The fact that there is no set formula, not to speak of a 'magic bullet', when it comes to institutional development should not, however, make us think that there is nothing we can do to improve the quality of institutions in today's developing countries.

First of all, being late-comers, today's developing countries have the benefit of being able to imitate institutions that exist in the more developed countries – of course, taking care that they choose the institutions that are right for their circumstances in right forms and in the right dosage – and thus cut down the costs associated with developing new institutions *de novo*. It is not just in terms of technologies but also in terms of institutions that the developing countries can reap the 'late-comer's advantage'.

Second, the historical experiences show that countries do not have to start with high-quality institutions before they start their economic development, as the orthodox discourse tends to imply. Our chapters show that, in many ways, institutional development is a consequence, rather than a cause, of economic development. More importantly, they also show that institutional development and economic development may be concurrently pursued – it is perfectly possible to improve the quality of institutions while the country is developing its economies, with both of them feeding into each other.

Third, despite the difficulties of identifying a better 'technology of institution building', there are some general principles that may be extracted that would help countries build better institutions. For example, if it is difficult to change deep-rooted institutions through political means, it may be possible to change them by introducing new economic activities that put demand for different kinds of institutions. For another example, we can take heart from the fact that some institutions with 'dark' political origins have been 'perverted' into serving good purposes.

Institutional development, especially if it is conceived as a means to promote economic development, is an area where finding a neat solution that applies to every country is simply impossible. However, our volume shows that, even in this inherently complex area, it is possible to extract some general principles and enrich our empirical knowledge, especially if we are willing to go beyond the rather narrow theoretical and empirical confines of today's orthodox discourse on institutions.

Notes

1.   I thank Peter Evans for his helpful comments on the first draft of this chapter.

References

Chang, H-J. 2001. 'Intellectual Property Rights and Economic Development – Historical Lessons and Emerging Issues', *Journal of Human Development*, 2(2).

Chang, H-J. 2002a. *Kicking Away the Ladder – Development Strategy in Historical Perspective*, London, Anthem Press.

Chang, H-J. 2002b. 'Breaking the Mould – An Institutionalist Political Economy Alternative to the Neo-Liberal Theory of the Market and the State', *Cambridge Journal of Economics*, 26(5).

Chang, H-J. 2005. 'Globalisation, Global Standards and the Future of East Asia', *Global Economic Review*, 34(4).

Chang, H-J. and Evans, P. 2005. 'The Role of Institutions in Economic Change', in G. Dymski and S. Da Paula (eds), *Reimagining Growth*, London, Zed Press.

Kapur, D. and Webber, R. 2000. 'Governance-related Conditionalities of the IFIs', G-24 Discussion Paper Series 6, Geneva, UNCTAD.

PART I

THEORETICAL OVERVIEW

CHAPTER 2
UNDERSTANDING THE RELATIONSHIP BETWEEN INSTITUTIONS AND ECONOMIC DEVELOPMENT – SOME KEY THEORETICAL ISSUES

Ha-Joon Chang[1]

1. Introduction

This chapter discusses how the theory on the role of institutions in development can be improved by critically examining the current orthodox discourse on institutions and highlighting some of its key theoretical issues that need further reflection.

After a discussion of some definitional problems (section 2), the chapter will discuss some problems arising from the widespread failure to distinguish between the forms and the functions of institution (section 3). Then it will critically examine the excessive emphasis on property rights in the orthodox literature on institutions and development (section 4) and discuss a number of problems that arise from the simplistic view on institutional change that underlies the orthodox view on institutional persistence (section 5). A short section of concluding remarks (section 6) follows.

2. Some definitional problems

One fundamental difficulty involved in the study of the relationship between institutions and economic development is that there is no widely accepted definition of institutions.[2] If we cannot agree on what we mean by institutions, it is difficult to imagine that we would have a consensus on what they are supposed to do, such as promoting economic development. When we have differences over the very definition of the term, 'institutions', it is not surprising that we do not have an agreement on the relationship between institutions and economic development.

At the very general level, we may say that there are certain functions that institutions have to serve if they are to promote economic development, and that there are certain forms of institutions that serve these functions the best. However, the difficulty is that we cannot come up with an agreed list of the 'essential' functions nor an obvious match between these functions and particular forms of institutions.

The problem is that there are many different ways and different levels of abstraction in which the conceptual 'pie' may be cut. For example, in one of my earlier articles, I had identified three key functions of institutions in promoting economic development: (i) coordination and administration; (ii) learning and innovation; and (iii) income redistribution and social cohesion (Chang, 1998b). However, why just these three functions? Why not add encouragement of investment or, following Amartya Sen's approach, the function of developing human capabilities? Also, the conceptual 'pie' could be cut at many different levels of abstraction. For example, why not define the functions at less abstract levels, such as the lender of last resort or the smoothing of income fluctuation, and so on? In the end, there is no one right way in which the functions necessary for economic development are defined.

Moreover, even if we can agree on the list of functions that are essential for economic development, this does not mean that we can agree on the exact kinds and forms of institutions that we need in order to fulfil those functions.

First, one institution could be serving more than one function. For example, budgetary institutions typically serve multiple functions, such as investment in productive assets (e.g., physical infrastructure, R&D facilities), social protection (the welfare state), and macroeconomic stability (e.g., through the 'automatic stabilizer' function). For another example, political institutions could also perform a number of functions such as distillation of different opinions into a decision, conflict resolution, provision of social cohesion, and nation-building. No institution performs only one function.

Second, there are many institutions that serve the same function, although they would all serve other functions as well, which may or may not overlap. So, for example, macroeconomic stability is achieved not simply by an independent central bank solely focused on inflation (as the current orthodoxy goes) but also by a host of other institutions, including the budgetary institutions, institutions of financial regulation, and wage- and price-setting institutions. For another example, investment is encouraged not just by strong protection of property rights (as the current orthodoxy goes) but also by financial institutions (which will determine the availability of 'patient' capital), labour institutions (which have implications on productivity of the investment), and the welfare state (which provides 'insurances' against failure of investment).

Third, the same function could be served by different institutions in different societies (or in the same society at different times). For example, social welfare is typically achieved by the welfare state in most European countries. The same is provided by a combination of a (weaker) welfare state, company welfare schemes, family provision, and other means in East Asia. If we looked at the welfare state only, we may misleadingly believe that the level of social welfare provision in East Asia is much lower than what it is. For another example, discipline of lax corporate management is provided by the stock market in the Anglo-American economies, whereas it is provided by the main lending banks in countries like Germany and Japan.

For all of these reasons, it is impossible to come up with a single list of functions and forms of institutions that are desirable, not to speak of essential, for economic development. This, in turn, makes the exploration of the relationship between institutions and economic development extremely complicated. Any theorization of the role of institutions and economic development will have to accept this limitation.

3.   Forms vs. functions

Another big problem that dogs the current orthodox literature on institutions and development is its inability to clearly distinguish between the forms and the functions of institutions.

For example, if we look at the papers by Kaufmann et al. (1999, 2002, 2003) that compile all major 'governance' indexes (or the indexes of institutional quality), we find that these indexes often mix up variables that capture the differences in the *forms* of institutions (e.g., democracy, independent judiciary, absence of state ownership) and the *functions* that they perform (e.g., rule of law, respect for private property, enforceability of contracts, maintenance of price stability, the restraint on corruption).

In response to this confusion, some have argued that the 'function' variables should therefore be preferred over the 'form' variables. For example, Aron (2000: 128) argues that, in studying the impact of institutions on economic development, we should use what she calls the 'performance or quality measures' for institutions (or what we would call the function variables), such as 'respect for contracts, property rights, trust, and civil freedom' rather than variables that 'merely describe the characteristics or attributes' of institutions (or what we would call the form variables). In other words, the functions that institutions perform may be more important than their forms.

I totally agree that particular forms of institutions do not guarantee particular outcomes, as we see in numerous failures of institutional transplantation. To put it another way, institutional forms may not matter that much, as the same function can be performed by different institutional forms, as I pointed out in the previous section.

However, this emphasis on functions over forms should not be taken too far. While a particular form does not guarantee the fulfilment of a particular set of functions, a complete neglect of forms makes it very difficult for us to make any concrete policy proposal. If we did that, we will be like a dietician who talks about eating a 'healthy, balanced diet' without telling people how much of what they should have. In other words, the emphasis on 'good' institutions may become empty without some statements on the forms to be adopted.

Having made this caveat, it should be emphasized that currently the orthodox literature errs on the other side – that is, there is simply too much fixation with particular forms. Such over-emphasis on forms is most vividly manifested in the so-called 'global standard institutions' (GSIs) argument (for a critic of this argument, see Chang, 2005).

The proponents of the GSI argument believe that there are particular (mostly Anglo-American) forms of institutions that all countries have to adopt if they are to survive in the ever-globalizing world: political democracy; an independent judiciary; a professional bureaucracy, ideally with open and flexible recruitments; a small public-enterprise sector, supervised by a politically independent regulator; a developed stock market with rules that facilitate hostile M&A (mergers and acquisitions); a regime of financial regulation that encourages prudence and stability, through things like the politically-independent central bank and the BIS (Bank for International Settlements) capital adequacy ratio; a shareholder-oriented corporate governance system; labour market institutions that guarantee flexibility.

This form-fetish has led to a dangerous denial of institutional diversity, a move whose folly is evident in light of the bio-diversity argument seriously. This transformation of the orthodox discourse on institutions into another 'one-size-fits-all' discourse is really unfortunate. To the heterodox economists who had initially drawn attention to the role of institution, the whole point of bringing institutions into the analysis was to expose the limits of the 'one-size-fits-all' argument regarding economic policy that had been deployed by the orthodox economists.

Even more problematical is the way in which their preferred institutional forms are propagated by the powerful. The GSIs are increasingly imposed upon unwilling countries through what Kapur and Weber (2000) call 'governance-related conditionalities' of the Bretton Woods institutions and the donor governments.

It may be easy to criticize the one-size-fits-all approach of the GSI discourse and say that we should not be constrained by the forms too much, but then we should be able to present a menu from which policy-makers can choose (of course, always acknowledging that there is room for innovation). Providing such a menu requires empirical knowledge of the diverse forms of institutions that perform similar functions in different contexts.

It may be equally easy to criticize the functionalist approach for being too abstract. The form-fetishists at least have a concrete suggestion to make, it may be said, even if it means exactly copying a particular form of institution that another country has, whereas the functionalists have nothing concrete to say. It may be easy to say that countries should have a rule of law or a professional bureaucracy, but how do policymakers put those suggestions into practice? Once again, without some knowledge of real-life institutions, it is difficult to say anything useful in this regard.

In the end, there needs to be some balance between forms and functions in our thinking about the role of institutions in economic development – while we don't want to ignore the importance of institutional forms, we should not recommend vague things like 'good property rights system' either.

4.   Which institutions? Property rights rules?

In the orthodox literature on institutions and development, property rights are accorded the most important role. It is because many of the developing and the transition economies lack a clearly-defined and secure private property rights system, it is argued, that the 'good' policies based on 'correct' theories recommended by orthodox economist have failed to work. This is because, according to this argument, in the absence of an appropriate guarantee for the fruits of their sacrifices, people would not make any investment, whatever the policies regarding macroeconomic balances, trade, and industrial regulations may be.

The emphasis on property rights in the orthodox literature is so strong that it has even attracted the criticism that it amounts to 'property rights reductionism' (Rodrik, 2004). This over-emphasis on property rights institutions is particularly problematic when the orthodox theory on the relationship between property rights and economic development suffers from a number of conceptual, theoretical, and empirical weaknesses, as I point out below.

4.1.   The 'measurement' problem

To begin with, unlike some other institutions, such as the bureaucracy or the fiscal system, the property rights system is a complex of a vast set of institutions – land law, urban planning law, tax law, inheritance law, contract law, company law, bankruptcy law, intellectual property rights law, and customs regarding common property, to name only the most important ones. And being made up of such diverse elements, it is almost impossible to 'aggregate' these component institutions into a single aggregate institution called the property rights system.

Given the impossibility of aggregating all elements of a property rights system into a single measurable indicator, empirical studies tend to rely on subjective measures of the overall 'quality' of the property rights system. Many rely on surveys among (especially foreign) businessmen, 'experts' (e.g., academics, chief economists of main banks and firms, etc.), or even the general public, asking them how they assess the business environment in general, and the quality of property rights institutions in particular.

As we can imagine, these kinds of measures are very problematic, as the survey results they can be strongly influenced by the general state of business, rather than the inherent quality of property rights system itself (Rodrik, 2004). For example, a lot of people who were quite happy to praise the good business environment in East and Southeast Asia suddenly started criticizing cronyism and other institutional deficiencies in these countries once the 1997 financial crisis broke out.

4.2.   The 'coverage' problem

The orthodox discourse on property rights does not recognize all possible forms of property rights. It essentially recognizes only three types of property rights – open access, pure private ownership, and state ownership – while ignoring other important forms of property rights.

For example, the literature on common-pool resources in environmental economics and that on 'open' software (or 'shareware') on the internet show that the absence of private property does not necessarily mean an 'open access' situation, where there is no property right for anyone. Unlike what is overlooked in the orthodox literature, there could be genuinely *communal property rights* that allow no individual ownership but are based on clear rules about access and utilization (e.g., communal rules for gathering firewood in communally-owned forest, rules on how one may not make money out of a software building on the free 'shareware').

Moreover, post-socialist developments in China have shown us that there even could be *hybrid forms of property rights* – for example, the TVEs (township and village enterprises) are *de jure* owned by local governments but in some cases operate under *de facto* (although unclear) private property rights held by powerful local political figures.

4.3. *Superiority of private property rights*

The orthodox literature on property rights is based on a rather simplistic and biased theory of property rights that glorifies private property rights. In this discourse, it is believed that all effective incentives have to be private and predominantly materialistic and therefore that no form of property rights other than private property rights can provide adequate incentive for good performance.

However, there are enough theories that question whether only individualized materialistic incentives, and therefore private property rights, work (Simon, 1983; Basu, 1983; Etzioni, 1988; Frey, 1997; and Ellerman, 1999). Unlike what is posited in the orthodox theory, human motivations are multi-faceted and there are just too many non-selfish human *behaviours* for us to explain without admitting a range of non-selfish *motivations* and without assuming a complex interaction between different types of motivations, both selfish and non-selfish.

At the empirical level, there are many examples that show the limits of the simplistic view on the superiority of private property rights. Once again, the recent Chinese experience, with a complex mixture of private, public, and hybrid ownership patterns, often with relatively unclear property rights (to add insult to injury to the orthodox theory, so to speak), is an obvious counter-example. Countries like France, Austria, Finland, Norway, and Taiwan have extensively used state-owned enterprises (SOEs) in engineering their impressive economic developments after the Second World War. For another example, the famous Korean steel producer, POSCO, was set up in the early 1970s as an SOE in a country that does not even produce the raw materials (iron ore or coking coal) at a time when such act was a clear defiance of comparative advantage (the country's main exports at the time were labour-intensive items like textiles and wigs) but went on to become the most cost-efficient steel producer in the world within a decade of its establishment and is now the second largest (now-privatized) steel producer in the world (for further discussions on the political economy of SOEs, see Chang and Singh, 2003).

4.4.   *Desirability of strong protection of property rights*

In the orthodox literature, it is uncritically assumed that a stronger protection of property rights is always better. However, this cannot be true as a general proposition.

The fact that some protection of property rights is good does not mean that more of it is always better. While it is probably true that a very weak protection of property rights is bad, too strong a protection may not be good either, as it can protect obsolete technologies and outmoded organizational forms. If that is the case, there may be an inverse-U-shaped relationship, where too weak a protection is not good but neither is too strong one. Or alternatively it may be that, as far as it is above a minimum threshold, the strength of property-rights protection may not matter too much. Whatever the exact relationship is, the relationship between the strength of property-rights protection and economic development is not likely to be linear, contrary to what is assumed in orthodox theories.

Moreover, and more importantly from the point of view of economic development, the growth-impact of a particular property right may not be constant over time.

A particular property right may become good or bad for the society, depending on changes in the underlying technology, population, political balance of power, or even ideologies. Indeed, there are many examples in history where the preservation of certain property rights proved harmful for economic development while the violation of certain existing property rights (and the creation of new property rights) was actually beneficial for economic development.

The best known example is probably the Enclosure in Britain, which violated existing communal property rights by confiscating the commons but contributed to the development of woollen manufacturing industry by promoting sheep farming on the land thus confiscated. De Soto (2000) documents how the recognition of squatter rights in violation of the existing property owners was crucial in developing the American West. Upham (2000) cites the famous Sanderson case in 1868, where the Pennsylvania Supreme Court over-rode the existing right of landowners to claim access to clean water in favour of the coal industry, which was a key industry of the state at the time. Land reform in Japan, Korea, and Taiwan after the Second World War violated the existing property rights of the landlords but contributed to the subsequent development of these countries. Many people argue that nationalization of industrial enterprises in countries like Austria and France after the Second World War contributed to their industrial developments, by transferring certain industrial properties from a conservative and non-dynamic industrial capitalist class to the professional public sector managers with a penchant for modern technology and aggressive investments.

The examples could go on, but the point is that, if there are groups who are able to utilize certain existing properties better than their current owners can, it may be better for the society not to protect the existing property rights and to create new ones that transfer the properties concerned to the former groups. And in this circumstance, too strong a protection of certain (existing) property rights may become a hindrance to economic development. This is, of course, a main insight from Marx's theory of social evolution.[3]

To summarize, the security of property rights cannot be regarded as something good *in itself*. What is important for economic development is *not* the protection of all existing property rights at all costs, but the ability to decide which property rights to protect to what extent under which conditions.

5. Theories of institutional change

5.1. *Institutional persistence and human agency*

In the mainstream theories, once institutions are in place, they are seen as perpetuating certain patterns of human interaction. And as institutions are seen as being determined by immutable (or at least very-difficult-to-change) things like climate, resource endowment, and cultural tradition, these patterns become almost impossible to change, which introduces a 'fatalist' bias in the argument.

So, for example, temperate climate in the USA is supposed to have made small-scale land ownership the natural institution, which then led to greater demands for democracy and education, whereas the tropical climate in many Latin American countries led to latifundia-dominated agriculture, producing the opposite results (Engerman and Sokoloff 1997, 2002). For another example, Botswana's consensus-oriented political culture with strong grass-root influence is supposed to have made its post-colonial leaders to create an inclusive property rights system, which promoted economic development (Acemoglu et al., 2003).

Now, at one level, persistence is what we should expect from institutions. Institutions are *meant to* be stable – otherwise they will have no use. And therefore some degree of self-reinforcing mechanism is inevitable when we look at the relationship between institutions and the economy. However, this view has a number of serious problems.

The first problem with this argument is that, a country's institutional complex contains various elements, and therefore can be described as pro-developmental, anti-developmental, or whatever we want, depending on which particular elements we choose to highlight. In this sense, explanations that rely on culture and institutions (as the embodiments of cultural values) can easily degenerate into *ex post* justifications.

The best example is Confucianism. If we highlight its emphasis on education, its notion of 'heavenly mandate' (which gives some important voice to the grassroots and justify dynastic changes), its emphasis on frugality, etc., you cannot have a better culture for economic development. However, if we emphasize its hierarchical nature (which is supposed to stifle creativity – Krugman, 1994), its penchant for bureaucracy, its despise for craftsmen and merchants, you cannot have a worse culture for economic development. Likewise, contrary to what Acemoglu et al. (2003) has done, it would be easy to identify anti-developmental elements of Botswanan traditional culture and institutions, if Botswana happened to be a failure.

The second problem with the orthodox argument is that there are almost always more than one 'tradition' in a country's culture and institutions. France is now seen as always having been a country of *dirigiste* culture and institutions at least since the days of Jean-Baptiste Colbert, Louis XIV's finance minister, but it was a very *laissez-faire* country between the fall of Napoleon and the Second World War – even more so than the then very liberal Britain in some respects (Kuisel, 1981; Chang, 2002).

The important thing is that for France liberalism was *not* an alien culture imported from the other side of the Channel. Though many Anglo-Saxons regard liberalism as their unique contribution to world civilization, liberalism is as much French as *dirigisme* – going back at least to the libertarian tendency in the French Revolution. France lurched towards liberalism in the nineteenth century as a reaction to the experience with Napoleon, while it revived its *dirigiste* tradition and its developmentalist tendency following the humiliation of the two World Wars.

If there is more than one 'tradition' in a country's culture and institutions, deliberate political choices, and the ideologies that influence such choices, become important in determining its developmental path.

Moreover, over the long term, 'traditions' are not immutable. Cultures and institutions themselves change, often dramatically. For example, contrary to the popular belief in the West today, the Islamic culture was more tolerant, scientifically-minded, and pro-commerce than the Christian ones until at least the sixteenth century. For another example, the Confucian societies, including China itself more recently, have defied cultural determinism to transform their 'traditions' (which had been believed to be anti-developmental until the 1950s) and engineer the biggest economic miracles in human history.

One reason for cultural and institutional shifts is that cultural/institutional changes and economic development influence each other, with complex chains of causality. In the mainstream theories, where individuals are seen as being born with a pre-determined 'preference', the causality runs from culture/institutions to economic development. However, once we accept the 'constitutive' role of institutions, we begin to understand that the causality could run the other way – from economic development to institutional changes to individual 'preference' (Chang and Evans, 2005).

For example, industrialization makes people more 'rational' and 'disciplined'. This is testified to by the fact that before their countries achieved a high degree of industrialization, people like the Germans and the Japanese were described by visitors from more advanced countries as lazy, irrational, and even congenitally incapable of dealing with machinery, completely different from their modern-day racial stereotypes. In 1903, the American missionary Sidney Gulick observed that many Japanese 'give an impression ... of being lazy and utterly indifferent to the passage of time' (Gulick, 1903: 117). Gulick was no casual observer. He lived in Japan for 25 years (1888–1913), fully mastered the Japanese language, and taught in Japanese universities. After his return to the USA, he was known for his campaign for racial equality on behalf of Asian Americans. Nevertheless, he saw ample confirmation of the then Japanese cultural stereotype of an 'easy-going' and 'emotional' people who possess qualities like 'lightness of heart, freedom from all anxiety for the future, living chiefly for the present' (Gulick, 1903: 82).

Before their economic take-off in the mid-nineteenth century, the Germans were typically described by the British as 'a dull and heavy people' (Hodgskin, 1820: 50, 2). Mary Shelley, the author of *Frankenstein*, wrote in exasperation after a particularly frustrating altercation with her German coach-driver; 'the Germans never hurry' (Shelley, 1843: 276). It wasn't just the British. A French manufacturer who employed German workers complained that they 'work as and when they please' (Landes, 1998: 281). Talking about excessive German emotion, Sir Arthur Brooke Faulkner, a physician serving in the British army, observed that 'some will laugh all sorrows away and others will always indulge in melancholy' (Faulkner, 1833: 155).

Another, and possibly more important, reason for cultural/institutional shift is that, to paraphrase Marx, it is humans that change institutions, albeit not in the institutional context of their own choosing. In the mainstream theory, this is impossible because there is no real human agency. Material interests that motivate people to change institutions (e.g., pressure for democracy from small independent farmers) are pre-determined by 'objective' economic (or even natural) conditions, and therefore there is no real 'choice' in what we do (Chang and Evans, 2005). Or alternatively we are just carriers of cultural 'memes' – such as Botswanan 'democratic' political culture or Confucian 'work ethic'. However, in reality, people make choices that are *not* totally determined by their 'objective' economic interests. Ideas and institutions that embody them, influence how people perceive their interests (and therefore there is no such thing as 'objective' interest in the final analysis) and sometimes even make people defy their own 'objective' interests because of the ideas they carry.[4]

To summarize, we can only break away from the cultural/institutional determinism so prevalent in the mainstream discourse only if we understand the complexity of culture and institutions, on the one hand, and accept the importance of human agency in institutional change, on the other. Only when we accept the multi-faceted nature of culture/institutions and the existence of competing cultural/institutional 'traditions' in a society, we begin to understand that what people believe and do matter in the real sense.

5.2.   *Imitation, adaptation, and innovation in institutional development*

If we take institutions as 'technologies for social management', then there is a strong case for using the Gerschenkronian 'catching-up' framework in understanding institutional development in the developing countries. In other words, the late-developing countries can import institutions from the developed countries and thereby use 'better' institutions without paying for the same 'prices'.

For example, it took today's developed countries a few centuries of financial crises (and all the economic and human costs that come from them) before they developed the institution of central bank.[5] However, because they have introduced the central bank relatively at lower levels of economic development, today's developing countries have been better able to cope with financial crises than were today's developed countries at comparable levels of economic development.

Indeed, the developing countries today are enjoying higher standards of political democracy, human rights, and social development than what were achieved by today's developed countries at similar levels of *economic* development (i.e., same per capita income) thanks to their institutional imitation (for further details, see Chang, 2002; ch. 3).

For example, in 1820, the UK was at a somewhat higher level of development than that of India today, but it did not even have many of the most 'basic' institutions that India has – universal suffrage (it did not even have universal *male* suffrage), a central bank, income tax, generalized limited liability, a 'modern' bankruptcy law, a professional bureaucracy, meaningful securities regulations, and even minimal labour regulations (except for a couple of minimal and hardly-enforced regulations on child labour in a few industries).

For another example, in 1875, Italy was at a level of development comparable to that of Pakistan today, but did not have universal male suffrage, a professional bureaucracy, even a remotely independent and professional judiciary, a central bank with note issue monopoly, and competition law – institutions that Pakistan has had for decades. Democracy is an obvious exception in this regard, but despite frequent suspension of electoral politics, suffrage in Pakistan, when allowed, has remained universal.

For still another example, in 1913, the US was at a level of development similar to that of Mexico today. However, its level of institutional development was well behind that we see in Mexico today. Women were still formally disenfranchised and blacks and other ethnic minorities were *de facto* disenfranchised in many parts of the country. It had been just over a decade since a federal bankruptcy law was legislated (1898) and it had been barely two decades since the country recognized foreigner's copyrights (1891). A highly incomplete central banking system and income tax literally only just came into being (1913), and the establishment of a meaningful (not to speak of being 'high quality') competition law (the Clayton Act) had to wait another year (1914). Also, there was no regulation on securities trading or on child labour, with a few state legislations that existed in these areas being of low quality and very poorly enforced.

Of course, institutional imitation is rarely enough, in the same way technological imitation is rarely enough, to guarantee a successful institutional development.

More importantly, in the same way in which there are a lot of *tacit* elements in technology, there are a lot of tacit elements in institutions. So some formal institution that seems to be working well in an advanced country may be working well only because it is supported by a certain set of not-easily-observable informal institutions. For example, it will be difficult to introduce VAT in countries where people do not have the habit of asking for and issuing receipts. Or introducing the JIT (Just-In-Time) production system in countries where people do not have 'industrial' sense of punctuality will be impossible. And so on. If this is the case, importing the formal institution is not going to produce the same outcome because the importing country may be missing the necessary, supporting informal institutions.

So, in the same way in which imported technology needs to be adapted to the local conditions, some degree of adaptation is needed in order to make imported institutions work. The best example in this regard is the far-reaching institutional reform in early Meiji Japan (details can be found in Westney 1986, ch. 1 among other things). Having been forced open by the Americans in 1853, the Japanese realized that they needed to import Western institutions if they are to industrialize. After scanning the Western world, they imported institutions that they thought were the most effective with suitable local adjustments – the Navy and the Post Office from Britain, the Army and the criminal law from Prussia, civil law from France, the central bank from Belgium. They also imported American educational system but ditched it in favour of a mixture of German and French systems, after it was revealed to be ill-suited to their country.

Of course, if imitation and adaptation were all we needed, other countries could have been as successful as Japan. Subsequently added to the imported institutions by the Japanese were lifetime employment system, enterprise union, long-term subcontracting network, the pre-war *zaibatsu* and the post-war *keiretsu* systems of enterprise grouping, and many other institutions that are 'unique' to Japan.

Same story of institutional innovation characterize many other 'success' stories – the American innovation in enterprise organization based on the multi-divisional firm and interchangeable parts, the German innovation in enterprise governance in the form of co-determination, the Nordic innovation in industrial relations in the forms of solidaristic wage and centralized wage bargaining, and so on. Indeed, institutional innovation has been a major source of economic success in many countries.

Of course, this does not mean that culture/institutions can be changed at will. Jacoby (2000) emphasizes the role of legitimacy in the process of institutional change. Unless the new institution commands certain degree of political legitimacy among the members of the society in question, it is not going to work. And in order to gain legitimacy, the new institution has to have some resonance with the existing culture/institutions, which limits the possible scope of institutional innovation.

6.   Concluding remarks

In this paper, I have reviewed some of the key theoretical issues involved in developing a good understanding of the relationship between institutions and economic development. The definitional issues, the failure to distinguish the forms and the functions of institutions, the excessive focus on property rights institutions, and the failure to build a sophisticated theory of institutional change have been pointed out as the major problems in the currently dominant literature on institutions and economic development.

While the very nature of the subject matter makes it unlikely that we will soon have a complete theory of institutions that will adequately address all the above-mentioned theoretical problems, identifying the problems with the currently dominant theory is the first step towards building such theory. As I have tried to argue throughout the paper, a more careful and ideology-free crafting of the basic concepts as well as a better knowledge of the historical and contemporary experiences are necessary if we are to make progress in this regard.

Notes

1. An earlier version of the paper was presented at the project conference on 18–19 April 2005. A revised version was presented at the WIDER Jubilee Conference on 17–18 June 2005. This chapter is a modified version of that paper. I thank the participants at both conferences for their helpful comments.
2. For a very informative early discussion of the definitional problem, see van Arkadie (1990). Van Arkadie points out that institutions are used to mean both the 'rules of the game' and the 'organizations'. While the former sense of the term has become more prevalent since the time when van Arkadie wrote the article, we still use terms like the Bretton Woods *Institutions*, which uses the word institution in the latter sense.
3. According to Marx, over time, societies evolve because 'productive forces' (technologies) outgrow the 'mode of production' (the property rights system), which become fetters that need to be thrown off if the productive forces are to develop further. Of course, he was wrong to build a teleological view of history upon it and he could have also more systematically incorporate things like ideologies and political power into his theory, but the insight behind the theory still remains valid.
4. One interesting example is the case of Korean planning agency, Economic Planning Board (EPB). Although it was the centre of government intervention until the 1970s, for various reasons many bureaucrats at the EPB adopted neo-liberal ideology since the 1980s. By the early 1990s, some EPB bureaucrats were even calling for the abolition of their own ministry. This flies directly in the face of the fundamental assumption of self-seeking in orthodox economics. Unless we accept the importance of human agency and the influence of ideologies on it, we will never be able to understand why these bureaucrats went against their 'objective' interests and campaigned for the reduction of their own power and influence. For further details, see Chang and Evans (2005).
5. The need for the lender of last resort, and thus for the central bank, was perceived from at least the seventeenth century but it was only after hundreds years of unnecessary financial crises that the developed countries of today have come to set up the central bank – between the second half of the nineteenth century and the first half of the twentieth century. Most market-oriented economists until that time believed that central banking would be harmful because it creates what we these days call 'moral hazard' on the part of the borrowers (Chang, 2000).

References

Acemoglu, D., Johnson, S. and Robinson, J. 2001. 'The Colonial Origins of Comparative Development: An Empirical Investigation', *American Economic Review*, 91(5).

Acemoglu, D., Johnson, S. and Robinson, J. 2003. 'An African Success Story: Botswana' in D. Rodrik (ed.), *In Search of Prosperity: Analytic Narratives on Economic Growth*, Princeton, Princeton University Press.

Aron, J. 2000. 'Growth and Institutions: A Review of the Evidence', *The World Bank Research Observer*, 15(1).

Basu, K. 1983. 'On Why We Do Not Try To Walk Off Without Paying After a Taxi-Ride', *Economic and Political Weekly*, 48: 2011–12.

Chang, H-J. 2000. 'The Hazard of Moral Hazard – Untangling the Asian Crisis', *World Development*, 28(4).

Chang, H-J. 2002. *Kicking Away the Ladder – Development Strategy in Historical Perspective*, London, Anthem Press.

Chang, H-J. 2002b. 'Breaking the Mould – An Institutionalist Political Economy Alternative to the Neo-Liberal Theory of the Market and the State', *Cambridge Journal of Economics*, 26(5).

Chang, H-J. 2005. 'Globlisation, Global Standards and the Future of East Asia', *Global Economic Review*, 34(4).

Chang, H-J. and Evans, P. 2005. 'The Role of Institutions in Economic Change' in G. Dymski and S. Da Paula (eds), *Reimagining Growth*, London, Zed Press.

Chang, H-J. and Rowthorn, R. 1995. 'Role of the State in Economic Change: Entrepreneurship and Conflict Management' in H-J. Chang and R. Rowthorn (eds), *The Role of the State in Economic Change*, Oxford, Clarendon Press for UNU-WIDER.

Chang, H-J. and Singh, A. 2003. 'Public Enterprises in Developing Countries and Economic Efficiency' in H-J. Chang, *Globalisation, Economic Development and the Role of the State*, London, Zed Press.

De Soto, H. 2000. *The Mystery of Capital*, London, Bantam Books.

Dore, R. 1987. *Taking Japan Seriously - A Confucian Perspective on Leading Economic Issues*. London: Athlone Press.

Ellerman, D. 1999. 'Helping Others to Help Themselves: The Challenge of Autonomy-Compatible Development Assistance', mimeo, Washington, DC, World Bank.

Engerman, S. and Sokoloff, K. 1997. 'Factor Endowments, Institutions, and Differential Growth Paths among New World Economies' in S. Haber (ed.), *How Latin America Fell Behind*, Stanford, Stanford University Press.

Etzioni, A. 1988. *The Moral Dimension*, New York, Free Press.

Evans, P. 1995. *Embedded Autonomy – States and Industrial Transformation*, Princeton, Princeton University Press.

Faulkner, A. 1833. *Visit to Germany and the Low Countries*, vol. 2, London, Richard Bentley.

Frey, B. 1997. *Not Just for the Money – An Economic Theory of Personal Motivation*, Cheltenham, Edward Elgar.

Gulick, S. 1903. *Evolution of the Japanese*, New York, Fleming H. Revell.

Hodgskin, T. 1820. *Travels in the North of Germany*, vol, I, Edinburgh, Archbald.

Jacoby, W. 2001. *Imitation and Politics: Redesigning Modern Germany*, Ithaca and London, Cornell University Press.

Johnson, C. 1982. *MITI and the Japanese Miracle*, Stanford, Stanford University Press.

Garraty, J. and Carnes, M. 2000. *The American Nation – A History of the United States*, 10th edn, New York, Addison Wesley Longman.

Kapur, D. and Webber, R. 2000. 'Governance-related Conditionalities of the IFIs', G-24 Discussion Paper Series 6, Geneva, UNCTAD.

Kaufmann, D., Kraay, A. and Zoido-Lobaton, P. 1998. 'Governance Matters I', Policy Research Working Paper, WPS 2196, World Bank, Washington, DC.

Kaufmann, D., Kraay, A. and Zoido-Lobaton, P. 2002. 'Governance Matters II', Policy Research Working Paper, WPS 2772, World Bank, Washington, DC.

Kaufmann, D., Kraay, A. and Mastruzzi, M. 2003. 'Governance Matters III', Policy Research Working Paper, WPS 3106, World Bank, Washington, DC.

Kuisel, R. 1981. *Capitalism and the State in Modern France*, Cambridge, Cambridge University Press.

Landes, D. 1998. *The Wealth and Poverty of Nations*, London, Abacus.

Rodrik, D. 2004. 'Getting Institutions Right', mimeo, Kennedy School of Government, Harvard University.

Shelly, M. 1843. *Rambles in Germany and Italy*, vol. 1, London, Edward Monkton.

Simon, H. 1983. *Reasons in Human Behaviour*, Oxford, Basil Blackwell.

Upham, F. 2000. 'Neoliberalism and the Rule of Law in Developing Societies', a paper presented at the UNRISD conference on 'Neoliberalism and Institutional Reform in East Asia', 12–14 May, Bangkok.

Van Arkadie, B. 1990. 'The Role of Institutions in Development', *Proceedings of the World Bank Annual Conference on Development Economics, 1989*, Washington, DC, World Bank.

Westney, E. 1987. *Imitation and Innovation: The Transfer of Western Organizational Patterns to Meiji Japan*, Cambridge, MA, Harvard University Press.

World Bank. 2002. *World Development Report 2002*, New York, Oxford University Press.

CHAPTER 3
EXTENDING THE
'INSTITUTIONAL' TURN:
PROPERTY, POLITICS, AND
DEVELOPMENT TRAJECTORIES

Peter B. Evans

Institutional approaches to the study of development now dominate the mainstream of development economics. In other social science disciplines they have long predominated. No one denies the centrality of traditional determinants of growth, such as investment or technological progress, but institutional analysis is considered fundamental to understanding the levels and effects of these traditional variables. Variations in institutional context are theorized as underlying variations in both levels of investment and the incorporation of technological progress. Likewise, the extent to which a given level of investment or a particular innovation actually results in a sustained increase in output is viewed as depending on the institutional context.

In their contribution to the *Handbook of Economic Growth*, Acemoglu, Johnson, and Robinson (AJR, 2005: 1) pull no punches: 'Differences in economic institutions are the fundamental cause of differences in economic development'. Dani Rodrik, in a co-authored paper (Rodrik et al. 2004)[1] called 'Institutions Rule' is equally straightforward: 'the quality of institutions 'trumps' everything else. Easterly and Levine (2003) and Bardhan (2005), among many others, offer further support for the primacy of institutions.

Dissenters continue to resist the rise of the institutional perspective. Jeff Sachs and his collaborators continue to push geography and disease as fundamental causes of differences in national wealth and incomes (Gallup et al. 1998; Sachs, 2001). Engerman and Sokoloff (1997; 2002) are more restrained, but argue that current explanatory frameworks have gone overboard in neglecting the way in which institutions are themselves shaped by natural factor endowments.

There is merit in these dissenting points of view, but the 'institutional turn' (Evans, 2004; 2005) is not likely to be reversed. Even if endowments, geography and disease would to gain purchase at the level of cross-national analysis, which they do not seem to be doing, these approaches would still be at a disadvantage. The logic of institutional analysis can be replicated at different levels of analysis, ranging from the very powerful district level comparisons recently executed by Banerjee and Iyer (2002) using Indian data to the carefully designed micro-level research of new generation of empirically oriented development economists (see, e.g., Miguel, 2004).

Institutional approaches also offer more fruitful forms of engagement with policy debates than natural endowment-based theories. Institutions can be constructed and reconstructed; natural endowments and geography must be lived with. Even if initial disadvantages are created by endowments (including 'negative endowments' like disease burden), ameliorating such disadvantages still requires institutional transformation. Future debates over the dynamics of development, both theoretical and empirical, will take place on the terrain of institutional analysis.

How will the institutional turn evolve? In its early 'Northian' manifestations institutional analysis was under-theorized. 'Property rights' was forced to carry far too heavy an explanatory burden. More recent work, by economists and other social scientists, has extended the institutional turn in ways that show promise of substantially enhancing our understanding of development with more sophisticated theorizing and consideration of a broader range of historical and contemporary data.

In this chapter, I will look briefly at the problems of an under-theorized, property-rights version of the institutional turn. Then I will turn to the way in which the property rights perspective becomes transformed in practice. I will focus particularly on the paradigmatic work of Acemoglu, Johnson and Robinson (AJR hereafter). To show how the institutional turn has been further extended, I will use the interaction of the work of a political scientist/sociologist, James Mahoney with the work of one of the AJR team (Robinson) in the specific historical context of nineteenth century Central America. Finally, I will use AJR's analysis of the case of Botswana, especially in contrast to the sociological analysis of Ann Swidler, to make the case for the necessity of additional extensions.

1.   Institutions, property rights, and development

Definitions of institutions are notoriously unspecific. The one offered by Douglass North (1994: 360), in his Nobel Prize lecture – 'The rules of the game: The humanly devised constraints that structure human interaction' – is a good example.[2] In practice, cross-national institutional analyses of development use a 'double-finesse' to surmount this lack of conceptual specificity. On the one hand, they tend to use simple, concrete empirical proxies to stand for complex combinations of institutions. Perhaps most popular are the various measures put out by commercial 'Political Risk' services such as those embodied in the ratings of the International Country Risk Guides. Exactly what 'institutions' are reflected in these measures is difficult, indeed often impossible, to figure out, but they are available for a full range of countries at varying points in time. This element of the finesse is the key to empirical feasibility.

The second element of the finesse is on the theoretical side. The specific concrete measures used are assumed to reflect 'institutions' at an abstract level reflecting the aggregate character of a whole complex of institutions – usually defined as 'property rights institutions'. It is a generically plausible finesse and an essential one given the low face validity of the empirical measures used. The theoretical finesse rests on a simple and very plausible logic in which propensities to make productive investments depend on the predictability of future rights to claim the returns from those assets. If people cannot count on maintaining future control of assets that they consider theirs, then investing in productive assets whose benefits are only accrued in the future makes less sense. Income consumed is hard to take away and hoarded assets are easier to defend than productive ones (which must be exposed to public view to reap their benefits). A combination of consumption and hoarding makes more sense than investment when assets are insecure.

The idea that people need predictable societal rules and equally predictable public enforcement if they are to engage in productive investments makes sense. The idea that historically specific property rights arrangements can be arrayed along a simple ordinal scale is anything but plausible. Any initial allocation of rights to different kinds of property – ranging from land to the broadcast spectrum to the human genome – is disputable and somewhat arbitrary. Enforcement of rights once they have been allocated is equally so. Sending the National Guard to evict peasants growing crops on a landlord's otherwise unused land is enforcing property rights. So is shutting down a factory whose pollution is making the surrounding neighbourhood unliveable. Development almost certainly depends on how property rights are allocated and what kind of property rights are enforced for what segments of the population. Exactly how these complex patterns of allocation and enforcement are related, positively or negatively, to development can hardly be taken for granted.

Neither the empirical proxies for institutions that have been used in most cross-national institutional analyses of development nor reliance on a simple ordinal notion of 'effective property rights' would seem propitious starting points for understanding developmental success or failure. Nonetheless, broad quantitative cross-national institutional analyses, stimulated theoretically by thinking about property rights, have generated intellectually exciting debates that belie the apparent foundational weaknesses of the approach. Some of the best examples have been generated by the collaboration of Daron Acemoglu, Simon Johnson and James Robinson.

2.   A paradigmatic example of extending the institutional turn

AJR have produced a prolific set of institutional analyses of development (e.g., 2001, 2002, 2003, and 2005). Here, I will use their already classic 2001 article in the *American Economic Review* as a starting point, in part because it conforms to the general 'double finesse' model that I have just laid out, but more important because it demonstrates the tendency for high quality analysis that begins from the double finesse to transcend it.

In their 2001 article AJR start with a traditional measure of 'good institutions' that has been used before. It is called 'Average Expropriation Risk 1985–95', was originally put forward by a consulting firm called 'Political Risk Services' and subsequently used by Steve Knack and Phil Keefer (1995) in a frequently cited article. The theoretical proposition that accompanies these results is a classic abstract Northian property rights argument:

> Countries with better '*institutions*', more secure property rights, and less distortionary policies will invest more in physical and human capital, and will use these factors more efficiently to achieve a greater level of income (e.g., Douglass North and Robert Thomas, 1973; North 1981…). (AJR 2001: 1)

What makes AJR's analysis more interesting than so many in this ilk is that they are so thoroughly aware of both the gap between their measure and their theory and the extent to which the concept of 'property rights institutions is underspecified. In the conclusion to their paper they say:

> There are many questions that our analysis does not address. Institutions are treated largely as a 'black-box'... . Institutional features, such as expropriation risk, property rights enforcement or rule of law, should probably be interpreted as an equilibrium outcome, related to some more fundamental 'institutions', e.g., presidential vs. parliamentary system, which can be changed directly. (AJR 2001: 27)

Despite their scepticism, AJR do an impeccable job at executing the empirical analysis. Their measure gives them good regression results and they do a thorough job of checking the robustness of the results in the face of the full gamut of possible statistical controls. In order to drive a stake into the heart of the endogeneity problem they use 'settler mortality rates' at the time of colonization as an instrument for early institutions. This turns out to be a statistically effective instrument. Perhaps more important, it leads them to undertake a much more historically oriented analysis than would have been the case had they focused simply on the contemporary relationship reflected by their primary measure.

By adding an historical dimension to their cross-sectional regression analysis, AJR have gotten themselves into some trouble with social scientists from other disciplines who question the accuracy of their comparisons of colonial institutions (see Mahoney, 2003; Lange et al. 2005). At the same time, AJR have been stimulated by their historical instrumental variable to open up the institutional 'black box' in interesting and potentially fruitful ways.

AJR's basic argument is that where there were large amounts of resources (mineral deposits or land suitable to crops in high demand on world markets) and large indigenous populations to exploit, colonialists created 'extractive institutions'. Where settlers had to survive largely on the basis of their own efforts, 'institutions of private property' emerged. AJR clarify what they mean by 'extractive institutions' and 'institutions of private property' by using a set of concrete historical examples.

Australia and New Zealand are used as archetypes of positive institutional development: In the case of Australia, AJR note that the main goal of the settlers was 'legal protection against the arbitrary power of landowners'. They go on to say, 'The settlers wanted institutions and political rights like those prevailing in England at the time. They demanded jury trials, freedom from arbitrary arrest, and electoral representation'. (AJR, 2001: 8). In the case of New Zealand, AJR focus on the effort to build up public infrastructure as represented by what they call an 'enormous boom in public investment' (AJR, 2001: 8).

Neither the idea that broad democratic rights are a key aspect of 'institutions of private property nor the key developmental role of state investment in infrastructure, is reflected in AJR's statistical modeling of institutions and growth, but these are reoccurring themes in AJR's subsequent work. For example, in their next paper (AJR, 2002: 17), 'institutions of private property' are defined as 'a cluster of (political, economic and social) institutions ensuring that *a broad cross-section of society* has effective property rights' [emphasis added]. In a 2003 paper they explicitly divide the requirements for effective property rights into two components. The first is the traditional Northian general provision of secure property rights. The second is the requirement that such rights are extended to a 'broad cross-section of the society'. Thus, they argue, a society in which a 'small fraction of the population' monopolizes control of property does not fully qualify as having 'institutions of private property', 'even if the property rights of this elite are secure' (AJR, 2003: 5).

Specification of the institutions that encourage investment in human capital and other kinds of productive assets is further elaborated when members of the AJR team turn their analytical lenses on regional and country case studies. Robinson's work on Central American, a set of cases that also happen to be the focus of the work of James Mahoney, one of AJR's most prominent critics, is a good example.

3.   A regional laboratory for comparative institutional analysis

Central America offers a fascinating comparative microcosm for examining questions of institutions and growth. Five countries share a similar colonial heritage, history of commodity exports and geo-political position.[3] Yet, once cut loose from the formal control of the Spanish empire at the beginning of the nineteenth century, they have strikingly different institutional histories and levels of economic success.

Robinson's analysis of Central America (done jointly with Jeffrey Nugent) focuses on a paired comparison of four coffee producers: Costa Rica and Colombia on the one hand and Guatemala and El Salvador on the other.[4] Coffee became the major export crop for all four countries during the latter part of the nineteenth century. Yet, the first two ended up with roughly double the incomes, and much higher levels of Human Development than the other two. Nugent and Robinson's argument is straightforward. In the former pair of countries (Costa Rica and Colombia), smallholders play a major or even dominant role, while in the latter pair (Guatemala and

El Salvador) coffee production is dominated by large landholders. In short, in Guatemala and El Salvador AJR's second requirement for institutions of private property, the 'broad cross-section requirement', is violated.

This difference in the structure of landholdings grew out of the institutions that re-shaped property rights in the mid to late nineteenth century. Land that was formerly communal, public or owned by the church was privatized in all four countries, but privatization took a different form in the two pairs. In Guatemala and El Salvador, new laws fostered a 'land grab' by elites. In Colombia and Costa Rica, smallholders were allowed to retain a share of the newly privatized lands. Since, according to Nugent and Robinson (2001: 4), smallholder coffee production is more economically efficient and associated with higher levels of investment, especially in human capital, the political-legal institutions of nineteenth-century Guatemala and El Salvador resulted in depressed rates of investment and growth over the course of the next 100 years.

How do Nugent and Robinson explain why Guatemalan and El Salvadorian elites chose the less efficient option? Because large plantations gave these elites control of labour as well as land and allowed them to extract monopsony rents from labour as well as returns from the land. Why didn't elites in Colombia and Costa Rica make the same choices? Because they were less unified, facing a greater level of political competition and, therefore, less able to turn legal and administrative institutions to exclusionary ends.

In Nugent and Robinson we see the evolution of the AJR perspective both toward a firmer focus on the distributional aspects of property rights as the key to their developmental efficacy and toward an emphasis on forms of political competition as the underlying determinants of distributional rules.[5] In outlining the political dynamics of elite strategies in nineteenth century Central America, Nugent and Robinson rely heavily on James Mahoney's 2001 book *Legacies of Liberalism*. It is, therefore, interesting to examine the way in which Mahoney's political science training results in a different reading of the process, based on essentially the same historical evidence.

Mahoney's interpretation of the institutional dynamics separating Costa Rica's development from that of El Salvador and Guatemala parallels Nugent and Robinson's paired comparison, but also differs in key respects.[6] Nugent and Robinson see legal and political institutions as reflecting a vector of elite economic interests which is summed through a process of political competition. It might even be argued that, for Nugent and Robinson, institutions are not real 'causes' at all but simply 'transmission belts' which instantiate the effects of pre-existing economic and political interests. Mahoney has a different view of how institutional change works, one which emphasizes both political agency, especially during what he calls 'critical junctures', and the subsequent effects of the institutional legacies generated by choices made during these 'critical junctures'.

Like Nugent and Robinson, Mahoney emphasizes the role of political competition, but he evaluates both its relative intensity in different countries and its effects differently. Like Nugent and Robinson, he sees elites in Guatemala and El Salvador as 'radical liberals', promoting the legal right of large landowners to control both land and labour much more aggressively than the 'reformist' liberal elites of Costa Rica. But, in contrast to Nugent and Robinson, Mahoney sees the motivation of elite choices as not simply, or even primarily, the promotion of the interests of large landholders. He argues that, while these elites did generally promote the interests of large landholders, the primary attraction of radical strategies was that such strategies appeared to be the most effective way of gaining and consolidating political control in the face of staunch opposition from conservative forces, such as the church and its traditionalist allies.

Mahoney also emphasizes the crucial role of building new institutions to enforce the radical new definitions of property rights. The construction of new national state apparatuses with vastly expanded powers of coercion was the heart of the institutional agenda of radical liberalism in Guatemala and El Salvador. Radical liberalism not only polarized rural class structures but also brought forth powerful military-coercive state apparatuses.

This is not to say that Mahoney sees state building in general as having a negative effect on development. State-building was an essential element for the export-led growth projects of both radical and reformist liberalizing regimes. In the same way that the state in the settler colonies discussed by AJR invested heavily in infrastructure, both radical and reformist regimes in Central America built powerful interventionist state apparatuses in order to help coffee producers take advantage of export market opportunities. There was, however, a fundamental difference between radical and reformist strategies. Just as Costa Rica's political leadership saw exclusionary transformation of property rights as creating more political risks than benefits, they were wary of the political risks involved in expansion of the military-coercive side of the state apparatus, and therefore refrained from expanding this facet of the state.

For Mahoney, the contrasting property rights institutions and state apparatuses that emerged in nineteenth century Central America cannot be read as transmission belts for previously defined interests in the way that Robinson and Nugent suggest. While antecedent conditions in Guatemala and El Salvador created an affinity for radical liberalism, reformist liberal strategies were still available to nineteenth century political leaderships in these countries. Furthermore, it is apparent in hindsight that the reformist option could have resulted in greater long-term economic gains even for local elites in Guatemala and El Salvador, say nothing of non-elites. Conversely, while antecedent conditions in Costa Rica created an affinity for reformist liberalism, its nineteenth century political leaders could still have seen the more radical option as the best strategy for remaining in power.

Once these political choices were made, institutions that resulted took on a causal life of their own. Once in place, military coercive apparatuses developed a set of preferences that went beyond those of economic elites, preferences that focused particularly on the preservation of the military's own power and privilege. The effects of the military's preferences and capacity persisted even after the agrarian export operations they had been created to defend fell into decay. When reform efforts generated political conflicts in mid-twentieth century Guatemala, the coercive apparatus played the determinative role in initiating a half century of state terror in order to prevent reform. When a similar set of reform efforts led to political conflict that deteriorated into civil war in Costa Rica in 1948, there was no military coercive apparatus capable of playing the deciding role. An evolution in the direction of real democratic elections and a long period of social reform was the result.

Both the points of consensus between Mahoney's perspective that of AJR and their points of difference provide useful signposts for the extension of the institutional turn. There are two key points of consensus. The first is on the developmental disadvantages of radically inegalitarian distributions of property rights. Mahoney's analysis firmly supports AJR's 'broad cross-section' requirement. The second is on the necessity of building a state apparatus whose capacities are focused on providing sufficient investment in infrastructure.

The two perspectives are, however, quite different in their analysis of the causes and consequences of political choices. In the model of AJR and Nugent and Robinson, once colonial rulers have set the institutional matrix in place, the enduring effects of constellations of endowments and interests generate institutional persistence. In Mahoney's 'critical juncture – legacy' model institutions emerge out of uncertain, politically motivated choices, made primarily during 'critical junctures' when developmental possibilities are in flux. These choices become embodied in new organizations and sets of social actors, with new interests and capacities, which become causal factors in their own right. Particularly important in this respect are the perverse consequences of the hypertrophy of the coercive side of the state apparatus.

The contrast between AJR and Mahoney may not, however, be as great as it appears in the Central American context. If we turn our attention to another case that has been the focus of AJR's work – the surprising economic success of Botswana, AJR sound much more like Mahoney. Political choices made during critical junctures, state-building and the avoidance of the over-investment in the coercive side of the state apparatus all play a key role in the emergence of an institutional context favourable to developmental success.

4.   Successful 'institutions of private property' in Africa

Like many other analysts of Botswana, AJR call it 'an African Success Story'. The data certainly support this view. From the seventies through the end of the twentieth century, Botswana's GDP per capita grew at a rate that made it look as though it was part of East Asia. By the end of the century, Botswana's PPP GDP was roughly four times the average for Southern Africa.

Sceptics of the institutional turn might try to reduce Botswana's success to a story of endowments: Diamond reserves sufficient to sustain a couple of billion dollars worth of exports a year and a population of only one and a half million. This facile explanation does not hold up to comparative scrutiny. As the sad case of Sierra Leone illustrates, diamond mines can as easily turn into a 'resource curse' as a resource bonanza. If we rephrase the question from 'Why did Botswana grow so fast?' to 'How did Botswana avoid the resource curse and take such exemplary advantage of its resources?', then 'good institutions' seems a reasonable answer.

What do we mean by 'good institutions' in this case? While AJR stick to the label 'institutions of private property', their actual historical analysis focuses on political institutions, political choices and the state apparatus in a way that is reminiscent of Mahoney's analysis of Central America. Providing appropriate incentives to local private investors seems to have had little to do with Botswana's success. Development seems instead to have depended on the ability of Botswana's leadership to build a state apparatus that avoided the coercive concentration of property rights and focused on building the capacity to provide effective infrastructure. Despite dramatically different endowments and historical circumstances, Botswana's strategy looks eerily similar to 'reformist liberalism' in nineteenth century Central America.

As in nineteenth century Central America, political choices in the immediate post-colonial period were crucial. AJR (2003: 1) emphasize the importance of 'a number of critical decisions made by the post independence leaders'. The essence of these choices was to focus on the construction of a relatively non-coercive, resource-based, mini-developmental state (see Leith, 2002). Botswana's political leaders were able, early on, to secure a contract with a transnational diamond mining company that gave the government 50 per cent of all export revenues. This, in turn, allowed the government to maintain a reasonably well paid, meritocratic bureaucracy in which 'probity, relative autonomy and competency have been nurtured and sustained' (Parsons 1984 quoted in AJR). About 40 per cent of all formal sector jobs are in public service, and the government invests a larger share of public expenditures in education than either the US or Canada.

Post-independence political elites made no effort to replicate the equivalent of the nineteenth century Central American land grab by looting the eminently lootable resources at their disposal, choosing instead to construct state institutions whose capacity to invest in infrastructure would mitigate the effect of existing inequalities. They also constructed a system of stable, relatively democratic, rule (i.e., a multi-party system with regular elections and a real possibility – though one never realized in practice – that the ruling party could lose). Post-hoc it is clear that their political instincts were correct, but prescience is a suspicious explanation of political choice. A more plausible explanation, and the one favoured by AJR, is that pre-colonial political models created an affinity for less coercive choices. These post-independence political choices, while certainly not determined by earlier political models, were consistent with them.

Fortunately for the Batswana, the extent of Botswana's resource wealth was not apparent during the period when colonial institutions were constructed. Botswana was more or less ignored during the colonial period, escaping the imposition of rapacious set of 'extractive institutions'. The traditional, pre-colonial leadership of the Batswana had managed to convince a population characterized by considerable diversity of ethnic origins that they were all part of a single socio-culturally grounded political entity.[7] At the same time, traditional Tswana political culture was characterized by a set of practices (*kgotla* assemblies) that gave adult males considerable leverage over the chiefs that ruled this unified political entity.

In short, exceptional resource endowments and a legacy of stable political institutions gave post-independence leaders the option of tolerating political constraints in return for continued adherence to the existing 'rules of the game' on the part of political competitors, instead of opting for maximizing their share of the wealth and investing in the means of violence necessary to keep political competitors from doing the same. They made the most of this option.

The Botswana case reinforces Central American lessons. Like nineteenth-century Costa Rican elites, Botswana's political leadership calculated that the possible economic rewards from trying to amass an even larger share of the national wealth and constructing the coercive apparatus necessary to enforce such a negative redistribution were not worth the political risks involved in expanding the means of violence. In twentieth-century Africa as in nineteenth century Central America, the political institutions that support this kind of choice appear to generate substantial economic returns.

A conundrum remains. Traditional property rights (primarily ownership of cattle) were highly unequally distributed in pre-independence Botswana and Botswana today is more unequal than either Guatemala or El Salvador. Does Botswana suggest that AJR's 'broad cross-section requirement' is not really a requirement? Public investment in human capital and the possibility of upward mobility via the public sector obviate the importance of the 'broad cross-section requirement'. Is there no developmental disadvantage to leaving the 'broad cross-section' relatively deprived of property rights as long as this deprivation takes the form of the maintenance of a long established, culturally validated traditional social hierarchy?

AJR don't comment on the implications of Botswana for their 'broad cross section requirement', but the reversal of fortune which Botswana has suffered in the last ten years as a result of HIV/AIDS suggests that violating the broad cross-section requirement had a price, even in Botswana. Even with rapid growth and democratic rule, quietly maintained hierarchies may result in a state apparatus unable to effectively engage a sufficiently broad cross-section of the population in developmentally essential projects when this becomes necessary.

5.   Redefining good institutions: Botswana and the challenge of AIDS

Throughout the 1990s everyone has been puzzled by Botswana's inability to deal with AIDS. It is not just that Botswana has done poorly, it has done worse than other African countries that seem to be much less well endowed – either in terms of material resources, or in terms of effective institutions. A common point of comparison is Uganda, which was devastated by dictatorship and civil war and ravaged by AIDS in the 1980s, but is now recorded as having a higher life expectancy than Botswana.

AJR (2003: 2) comment: 'Not everything in Botswana is rosy. Though the statistics are not fully reliable, Botswana has one of the highest adult incidences of AIDS in the world'. They add that this 'probably represents, above all else, a serious public policy failure', but this failure does not figure in their evaluation of Botswana's institutions. To fill this lacuna we are forced to move beyond economics and political science to Ann Swidler

(2004), a sociologist who provides a provocative, even though preliminary, new perspective.

Swidler takes AJR's analysis of Botswana's successful institutions as her starting point. Like others (e.g., Allen and Heald, 2004), she begins by noting that the public policy response in Botswana has been precisely what one would expect on the basis of AJR's institutional analysis – modern, competent and thorough. Yet, the impact of the government's effort on people's behaviour appears to have been minimal, or even perverse. Allen and Heald (2004: 1144) note that following the government's educational campaign on the radio, AIDS became known as the 'radio disease' and a traditional Tswana interpretation of AIDS developed in which condoms were 'an agent, not in the control of the disease, but rather in its very origin and spread' and in which the disease was due to 'disrespect for the mores of traditional culture'. For too many Batswana, avoiding the stigma of the disease still appears to be a more compelling motivation than engaging in treatment that requires publicly acknowledging having the disease. And the devastation continues.

What went wrong? Swidler's tentative answer (2004: 15–16) is that the government of Botswana lacks the ability to spark 'the activation of social solidarities, the sense of community and the mobilization of collective identities' necessary to break through the stigma and denial that are natural responses to AIDS and generate real behaviour change. Mobilizational capacity, rather than regulatory or administrative, was what was needed. Mobilization was a task for which the Botswana political institutions had not been equipped by prior developmental successes. Nor had Botswana's political leaders had to figure out how to create the political and social space in which NGO and community groups, which must play a key role in changing behaviour and values on the ground, could flourish.

Whether or not Swidler's analysis of the Botswana is eventually confirmed, it represents an important conceptual extension of the institutional turn. Swidler takes us beyond the classic 'instrumental' vision of the relationship between institutions and individual motivations, in which institutions enable individuals to pursue their own exogenous and taken for granted aims.[8] In Swidler's vision, an even more important role of institutions is enabling people to re-shape their preferences and motivations, creating new definitions of desirable, culturally-valued behaviour, in response to changing circumstance.

At this point, we have left property rights behind, but perhaps not the political institutions that are associated with sustaining the 'broad cross-section' requirement. From AJR's initial settle colony examples to Mahoney's description of 'reformist' liberal regimes in Central America, one of the central requirements of maintaining the property rights of the 'broad cross-section' is that the broad cross-section be mobilized and active. In Swidler's view of Botswana, what is needed is mobilization focused on changing goals and values rather than a more instrumental sort of mobilization, but in both cases broad-based mobilizational capacity is the key.

6.   Extending the institutional turn

When we follow the trail of AJR and juxtapose their analysis with that of others working on the same cases, the heuristic potential of the institutional turn becomes apparent. No less apparent is the extent to which 'institutions of private property' is a conceptual procrustean bed, even for AJR themselves. As soon as cases are examined in detail, contestation over the distribution of political rights and power and the institutions that shape this contestation comes to the fore.[9]

From the work of both AJR and Mahoney it would seem to follow that political institutions which discourage elites from grabbing a disproportionate share of national assets for themselves are the first key to developmentally effective private property rights. This proposition in turn suggests five important foci: What determines the collective rationalities and shared political preferences of elites themselves? What determines the balance between the state's exercise of its role as coercive apparatus and its role as essential source of investment in crucial collective goods? What possibilities for mobilization and access to state power do political institutions affords non-elites? What kinds of historical circumstances turn these options into available political choices and what kinds of circumstances increase the determinative weight of prior institutional legacies? And, finally, as Swidler's analysis reminds us, none of this can be analysed simply in terms of the instrumental realization of a taken for granted goals and interests. Institutions enable individuals and societies to constitute new goals as well as enabling the satisfaction of goals and values already in place.

Quests for answers to the first three questions must be tightly intertwined. Elite propensities to grab assets depend on shared perceptions that doing so is both feasible in terms of the relative political strength of both competitors and non-elites and necessary in order to maintain their dominant political status. The choices that elites make with regard to asset grabs have, in turn, strong implications for the character of the state. Grabbing assets and privileging the coercive side of the state apparatus are likely to go together. If the construction of state institutions focused on the provision of infrastructure rather than amassing coercive capacity is an essential element of developmental success, then elite asset-grab strategies will undercut development both directly through their distortion of the distribution of property and indirectly through their effect on the state.

The political focus of the extended institutional turn gives non-elite mobilization a valence quite different from the one assumed in the old property rights version. Rather than property rights being threatened by the potential redistributional consequences of non-elite mobilization, the potential strength of non-elite mobilization becomes a key check on both elite asset grabs and elites' tendencies to hyper-develop the coercive side of the state apparatus.

For most of the global South, all of this takes place under circumstances in which success requires escaping institutional nightmares imposed by history, with AJR's colonially-imposed 'extractive institutions' being the primary case in point. It is, however, a central premise of the extended institutional turn that such escape is indeed possible. Denying the possibility of political choice would negate the very historical narratives on which the extension of the institutional turn is predicated.

At the same time, the extension of the institutional turn requires accepting the idea that exogenous challenges may turn what seem to be institutional dreams into nightmares. Botswana offers a heart-rending example of how institutions that appeared for decades to epitomize effectiveness can suddenly be revealed as incapable of dealing with the challenge at hand, creating a critical juncture forged from failure rather than opportunity.

And this brings us back to Swidler's fundamental proposition. An institutional analysis that takes goals and interests for granted would be intellectually impoverished. The better part of human needs and desires are culturally constructed. Enabling people to construct and reconstruct their aims is as basic a task of institutions as enabling people to satisfy the needs and desires that have been constructed. Just because this complicates linear explanatory logics does not give us an excuse for ignoring it.

The extension of the institutional turn has a long way to go before it succeeds in providing consistently compelling explanations of developmental outcomes to replace the deceptively parsimonious proofs offered by the old double finesse version of institutional analysis. Nonetheless, it has come a long way from its Northian origins. It continues to generate exciting debates across disciplines as well as within them. It is an agenda of both heuristic and practical value, well worth pursuing.

Notes

1. Citations to this and most other recent papers are based on the versions available on authors' websites. Pages numbers do not conform to those in the published version and quotations may vary from published version.
2. For an equally broad variant definition see Chang and Evans, 2005.
3. Panama and Belize are usually excluded from comparative analyses despite being geographically in Central America because they don't share to the same degree the historical features that unite the other five.
4. Colombia is, of course, not technically speaking part of Central America, but its geographical proximity, shared colonial history and reliance on coffee exports make it a reasonable addition.
5. Baland and Robinson (2005) provide a concrete confirmation and extension of the Nugent and Robinson perspective. Their analysis demonstrates that in the Chilean case, it was not just an initial allocation of land rights that was key to the economic returns of landlords but also the persistence of specific political institutions (i.e., the absence of the secret ballot) that reinforced landlords' control over those who worked the land.
6. Mahoney focuses on Central America *per se* and therefore doesn't include Colombia. Mahoney also includes Honduras and Nicaragua. I will leave them out here in order to maximize the parallels between his analysis and Nugent and Robinson's.
7. The analogies to Miguel's (2004) analysis of post-colonial nation-building in Tanzania are provocative.
8. AJR (2001:7) epitomize the 'instrumental' version of institutions in their description of settler colonies as having 'representative institutions which promoted what the settlers wanted and that what they wanted was freedom and the ability to get rich by engaging in trade'.
9. This observation is, of course, fully consistent with AJR's own admonition (2001: quoted above) that the institutional turn should shift its focus toward institutions that are 'more fundamental'.

References

Acemoglu, D. and Robinson, J. 2000. 'Why Did the West Extend the Franchise? Growth, Inequality and Democracy in Historical Perspective', *Quarterly Journal of Economics*, CXV: 1167–99.

Acemoglu, D. and Robinson, J. 2001. 'A Theory of Political Transitions', *American Economic Review* 91: 938–63.

Acemoglu, D., Johnson, S. and Robinson, J. (AJR) 2001. 'The Colonial Origins of Comparative Development: An Empirical Investigation', *American Economic Review* 91: 1369–1401.

Acemoglu, D., Johnson, S. and Robinson, J. (AJR) 2002. 'Reversal of Fortune: Geography and Institutions in the Making of the Modern World Income Distribution', *Quarterly Journal of Economics* 117: 1231–94.

Acemoglu, D., Johnson, S. and Robinson, J. (AJR) 2003. 'An African Success Story: Botswana', in Dani Rodrik (ed.), *In Search of Prosperity: Analytic Narratives on Economic Growth*, Princeton: Princeton University Press, pp. 80–122.

Acemoglu, D., Johnson, S. and Robinson, J. (AJR) 2005. 'Institutions as the Fundamental Cause of Long-Run Growth', in P. Aghion and S. Durlauf (eds), *Handbook of Economic Growth*.

Allen, T. and Heald, S. 2004. 'HIV/AIDS Policy in Africa: What has worked in Uganda and what has failed in Botswana?', *Journal of International Development*, 16: 1141–54.

Baland, J-M. and Robinson, J. A. (forthcoming) 'Land and Power: Theory and Evidence from Chile', *American Economic Review* [currently available as CEPR Discussion Paper 3800].

Banerjee, A. and Iyer, L. 2002. *History, Institutions and Economic Performance: The Legacy of Colonial Land Tenure Systems in India*, manuscript, Department of Economics, MIT.

Bardhan, P. 1989. 'The New Institutional Economics and Development Theory: A Brief Critical Assessment', *World Development*, 17(9): 1389–95.

Bardhan, P. 2005. *Scarcity, Conflicts and Cooperation: Essays in the Political and Institutional Economics of Development*, Cambridge MA: MIT Press.

Chang, H-J. and Evans, P. 2005. 'The Role of Institutions in Economic Change', in Gary Dymski and Silvana de Paula (eds), *Reimagining Growth: Institutions, Development, and Society*, New York: Edward Elgar.

Easterly, W. and Levine, R. 2003. 'Tropics, Germs, and Crops: How Endowments Influence Economic Development', *Journal of Monetary Economics* 50: 3–39.

Engerman, S. L. and Sokoloff, K. L. 1997. 'Factor Endowments, Institutions, and Differential Growth Paths among New World Economies', in Stephen Haber (ed.), *How Latin America Fell Behind*, Stanford CA: Stanford University Press.

Engerman, S. L. and Sokoloff, K. L. 2002. 'Factor Endowments, Inequality, and Paths of Development among New World Economies', *Economia*, 3: 41–88.

Evans, P. 2004. 'Development as Institutional Change: The Pitfalls of Monocropping and Potentials of Deliberation', *Studies in Comparative International Development*, 38(4): 30–53.

Evans, P. 2005. 'The Challenges of the 'Institutional Turn': New Interdisciplinary Opportunities in Development Theory', in V. Nee and R. Swedberg (eds), *The Economic Sociology of Capitalist Institutions*. Princeton: Princeton University Press, pp. 90–116

Gallup, J. L., Sachs, J. D. and Mellinger, A. D. 1998. 'Geography and Economic Development', NBER Working Paper 6849 (December), Cambridge MA: NBER.

Hoff, K. and Stiglitz, J. 2001. 'Modern Economic Theory and Development' in G. Meier and J. Stiglitz (eds), *Frontiers of Development Economics*, New York: Oxford University Press for the World Bank, pp. 389–460.

Knack, S. and Keefer, P. 1995. 'Institutions and Economic Performance: Cross-country tests using Alternative Institutional Measures', *Economics and Politics* 7(3): 207–27.

Lange, M., Mahoney, J. and vom Hau, M. (forthcoming). 'Colonialism and Development: A Comparative Analysis of Spanish and British Colonies', *American Journal of Sociology*.

Leith, J. C. 2002. *Why Botswana Prospered*, manuscript. University of Western Ontario.

Mahoney, J. 2001. *Legacies of Liberalism: Path Dependence and Political Regimes in Central America*, Baltimore MD: Johns Hopkins University Press.

Mahoney, J. 2003. 'Long-Run Development and the Legacy of Colonialism in Spanish America', *American Journal of Sociology*, 109: 50–106.

Meier, G. and Stiglitz, J. (eds) 2001. *Frontiers of Development Economics*, New York: Oxford University Press for the World Bank.

Miguel, E. 2004. 'Tribe or Nation? Nation-Building and Public Goods in Kenya versus Tanzania', *World Politics* 56(3): 327–62.

North, D. C. 1981. *Structure and Change in Economic History*. New York: Norton.

North, D. C. 1994. 'Economic Performance through Time', *American Economic Review*, 84(3): 359–68 (Nobel Prize lecture given on 19 December 1993).

North, D. C. and Thomas, R. P. 1973. *The Rise of the Western World: A New Economic History*, Cambridge: Cambridge University Press.

Nugent, J. B. and Robinson, J. A. 2001. 'Are Endowments Fate? On the Political Economy of Comparative Institutional Development', CEPR Discussion Paper 3206, London: Centre for Economic Policy Research.

Rodrik, D., Subramanian, A. and Trebbi, F. 2004. 'Institutions Rule: The Primacy of Institutions over Geography and Integration in Economic Development', *Journal of Economic Growth*, 9(2): 131–165.

Sachs, J. D. 2001. 'Tropical Underdevelopment', NBER Working Paper 8119, Cambridge MA: NBER.

Swidler, A. 2004. *The Politics of AIDS in sub-Saharan Africa*, Manuscript, Department of Sociology, University of California, Berkeley.

CHAPTER 4
INSTITUTIONALISM ANCIENT, OLD, AND NEW: A HISTORICAL PERSPECTIVE ON INSTITUTIONS AND UNEVEN DEVELOPMENT

Erik S. Reinert

1. Introduction

As a result of the inability of mainstream economics to tackle prominent problems of the global economy, some of its basic assumptions are increasingly being questioned. In this context, the standard emphasis on methodological individualism is gradually being eased in favour of studying the institutional structures necessary for economic development: The social, cultural, and political norms and habits economists had come to take for granted. This 'institutionalist' approach is most often traced back to the work of Thorstein Veblen in the late nineteenth and early twentieth century. My chapter shows how an acute awareness of the importance of institutions, and more specifically of a certain *kind* of institutions, in fact has been explicitly present in the history of economic thought and policy at least since the Renaissance. Therefore, in addition to the 'new' institutional economics of Douglass North and the 'old' institutional economics of Veblen and Commons, there existed an 'ancient' tradition of institutional economics which, among other things, informed the policies responsible for the European economic miracle in the early modern period.

In light of this 'ancient' institutionalism, I wish to explore its relevance for economic development. Whereas today's literature tends to discuss institutions independent of the type of productive structure they support, both the 'ancient' and the 'old' institutional schools saw institutions as an integral part of a particular production system. Different technological systems, or modes of production, were seen as requiring different institutions, and an institution *per se* could not change the technological system. Whereas institutions like property rights and universal suffrage today often are seen as promoting economic development, I wish to show that the arrows of causality historically have been considered going in both directions. In fact, the institution of insurance came about *after* the need for it developed out of risky long-distance trade, and modern democracies, in any meaningful sense, were the fruits of literate urban artisan and working classes rather than of feudalism.

It is therefore not entirely clear that the Masaai are poor and stuck in subsistence agriculture because they lack property rights. Perhaps, I would argue, they lack property rights because they are poor and stuck in subsistence agriculture. In other words the problem lies in their mode of production – subsistence agriculture rather than e.g., manufacturing – and *not* narrowly in an institutional arrangement in a restricted sense. An institution that suits one production system may not suit another. It can for example be argued that the sequential usufruct of land found in pastoral societies[1] is much better suited to that particular mode of production than are capitalist property rights. Precisely because institutions and mode of production of a society obviously evolved together, institutions cannot be meaningfully studied separately from a technological system which needed and created them. Today one side of the equation – institutions in isolation as instruments favouring development – has too often been emphasized, skewing our understanding of economic and institutional development.

'The discipline of daily life acts to alter or reinforce the received habits of thought, and so acts to alter or fortify the received institutions under which men live' says Veblen (1961: 314). In this chapter I argue that a conscious element should be added to this theory: There are, I will argue, enabling institutions that are deliberately created in order to induce change, as integral parts of the dynamics of evolving systems of production. Some institutions, I will argue, are of a Schumpeterian nature created pro-actively in order to promote change (e.g., patents, scientific academies), others appear through a more re-active process as solutions to 'reverse salients' (e.g., insurance facilitating long-distance trading) that hinder the desired development of the system (Hughes, 1987).[2] These two forms are clearly closely related, but differ qualitatively in being more or less pro-active or re-active in nature.

A fundamental fault line in economics over the centuries is Werner Sombart's classic distinction between *passivistic-materialistic* and *activistic-idealistic* economics. The latter focuses on production rather than trade and anchored its analysis of economic development in institutions and social synergies, using the human body as the basic metaphor for society. The former – founding economics on physics-based metaphors – focuses on trade rather than production and dismisses institutions and social synergies. The practical consequences of this dismissal are, I will argue, highly dramatic. One fundamental problem of today's development debate is that the vast majority of participants come from the *passivistic-materialistic* tradition which – since Adam Smith – has largely exogenized production and unlearned Werner Sombart's definition of capitalism as consisting of (1) the entrepreneur, (2) the modern state, and (3) the *industrial system*. At its core the history of institutions is a history of the Schumpeterian institutions that enabled the growth and spread of this industrial system across the developed world. By this definition, capitalism never reached the production system of the colonies, colonialism was for centuries in effect a technology policy aimed at keeping industry out of the colonies. Herein lies the core of the problems of Third World poverty, not in their geography or climate.

I have previously argued (Reinert, 1999) that economic development is *activity-specific*, tied to certain economic activities exhibiting high productivity growth and increasing returns in a synergetic system formed by the presence of a large division of labour, in short what Werner Sombart calls 'the industrial system'. That only the presence of such an industrial system will create efficient agriculture was a key insight of the 1700s (Reinert and Reinert, 2005) that was also at the core of US development and industrial policy into the twentieth century. The inability of neo-classical tools to capture these production-specific variables has lead to the 'Geography, Climate and Disease School of Poverty', which in a sense is right for the wrong reason. What this school fails to see is that it was the policy of diversification away from raw materials, creating an industrial system, which made the presently developed countries rich. Climate enters the picture only indirectly, via Veblenian vested interests. The temperate zone attracted enough immigration to create a vested interest for protecting local industry even against the mother country (e.g., Australia, Canada, New Zealand, South Africa), whereas the settlers in the tropical countries were mainly exporting raw materials. The experience of Rhodesia shows how real wages increased dramatically when the boycott forced the white settlers there to industrialize. As was the case with the United States under the Napoleonic Wars, a boycott created a highly beneficial involuntary import substitution.

Finally, I will show how institutions can change character over time, and how our taxonomy of institutions might benefit from a broader analysis of their costs and benefits in different contexts, an approach that was far from unknown to the 'ancient' institutionalists. Institutions that at one point were beneficial can also, with the passage of time, become roadblocks for development. In terms of economic development, we must therefore never forget that the institutions necessary for Third World development may – at any point in time – be very different from those beneficial to the industrialized world, and that our past, the only real laboratory of the economics profession, still is able to shed light on the future development of the world's poor.

2.   The Renaissance and the birth of Schumpeterian institutions

'It is not sufficient to inquire whether an institution of the state is attested to have been founded by our ancestors. Rather it is necessary that we understand and explain *why* it was instituted. For it is by knowing the *cause* that we gain knowledge of a thing.' This statement on methodology is found in an analysis of the Florentine Constitution written in 1413 (Baron, 1966: 207) at the request of Emperor Sigismund of the Holy Roman Empire. The author, Leonardo Bruni (1369–1444), represents what has become known as the school of *civic humanism*, the ideology of the successful Italian city-states of the Renaissance.

Bruni's description of Florence and its institutions represents something of a watershed in the social sciences. While earlier literature tended to focus on mere descriptions of facts, Bruni creates an analysis of economic institutions combining both the dynamics of *causality* and *deliberate design*. Institutions, he argued, tend to be created with a clear purpose in mind, as part of a conscious strategy aimed at achieving defined dynamic political and /or economic goals. These were institutions aimed at breaking the equilibrium of the Middle Ages: They were change-inducing and change-enabling institutions that I suggest calling *Schumpeterian Institutions*. The ability to create such Schumpeterian institutions that enables the structural change that we call economic development – and to change these institutions when new conditions so require – comes across as a key feature of the organizational capability of any society.

While the study of institutions themselves seems to grow out of the mediaeval legal tradition, the appearance of this change-inducing type of institutions increased in importance as a new cosmology unlocked the previous zero-sum worldview (Reinert and Reinert, 2005). Many of the necessary elements can be traced far back in time, but only during the period we have come to call the Renaissance did they achieve a critical mass sufficient to profoundly change society in the whole Italian peninsula, and later, the rest of Europe. First of all, the undeniable urban bias of wealth creation was, at the time, identified as the result of *synergic effects*, what Florentine chancellor Brunetto Latini (c.1210–94) had called the 'common weal' or 'common good' (Latini, 1993). This *ben comune* that made some cities so wealthy sprang from an organic social synergy, seeing the body as the metaphor for society. This idea of a synergic *common good* forms the nexus from which the ideas of enabling institution grew.

The Medieval scholastics saw the universe as fundamentally static, while the Renaissance envisioned the cosmos as expanding, permanently in flux. Based on this, they created institutions in order to promote and spread economic growth: Among them tax breaks and bounties to firms bringing in new technology, the establishment of scientific academies and, in England under Elizabeth I, an apprentice system (for a more complete list see Reinert, 1999).

The same 1400s, when Leonardo Bruni wrote, saw the birth of two important economic institutions: both children of the same *Weltanschauung*, both created specifically in order to increase and spread knowledge: *patents* (to make new inventions profitable) and *strategic tariff protection* (in order to make it profitable to spread inventions to new geographical areas: to spread manufacturing). Although tariffs had been used to raise revenue since 'three-score years after the Birth of Christ' according to a seventeenth century author, their use as part of a strategy of change is only clear with Henry VII of England in 1485.[3] The first patents also appear during the last two decades of the *quattrocento,* in Venice. In the right circumstances and in the appropriate doses, these institutions have remained successful and visible hands of economic development ever since.

The study of institutions, then, has been part of social and political science for a very long time. Jakob Friedrich von Bielfeld's cameralist treatise in economics entitled *Institutions politiques* was first published in 1760, and reached a total of 12 editions in French, German, Italian, Spanish and Russian (Bielfeld, 1760). However, as we shall discuss later, this venerable emphasis on the importance of institutions in economic and political development was excluded from the toolbox when Adam Smith set the stage of modern economics. Smith's economics became what nineteenth century continental economists called *catalectics*, that is, the science of exchange, not of production. In this science of barter, trade and exchange, the dynamics of knowledge, technology and production and the Schumpeterian institutions that are needed to support them tended to disappear.

Consequently, important aspects of the scholastic equilibrium world view returned with physics-based equilibrium economics (neo-classical economics). Here economics became a theory of accumulation of capital and allocation of resources, rather than of the creation and assimilation of new knowledge. The dynamic institutions that were products of the Renaissance world view – such as patents and protection – became foreign bodies in neo-classical economic theory. With the methodological individualism of neo-classical theory, the fifteenth century view of wealth as a synergetic phenomenon in society – so important for understanding institutions – also disappeared.

I suggest then that in addition to the 'old' institutional school originating with Thorstein Veblen and associated with the later US institutionalists and the 'new' institutional school built on neo-classical economics, an 'ancient' institutional school also exists. This is not a radical preposition *per se*, as the nineteenth century American historiography out of which Veblen's *Theory of the Leisure Class* emerged was well versed in the study of ancient institutions. Henry Sumner Maine's seminal 1875 *Lectures on The Early History of Institutions*, which ventured as far back as the institutional structures of the pre-Christian druids, can indeed be seen as forming a bridge between the 'ancient' and the 'old' institutional schools. Veblen quoted the book often, and studied with Maine's heirs at Cornell in the early 1890s (Viano, 2006).

3.   Institutions and economic traditions in the context of the present development debate

From this vantage point, the present debate on the role of institutions in economic development – ably described in Chang (chapter 2) and Evans (chapter 3) in this volume – unveils a fault line that has been a dominant feature of economics since the eighteenth century. Werner Sombart (Sombart, 1928: 919), the great analyst of capitalism, generally distinguished between the *activistic-idealistic* Renaissance tradition – which I refer to as The Other Canon (Reinert and Daastøl, 2004) – and the *passivistic-materialistic* tradition which originated in the eighteenth century with Bernhard Mandeville, physiocracy, and Adam Smith.

The tradition in which Leonardo Bruni wrote is the prototypical *activistic-idealistic* type of economics, a tradition that considered economic development the result of *deliberate design*. In this tradition Italian economists Giovanni Botero (1590) and Antonio Serra (1613) explained uneven economic development as resulting from differences in the productive structures of nations; of scale, increasing and diminishing returns, 'windows of opportunity' for innovation, degree of division of labour and synergies. The large division of labour in the Italian city states – compared to the situation in the countryside – gave birth to relative political freedom, to the rule of law, and to the institutions protecting property rights. Strikingly, the first cadastral register in Venice was created already in the years 1148–1156.

The analysis of the *activistic-idealistic* tradition also included factors like geography and climate. While it was exceedingly obvious to economic writers at the time that wealth often depended on geographical factors, it was certainly viable to compensate for 'bad' geography with *good economic policy*. It was clear to most observers in the activistic-idealistic tradition that the few wealthy areas of Europe tended to be islands, and that this was no coincidence. In the 'commodity lottery' the winners seemed to be areas that had little or no arable land. The geographical position and the lack of arable land in places like Venice, Genoa, and the Dutch Republic had forced the inhabitants into making a living from manufacturing and trading. However, the nations that had drawn worse lots – e.g., rather counterintuitively having much arable land – could compensate for that disadvantage through *conscious economic policies*, to which Serra (1613) devotes a whole chapter. It is clear that much early economic theory indeed was born, as a reaction to this lottery, in the poor countries that tried to emulate the productive structures of the wealthier areas of Europe. Their strategic geographical positions and the lack of arable land had made Venice and the Dutch Republic wealthy by creating an industrial system with a huge division of labour. Other countries could create copies of these wealth-producing economic structures by promoting the same kind of activities found there. This required conscious economic policies.

The forces of Fate and Providence could thus be counteracted by wise economic policies. It is crucial to understand, however, that such economic policies, ever since Henry VII's successful industrialization of England (Reinert, 1996), initially – and sometimes for centuries – required making *a less efficient* copy of the productive structure observed in the leading nations (Reinert and Reinert, 2005). This required tariffs. A key objective of economic policies was for centuries to achieve the right balance between *agriculture, manufacturing*, and *trade* – activities that were seen as being *qualitatively different* – that would maximize human welfare. Even with the advantage of lower wages enjoyed by poor nations in competing for world markets, the dynamics of learning, technology, scale, and market sizes made it impossible to catch up with the 'naturally rich' nations like Venice and the

Dutch Republic without some kind of 'artificial' support of the targeted industries. Only by creating production units that from a business point of view initially were less efficient than those of the leading countries, laggard nations could raise their standard of living. Thus, in the short term the interests of the nation's inhabitants as *consumers* were sacrificed in the interest of the same inhabitants as *producers*. When the desired economic structure had been achieved, it was clear to all that the increased level of income more than compensated for the increased price level. Through economic policy nations without the natural and geographical advantages of Venice and the Dutch Republic were able to catch up with these leaders. Their toolbox for catching up has now essentially been outlawed by the 'conditionalities' of the Washington institutions.

However, the *timing* of this protection was crucial: The same institution that in one context would cause *increased* welfare would, in another context, *decrease* welfare. Once a certain domestic industrial capacity was reached, access to larger markets was deemed more important than continuing protection: '*tariffs*', as an anonymous Italian political economist travelling in Holland observed, '*are as useful for introducing the arts in a country, as they are damaging once these are established*' (Anonymous, 1786: 31).

In this framework economic development is *activity-specific*: Intimately tied to diversified economic structures that both individually and as a whole are subject to dynamic increasing returns. Institutions therefore become *context specific*, the same institutions that are appropriate in one context may become totally inappropriate in another. As we shall discuss later, in a technologically dynamic system institutional unlearning becomes as important as institutional learning and – as Chang points out in this volume – an institution like property rights cannot be regarded as 'something good in itself'. Context is again the key. There can be both 'too much' and 'too little' property rights, as well as institutional perversion, as we shall see under the discussion of patents.

Institutions, then, are only fully comprehensible as they relate to a future goal to be achieved. In this evolutionary world view, the economy is not on its way to any equilibrium, but rather towards some future optimum that is never reached, because the dynamics of new knowledge and technology continuously change both the present and the prospects for the future. In the activistic-idealistic tradition this goal is economic *progress* or economic development. Both in the eighteenth and nineteenth centuries this progress was generally seen as moving through qualitatively different stages, e.g. from a hunting and gathering society to a pastoral society to an agricultural society to a society based on handicraft, and finally through an industrial society (Reinert, 2000). It was obvious to all that an industrial society would create a higher standard of living than a hunting and gathering society. Institutions were tools from which this progress from one stage to another was crafted, and their dynamics had to be understood in the context of the productive structure.

This tradition contrasts with the *passivistic-materialistic* tradition. Starting with Adam Smith, three methodological innovations evolved – peaking with the work of David Ricardo – creating a fundamental change in the nature of economics.

1. Production and trade were unified and converted into 'labour' (Biernacki, 1995: 252).
2. Society as a unit of analysis disappeared in favour of 'methodological individualism': With this the synergetic elements disappeared and private rate of return became identical with societal rate of return.
3. Inventions and innovations were exogenized from the economic theory.

Collectively, these assumptions radically changed economics in a variety of ways: First of all, in this theory all economic activities became qualitatively alike as carriers of economic activities ('the equality assumption'). Markets thus became institutions that automatically created harmony. A major innovation brought by this kind of economic theory was that, for the first time, colonialism became morally defensible (Reinert and Reinert, 2005). Previously it had been clear to most social scientists that the key element of colonialism – prohibiting the establishment of manufacturing – was tantamount to poverty.

With Adam Smith the metaphor on which the science of economics was based also changed. Since Roman Law, the basic metaphor in understanding society had been the human body, where synergies are obvious. When the basic metaphor for economics became physics-based – either with the invisible hand that kept the social system together or later with equilibrium physics – the need for institutions in order to oil the machinery of progress disappeared. Since its conception with Adam Smith, an important hallmark of *laissez-faire* theory has therefore been its *neglect* of institutions. Harvard economic historian Thomas McCraw puts it this way: 'Smith exhibits a powerful aesthetic aversion to any type of collective action, a visceral distaste bordering on revulsion. For him, '"human institutions" so invariably produce "absurd" results that they have no presumptive legitimacy' (McCraw, 1992: 364).

4.   Institution-building and development: Co-evolution and the direction of arrows of causality

This section looks at how the question of causality between institutional change and productive structures has been evaluated by social scientists. In my opinion the virtually unanimous consensus across Europe from very early on was that – in spite of obvious elements of co-evolution – that *the mode of production of a society* would create the demand for new institutions and itself mould, shape and determine these.

'Industry moulds people' is the title of a 1929 book, recently reprinted (Kautz, 1929/1994). Industrialization changed attitudes and institutions, changes that would have been both impossible and undesirable in the absence of that industrialization. Feudal societies cannot have the institutions of industrial societies, so human attitudes and institutions are more a product of their mode of production than the other way around. As Thorstein Veblen puts it:

> It may be said that institutions are of the nature of prevalent habits of thought, and that therefore the force which shapes institutions is the force or forces which shape the habits of thought prevalent in the community. But habits of thought are the outcome of the habits of life. Whether it is intentionally directed to the education of the individual or not, the discipline of daily life acts to alter or reinforce the received habits of thought, and so acts to alter or fortify the received institutions under which men live. And the direction in which, on the whole, the alteration proceeds is conditioned by the trend of the discipline of daily life. (Veblen, 1961: 314)

In 1620 Francis Bacon formulated a view that was to dominate in the social sciences for centuries: 'There is a startling difference between the life of men in the most civilized provinces of Europe, and in the wildest and most barbarous districts of New India. This difference comes not from the soil, not from climate, not from race, but from *the arts*'. Francis Bacon is clear on the causality in question: Man's activities – his modes of production – determine his institutions. Further geographical discoveries were only to reinforce this view. William Robertson's *The History of America* (1777) emphasizes Bacon's point: 'In every inquiry concerning the operations of men when united together in society, the first object of attention should be their mode of subsistence. Accordingly as that varies, their laws and policies must be different' (Reinert, 2000).

When Johan Jacob Meyen, a German scientist, in 1769 stated, 'It is known that a primitive people does not improve its customs and institutions, later to find useful industries, but the other way around' he expressed an understanding of causality that was considered common sense at the time. In the *Communist Manifesto* Karl Marx and Friedrich Engels follow the same line of reasoning: Technical change brought on by manufacturing is the driving force of change; it is manufacturing that rescued people from what they call the idiocy (isolation/stasis) of rural life.

> The bourgeoisie, by the rapid improvement of all instruments of production, by the immensely facilitated means of communication, draws all, even the most barbarian, nations into civilization... . The bourgeoisie has subjected the country to the rule of the towns. It has created enormous cities, has greatly increased the urban population as compared with the rural, and has thus rescued a considerable part of the population from the idiocy of rural life.

This *mode-of-production-based* view of institutions is in my view strongly at odds with the present World Bank view, where institutions *per se* – freed from any understanding of the system of production – are supposed to solve problems of development. By looking at institutions *per se*, crucial factors involving demand, knowledge, synergies, cumulative causations and the activity-specific nature of economic growth are all excluded. To early modern 'mercantilist' writers it would not be meaningful to attempt to understand the institutional development of Europe independent of the underlying strategy of industrialization that prompted the establishment of so many key institutions. The establishment of an apprentice system in England under Elizabeth I cannot be understood outside the context of a highly successful Tudor strategy of building English woolen manufactures during the 1500s. The establishment of countless scientific academies in the 1700s all over Europe must also be understood as part of a strategy to establish economic activities outside the agricultural sector. The success of these diversification strategies in turn created new institutional arrangements.

'Mercantilist' institutions cannot be understood outside a context of nations seeking to escape a comparative advantage in producing raw materials. The present focus on institutions tends to see them statically and context-free rather than as parts of a complex dynamic link of causality of economic development. In reality a large number of institutions are part of a much broader process of economic development that is incompatible with the internal logic of present mainstream economics. Seeing institutions independently of the productive system they support and sustain is not meaningful. Attempting to establish scientific academies in hunting and gathering tribes is therefore attacking the problem from the wrong end. *History shows that only societies that have achieved a certain level of manufacturing and/or other increasing return activities have ever achieved the 'right' institutions or any degree of 'competitiveness'. Hundreds of years of accumulated experience show that today's maxim 'get the institutions right' cannot be solved independently of 'getting into the right kind of economic activities'.*

Historically, we can often observe that the economic activity establishing a demand for the institution in question would appear before the institution itself. A 'reverse salient' that hindered the evolution of the system was solved by establishing a new institution. Insurance was created as the result of high-risk camel caravans and other long distance trading. The caravans and the ocean trade were there long before the important institution of insurance, and without these high-risk ventures such institutions are much less likely to evolve. Banking was created in the Italian city-states, where certain economic activities created a demand for such institutions, and introducing banking in a society which is not ripe for such institutions may therefore easily fail. Over the centuries, manufacturing industries in particular were seen as a necessary ingredient in creating the most desirable institutions, including political freedom. Beneficial institutions were, to some extent, seen as unintended secondary effects of establishing certain types of economic activities.

It can be argued that even as late as after the Second World War – with the Marshall Plan to reindustrialize Europe – the 'technology of institution building' in terms of *creating* wealth was based on targeting the kind of activities that would bring the right kinds of institutions, not the other way around. Also, particularly since the 1870s, the *distributive* institutions aimed at solving the social problems brought by industrialization were systematically and consciously created by accumulation of case studies by the German *Verein für Sozialpolitik* (1872–1932). Their construction of the institutions that created the welfare state – from health plans to unemployment benefits – played a key role in all of Europe.

German economist Karl Diehl (1941) used a piece by Swedish playwright August Strindberg to discuss the relationship between modes of production and economic institutions, reaffirming the tradition that institutions are determined by the mode of production, and that it is not really constructive to attempt reversing the arrow of causality. In Strindberg's novel *De lycksaligas ö* ('The island of the blissful') a group of eighteenth century Swedish convicts, including two young students who had insulted the King, experience a sequence of Robinson Crusoe type shipwrecks on their way to a far-away colony that they never reach (Strindberg, 1882/1913). Led by the students, the convicts — by now free from any authority — establish their own society and consciously discuss the abolishment or establishment of the institutions they are used to at home. While at the most tropical of the islands visited, they decide to abolish most of the known institutions. You need no inheritance law if you walk around naked and harvest the fruits of the earth, they argue. When, after a second shipwreck, they reach an island with a more temperate climate, they discover that their new life-style requires the reintroduction of institutions that they had previously abandoned as useless. August Strindberg shows us Francis Bacon's point: An institutional system is mainly moulded around the needs determined by the mode of production, not the other way around.

Having lost a qualitative type of understanding which can only be achieved by understanding production, rather than just barter and trade, neo-classical economics has lost this connection between production and institutions: The activity-specific element of institutional development which for centuries was commonly known to social scientists. This loss is much to the detriment of many developing countries today. Thus, we would argue that the problem of 'failed states' and their institutional failures cannot meaningfully be discussed independently of the kind of economic activities in which these states engage.

Historically institution-building has been intimately tied to strategies of learning and change, of changing the economic fabric of a society, a way of thinking not easily captured within a neo-classical *laissez-faire* framework. In 1404 the magistrates of Bruges, in Flanders, requested the magistrates of Barcelona to inform them what the common practice was in regard to bills of exchange (Beckmann, 1797: 482). This is an example of a conscious attempt to import an institution in order to increase production and trade in their city. Again, studying institutions *per se* in an equilibrium framework, outside the context of the desired process of change, is in our view generally not meaningful. Likewise, we would argue that it is not meaningful to study institutions divorced from the historical setting that made the desired change feasible. Institutional change must therefore be seen, as traditionally it has been, in a dynamic context of technological change where different economic activities, operating in a system of synergy, are seen as playing different roles, demanding and creating very different institutional frameworks.

5.   Institutions as roadblocks to change: Institutional inertia, institutional overdoses, and institutional perversions

Just as they may open the path for Schumpeterian creative destruction, institutions may – if they have been created in order to further an old order to be destroyed – function as roadblocks for change. Karl Marx and Thorstein Veblen both discuss institutional inertia as such roadblocks impeding change. As Carlota Perez argues, fundamentally new technologies require not only new institutions, they simultaneously require and develop a new type of organizational common sense (Perez, 2004). The slow speed of institutional unlearning thus hinders technological change. Feudalist institutions hindered industrialization, and had to be demolished. Similarly Thorstein Veblen – that quintessential institutional economist – argued that new technologies spread better in new environments where old institutions do not hold them back. This is clearly an important mechanism that explains why periods of radical technological change are also periods when new nations – uninhibited by institutions that preserve the old order – are able to leapfrog into world leadership.

It is natural that the observation of institutional inertia serving as a roadblock to further development will appear in periods with radical technological change, in the transition period between techno-economic paradigms. The timing of the references of Marx, Nietzsche, Veblen, and Perez/Freeman all testify to this.

This same type of argument is often used to explain why immigrants tend to be more entrepreneurial than locals: They are unbound by the existing institutional framework in their new country. Again, with Veblen the *activities themselves* tend to push the institutional change, not the other way around. The technology of institution-building must therefore, in our view, be deeply integrated into Leonardo Bruni's question from 1413: The question of *why* it was instituted. A failure to do this leads down today's slippery slope where mainstream policy-making seems to indicate that what African hunting and gathering tribes need are better property rights rather than a different production structure.

Also Friedrich Nietzsche describes, in a quite poetic way, an institutional inertia where ideas come first and only slowly are able to change institutions: 'The overthrow of institutions does not follow immediately upon the overthrow of opinions, instead, the new opinions live for a long time in the desolate and strangely unfamiliar house of their predecessors and even preserve it themselves, since they need some sort of shelter' (Nietzsche, 2000: 4708).

Technological dynamics requires that institutions be seen dynamically as they relate to changes in the productive sectors. In this context institutions must be understood as *context-specific* tools in a setting where economic development is *activity-specific* and where the factor bias of economic development changes over time. A changing factor-bias of economic development means that some economic periods need one factor of production more intensely than other periods, as e.g., the age of railways was relatively intensive in the use of capital. This would in turn change the institutional requirements of one era from those of another. It is also possible that institutions that are productive and legitimate in a certain dose may – in a larger dose – become either unproductive or illegitimate or both. Institutional overdoses are entirely possible, and they may bring with them a perversion of institutions as compared to their original intent.

The Inca Empire, or *Tahuantinsuyu*, is the largest society known to have functioned without the use of money, with an estimated 12 million inhabitants ranging from the north of present-day Chile to the south of Colombia, including large parts of Bolivia, Peru and Ecuador. In a society without money, taxes are paid by working a certain number of days a year for the community. In many countries military conscription represents to this very day this type of tax-by-labour. In the Inca Empire this tax institution was known as the *mita* (Murra, 1978). In a year with 365 days, 36.5 days of work per year would represent a tax rate of 10 per cent.

When the Spanish arrived and needed labour for the mines, they extended the *mita* to what in effect became slavery. This is an early example of how legitimate institutions are used in a way that makes them ethically illegitimate. Today the changes taking place in the fifteenth century institution of patents may be not only be comparable to the 'illegitimate' change in the Inca institution of *mita*, but also be unproductive in the sense that the institution of patents in some cases may hinder rather than foster innovations (Perelman, 2002).

There are examples of too broad patents previously awarded being revoked because they blocked further innovations. Today, allowing patents to move upstream from products to e.g., genes may block rather than promote further research. This is a case of 'institutional perversion' similar to one observed by Adam Smith. At the time of Smith's writing, the institution of patents in England had clearly partly become perverted. Instead of supporting innovations, the kings would sell monopolies in order to finance expensive wars. In this way patents become vehicles of static rent-seeking rather than of dynamic Schumpeterian rent-seeking as they were supposed to.

In 1943 the Supreme Court of the United States held the broad claims of Guglielmo Marconi's patent for improvements in apparatus for wireless telegraphy to be invalid. In a similar way, the Wright brothers were granted a patent by the US Patent Office in 1906 for a flying machine. An array of patent litigations was to follow. This ended only with the advent of the First World War, when the aircraft manufacturers formed a patent pool with the approval of the US government, causing all patent litigation to cease automatically (Perelman, 2002). In the new knowledge-based economy, the encroachment of patents into the areas closest to the frontier of knowledge makes catching-up through reverse engineering – a common tool for catching up under Fordist mass production – increasingly impossible. This is no doubt an issue that will grow in importance in the years to come.

Some institutions importantly serve dual, multiple, and systemic purposes. Indeed, industrialization was seen as the nucleus of the virtuous circles of growth and development. Customs duties for a long time played the dual role of creating fiscal income and industrialization. This combination was particularly important in weak nations in the economic periphery, as in Latin America, where the ports were one of the few geographic areas that the state fully controlled. Going back to the original sources, however, not a minimal doubt exists that a primary purpose of import duties after 1485 was a strategy to change the economic structure of a nation rather than to increase fiscal income.

6.   Conclusion: Bringing production and institutions back *together*

Long before the 1532 arrival of the Spaniards in Peru, Nicolas Oresme – in his 1355 treatise on the invention of money – complains about another kind of institutional perversion: That money is no longer used only as it was intended (Oresme *c.*1355/1956). Too much money was hoarded as treasure rather than being used in order to foment trade and production, which was the reason money had been invented in the first place. Both the Leonardo Bruni 1413 quote at the start of section 2 of this chapter and Oresme's insistence on how consciously institutions were made in order to achieve specific dynamic economic goals should stand as examples leading us away from the static neo-classical view of institutions and into the rediscovery of the 'ancient' and dynamic institutional school of economics. Here we find an extremely rich literature, covering close to 800 years, on the dynamic role of institutions and production working together to create economic growth and welfare.

I have argued that around the fifteenth century this 'ancient' institutional school acquired a dynamic and Schumpeterian character, emphasizing innovations and structural change. This tradition looked at institutions as they affected the dynamics of changing modes of production, much as these two elements were combined in the writings of Thorstein Veblen. The people who in the late 1400s established both patents (in order to make it profitable to create new knowledge) and dynamic tariffs (in order to resettle newly created knowledge and technologies in new nations) obviously had a very clear model of economic development in their heads: A model where the creation and diffusion of new knowledge were at the core of an economic strategy creating wealth. Patents and tariffs, when used for this purpose, are typically *Schumpeterian institutions*. When Adam Smith later exogenized the production of knowledge, and to a large extent also production itself, from economic theory, economics became catalectics – a science of exchange – and mainstream institutionalism rarely ventures beyond the study of the institutions needed for this exchange to take place and those needed to protect property. Such equilibrium-producing institutions are typically the focus points of 'new' institutional theory.

What is so serious about today's situation is that mainstream economics – with catalectics at its very core – generally ignores that institutionalism outside their own 'new' institutionalism possesses a theory. We are, as I see it, back to the perennial fault lines in the economics profession as defined above by Werner Sombart. Ronald Coase's dismissal of 'old' institutionalism is typical: 'Without a theory they had nothing to pass on except a mass of descriptive material waiting for a theory, or a fire' (Coase, 1984: 230). In this spirit, solutions to the poverty problems of today are not sought where they are to be found – in the application of inappropriate models of standard textbook economics – but way outside economics itself, in the realm of Providence, climate, disease, and geography.

Werner Sombart understood capitalism as a system of production consisting of 1) the entrepreneur, 2) the modern state, and 3) *the industrial system*. By studying how institutions strategically affect such production systems, it is possible to unveil the mechanisms creating and distributing wealth and poverty. Today however, Adam Smith's reduction of production and trade to a common unity of 'labour' – thereby leaving out the study of production – continues to haunt the economics profession as a nemesis. Having lost the necessary understanding of production, mainstream economics instead brings back peripheral factors like climate, geography and disease to the core of mainstream development economics. In this way an irrational belief in the invisible hand of the market as an equalizer of world income combines with a primitive belief in Fate and Providence. In my view this leads to a primitivization of the theory itself; to a pre-Renaissance world view where Mankind is helplessly left at the mercy of outside forces rather than being in charge of its own destiny. In this spirit, the basic problem facing poor countries is that the tools and policy instruments that historically subjugated Fate and Providence – allowing poor nations to catch up by creating industrial systems – are today outlawed by the Washington institutions.

Notes

1. Sequential usufruct means that, rooted in traditional usage, different groups use the same land at different times of the year. Property rights in the capitalist sense do not exist. The system can best be compared to 'time-sharing' of apartments as practiced in many holiday resorts today.
2. I am consciously comparing the structural development of an economy to that of an evolving technological system, and adopting the term reverse salient from the technological systems literature. 'A salient is a protrusion in a geometric figure, a line of battle, or an expanding weather front. As technological systems expand, reverse salients develop. Reverse salients are components in the system that have fallen behind or are out of phase with the others' (Hughes, 1987).
3. We know that Henry's strategy from 1485 was an attempt to replicate the economic structure in the part of France where he had grown up (Reinert, 1996), but it is also quite possible that it was built on observation of how previous revenue tariffs in England had, as beneficial unintended by-products, changed economic structures and created more wealth.

References

Anonymous 1786. *Relazione di una scorsa per varie provincie d'Europa del M. M... a Madama G. in Parigi*. Pavia: Monastero di S. Salvatore.

Arthur, B. 1989. 'Competing Technologies, Increasing Returns and Lock-in by Historical Events'. *Economic Journal*, 99: 116–31

Bacon, F. 1930. 'New Atlantis', in Charles M. Andrews (ed.), *Famous Utopias*, New York: Tudor Publishing.

Baron, H. 1966. *The Crisis of the Early Italian Renaissance*, Princeton: Princeton University Press.

Beckmann, J. 1797. *A History of Inventions and Discoveries*. Translated from the German by William Johnston, London: printed for J. Bell, 3 volumes.

Bielfeld, J. F. 1760. *Institutions Politiques*, The Hague: Pierre Gosse Junior.

Biernacki, R. 1995. *The Fabrication of Labour: Germany and Britain, 1640–1914, Studies on the History of Society and Culture*, 22. Berkeley: University of California Press.

Botero, G. 1590. *Della ragione di stato. Libri dieci, this work also contains Delle cause della grandezza delle città, libri tre*, Rome: Vicenzio Pellagalo.

Carpenter, K. 1975. *The Economic Bestsellers Before 1850*, Bulletin No. 11, May, of the Kress Library of Business and Economics, Boston: Harvard Business School.

Coase, R. H. 1984. 'The New Institutional Economics', *Journal of Institutional and Theoretical Economics*, March.

Diehl, K. 1941. *Die sozialrechtliche Richtung in der Nationalökonomie*, Jena: Fischer.

Ely, R. 1903. *Studies in the Evolution of Industrial Society*, New York: Chautauqua Press.

Fanfani, A. 1955. *Storia delle dottrine economiche dall'antichità al XIX secolo*. Milan: Giuseppe Principato.

Ferguson, J. M. 1938. *Landmarks of Economic Thought*, New York: Longmans, Green & Co.

Hamilton, A. 1791. *A Report on the Manufactures of the United States*. On http://www.juntosociety.com/i_documents/ah_rom.htm

Hughes, T. P. 1987. 'The Evolution of Large Technological Systems' in W. E. Bijker, T. P. Hughes and T. J. Pinch (eds), *The Social Construction of Technological Systems. New Directions in the Sociology and History of Technology*. Cambridge: Cambridge University Press.

Kautz, H. 1929. *Industrie formt Menschen. Versuch einer Normierung der Industriepädagogik*. Einsiedeln: Benzinger (republished Hildesheim, Olms 1994)

King, C. 1721. *The British Merchant; or, Commerce Preserv'd*, London: John Darby, 3 volumes.

Latini, B. 1993. *The Book of the Treasure (Li livres dou tresor)*, New York: Garland Publishing.

List, F. 1841. *Das Nationale System der Politischen Ökonomie*, Stuttgart: Cotta.

Maine, H. S. 1875. *Lectures on The Early History of Institutions*, London: John Murray.

McCraw, T. 1992. 'The Trouble with Adam Smith', *The American Scholar*, 61(3, Summer).

Meek, R. 1976. *Social Science and the Ignoble Savage*, Cambridge: Cambridge University Press.

Murra, J. 1978. *La organización económica del estado inca*, México: Siglo XXI.

Muthu, S. 2003. *Enlightenment against Empire*, Princeton: Princeton University Press.

Myrdal, G. 1956. *Development and Underdevelopment. A Note on the Mechanisms of National and International Economic Inequality*, Cairo: National Bank of Egypt.

Nietzsche, F. 2000. *Werke*, Digitale Bibliothek Band 31, Berlin: Directmedia (CD-Rom).

North, D. C. 1991. 'Institutions', *Journal of Economic Perspectives*, 5: 97–112.

Oresme, N. (*c.*1355/1956) *De moneta of Nicholas Oresme and English Mint Documents*, edited and translated by Charles Johnson, London: Thomas Nelson.

Perelman, M. 2002. *Steal This Idea: Intellectual Property Rights and the Corporate Confiscation of Creativity*, New York: Palgrave Macmillan.

Perez, C. 2004. 'Technological Revolutions, Paradigm Shifts and Socio-Institutional Change', in E. S. Reinert (ed.), *Globalization, Economic Development and Inequality: An Alternative Perspective*, Edward Elgar: Cheltenham.

Polanyi, K. 1944. *The Great Transformation*, New York: Rinehart and Co.

Reinert, E. S. 1996. 'The role of technology in the creation of rich and poor nations: Underdevelopment in a Schumpeterian system' in D. H. Aldcroft and R. Catterall (eds), *Rich Nations – Poor Nations. The Long Run Perspective*, Aldershot: Edward Elgar.

Reinert, E. S. 1999. 'The role of the state in economic growth'. *Journal of Economic Studies* 26 (4/5). On www.othercanon.org

Reinert, E. 2000a. 'Karl Bücher and the Geographical Dimensions of Techno-Economic Change', in J. Backhaus (ed.), *K. Bücher: Theory – History – Anthropology – Non-Market Economies*, Marburg: Metropolis Verlag.

Reinert, E. 2000b. 'Full Circle: Economics from Scholasticism through Innovation and back into Mathematical Scholasticism. Reflections around a 1769 price essay: "Why is it that Economics so Far has Gained so Few Advantages from Physics and Mathematics?"', *Journal of Economic Studies* 27(4/5). On www.othercanon.org

Reinert, E. S. (ed.) 2004a. *Globalization, Economic Development and Inequality: An Alternative Perspective*. Edward Elgar, Cheltenham.

Reinert, E. S. 2004b. 'Benchmarking Success: The Dutch Republic (1500–1750) as seen by Contemporary European Economists', in *How Rich Nations got Rich. Essays in the History of Economic Policy*. Working Paper 1, SUM – Centre for Development and the Environment, University of Oslo. http://www.sum.uio.no/publications

Reinert, E. S. 2005b. 'Development and Social Goals: Balancing Aid and Development to Prevent 'Welfare Colonialism', in *Post-Autistic Economics Review*, 30 (21 March), article 1, http://www.btinternet.com/~pae_news/review/issue30.htm

Reinert, E. S. 2006. *How Rich Nations Got Rich and Why Poor Countries Stay Poor*, London: Constable and Robinson (Norwegian edition 2004, Spartacus, Oslo).

Reinert, E. and Daastøl, A. 1997. 'Exploring the Genesis of Economic Innovations: The religious gestalt-switch and the duty to invent as preconditions for economic growth', *European Journal of Law and Economics*, 4(2/3): 233–83, and in *Christian Wolff. Gesammelte Werke, Materialien und Dokumente*, Hildesheim: Georg Olms Verlag, 1998.

Reinert, E. S. and Daastøl, A. 2004. 'The Other Canon: The History of Renaissance Economics. Its Role as an Immaterial and Production-based Canon in the History of Economic Thought and in the History of Economic Policy', in E. S. Reinert (ed.) (2004) *Globalization, Economic Development and Inequality: An Alternative Perspective*. Cheltenham: Edward Elgar.

Reinert, E. S. and Reinert, S. 2005. 'Mercantilism and Economic Development: Schumpeterian Dynamics, Institution Building and International Benchmarking', in Jomo, K. S. and E. S. Reinert (eds), *Origins of Economic Development*, London: Zed Publications.

Ross, E. 1998, *The Malthus Factor: Poverty, Politics and Population in Capitalist Development*, London: Palgrave Macmillan.

Schmoller, G. 1897/1967. *The Mercantile System and its Historical Significance*, New York: Macmillan/Kelley (translated from articles in the journal *Schmoller's Jahrbuch*).

Serra, A. 1613. *Breve Trattato delle Cause che Possono far Abbondare l'Oro e l'Argento dove non sono Miniere*, Naples: Lazzaro Scorriggio.

Smith, A. 1759/1812. *The Theory of Moral Sentiments*, in *Collected Works*, London: Cadell and Davies.

Sombart, W. 1928. *Der Moderne Kapitalismus, Vol. 2, Das Europäische Wirtschaftsleben im Zeitalter des Frühkapitalismus*, München and Leipzig: Duncker and Humblot.

Sombart, W. 1930. *Die drei Nationalökonomien*, München and Leipzig: Duncker and Humblot.

Strindberg, A. 1882/1913. *De lycksaliges ö och andra berättelser. Svenska öden och äventyr*, Stockholm: Åhlén and Åkerlund (additionally there are translations into German and Italian).

Veblen, T. 1961. 'Industrial and Pecuniary Employment' in *The Place of Science in Modern Civilization and Other Essays*, New York: Russel and Russel.

Viner, J. 1972. *The Role of Providence in the Social Order. An Essay in Intellectual History*, Philadelphia: American Philosophical Society.

PART II

EVOLUTION OF PARTICULAR INSTITUTIONS

CHAPTER 5
MODERN BUREAUCRACY

John Toye

1. The modernity of bureaucracy

Max Weber's account of the evolution of bureaucracy started from the claim that modern officialdom could be identified by a set of typical characteristics. These were that officials were full-time salaried employees, whose appointment, promotion and retirement was contractually based (and not derived from their ownership of their offices); that they were technically trained and that this was a condition of their employment; and that official rights and duties were well-defined in public written regulations. His study of history told him that this had not always been so, and that in previous centuries state administration had been much more personalized and part-time. He argued, however, that these novel characteristics did not apply just to modern state administrators, but rather applied to the institutions of modern society much more broadly. He saw the typical characteristics of modern bureaucracy emerging not just in state administration, but also in the church, the law, the military, political parties, science, university research and even in private enterprises. Because of the wide range of institutions that he believed modern bureaucracy to be permeating, one might say that Weber viewed bureaucracy as a horizontal phenomenon spreading throughout society.

He was interested in the emergence of bureaucracy as a long-term and pervasive macro-social process, one that he took to be a key element in the advent of modernity. The diffusion of bureaucracy in society was, for Weber, an important component of a grander trend. That was the movement away from the magical thinking of the European Middle Ages (he called this trend 'disenchantment') and the establishment in its place of secular rational values (a process he called 'rationalization'). The historical evolution of bureaucracy was thus a central part of his entire theory of history.[1] Yet the evolution of bureaucracy was also something that Weber feared and distrusted. His idea of the spread of modern bureaucracy almost amounted to a personal vision of dystopia. He interpreted it as a powerful force for increasing the efficiency of state action, by a process of de-humanizing the agents of the state (Gerth and Mills, 1991: 215). Manifestly, political developments in the second quarter of the twentieth century, not only in the Soviet Union but also in Germany itself, lent substance to this interpretation and its associated anxieties.

Sociologists have made many criticisms of Weber, but here I just note two important ones. For the sake of clarity, it is better to substitute the idea of 'the rise of the professional' for Weber's 'bureaucratization'. The idea of 'the professional' encompasses the criteria of full-time work, contractually based, and conditional on standards of expertise and training, but it has the advantage of allowing us to distinguish a general social phenomenon from what was happening specifically to the state administration. It is the latter that is the focus of this paper.

The other main problem with Weber's analysis was his confident assumption that the personal motives and attitudes of state officials could be made fully congruent with the behaviour required by their formal roles. It was assumed that the distribution of power in the official hierarchy could become identical with the delegation of authority. Even in countries with authoritarian forms of government, this is not necessarily the case. Actual power depends on the possession of information, the control of incentives and having the motive and skill to make rational use of them. Unless those at the top have these things sufficiently, autocratic regimes may not be particularly effective performers when it comes to governing. Although Weber saw that power had in the past been accumulated in the lower levels of a formal hierarchy, and that bureaucratic power struggles therefore had taken place, he thought that this bureaucratic unruliness would in future be gradually but completely eliminated (Rudolph and Rudolph, 1979: 207–10).

The new institutional economists reinforce this sociological correction of Weber. Principal-agent theory makes the very notion of perfect instrumentalism problematic. On the contrary, it assumes that the goals and preferences of the principal (the superior in the hierarchy) and those of the agents (the subordinates in the hierarchy) do normally differ. It assumes that the agents normally have more information about the rights and duties that are delegated to them than does the principal. It assumes that the principal can redress this information imbalance, but only at an increasing cost. The question then is: How can a form of delegation be designed with incentives that minimize the deviation of the agents' behaviour from the principal's goals? The debate around this question has superseded theories assuming an official habit of obedience, bred either by perfect oppression (the slavery solution) or by perfect socialization (Weber's false assumption).

Weber's ideal type cannot tell the whole story of modern bureaucracy, and Weber (to do him justice) was well aware of the different situations of the bureaucracy that existed in the United States and Britain. As he readily conceded, in the real world, some bureaucracies did not conform to this ideal type. What he saw, however, was just a variety of close approximations to it, exhibiting divergences that he thought were destined to disappear over time. It is instructive to re-examine three of Weber's historical examples of bureaucracy, plus that of Japan, in order to see whether they support his expectation of the disappearance of divergences. I take a contrary view, arguing two theses. The first is that the diversity of paths to bureaucratic modernity is much more fundamental than Weber allows when he speaks of the slow emergence of his ideal type in different countries. The second is that the vertical linkages between bureaucracies and high-powered politics can explain this more fundamental diversity, linkages that Weber's horizontal approach to the evolution of bureaucracy tends to obscure.

2.   Varieties of successful bureaucracy-building

2.1.   *Prussian bureaucracy*

Much of Weber's core model of what a modern bureaucracy should be came from his understanding of Prussian bureaucracy, which was virtually all that was left of Germany's institutional inheritance by the time of his death in 1920. Yet it is hard to understand that inheritance apart from its political context, the rise and fall of the Hohenzollern dynasty. The Hohenzollerns, a noble family from southwest Germany, by 1648 had acquired by dynastic marriages a scattering of non-contiguous territories across the north of Germany.[2] The strategic and driving aim of the ruler, Frederick William (1640–88) was to secure this collection of domains from a return of the ravages of war. The recent Thirty Years War had been the most ferociously destructive war that Germany had yet known. In order to avoid the damage of future such holocausts, the least Frederick William needed to do was to establish a small standing army, and then to find the means of raising continuous finance for it.

The traditional method of raising war finance had been to seek a grant from the local Diets, or parliaments, but one effect of the long war had been markedly to reduce the prosperity of the towns. This allowed Frederick William to dispense with their consent in the Diets and to impose excises collected by his own servants. The origins of Prussian bureaucracy were thus linked both to active revenue gathering and to the ignoring of existing mechanisms of consultation and consent. In the 1670s, the independence of the towns was eroded, as they were placed under the rule of a body of officials appointed by Frederick William.

The un-free status of the peasantry made it easier to recruit and train military manpower, allowing Brandenburg-Prussia to become not just a country with an army, but rather, as it was often said, an army with a country. This aphorism could be applied with equal justice to the bureaucracy. In Brandenburg-Prussia, it was the bureaucracy that acquired a country, rather than vice versa. In 1723, bureaucratic centralization was achieved when war and finance administration were integrated in the General Directory, as a means of giving some practical effect to the theoretical unity of the state, which had been proclaimed in 1713. However, it was only after Frederick the Great had gained Silesia during the Austrian Succession and Seven Years War, and after he took West Prussia in the 1772 partition of Poland that the territorial integrity of the kingdom of Prussia was indeed consolidated.

Once the towns were subordinated, the building of the Prussian bureaucracy was a matter of displacing the rule of the local notables in the countryside. To appoint them directly as royal servants in their own localities would have obvious limits in ensuring their loyalty to the king. Instead, nobles were only allowed to serve the king in distant provinces far from their own local power bases. Moreover, the king was willing to promote commoners to the nobility in exchange for service to the state. Official basic salaries remained low, but there were rewards for good and loyal service. In order to further ensure bureaucratic reliability, Frederick II set up a cadre of secret inspectors to spy on his own officials. Moreover, in part to spy on his own spies, he continuously toured around Prussia to keep himself informed about the condition of the country.

It is straightforward to translate these historical facts into the new institutional economist's jargon of negative and positive incentives and the costs of supervision. Yet it would be too mechanical to suppose that the success of the Prussian bureaucracy depended solely on the putting in place of the sticks and carrots required to motivate its performance. More subtle ideological influences also favoured its success. One was the royal sponsorship of Pietism as the official religion. While replacing the Lutheran Church, which tended to support the local nobility, it also encouraged a widespread belief in the values of education and meritocracy, values that legitimized the bureaucratic order. Moreover, the absolutism of Prussia was an enlightened one, with the bureaucracy was an instrument of benevolent government. Frederick had tried to introduce a national system of primary schooling (1763), a limited land reform (1765–70), a customs and excise reform (1766) and a legal codification (1780–94) (Fulbrook, 2004: 94–5). The introduction of entrance examinations for high administrative posts in 1771 set limits on his right to select, and gave senior officials greater autonomy.

Prussia's tariff reform of 1818 paved the way for the establishment of a more general customs union, the Zollverein, in 1834. As a result, a Germany unified by Prussia (1863–71) was well placed to undergo rapid economic development and rapid population growth thereafter. Nevertheless, the bureaucracy had developed some weaknesses, particularly at the middle level where group responsibility inhibited initiative. There is some evidence of bureaucratic obstruction of the growth of railways, for example (Armstrong, 1973: 284–6).

However, the great failure of the later Hohenzollerns was not in the bureaucratic realm as such. It lay in their continuing inability to develop a political system that can cope with the socio-economic changes of capitalist industrialization. Prussia was late in moving to representative government, and when it finally did so, the 1850 constitution entrenched the representation of an economically declining class – the Junker nobility of East Prussia. The constitution of the German Empire (1871) did move to universal manhood suffrage to elect the Reichstag, but the initiating power was reserved for the Bundesrat (Federal Council) and, above that, the Emperor, Chancellor, ministers, army chiefs and senior officials were the effective political masters. Bismarck's political juggling successfully disguised the lack of a broadly-based political consensus until 1890, but it emerged clearly under Emperor Wilhelm II. By 1914, the bureaucracy was still under the control of the Emperor, the army and an old aristocratic elite, which had come to believe that domestic political tensions could somehow be resolved by external national assertion. Given that the bureaucracy had done little to prepare the economy for war conditions, this was a gamble that led to monumental disaster in the First World War.

The old elites then had to live with the consequences of military defeat – national humiliation, foreign demands for impossible reparations, self-inflicted hyperinflation and extreme social and political turbulence. When they could no longer do so, they turned to the leader whose bizarre and irrational mass movement promised them a national transformation. Hitler removed all vestiges of democracy, and then purged the bureaucracy of all opponents of Nazism, rendering it a pliable tool of his personal power.[3] Ironically, he did this by passing a 'Law for the restoration of the professional civil service', which provided for the demotion, retirement and dismissal of any official suspected of disloyalty to the Nazis (Haffner, 2002: 183–5). In fact, such a restoration arrived only after a reverse process of purging ex-Nazis and the adoption of the American-designed constitution of the Federal Republic of Germany in 1949.

2.2.   *British administration*

While the Thirty Years War raged in Germany, the civil war in England preserved a mixed form of government, in which legislation required the assent of the monarch and a parliament of nobles and commoners. Although over the following hundred years James II and the Jacobites made sporadic attempts to reverse this outcome, the constitutional ascendancy of Parliament *vis à vis* the Crown increased rather than diminished. This implied that the King increasingly needed the support of advisers who could procure for his legislation a reliable majority of votes in both Houses of Parliament. Conversely, those members of Parliament who wanted to advise the King had to be able to show that they could command the votes of the majority. The friction engendered by this mutual need produced two opposing forms of political paranoia. Parliament feared that royal manipulation was undermining its independence, while the King feared the 'storming of the closet' by powerful parliamentarians whose principles and policies he detested. Yet despite the mutual distrust, the early eighteenth century witnessed the growth of political stability in England (Plumb, 1967).

Most British government in the eighteenth century was local government, carried out by local volunteers, the Justices of the Peace. As far as the central government was concerned, the form that 'royal interference' took was allowing the chief minister to distribute Crown patronage, which he used to consolidate his majority in Parliament. Royal appointment to civil offices – something that did not extend to ecclesiastical or military offices – was dispensed by the prime minister of the day, whose choice of recipient was made with a view to bolstering his ability to carry on the King's business in Parliament, rather than on criteria of fitness for the particular office. This was the 'old corruption' that Walpole, Pelham and Newcastle reduced to a fine art. Since, if he distributed Crown patronage unwisely, the prime minister would lose his own office, the 'old corruption' necessarily involved a strong internal disciplining mechanism.

The return of war in the 1740s and 1750s strained British public finances. As the real value of land tax declined, Parliament granted increasing revenues from stamp duties, customs revenue and excises and other forms of indirect taxation to fund the expansion of the navy and army (see chapter 10, this volume). Growing numbers of revenue and excise officers swelled the 'offices of profit under the Crown' that could be used for political patronage. After the loss of the American colonies strengthened opposition to the influence of the Crown, various measures of 'economical reform' were legislated in 1780, including bringing the Civil List under the control of Parliament and setting up a Public Accounts Commission. The reports of the Commissioners of Public Accounts (1780–86) laid down the principles of administrative reform. These included performance of official duties in person, not by deputies; payment by fixed salary, and not by levying fees; and strict obedience to the regulations governing the discharge of duties (Langford, 1989: 696). However, the conservative reaction to the French Revolution delayed the implementation of these principles until the next century.

The Northcote-Trevelyan report (1853–54) provided further recommendations for reform, namely, that recruitment should be by open examination and that promotion should be on merit. Defeat in the Crimea and the Indian Mutiny finally galvanized the governments to put these principles into action, first in the Indian Civil Service, and finally at home. The presiding spirit was that of Gladstone, who, as Chancellor of the Exchequer from 1859 to 1866, asserted firm Treasury control over the numbers of and expenditure on the civil service, and introduced new bodies to support it – the Exchequer and Audit Department, the Public Accounts Committee of the Commons and the Civil Service Commissioners. He instituted open examination and merit promotion in the home civil service in 1870. Crown patronage was now severely circumscribed, and the expansion of government regulation – of factories, prisons, transport, postal services, and so on – was de-linked from it.

As Weber observed, the bureaucratization of the British administration went on slowly (Gerth and Mills, 1991: 228). For a further century after Gladstone's reforms, technical training was not made a condition of employment at the highest administrative level. Nor was it given after selection, except for recruits to the Indian Civil Service and (from 1929) to the Colonial Service. The written entrance examinations were closely modelled on the examinations of Oxford and Cambridge, whose graduates for long dominated among the successful recruits. This Oxbridge elite operated as a cadre of high-level generalist administrators, a self-image that was increasingly challenged as the tasks of government expanded and became increasingly enmeshed with scientific and technical activities.[4] The issue of improving specialist skills in the civil service was addressed by the report of the Fulton Committee (1966–68), but its moderate recommendations met internal resistance that limited the extent of change. Nevertheless, a civil service training college was finally set up in the 1970s.

Britain was also slow to achieve a unified civil service. Even after recruitment was centralized, new recruits entered Departments that were separate and independent, and then were promoted within them (Salter, 1961: 36). It was not until the pressures of the World Wars and the rapid expansion of public administration that the limitations of excessive departmentalism even started to be overcome. In operational terms, the novelty was inter-departmental committees of officials that reported to equivalent committees of the Cabinet. The official committee charged with planning public expenditure was a particularly powerful centralizing force. In management terms, unifying changes included central appointment to the key administrative posts in each department, as well as inter-department transfers of personnel. Yet although Britain was politically centralized, it was still struggling to achieve 'joined-up government' under Tony Blair at the end of the twentieth century.

2.3.   *The US Executive Branch*

The statesmen of the fledgling United States of America designed a new constitution, conscious that in doing so they were addressing a larger question: 'whether societies of men are really capable or not of establishing good government from reflection and choice, or whether they are forever destined to depend for their political constitutions on accident and force' (Hamilton, 1937: 3). The fact of their deliberate reflection and choice makes it easier for us to re-capture the vision behind the institution of bureaucracy in the US.

The constitution makers wanted to start again, avoiding the mistakes of the past. The major source of the mistakes to be avoided was not local; it was Britain. First, the exercise of political power by a hereditary monarchy and aristocracy was deemed objectionable in itself, so direct or indirect popular election was made into the foundation of all political power. Second, the influence of the British Crown in Parliament was seen as malign, and, to avoid anything similar, the doctrine of separation of powers debarred legislators from holding executive office and members of the executive branch from being elected as legislators. Third, faction or 'party interest' was seen as a source of political instability, so the intervals between elections (and thus the terms of office) for the legislature and the President, the head of the executive, were fixed. At the same time, to avoid creating instability by a complete turnover of personnel every four years, legislators and the President were allowed to stand for re-election. Fourth, the founding fathers were generally suspicious of the evils of government, so the different branches of government were made to 'check and balance' each other. This meant that the President had the right to propose the appointment of officials, but that the Senate must consent to each nomination before it could be effective (*ibid*: 491–6).

Did the US constitution succeed in establishing good government by reflection and choice? History's answer to Hamilton's rhetorical question was a dusty one. Why so? Faction or the spirit of party could not realistically be expected to be permanently absent in a political system in which elections had been given such a prominent part. With the passing of the revolutionary generation, parties were formed more tightly and competed with increasing ruthlessness. The first Tenure of Office Act (1820) gave the President and the Senate the power to re-appoint to every office of the government (except federal judgeships) every four years, after the Presidential election. This was justified by the argument that rotation of offices would prevent the emergence of an official aristocracy able to pass office on to its children. It certainly did that, but it also stopped dead the emergence of a class of professional public servants similar to what J.S. Mill described as 'the permanent strength of the public service' in mid-Victorian Britain (Mill, 1962 [1861]: 341).

What emerged instead was the American spoils system, where public office holders were dependent for their tenure on the electoral success of one political party, with which they had wholly to identify themselves. This was not just a matter of declaring a party affiliation, but of paying part of their salary to the party when in office, and working for the party organization when out of office, in the hope that it would be re-elected (Brogan, 199 [1985]: 268–9). The power of appointment effectively passed from the President to the Senate. The scramble of the hordes of office-seekers brought other government business to a near standstill every four years, but without the compensation of appointing the most meritorious candidates. It was only after a disappointed office-seeker assassinated President Garfield in 1881 that the Pendleton Act (1883) introduced a merit-based appointment mechanism.

Weber was surely right to say that in the US the social esteem of officials was low because the demand for expert administration remained low, and that dependence on popular election both lowered the expert qualifications of officials, and weakened the functioning of the bureaucratic regime (Gerth and Mills, 1991: 199 and 201). The worst excesses of American machine politics were mitigated by the slow spread of merit-based recruitment within the federal civil service and reforms placing restrictions on the methods of funding political parties.[5] Yet still today political appointees have various entry channels into the federal bureaucracy – Presidential appointments, Schedule C jobs, and non-career executive assignments that together account for one per cent of personnel. In addition, jobs are often filled on a 'name request' basis, where the agency has already identified the candidate that it wishes to appoint – usually on the basis of shared views about policy (Wilson and DiJulio, 1995 [1980]: 394–6). Moreover, in a federal system, state governments are responsible for much civil service recruitment. They do this by various methods, some of which include electing officials, including judges.

2.4.   *The Japanese bureaucracy*

During the Tokugawa period, samurai warriors transformed themselves into government officials, becoming a high status nobility of service rather than a professional cadre. After the Meiji Revolution of 1868, Meiji leaders countered the power and privileges `of Satsuma and Chōshū feudal groups by establishing a bureaucracy of Higher-level Public Officials, who shared the status of their predecessors but were also evidently modern in being university-trained and recruited by public examination. Under the Emperor, they exercised an authoritarian rule that was hardly diluted when a National Diet and political parties were authorized in the Constitution of 1889. At the end of the nineteenth century, Japan's political system closely resembled the form of government that Bismarck had created for Imperial Germany, in which a prime minister, his Cabinet, and the civil and military bureaucracies were responsible to the Emperor – and not to the Diet. By the 1930s, this form of monarchical constitutionalism – to use Weber's term – had stabilized and was following a very similar militaristic trajectory to that of Wilhelmine Germany, ending in the military disaster of the Pacific War of 1941–5.

However, Japan did not undergo the same post-war reconstruction as West Germany, and the economic bureaucracy emerged from it stronger than previously. While the military bureaucracy disappeared and the powerful Home Ministry was broken up, few economic bureaucrats were purged. The extensive controls operated in the economy during the US occupation of 1945–52 even tended to enhance the powers of the economic ministries. The National Public Service Law 1947 (no. 120) did not provide a strong basis for civil service reform. It did set up a National Personnel Authority with responsibility for public service examinations, pay scales and grievance procedures, but control of budgets remained with the Ministry of Finance, and central co-ordination machinery in the prime minister or Cabinet Office was omitted.

The result was a system in which the Diet, a significant portion of whose members were now ex-bureaucrats, acted as the ratifying body for legislation drafted by the ministries. After 1955, the Liberal Democratic Party, as the dominant party, acted as a defender of minority interests (farmers, small enterprises) against the ambitions of the economic bureaucracy, which were generally seen as representing the national interest of Japan Inc. The prime minister and his Cabinet were able to bring relatively little political leverage to the making of policy. Indeed, it has been said: 'the norm is for the minister to fear his bureaucrats' (Johnson, 1982: 52). The bureaucrats were in the happy position of being able to give informal advice and guidance, and having it implemented voluntarily by members of the public. Where the bureaucracy enjoys so much power, status and respect, there is inevitably fierce competition for posts, fierce internal struggles for promotion, and fierce territorial battles between departments for new jurisdiction and control of agencies that are intended to co-ordinate. Competition extends after retirement to securing the possession of top jobs in private and public corporations, banks, and politics.

None of this prevented Japan from enjoying a period of extremely rapid economic growth. Between 1946 and 1976, the Japanese economy increased 55-fold (*ibid*: 6). Although its causes remain controversial, many scholars believe that the economic bureaucrats were instrumental in managing this 'miracle'. Since 1976, however, the Prussian-style system of administrative guidance has been much attenuated. Partly this is due to deliberate policy efforts towards de-regulation; partly to the arrival of information age technologies the production of which the economic bureaucrats would have had difficulty directing; and partly to increased judicial review of administrative actions (see chapter 9, this volume).

3.   Bureaucracy, the legislature, and the electorate

It is instructive to see, from these four examples, how markedly the bureaucracies of these economically developed states differ from each other in their genesis, structures, and abilities to exercise power. They also demonstrate that a comparison confined only to the ideal typical characteristics of bureaucracy – the method of recruitment, terms of appointment, remuneration, training and method of operation – is likely to provide only modest insight into the reasons why bureaucracies differ, and how they have evolved. This is because state bureaucracies cannot be understood by examining them in isolation. If they are instruments, their fitness cannot be judged just by looking at their characteristics. These qualities become relevant only when we know who is meant to use the instrument, and for what purpose.

Each bureaucracy exists in its own special web of politics. Whether evolving out of traditional political practice (Prussia, Britain and Japan) or in the context of a newly and consciously designed constitution (USA), bureaucracies have to be understood in relation to the larger political system of which they form a part. The larger political system will be subject to its own evolutionary pressures. Our case studies confirm that a critical question is how far the political system will go on the path of democratization (Acemoglu and Robinson, 2000: 1167–99). The resolution of this question will establish who are the ultimate masters of the bureaucracy, and determine the breadth of the power of the political engine that attempts to drive it.

When pressures for democratic reform become active in society, the policy agenda itself changes in favour of greater income and wealth redistribution. If the elite politicians do not find ways of attending to the new policy agenda, they will erode their political legitimacy and bring ultimate grief upon themselves, and on their public servants – however well attuned to their purposes their servants are. This is the moral of Prussian history after 1850 and Japanese history from 1890–1945. Politicians' ability to respond to the challenges of incipient socio-economic development is improved if they are already linked to their society, however imperfectly, by a political system with representative elements, as in Britain and, to a much greater degree, the USA. Yet when politicians do adjust to a new policy agenda, they encounter a new problem in their relations with bureaucracy. They find that the bureaucratic instrument that was fit for their purposes yesterday is no longer fit for their new purposes.

To maintain their legitimacy, democratic politicians have to strive regularly for a popular mandate. In the first half of the twentieth century, this form of competition produced decisions to extend the functions of government into the areas of health, education and welfare; after the Depression of the 1930s, into regulation of the economy; and into military-related functions that were not fully phased out after each World War, such as scientific and technological research. The decisions to extend government functions were themselves driven by long-term structural changes in Western society, such as population growth, urbanization, industrialization and international economic integration. They represented a new grand bargain in which the electorate's greatly enhanced willingness to pay personal taxes was exchanged for the greatly expanded welfare and social security services.

Once absolutism has given way to representative government, the application of principal-agent theory necessarily becomes more complex. Instead of one, two principal-agent problems now present themselves. One is the relation between the legislature and the bureaucracy, and the other, newly added, is the relation between the electorate and the legislature. The legislature is a party to both relations, which means that the two agency problems are not independent of each other and so cannot necessarily be resolved in sequence. Instead, they interact in complicating ways. In particular, the legislature may be tempted to try and make its policy commitments to the electorate more credible by delegating their implementation to bodies with a longer life span than its own fixed electoral period (Horn, 1995: 24). Delegating important functions to permanent agencies is a further step by which the legislature restricts its powers of day-to-day control to reassure the electorate that promises previously made to it cannot be easily reneged on. The recent proliferation of agencies of restraint, such as 'independent' central banks, suggests that the need for such reassurance has not diminished.

The interlocking of the two agency problems creates the time inconsistency of incentives for the legislature and bureaucracy. Tax-financed bureaus with a permanently employed staff and a fixed hierarchy operate with a different time horizon than legislators, who in a democracy must submit to regular re-election. This makes civil servants more risk averse, and less responsive to short-term political impulses than politicians. In particular, permanent tenure gives bureaucrats a key advantage in struggles with their principal. They can try to wait out a political master whose policies they oppose. They have an incentive to slow down necessary political and administrative processes in the hope that he or she will be replaced before the disliked policy is fully implemented. This is one reason why it is naïve to suppose that the introduction of democratic politics will very easily bring bureaucracies under democratic control.

4.   The ambiguity of bureaucracy

Is bureaucracy a vital institution that has to be built up by poor countries that are in pursuit of economic development? Or is it an institution that persistently threatens, like a fast-growing riverweed, to choke the channels of public administration? That 'bureaucracy' has a pejorative connotation is well known. Yet recently a World Bank report explained the East Asian economic miracle by noting that, from an institutional perspective, 'the first step was to recruit a competent and relatively honest technocratic cadre and insulate it from day-to-day political interference'. It remarked that 'in Japan, Korea, Singapore and Taiwan, China', where fast economic growth had occurred, 'strong well-organized bureaucracies wield considerable power' (World Bank 1993: 14). Some international organizations evidently see insulation of the bureaucracy from democratic control as an institutional requirement of poor countries wanting to develop economically.

To understand the ambiguity of bureaucracy, we need to distinguish between the abstract and the concrete senses of 'bureaucracy'. It is abstract bureaucracy that bears the negative connotation, while the concrete noun – 'a bureaucracy', a synonym for an organized civil service – does not necessarily do so. This distinction allows us to imagine that there could be bureaucracies that are not bureaucratic in the pejorative sense. From this one might conclude that the essential problem for poor countries is to design the institutional context for a non-bureaucratic bureaucracy. Before jumping to this conclusion, however, it is necessary to be more precise about what is wrong with bureaucracy in the abstract sense.

Those who use 'bureaucracy' as a term of abuse are probably making one or more of five complaints. The first – and perhaps the most fundamental – is that officials are accountable only to their superiors, and not to those whose affairs they administer. Officials are empowered first of all by the prevailing laws, but then, under the law, by their superiors delegating powers and duties down to them through an organized official hierarchy. None of this implies any accountability to the governed.[6] Bad bureaucracy then is the lack of popular accountability of officials.

The second complaint is a more recent one, advanced by economists. The bureaucracy, to the extent that it provides goods and services, operates without competition, and in the absence of competition, has no incentive to force down the costs of production of public services. Bad bureaucracy is pervasively inefficient.[7]

The third complaint, also due to economists, runs parallel to the previous one. To the extent that the bureaucracy is providing regulatory services, it is in danger of being 'captured' by the private interests whose activities it is intended to regulate. When regulatory capture has taken place, bad bureaucracy becomes the creator and distributor of rents and vested interests in the private sector (Stigler, 1975).

The fourth complaint arises because modern bureaucracies operate by making and enforcing rules that apply to categories of people. The purpose of this practice of making general rules is to eliminate arbitrariness, personal favouritism and objectionable discrimination in administration. Examples of such category-based rules are: All pregnant women are entitled to collect free vitamin supplements; or all who receive public money to which they are not entitled must pay it back. However, all such general rules usually have some exceptions, from the point of view of complying with common sense – exceptions that are not foreseen or written into the general rule. Yet officials may apply the written rule literally and exactly, and without the exercise of any judgement and discretion. Bad bureaucracy is the legalistic implementation of category-based rules.

The fifth complaint is the multiplication of offices and departments, which then operate without adequate co-ordination. The proliferation of different offices induces a failure of overall control of the bureaucracy. In these conditions, delegation becomes incoherent, and bureaus operate with overlapping and conflicting functions. As a result, people suffer unnecessary delays while trying to find out which official is responsible for the matter concerning them. Bad bureaucracy is bureaucratic expansion and the blurring of responsibilities that it induces.

Is it possible then to eliminate these negative features and design non-bureaucratic bureaucracies to be the institutional tool to facilitate the aims of development? What are the correctives to these five complaints? Peter Evans (2003) has proposed that 'the effectiveness of public institutions depends on 'hybridity', an integrated balance among three different (sometimes contradictory) modes of guiding public action'. The three modes are: Enhancing bureaucratic capacity, defined in terms of Weber's ideal-type characteristics; following market signals, conveying the costs and benefits of public resource use; and empowering bottom-up democratic participation to check that state action reflects the needs and desires of ordinary citizens. Evans's 'tripod model' is depicted in Figure 5.1.

By the mid-nineteenth century, bureaucracy was attracting popular criticism precisely because the monarch had successfully subordinated it, and it had become the well-honed instrument of powerful but undemocratic monarchies (Heizen, 1845). Since then, the democratic control leg of the Evans tripod has been much strengthened. Yet even elected politicians in long-established democracies have to struggle to maintain the upper hand in relation to their bureaucrats. That fact was the source of the humour in the well-observed British television series *Yes, Minister*. It would be naïve to suppose that the recent spread of democratic regimes to Latin America, the former Soviet Union, Asia and Africa has eliminated the problem of democratic accountability there. As Evans observes:

Election does not increase the range of policy options available to political leaders and the prerogative of electing leaders does not necessarily result in concrete democratic input into the policy making process. While there are encouraging instances of expanded democratic input, they are still not sufficiently generalized to challenge the overall tendency towards imbalance.

Figure 5.1 The Tripod Model of State Control

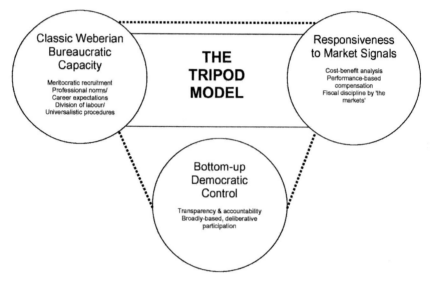

Much more work is still needed, despite the wave of democratization of the last two decades, to devise novel ways by which ordinary citizens can increase the transparency and accountability of bureaucratic action.

There is clearly a fear in some powerful international organizations that any increase in democratic control could disable a bureaucracy from being effective for development. The authors of the World Bank's East Asian Miracle study thought that East Asian bureaucracies were effective because they were insulated from day-to-day political interference. Yet what constitutes 'political interference', and what is the right degree of insulation? When does democratic control stop and political interference begin? These central unresolved issues of modern bureaucracies must continue to be the subject of discussion and the object of political contest.

The market signals leg of the Evans tripod addresses the issue of reducing government inefficiency. Yet that issue is clouded by the fundamental difficulty of measuring government output. The budget provides information on the costs of the inputs, but unless these can be compared with the value of the output, it is hard to calculate what has happened to efficiency. This is a fundamental problem of applying cost/benefit analysis to government services. If the market signals could have induced the provision of these services, no government intervention would have been justified in the first place. In this situation, there is no easy market-based solution. Nevertheless, some improvement in efficiency can probably be achieved by n-th best measures, such as finding small components of a public service that can be out-sourced, by simulating the conditions of competition where they cannot naturally prevail, or simply by insisting that departments surrender a regular small percentage of their expenditure as 'efficiency savings'.

Regulatory capture, however, arises because of concentrations of political and economic power that become mutually dependent. In industries where oligopoly prevails, existing firms have an incentive to capture the political power to regulate, as a means of deterring potential new entrants. Political parties have an incentive to promise anti-competitive forms of regulation in return for financial contributions to their operating expenses. The bureaucrats may have an incentive to prefer any type of regulation to a scrupulous insistence on enforcing only regulations that are a genuine public benefit. The pressures for collusion are then powerful, and to lessen them once collusion has taken hold cannot be a matter of following market signals because the market is being rigged. Breaking the problem of regulatory capture would have to involve radical political change initiated from outside the system of collusion. Nothing less than the rise of a new social movement would have a chance of success.

What of the other two categories of complaint? The implementation of bureaucratic rules, like that of legal rules, will always remain problematic. There is an inherent difficulty in anticipating within the written rule itself all the circumstances under which it might be implemented. The attempt to deal with every possible case always increases the complexity of the rule, which reduces people's ability to understand it. If, on the other hand, the rules are kept simple but officials are granted discretion to interpret them, other problems arise. Some will not use their discretion, while those that do may take different views about what common sense requires. The governed will then be subject to the so-called 'post code lottery', namely, while the rules appear to be the same everywhere, what actually happens will depend on the jurisdiction where one lives or registers one's business. The enlargement of official discretion opens the door for the return of personal favouritism in the application of rules. Once discretion is permitted, the next step is that some officials will start selling their favours to those who pay, fuelling the growth of official corruption.

The problem of blurred lines of responsibility is not easy to remedy either. Some remedial steps are feasible. In the short run, one can just demarcate official rights and duties more sharply. In policy-making, campaigns for 'joined-up government' can do something to mitigate the follies of excessive departmentalism. In service delivery, there is often scope for organizing a 'one-stop shop' at the point of public access. The trouble is that such moves, worthy as they are, can never be once-for-all operations. The management of a civil service must be viewed dynamically.

The definitions of responsibilities and the lines of hierarchical delegation are always changing, and some fuzziness about where they lie at any one time is therefore a more or less permanent feature of the bureaucratic scene. This is one factor – let us call it the defensive motive - that fuels bureaucratic turf wars: No one wants to lose out in the forthcoming reorganization. Turf wars themselves then make the picture muddier, as individual units make claims and counter-claim about the appropriate lines of demarcation, and seek to bolster such claims by behaving as if the issue was already settled in their favour. Powerful high-level management can subdue this kind of conflict, but never eliminate it.

The foregoing discussion has shown that the ambiguous evaluation of bureaucracies is not the result of superficial defects in the ways that they operate. On the contrary, the ambiguity is fundamental and deeply seated, since measures to address bureaucratic defects are often the source of new and different problems, and in any case need to be applied on a continuing basis. Thus, the prospects of smart designers producing successful blueprints for a non-bureaucratic bureaucracy are not particularly promising. The hybridity model of Evans is a useful heuristic device for summarizing key elements of the bureaucratic problem, but it also emphasizes that the task is to maintain eternal vigilance, and to balance continuously the trade-offs between further reforms of each leg of the reform tripod.

Notes

1. 'We nevertheless feel justified in holding that a unilinear construction is clearly implied in Weber's idea of the bureaucratic trend', Turner (1995: 51).
2. From west to east these parcels of land were Cleves, Mark, Brandenburg and East Prussia. By the Treaty of Westphalia of 1648, they made the modest gains of Minden, Magdeburg, and Eastern Pomerania.
3. See Tooze (2000) for how this affected the German Statistical Office.
4. Edward Bridges (1950) explained and argued the case for the generalist administrator, while Thomas Balogh (1967: 11–52) fiercely attacked it.

5. These restrictions have had the unfortunate side-effect of delivering the political parties and their candidates into the hands of wealthy individuals and corporations, to an extent that was not the case under the nineteenth century spoils system.

6. As the etymology of the word indicates, bureaucracy has been and still can be understood as a form of government that stands as an alternative to representative government and democracy. As John Stuart Mill puts it: 'The only governments, not representative, in which high political skill and ability have been other than exceptional, whether under monarchical or aristocratic forms, have been essentially bureaucracies. The work of government has been in the hands of governors by profession; which is the essence and meaning of bureaucracy' (Mill, 1962 [1861]: 245).

7. This argument has an analogue that is often overlooked. If the bureau is a monopoly provider, it is also a monopsonist in the market for administrative labour. It is therefore able to keep the price of its inputs lower than would be the case in a competitive situation. Thus bureaus may not use their inputs efficiently, but this matters less because the dominant input – labour – is artificially cheap.

References

Acemoglu, D. and Robinson, J. 2000. 'Why did the West Extend the Franchise? Growth, Inequality and Democracy in Historical Perspective', *Quarterly Journal of Economics*, Vol. CXV, No. 4.

Armstrong J. A. 1973. *The European Administrative Elite*, Princeton, Princeton University Press.

Balogh, T. 1967. 'The Apotheosis of the Dilettante' in H. Thomas (ed.), *Crisis in the Civil Service*, London, Anthony Blond.

Bridges, E. 1950. *Portrait of a Profession*, Rede Lecture, Cambridge, Cambridge University Press.

Brogan H. 1999. [1985]. *The Penguin History of the USA*, Harmondsworth, Penguin.

Evans, P. B. 2003. 'Harnessing the State: Rebalancing Strategies for Monitoring and Evaluation', mimeo.

Fulbrook, M. 2004. *A Concise History of Germany*, Cambridge, Cambridge University Press.

Gerth, H. H. and Mills, C. W. (eds) 1991. *From Max Weber: Essays in Sociology*, London, Routledge.

Haffner, S. 2002. *Defying Hitler: A Memoir*, London, Weidenfeld and Nicolson.

Hamilton, A. 1937. *The Federalist*, New York, The Modern Library.

Heinzen, K. 1845. *Die preussiche Büreaukratie*, Darmstadt, Leske.

Horn, M. J. 1995. *The Political Economy of Public Administration. Institutional Choice in the Public Sector*, Cambridge, Cambridge University Press.

Johnson, C. 1982. *MITI and the Japanese Miracle: the Growth of Industrial Policy, 1925–1975*, Stanford, Stanford University Press.

Langford, P. 1989. *A Polite and Commercial People: England 1727–1783*, Oxford, Oxford University Press.

Mill, J. S. 1962 [1861] *Representative Government*, London, Everyman's Library.

Plumb, J. H. 1967. *The Growth of Political Stability In England, 1675–1725*, London, Macmillan.

Rudolph, L. I. and Rudolph S. H. 1979. 'Authority and Power in Bureaucratic and Patrimonial Administration: A Revisionist Interpretation of Weber on Bureaucracy', *World Politics*, 38.2.

Salter, A. 1961. *Memoirs of a Public Servant*, London, Faber.

Stigler, G. 1975. *The Citizen and the State: Essays on Regulation*, Chicago, University of Chicago Press.

Thomas H. (ed.) 1967. *Crisis in the Civil Service*, London, Anthony Blond.

Tooze, J. A. 2000. *The German Statistical Service*, Cambridge, Cambridge University Press.

Turner, B. S. 1991. 'Introduction: the Man and his Work' in H. H. Gerth and C. W. Mills (eds), *From Max Weber: Essays in Sociology*, Routledge.

Wilson J. Q. and DiJulio, J. J. 1995 [1980] *American Government*, Lexington DC, Heath and Co.

World Bank. 1993. *The East Asian Miracle. Economic Growth and Public Policy*, New York, Oxford University Press.

CHAPTER 6
CENTRAL BANKS AS AGENTS OF ECONOMIC DEVELOPMENT

Gerald Epstein[1]

1.   Introduction

In the last two decades, there has been a global sea change in the theory and practice of central banking.[2] The 'best practice' commonly prescribed by the international financial institutions and by many prominent economists, is the 'neo-liberal' approach to central banking (Epstein, 2003). Its main components are: (1) central bank independence (2) a focus on inflation fighting (including adopting formal 'inflation targeting') and (3) the use of indirect methods of monetary policy (i.e., short-term interest rates as opposed to direct methods such as credit ceilings) (Bernanke et al. 1999).

   These principles have far reaching implications. Central bank independence implies, first and foremost, that the central bank should not be subject to pressure from the government to finance government activities (deficits). The focus on inflation means that the central bank should not be concerned with other goals such as promoting full employment, supporting industrial policy or allocating credit to sectors of special social need, such as housing. Neither should the central bank attempt to manage exchange rates through monetary policy, and certainly not through using controls on capital flows. Using indirect tools of monetary policy means that central banks should not use credit allocation techniques such as subsidized interest rates, credit ceilings, and capital controls to affect the quantity or the allocation of credit. These tenets are promoted not only in developed countries, but also with great vigour in the developing world.

   As I show, this recipe is a highly idiosyncratic one: As a package, it is dramatically different from the historically dominant theory and practice of central banking, not only in the developing world, but, notably, in the now developed countries themselves.[3] Throughout the early and recent history of central banking in the US, England, Europe, and elsewhere, financing governments, managing exchange rates, and supporting economic sectors by using 'direct methods' of intervention have been among the most important tasks of central banking and, indeed, in many cases, were among the reasons for their existence. The neo-liberal policy package currently proposed, then, is drastically out of step with the history and dominant practice of central banking throughout most of its history.

Indeed, historians of central banking will agree that financing governments and managing exchange rates were key for central banks for decades, if not centuries. But they would deny that central banks have commonly given support to selected economic sectors. Following Gerschenkron's (1962) seminal discussion, the standard story draws an important distinction between banking systems in late developers, such as France, and early developers, primarily England. Among the former, banks had to accumulate and allocate long-term credit so that local firms could catch up with those in England.

Less noted is an associated presumptive difference in the role of central banks in these two types of countries. In the common historiography, the UK and the US had *macro-oriented* central banks that have used primarily indirect tools of policy and on the continent and in Japan there are the *credit allocating* central banks, that supported industrial policy. For many economists, achieving modernism in central banking means transforming the central bank from the anachronistic European mode into the modern mode of the Bank of England or Federal Reserve.

Significantly, this story misses an important fact: Virtually all central banks, *including* the Bank of England (BOE) and the US Federal Reserve (the Fed) have used direct means to support economic sectors. And this has not simply been a matter of historical aberration. It has been an essential aspect of their structures and behaviour for decades on end. Both the BOE and the Fed have promoted the *financial sectors* of their economies, and especially, to support the *international role* of their financial services industries. They have done this by using subsidized interest rates, legal restrictions, directed credit and moral suasion to promote particular financial markets and institutions. Moreover, at times, they have even oriented their overall monetary policy toward promoting the development of this particular economic sector.

The historical role of the BOE in promoting the City of London is well known, but the Fed's similar role with respect to the US financial markets and the international role of the dollar is less discussed (Broz, 1997; Epstein,

1981; Greider, 1987). Still, when acknowledged, these cases have usually been viewed simply as a way of redistributing income from one sector (industry and labour) to another (finance). But – and this is the important point here – they should also be seen as mechanisms of 'industrial policy' an attempt by the central bank to build up a 'targeted' sector of the economy, not *only* to deliver benefits to their friends and political allies, or to provide 'macro stability', but *also* because they are considered an important, dynamic sector for the economy as a whole.

The point, then, is this: Virtually all central banks have engaged in 'industrial policy' or 'selective targeting'. The difference lies in which industries they have promoted. Significantly, the whole tenor of economic development can be fundamentally affected by which of these industries the central bank and associated institutions promoted. Sorting this out is complex, however. Evidence suggests that central banks that are more oriented to industrial and social development are likely to have a more productive role as agents of development than those that build up only their financial sectors.

The rest of the chapter is organized as follows: In the next section, by way of background, I discuss the functions of central banks in the development process. Section 3 discusses the evolution of major 'OECD' central banks prior to the Second World War. I focus on their roles of financing governments, managing exchange rates, and promoting economic sectors. In section 4, I discuss the issue of sectoral policy in the post Second World War period. Section 5 extends the argument to central banking in developing countries. Section 6 summarizes and concludes.

2.   The role of central banks in development

Most developed country central banks evolved from private banks, not in a bang, but over a long period of time (Goodhart, 1998; Capie et al. 1994). Historians of central banking therefore debate the question: 'when did each 'proto' central bank become a 'real' central bank?' This naturally raises the question: What exactly is the definition of a central bank, and as a related matter, what functions must a bank perform to be properly called a central bank?

Most historians identify the following functions as being historically essential to the operations of central banks: (1) unifying and issuing the country's bank notes; (2) acting as the government's bank; (3) acting as the commercial banks' bank; (4) serving as a lender of last resort to the banking sector and possibly the whole financial system; (5) conducting monetary policy to manage the foreign exchanges and the price level; (6) conducting monetary policy to manage the overall level of economic activity and (7) allocating credit to promote national goals. This list is contentious with historians, with many claiming that one or the other of these is the *sina qua non* of central banking, and with most authorities ultimately throwing up their hands and declaring that maybe they can't agree on how to define a central bank, but they know one when they see it.[4]

There are at least three other roles of central banks that are less considered. One is the *distributive* role of central bank policy. Central banks' policies can have differential impacts on different classes and groups: Workers and capitalists, debtors and creditors, finance and industry, those operating in traded and non-traded goods. Linking this to the political economy of central banking, for example, bankers may oppose expansionary monetary policy because they believe it will lower real interest rates and raise inflation, whereas workers and industrialists may prefer looser policy.

A second less-known role is the *political* role of central banks. In this regard, the most discussed issue is focused on the impact of central bank *independence* on inflation. But central banks' potential political role is much broader than this. During the period of de-colonization central banks played an important political role in helping to establish national sovereignty and unity. More recently, central banks which are relatively independent from government often represent and promote particular interests, constituencies and ideologies and thereby affect the overall tenor of economic debate. In recent times, central banks have often been aligned with those in financial circles, including external actors like the IMF, in promoting financial liberalization, inflation targeting and the elimination of capital controls. By contrast, central banks that are more integrated into government are more likely to promote policies and procedures that are framed more closely by government priorities and reigning ideologies.

A third underappreciated role is the central banks' *allocative role* in which their policies can affect the profitability and access to credit of different industries.

In short, historically central banks have played many and diverse roles and, it is clear, that the neo-liberal version of central banking has picked a highly truncated version of this list.

What, then, do we mean by 'central banks as agents of economic development? The term 'agent' implies that the central bank *deliberately* tries to promote development. By contrast, the current fashion is for central banks to take a narrow view of this by focusing only on 'macroeconomic and financial stability'. In our histories, however, we will see that for much of central banking history, many central banks have aspired to do much more than that, with a number of them even seeing themselves as 'agents of development' in the self-aware meaning of the term.

3.   The development of central banking in the US, UK, Europe, and Japan

3.1.   *Financing the state*

Recently, historians have noted the critical role of the state in the development of banking and central banking, emphasizing in this regard the state's need for finance. According to three of the most prominent historians of banking:

> The more one studies the historical origins and development of modern financial systems, the more it becomes apparent that at most of the critical points when financial systems changed, sometimes for the better, sometimes for the worse, the role of the state was of paramount importance ... Long before private economic entities ... came to require financing on a scale beyond the capabilities of individual proprietors and partners, governments had needs for large scale finance... . Among the needs for which states needed financing were: solidifying and extending their authority, unifying the disparate components of their states under a central administration, promoting state-led and state-financed economic development projects as means of increasing state power, and, perhaps most important of all, waging wars against other competing states. (Sylla et al. 1999: 1)

To raise money, states often made arrangements with existing banks or created special banks typically by issuing a bank charter. In exchange for giving these banks monopoly over note issue and other privileges, the banks would promise to finance the state. Among other means, the bank would then generally take the debt issue of the government and distribute it among a decentralized group of lenders. This would facilitate the government's borrowing, and would also allow the lenders to create a 'lender's cartel' thereby improving their enforcement of debt repayment by the government. (North and Weingast, 1989). It is these banks that often evolved into central banks.

The initial creation of the BOE in 1694, in the midst of a major war with France, is, perhaps, the classic example of this role of central banking. In effect, a deal was struck: The state would get badly needed loans at a preferential rate in exchange for granting extensive legal privileges to a private banking corporation, a corporation that eventually became the BOE (Broz, 1997: 215). The role of the BOE in financing the crown is commonly cited as an important factor in the war-making prowess of Britain and, particularly, in its success in the Napoleonic Wars. There are many other prominent examples: the first two banks of the United States in the nineteenth century, the Bank of France (1800) the National Bank of Belgium (1850), the Bank of Spain (1874) and the Reichsbank (1876). (Capie et al. 1994: 1–231; Broz, 1997: ch. 6).

Central banks, then, at their inception, were designed to finance the state. How ironic it is, then, that the current fashion in central banking is to severely limit the ability of central banks to carry out this function, especially when state capacity in developing countries have been eviscerated by years of structural adjustment.

3.2.   *Managing exchange rates and the price level*

Since most of the European countries were on a specie standard in the nineteenth century, a crucial task of these central banks was to maintain the convertibility of the county's currency into specie at the fixed price. In practice, this meant managing the country's money, credit and gold reserves so as to maintain convertibility. Maintaining convertibility at the fixed rate also served to limit increases in price levels and, therefore, the task of these central banks was to target the exchange rate and, in doing so, also implicitly manage the price level.

Yet, in practice, most central banks had additional goals. These included directing credit to specific uses, and limiting economic instabilities associated with inflows and outflows of capital and gold. Some central banks also tried to maintain trade surpluses, rather than automatically adjust according to gold standard rules of the game that were supposed to automatically lead to international trade balance. To pursue these additional objectives, central banks employed numerous 'gold devices' to give the central bank some freedom to manage monetary and credit conditions as seemed appropriate for domestic business (Yeager, 1976: 307, fn. 25) and other domestic goals. In Germany, for example, interest free loans were given to importers of gold, and exports of gold were impeded. (Yeager, 1976: 306). This, amounts to a type of exchange control. Similar devices were used in France where, for example, the central bank sometimes insisted on its legal right to redeem its notes in silver five-franc pieces rather than gold, a clear tax on the export of gold (*ibid.*). These devices 'put some slight variability into the gold values of monetary units and slightly increased the range of possible exchange rate fluctuations' (*ibid.*). These and related devices clearly undermine the notion of a rules based automatic system of central bank policy, as well as one single-mindedly devoted to price stability.

In short, even within the confines of the international gold standard, central banks used exchange and capital controls to buy some modest freedom of manoeuvre to pursue domestic objectives. This violates the neo-liberal recipe of today, but was used to good effect in the (old) liberal period of the nineteenth century.

3.3. *Sectoral policies*

Central banks, both on the European continent and off, promoted important sectoral goals.

3.3.1. *Continental European central banks in the nineteenth century*

Central banks in Europe were not only important lenders to the state, but also very involved in lending to industry (Capie et al. 1999: 69). The Bank of France, the Bank of the Netherlands, and the Bank of Italy all had widespread branch networks, and had very close relationships with industry. The Reichsbank of Germany also had important industrial customers (*ibid.*).

Many of these 'central' banks were private banks with special government privileges, and were profit oriented. But this fact should not obscure the 'public' role they played in helping to direct credit. These banks had special privileges included a monopoly on note issue and they also often benefited from the requirement that the government and other banks place reserves with them. These privileges gave these banks subsidized access to credit, allowing them to make loans at subsidized rates to industry (Cameron and Neal, 2003). Indeed, Knodell reports that countries that had central banks during this period had, on average, lower nominal and real interest rates, than countries that did not (Knodell, 2004).

Of course, one should not over-estimate the extent to which these central banks were 'agents' of development in the sense of having a developmental 'vision' and intent. Often, these central banks were private, not public. Still, however imperfectly, these central banks often played an important role in mobilizing and allocating finance to industry and to government in the service of economic development; sometimes even directed by a developmental vision from the state.

3.3.2.   *Britain and the US*

The BOE and the US Fed are often seen has lacking in 'sectoral' policy during their early years. But, this argument ignores the fact that these banks were very much involved in promoting sections of the financial sector in their economies. We first discuss the Fed and then take on the more familiar story of the BOE.

a.   The Federal Reserve[5]

The common explanation of the founding of the Fed in 1913 was that it was designed to enhance the country's lender of last resort function to prevent the cyclical drains of reserves from regional banks and resulting financial panics that had characterized earlier decades. While this is certainly part of the story, another key factor was the desire on the part of New York bankers to enhance their ability to compete with London banks in the global financial market. As Carter Glass, who was instrumental in the creation of the system, told a Washington audience during the First World War:

> The proponents of the Federal Reserve Act had no idea of impairing the rightful prestige of New York as the financial metropolis of this hemisphere. They rather expected to confirm its distinction, and even hoped to assist powerfully in wresting the scepter from London, and eventually making New York the financial center of the world. (quoted in Kolko, 1963: 254)

As Broz describes in great detail, relative to the prior National Monetary System the key changes in the Federal Reserve Act concerned creating markets in bankers and trade acceptances that would allow New York Banks to compete with British banks in the highly lucrative financing of international trade (Broz, 1997: ch. 1). Key was to create a central bank that would allow the bank to discount these acceptances. As Paul Warburg, a New York banker and one of the master-minds behind the Federal Reserve Act put it: American discounting practices prior to the founding of the Fed was 'as backward as Europe at the time of the Medicis, and Asia, in all likelihood, at the time of Hammurabi' (quoted in Broz, 1997: 40.) The authors of the Federal Reserve Act chose to privilege instruments that would help develop financial markets to improve the competitiveness of US banks with their London counterparts. These instrument included bills of exchange, or trade acceptances drawn within the United States, which was not used extensively to finance domestic transactions (Broz, 1997: 48).

Key components of the Federal Reserve Act were also designed to enhance the ability of the US financial system to manage the gold standard. Since the resumption of the gold standard in 1879, the US had perhaps the freest market for gold in the world, and did not have a central bank to protect the supply in case of crisis (Broz, 1997: 49). In addition, the US did not have a central bank that could employ gold devices to help create policy space to pursue other goals.

Promoting the US dollar as an international currency was also a goal of the founders of the Fed. Despite the fact that the US had accumulated massive amounts of foreign assets and was becoming the world's largest creditor, the US dollar was still not widely used in international finance. The Federal Reserve Act was also intended to rectify that situation to enhancing the global competitiveness of New York banks. To some extent, this promotion of the international aspects of the Federal Reserve Act in order to help New York bankers compete with London was simply a matter of 'rent seeking'. Still, at the same time, this was clearly a targeted policy to subsidize and promote a particular sector in its quest to become more internationally competitive.

b.   The Bank of England

The case of the BOE and its connection to the City of London is well known. London had been the financial centre of the world, or had a monopoly of capital exports at least up to 1850. Rivalry with the French heated up around mid-century, but the Franco-Prussian War destroyed French chances. By 1875 London was supreme in both domestic and international money markets (Kindleberger, 1993: 261). By the late nineteenth century, during the heyday of the classical gold standard, British banks and bond houses were dominant in international capital markets and in the financing of trade. For example, during the boom in foreign securities from 1904 to 1913, British bond and banking houses sent abroad close to half of British savings and 5 per cent of national income (Kindleberger, 1996: 136).

A major reason for British financial primacy was the structure and stability of the international gold standard. Indeed, at times, the gold standard operated more like a sterling standard (Kindleberger, 1996: 136). A French study quoted by Kindleberger emphasizes the importance of the gold standard for the competitiveness of British financial institutions. 'Paris was especially handicapped by the practice of bimetallism, which gave the Bank of France the choice of whether it would pay off its notes in gold or silver – whereas in London one could get all the gold one wanted without hesitation on the part of the authorities or any doubt' (quoted in Kindleberger, 1993: 262).

For our purposes, the relevant lesson is this: While other factors such as the efficiency and sophistication of the British financial institutions were important, the stability of the gold standard, with sterling at its centre was enormously important in the success and global competitiveness of the British financial system. *Hence, the efforts and support that the Bank of England made to develop and maintain the gold standard were, in effect, a major subsidy and support of the city of London financial institutions themselves.* The BOE's policy to maintain the convertibility of sterling was therefore not only a macroeconomic policy but also a sectoral policy designed to support the international competitiveness of British financial institutions.

Thus, even during the classical liberal period of the late nineteenth and early twentieth century, all the central banks considered here have engaged in sectoral policies. After the Great Depression and the Second World War, this use of selective policies became even more integral to central bank policies, and even more widespread.

4.   Western central bank policies after the Second World War: Credit allocation for social goals

Following the disasters of the Great Depression and the Second World War, governments in the UK, Europe, Japan and even the US asserted much greater control over central banks and the banking industries (Capie et al. 1999). Central banks again became important institutions for financing and managing government debts accumulated during the war; and after the war, central banks became important tools for rebuilding and restructuring national economies and providing for social needs, often under government's direction. Central banks utilized a variety of credit allocation techniques to accomplish these goals, and in most cases, these techniques were supported by capital and exchange controls on international capital movements (see Epstein and Schor, 1992).

The types of controls, the goals they were directed to and their degree of success varied. Still, no matter how successful, virtually all of these central banks had ended or severely limited their use of these controls by the mid 1980s. Under the neo-liberal play book, these controls, despite their long histories and many successes, were thrown in the dust bin of history.

4.1.   *Developed country central banks as agents of economic development during the 'golden age of capitalism'[6]*

The Great Depression of the 1930s and then the Second World War was a watershed for central banks in the industrialized world. Virtually all were brought under more government control and were reoriented to promote government priorities. In the United States, the Fed was brought under tighter government control in the late 1930s and then, at the start of the Second World War, was required to help the Treasury finance the war effort at relatively low interest rates. It remained under Treasury control until 1951, but even after that, was subject to significant government pressures to support the market for wartime US government debt. In addition, the Humphrey-Hawkins bill obligated the Fed to pursue polices to support high employment while controlling inflation. The era of Keynesian policies was at hand (Epstein and Schor, 1990).

The US government had a myriad financial institutions, moreover, that supported national goals, notably housing (Dymski, 1993; Wolfson, 1993). The Savings and Loan banks, along with other government supported financial institutions, for example, supported housing. During this period, the Fed policy was quite sensitive to the needs of the housing market concerns and even tailored its monetary policy to avoid significantly harming it (Maisel, 1973).

In Europe and England, central banks that had been independent before the War found themselves subject to state control after 1945 (Capie et al. 1999: 72). During the War, monetary policy was often implemented through direct controls while interest rates were held low and constant. Direct controls continued in the aftermath of the war with various credit allocation techniques (Capie et al. 1999: 25).

4.2.   *Credit allocation techniques*

Credit controls are measures by which the authorities seek to modify the pattern and incidence of cost and availability of credit from what markets would generate on their own (Hodgman, 1972: 137). Credit controls seek to influence credit allocation and interest rate structures (*ibid.*). In Europe credit controls have served a number of purposes: (1) to finance government debt at lower interest rates (2) to reduce the flow of credit to the private sector without raising domestic interest rates (3) to influence the allocation of real resources to priority uses and (4) to block channels of financial intermediation and thus to assist restrictive general monetary policy and (5) to strengthen popular acceptance of wage-price controls by holding down interest income (*ibid.*).

European experiences with credit controls varied. In Germany, controls were used only briefly after the Second World War. In the Netherlands and the United Kingdom, extensive use was made of them, but they were always seen as temporary and short-run expedients. In the Netherlands, credit controls were used to support macroeconomic policy, rather than credit allocation. In the United Kingdom, the principal aim of controls was to facilitate low cost government debt since the government wanted to reduce the negative impacts of high interest rates on the bond market, on income distribution and on the balance of payments. A more limited aim of the quantitative ceilings was to guarantee a flow of short-term credit at favourable interest rates to high priority activities such as ship building, exports and manufacturing. This was achieved by putting credit ceilings into place, and giving exemptions to priority sectors (Hodgman, 1972: 144). Moreover, the BOE identified sectors for which credit should be limited, such as consumption and the financing of imports. In England, as elsewhere, these credit controls were accompanied by exchange and capital controls.

In France, Italy and Belgium the principle of controlling credit flows and interest rates to serve national interests was more widely accepted. France had among the most extensive and successful sets of controls and they were key parts of the government's industrial policy. The Bank of France was nationalized in 1945, and placed under the National Credit Council, the institution in charge of implementing the financial aspects of the government plan (Hodgman, 1972: 147; Zysman 1987). The broad aim of credit policy in France was to contribute to the modernization of the French economy and its ability to compete in international markets.

To influence the volume and allocation of credit, the Bank of France used various methods. Variable 'asset based reserve requirements' were widely used. These require that banks have to observe minimum reserve requirements based on the assets they hold, but the central bank varies these to promote lending to desired sectors by allowing lower required reserve rates on privileged assets. Ceilings on credit extension with extensions for priority sectors were also widely used on the continent. These included short-term export credits, and medium-term loans for construction. These ceilings applied to a large range of financial institutions, and were accompanied, as well, by capital and exchange controls (Hodgman, 1972: 148–149; Zysman, 1987). A third tool was careful Central Bank scrutiny of individual credits made by commercial banks. This allowed the Bank of France, for example, to approve loans for privileged purposes. Another approach affecting the allocation of credit involved the use of rediscounting of bills at lower interest rates for priority purposes (Hodgman, 1972: 151).

Zysman (1987) has emphasized the role of these credit allocation techniques in helping to revive the French economy and help it adjust to structural challenges in the post-war period. Italy and Belgium also used similar policies. In the case of Italy, a major goal was to help develop the southern part of the country (US House of Representatives 1972: 11).

Unfortunately, there has not been a comprehensive statistical analysis of the effectiveness of these controls, though limited studies report that the controls were effective (Hodgman, 1972: 145). Still, lessons can be drawn from these experiences: These policies are most successful when the controls apply to a broad swath of the financial sector, to avoid arbitrage and avoidance; when they are accompanied by capital and exchange controls, to avoid capital flight; and when they are part of a coherent plan of economic promotion and development.

4.3.   *The neo-liberal order*

To be sure, not all of these efforts were successful. Yet most accounts suggest that many of them were very helpful in reaching important social goals including rebuilding industry, supporting housing and financing the overhang of government debt acquired during the war while avoiding massive shifts in wealth toward rentiers. By the 1990s many if not most of these programme had been swept away. The increase in inflation, elimination of exchange and capital controls, and the break-down of the Bretton Woods System all contributed to these dramatic changes in financial markets and policies. Still, rather than seeing this evolution to liberalized financial markets and central banking policy as simply a conjunctural change, economists and policy makers have identified the current complex of policies and structures as somehow 'modern', even optimal, and therefore the only policy structures worthy of emulation throughout the globe.

5.   Central banks as agents of economic development in developing countries

After the Second World War, there was a major transformation of central banking in the developing world as well. In many respects, these changes paralleled those in the developed world, but in developing countries, central banks were much more emphatically *agents* of economic development then in many richer countries. As renowned monetary historian of the New York Federal Reserve, Arthur I. Bloomfield reported in 1957:

> During the past decade there has been a marked proliferation and development of central banking facilities in the underdeveloped countries of the world, along with an increasing resort to the use of monetary policy as an instrument of economic control. Since 1945,

central banks have been newly established and pre-existing ones thoroughly reorganized, in no less than some twenty-five underdeveloped countries. In other cases the powers of pre-existing central banks have been broadened ...in large part the recent growth of central banking in the economically backward areas has also reflected a desire on the part of the governments concerned to be able to pursue a monetary policy designed to promote more rapid economic development and to mitigate undue swings in national money incomes. (Bloomfield, 1957: 190)

Bloomfield goes on to describe the functions, powers, and goals of these central banks.

Many of the central banks, especially those established since 1945 *with the help of Federal Reserve advisers* are characterized by unusually wide and flexible powers. A large number of instruments of general and selective credit control, some of a novel character, are provided for. Powers are given to the central bank to engage in a wide range of credit operations with commercial banks and in some cases with other financial institutions... . These and other powers were specifically provided in the hope of enabling the central banks ... to pursue a more *purposive* and effective monetary possible than had been possible for most .... that had been set up ... during the twenties and thirties ... [that] for the most part [had] been equipped with exceeding orthodox statutes and limited powers which permitted little scope for a monetary policy *designed to promote economic development and internal stability...* (Bloomfield, 1957: 191, emphasis added)

Somewhat surprisingly from the perspective of today's financial orthodoxy, the Federal Reserve Bank of New York helped to establish developing country central banks and encouraged them to have a broad range of monetary and credit powers, especially in contrast to the orthodoxy of the 1920s and 1930s. Of course, the Fed continued to be concerned with stabilization, controlling excessive credit creation and maintaining moderate inflation. Still, Bloomfield emphasized (1957: 197): '[the central bank's] efforts need not, and in fact should not, stop here. The majority of central banks in underdeveloped countries have in actual practice adopted a variety of measures designed more effectively to promote the over-all development of their economies...'.

Bloomfield describes the same tools of credit manipulation described earlier with respect to Europe, Japan and even the United States:

Selective credit controls applied to the banking system, through help in establishing and supporting special credit institutions catering to specialized credit needs, and through influence over the lending policies of such institutions, it can help to some degree to re-channel real resources in desired directions, both between the public and private sector and within the private sector itself. (1957: 198)[7]

Writing about the same issue almost fifteen years later (in 1971), another prominent Fed official, Andrew F. Brimmer, a member of the Federal Reserve Board of Governors, looks back on the experience with 'developmental' central banking in the developing world; 'during the last ten years, a number of central banks concerned themselves with problems of economic development almost as much as they did with the traditional functions of central banking' (Brimmer, 1971: 780). But by 1971, monetary officials, as represented even by a pro-Keynesian economist like Brimmer, had become more sceptical of the developmental role of central banks in developing countries.

Brimmer and his associates describe a variety of techniques that central banks pursued in the 1960s. These included: Providing capital to development institutions, such as industrial and agricultural development banks; extending credit to development banks in purchasing their securities; buying a small part of the equity of development banks; establishing a 'securities regulation fund' to create a market for the securities of various development finance institutions, by using the profits from the ordinary operations of the central bank (1971: 785); using differential discount rates to allocate credit to capital development projects;[8] the establishment of portfolio ceilings on activities having a low priority; various types of reserve requirements, including differential reserve requirements to influence the allocation of credit;[9] using import deposit requirements, (primarily intended to deal with balance of payments difficulties) to also influence the allocation of bank credit.[10]

Brimmer on the whole is somewhat negative about the effectiveness of many of these techniques. The possible trade-off between developmental central bank and the maintenance of financial and macroeconomic stability was a major concern of Brimmer and his colleagues. To be sure, this possible trade-off is a key issue in designing developmental central bank policies.

From the research available, it is clear that support by the central bank of the government's policy for industrial development made a key contribution to the rise of many of the more successful developing countries in the late twentieth century. Alice Amsden reports, the role of medium and long-term financing, often supported by central banking mechanisms as just described, were key to the 'Rise of the Rest'.[11] The countries of the 'rest', according to Amsden, acquired a manufacturing base in the years prior to the Second World War and then, after the war, industrialized rapidly, moving, eventually into mid-level and even high-technology production (2001: 1–2). Among many other factors, Amsden stresses the important role of finance in the success of these countries, and especially the mobilization and allocation of medium term and long-term finance for industrialization.

The state's main agent for financing investment was the development bank. Sometimes, the whole banking sector in these countries was mobilized to direct long-term credit to targeted industries, thereby 'acting as a surrogate development bank'. (Amsden, 2001: 129). The lending terms of these development banks were almost always concessionary (Amsden, 2001: 132). The public finance behind the 'rest's' development banking was often 'off-budget' and related to non-tax revenues. It came from foreign sources, deposits in government-owned banks post office savings accounts, and pension funds. As we just saw, many central banks played a key role here as well, just as they had in Europe, financing the important roles of the state.

Central banks played an important role in accommodating the development oriented policies of these governments. Most kept effective real interest rates were often low, even negative. They also used capital controls to insulate domestic markets from hot money flows that could lead to over-valued exchange rates and crises. Furthermore, central banks also played an important role in the 'off-budget' financing of a number of these countries using the techniques described by Bloomfield and Brimmer as described above. Of course, these policies in some cases eventually had negative consequences, contributing to excessive inflation, financial instability and sometimes misallocation of credit. These problems bring us back to the question of the delicate balance between the developmental and stabilization roles that central banks must play to be successful agents of economic development. Still, in many cases, as part of a government policy, they helped underwrite significant economic development in many countries.

6.   Conclusion

I have argued that throughout most of their history, central banks have financed governments, used allocation methods and subsidies to engage in 'sectoral policy' and have attempted to manage the foreign exchanges, often with capital and exchange controls of various kinds. The current neo-liberal central banking 'best practice recipe', then, goes against the history and tradition of central banking in the countries now most strongly promoting it.

The question, then, is NOT whether central banks have or should pursue developmental policy, but rather: What *kind* of developmental policy should they conduct? Here history also gives some guidance. Central banks have been most effective in helping to foster development, especially in 'late developers', where they have been part of the governmental apparatus of industrial policy.

Throughout this history, a tension has existed between central banks' developmental and stabilizing roles. Yet there is little evidence that the optimal solution to this tension is to abandon the developmental role entirely. Worse yet is to follow the lead of England and the US and focus the developmental role entirely on promoting the financial sector, especially the fashionable 'stock market based' financial sectors. There is little evidence that the stock-market based financial sectors so actively promoted these days in many developing countries leads to faster economic growth or more development (Zhu et al. 2004). Worse yet, promoting the financial sector through internal and external financial liberalization can make developing countries highly vulnerable to financial panics and crises. Thus, far from resolving the tension between the developmental and stabilization central bank roles, focusing on financial and capital account liberalization poses the danger of making this conflict even worse. It would be far better to go back to the history of central banking and rebuild the capacity of central banks to act as true agents of economic development as they have in the past.

Notes

1. I thank Ha-Joon Chang, Meredith Jung-En Woo, Eric Rauchway, Howard Stein, Leonardo Burlamaqui, Thomas David, Erik Reinert, and the other participants at the WIDER conference for many helpful comments, and Kade Finnoff and Lynda Pickbourn for excellent research assistance. All remaining errors are mine.
2. For reasons of space, bibliographical references will be kept to a minimum. For a full set of references, and elaboration of these arguments and evidence, see Epstein 2006.
3. See Chang (2002), for parallel argument for a range of other policies and institutions.
4. Capie (1999), for example, claims that the lender of last resort function is the true sina qua non of central banking.
5. This section draws heavily on the fascinating book by Broz (1997), as well as the more familiar work of Greider (1987). See also Epstein (1981). Limited space prevents me from discussing many other issues here, including the role of wildcat banking and the J.P. Morgan banks' central banking roles.
6. I have drawn the material for this section mainly from US House of Representatives (1972), Zysman (1987), Hodgman (1972), and US Senate (1981). See also Pollin (1995).
7. Of course, Bloomfield cautions that: 'Such measures would for the most part be justified, however, only to the extent that they do not conflict with the overriding requirement of financial stability or involve the central bank in details of a sort that

might distract its attention and energies from the effective implementation of a policy aimed at stability' (1957: 197).

8. These have been used in many countries: Argentina, Bolivia, Brazil, China, Colombia, Costa Rica, the Dominican Republic, Ecuador, Peru, Venezuela, Israel, India, Indonesia, Korea, Pakistan, the Philippines, and Thailand. The central bank charges a preferential rate on discounts or advances against favoured types of paper to induce commercial banks to increase their lending (Brimmer, 1971: 786).

9. These have been used in: Mexico, Argentina, Brazil, Chile, Colombia, the Dominican Republic, Israel, and Peru among other countries (Brimmer, 1971: 788).

10. Imports of developmentally important goods are subject to lower deposit requirements and hence are favoured. This has been used in Argentina, Brazil, Chile, Colombia, Ecuador, Indonesia, Israel, Pakistan, Paraguay, the Philippines, Uruguay, and Vietnam (Brimmer, 1971: 789).

11. Amsden's 'rest' consist of China, India, Indonesia, South Korea, Malaysia, Taiwan, and Thailand in Asia; Argentina, Brazil, Chile and Mexico in Latin America; and Turkey in the Middle East (Amsden, 2001: 1). Here we briefly discuss six of these countries: China, India, South Korea, Thailand, Brazil, and Mexico.

References

Amsden, A. H. 2001. *The Rise of 'The Rest'; Challenges to the West from Late-Industrializing Economies.* Oxford: Oxford University Press.

Bernanke, B. S., T. Laubach, A. S. Posen and Mishkin, F. S. 1999. *Inflation Targeting: Lessons from the International Experience.* Princeton, NJ: Princeton University Press.

Bloomfield, A. I. 1957. 'Some Problems of Central Banking in Underdeveloped Countries', *The Journal of Finance*, 12, 2 May: 190–204.

Brimmer, A. F. 1971. 'Central Banking and Economic Development: The Record of Innovation', *Journal of Money, Credit and Banking*, 3, 4 November: 780–92.

Broz, J. L. 1997. *The International Origins of the Federal Reserve System.* Ithaca: Cornell University Press.

Cameron, R. and Neal, L. 2003. *Concise Economic History of the World; From Paleolithic Times to the Present.* Oxford: Oxford University Press.

Capie, F., C. Goodhart, S. Fischer and Schnadt, N. 1994. *The Future of Central Banking; The Tercentenary Symposium of the Bank of England.* Cambridge: Cambridge University Press.

Capie, F. 1999. 'Banking in Europe in the 19th Century: The Role of the Central Bank', in R. Sylla, R. Tilly and G. Tortella (eds), *The State, the Financial System and Economic Modernization.* Cambridge: Cambridge University Press, pp. 118–133.

Chang, H-J. 2002. *Kicking Away the Ladder – Development Strategy in Historical Perspective.* London: Anthem Press.

Dymski, G. A. 1993. 'How To Rebuild the U.S. Financial System: Level the Playing Field and Renew the Social Contract' in G. A. Dymski, G. Epstein and R. Pollin (eds), *Transforming the U.S. Financial System; Equity and Efficiency for the 21st Century.* Washington: Economic Policy Institute, pp. 101–31.

Epstein, G. 1981. Domestic Stagflation and Monetary Policy: The Federal Reserve and the Hidden Election, in T. Ferguson and J. Rogers (eds), *The Hidden Election*, New York: Pantheon Press.

Epstein, G. 2003. 'Alternatives to Inflation Targeting Monetary Policy For Stable and Egalitarian Growth: A Brief Research Summary', www.umass.edu/peri

Epstein, G. 2006. 'Central Banks as Agents of Economic Development', WIDER Research Paper 2006–54. Helsinki: UNU-WIDER.

Epstein, G. and Schor, J. 1990. Macropolicy in the Rise and Fall of the Golden Age, in S. Marglin and J. Schor (eds), *The Golden Age of Capitalism: Reinterpreting the Postwar Experience.* New York: Oxford University Press for UNU-WIDER.

Epstein, G. and Schor, J. 1992. 'Structural Determinants and Economic Effects of Capital Controls in OECD Countries', in T. Banuri and J. Schor (eds), *Financial Openness and National Autonomy.* Oxford: Clarendon Press for UNU-WIDER, pp. 136–161.

Epstein, G., Grabel, I. and Jomo, K.S. 2005. 'Capital Management Techniques in Developing Countries,' in G. Epstein (ed.), *Capital Flight and Capital Controls in Developing Countries.* Northampton: Edward Elgar.

Gerschenkron, A. 1962. *Economic Backwardness in Historical Perspective.* Cambridge, MA: Harvard University Press, Belknap Press.

Goodhart, C. 1988. *The Evolution of Central Banks.* Cambridge MA: MIT Press.

Greider, W. 1987. *The Secrets of the Temple.* New York: Simon and Schuster.

Hodgman, D. R. 1973.'Credit Controls in Western Europe: An Evaluative Review', in The Federal Reserve Bank of Boston, *Credit Allocation Techniques and Monetary Policy.* Boston: Federal Reserve Bank, pp. 137–161.

Kindleberger, C. 1993. *A Financial History of Western Europe.* 2nd edn. Oxford: Oxford University Press.

Kindleberger, C. 1996. *World Economic Primacy, 1500–1990.* Oxford: Oxford University Press.

Knodell, J. 2004. 'Central Banking in Early Industrialization', in M. Lavoie and M. Seccareccia, *Central Banking in the Modern World; Alternative Perspectives.* Cheltenham: Edward Elgar, pp. 262–81.

Kolko, G. 1963. *The Triumph of Conservatism.* New York: Free Press.

Maisel, S. 1973. *Managing the Dollar.* New York: Norton.

North, D. C. and Weingast, B. R. 1989. 'Constitutions and Commitment: The Evolution of Institutions Governing Public Choice in Seventeenth-Century England', *Journal of Economic History*, 49, December: 803–32.

Pollin, R. 1995. 'Financial Structures and Egalitarian Economic Policy', in *New Left Review*, 214: 26–61.

Sylla, R., Tilly, R. and Tortella, G. 1999. *The State, the Financial System and Economic Modernization.* Cambridge: Cambridge University Press.

US Congress, House of Representatives, 92nd Congress, 2nd Session. 1972. *Foreign Experiences with Monetary Policies to Promote Economic and Social Priority Programs.*

US Congress, Joint Economic Committee. 1981. *Monetary Policy, Selective Credit Policy and Industrial Policy in France, Britain, West Germany and Sweden.* Washington DC: Government Printing Office.

Wolfson, M. 1993. 'The Evolution of the Financial System and the Possibilities of Reform', in G. A. Dymski, G. Epstein and R. Pollin (eds), *Transforming the U.S. Financial System; Equity and Efficiency for the 21st Century.* Washington DC: Economic Policy Institute, pp. 133–155.

Yeager, L. B. 1976. *International Monetary Relations; Theory, History and Policy,* 2nd edn, New York: Harper and Row.

Zhu, A., Ash, M. and Pollin, R. 2002. 'Stock Market Activity and Economic Growth: A Critical Appraisal of the Levine/Zervos Model', PERI Working Paper 47. www.umass.edu/peri

Zysman, J. 1983. *Governments, Markets and Growth.* Ithaca: Cornell University Press.

CHAPTER 7
CORPORATE GOVERNANCE, INNOVATIVE ENTERPRISE, AND ECONOMIC DEVELOPMENT[1]

William Lazonick

1.   Innovative enterprise and 'shareholder value'

In all of the richest economies, business corporations are repositories of large, and in many cases vast, quantities of resources over which corporate managers, rather than markets, exercise allocative control. Indeed, it can be argued that corporate control, as distinct from market control, of resource allocation represents the defining institutional characteristic of twentieth-century capitalist economies (Chandler, 1977; 1990). Whereas conventional neoclassical economic theory would have it that markets should allocate resources to achieve superior economic performance, the actual pervasiveness of corporate control over resource allocation demands a theory of the ways in which corporate governance affects economic performance.

During the 1980s and 1990s the argument that 'maximizing shareholder value' results in superior economic performance came to dominate the corporate governance debates. This perspective represents an attempt to construct a theory of corporate governance that is consistent with the more general theory of the market economy. Like the theory of the market economy, however, the shareholder-value perspective lacks a theory of innovative enterprise (see O'Sullivan, 2000b; Lazonick, 2003b; 2005b). Yet economic development depends on innovation. The result, as I show in this chapter, is that, lacking a theory of innovative enterprise, the perspective fails to comprehend how and under what conditions the corporate allocation of resources can generate higher incomes for larger numbers of people over a sustained period of time.

In Section 2 of this chapter, I outline the rationale for the shareholder-value perspective. Section 3 provides a critique of it, based on the ways in which an innovative corporate economy actually operates. In Section 4 I define the 'social conditions of innovative enterprise' as central concepts of a theory of innovative enterprise, and consider their implications for understanding the relation between corporate governance and economic performance, and Section 5 concludes with some remarks on the relation between corporate governance and economic development.

2.   Maximizing shareholder value[2]

For adherents of the theory of the market economy, 'market imperfections' – for example, 'asset specificity' in the work of Oliver Williamson (1985, 1996) – necessitate managerial control over the allocation of resources, thus creating an 'agency problem' for those 'principals' who have made investments in the firm. The agency problem derives from two limitations, one cognitive and the other behavioural, on the human ability to make allocative decisions. The cognitive limitation is 'hidden information' (also known as 'adverse selection' or 'bounded rationality') that prevents investors from knowing *a priori* whether the hired managers are good or bad resource allocators. The behavioural limitation is 'hidden action' (also known as 'moral hazard' or 'opportunism') that reflects the proclivity, inherent in an individualistic society, of managers as agents to use their positions as resource allocators to pursue their own self-interests and not necessarily the interests of the firm's principals. These managers may allocate corporate resources to build their own personal empires regardless of whether the investments that they make and the people whom they employ generate sufficient profits for the firm. They may hoard surplus cash or near-liquid assets, thus maintaining control over uninvested resources, rather than distributing extra revenues to shareholders. Or they may simply use their control over resource allocation to line their own pockets.

The manifestation of a movement toward the more efficient allocation of resources, it is argued, is a higher return to shareholders. But why is it shareholders for whom value should be maximized? Why not create more value for creditors by making their financial investments more secure, or for employees by paying them higher wages and benefits, or for communities in which the corporations operate by generating more tax revenues? Neoclassical financial theorists argue that among all the stakeholders in the business corporation only shareholders are 'residual claimants'. The amount of returns that shareholders receive depends on what is left over after other stakeholders, all of whom have guaranteed contractual claims, have been paid for their productive contributions to the firm. If the firm incurs a loss, the return to shareholders is negative, and vice versa.

By this argument, shareholders are the only stakeholders who have an incentive to bear the risk of investing in productive resources that may result in superior economic performance (O'Sullivan, 2002). As residual claimants, moreover, they are the only stakeholders with an interest in monitoring managers. Furthermore, by selling and buying corporate shares on the stock market, public shareholders, it is argued, are the participants in the economy who are best situated to reallocate resources to more efficient uses. The agency problem – the fact that public shareholders as the (purported) 'principals' who bear risk are obliged to leave the corporate allocation of resources under the control of managers as their 'agents' – poses a constant threat to the efficient allocation of resources.

Within the shareholder-value paradigm, the stock market represents the corporate governance institution through which the agency problem can be resolved and the efficient allocation of resources can be achieved. Specifically, the stock market can function as a 'market for corporate control' that enables shareholders to 'disgorge the free cash flow'. As Michael Jensen (1986: 323), the leading academic proponent of maximizing shareholder value, has put it:

> Free cash flow is cash flow in excess of that required to fund all projects that have positive net present values when discounted at the relevant cost of capital. Conflicts of interest between shareholders and managers over payout policies are especially severe when the organization generates substantial free cash flow. The problem is how to motivate managers to disgorge the cash rather than investing it at below cost or wasting it on organization inefficiencies.

How can those managers be motivated, or coerced, to distribute cash to shareholders? If a company does not maximize shareholder value, shareholders can sell their shares and reallocate the proceeds to what they deem to be more efficient uses. The sale of shares depresses that company's stock price, which in turn facilitates a takeover by shareholders who can put in place managers who are willing to distribute the 'free cash flow' to shareholders in the forms of higher dividends and/or stock repurchases. Better yet, as Jensen (1986) argued in the midst of the 1980s corporate takeover movement, let corporate raiders use the market for corporate control for debt-financed takeovers, thus enabling shareholders to transform their corporate equities into corporate bonds. Corporate managers would then be 'bonded' to distribute the 'free cash flow' in the form of interest rather than dividends. Additionally, as Jensen and Murphy (1990) among others, contended, the maximization of shareholder value could be achieved by giving corporate managers stock-based compensation, such as stock options, to align their own self-interests with those of shareholders. Then, even without the threat of a takeover, these managers would have a personal incentive to maximize shareholder value by investing corporate revenues only in those 'projects that have positive net present values when discounted at the relevant cost of capital' (Jensen, 1986: 323), and distributing the remainder of corporate revenues to shareholders in the forms of dividends and/or stock repurchases.

3.   A critique of the shareholder-value perspective

During the 1980s and 1990s 'maximizing shareholder value' became the dominant ideology for corporate governance in the United States, and from there was disseminated around the world. Top managers of industrial corporations became ardent advocates of this perspective, and with their stock-based compensation, they reaped ample returns that inured them to 'maximizing shareholder value' (Hall and Leibman, 1998, 661). In 2000 the average CEO compensation at the top 200 US corporations by sales revenues was $11.3 million, of which stock options generated 60 per cent, restricted stock 11 per cent, bonuses 18 per cent, and salary 9 per cent (Pearl Meyer, 2001).

During the decade of the 1970s the stock market had languished, and inflation had eroded dividend yields. In the 1980 and 1990s, however, with 'maximizing shareholder value' as the new corporate ideology, high real yields on corporate stock characterized the US corporate economy. As can be seen in Table 7.1, these high yields came mainly from stock-price appreciation as distinct from dividends yields, which were low in the 1990s despite high payout ratios.

High price yields reflected a combination of three distinct forces at work: a) *redistribution* of corporate revenues from labour incomes to capital incomes, mainly by older industrial corporations, in the form of stock repurchases; b) *innovation*, especially by newer technology companies, that boosted earnings per share; and c) *speculation* by stock market investors, encouraged, initially at least, by stock price increases due to the combination of redistribution and innovation. An understanding of these three sources of an ebullient stock market is essential for a critical evaluation of the efficiency claims of the shareholder-value perspective.

Table 7.1 US corporate stock and bond yields, 1960–2005

Average annual per cent change

	1960–69	1970–79	1980–89	1990–99	2000–05
Real stock yield	6.63	-1.66	11.67	15.01	-1.87
Price yield	5.80	1.35	12.91	15.54	-0.76
Dividend yield	3.19	4.08	4.32	2.47	1.58
Change in CPI	2.36	7.09	5.55	3.00	2.67
Real bond yield	2.65	1.14	5.79	4.72	3.60

Notes: Stock yields are for Standard and Poor's composite index of 500 US corporate stocks (about 75 per cent of which are NYSE). Bond yields are for Moody's Aaa-rated US corporate bonds.

Source: Updated from Lazonick and O'Sullivan (2000a), using US Congress (2005: tables B-62, B-73, B-95, B-96).

First, in the 1980s and 1990s, older companies, many with their origins in the late nineteenth century, engaged in a process of redistributing corporate revenues from labour to capital. Engaging in a 'downsize-and-distribute' allocation regime, they downsized their labour forces and increased the distribution of corporate revenues to shareholders (Lazonick and O'Sullivan, 2000a). This allocation regime represented a reversal of the 'retain-and-reinvest' regime that had characterized these companies in the post-Second World War decades. Coming into the 1980s employees – both managerial personnel and shop-floor workers – had expectations, based on over three decades of experience of 'retain-and-reinvest', of long-term employment with these corporations (Lazonick, 2004a).

Downsizing the enhanced 'free cash flow' that could be distributed to shareholders. In the early and mid-1980s, this redistribution of corporate revenues often occurred through debt-financed hostile takeovers, favoured by the proponents of the 'market for corporate control'. Post-takeover downsizing facilitated the servicing and retirement of the massive debt that a company had taken on (Shleifer and Summers, 1988; Blair, 1993). From the mid-1980s it increasingly took the form of corporate stock repurchases, which boosted stock prices, and complemented dividend payments. In 1984 repurchases represented 13.5 per cent of the earnings of US corporations; dividends 35.8 per cent. In 1997 the amount of repurchases surpassed dividends, and in 1999 repurchases were 35.8 per cent of earnings while dividends were 26.3 per cent (Dittmar and Dittmar, 2004). By the late 1990s large-scale repurchases had became a fact of financial life for many newer technology companies as well, primarily to offset the dilution of shareholdings that' resulted from the use of their own stock as a compensation currency in the form of stock options and a combination currency to acquire other companies (Carpenter et al. 2003).

Second, newer technology companies such as Intel, Microsoft, Oracle, Sun Microsystems, and Cisco Systems experienced significant growth in both revenues and employment during the 1980s and 1990s by means of a 'retain-and-reinvest' allocation regime; they retained corporate revenues, paying little if any dividends, and reinvested them in innovative products and processes. In general both the revenues and employment levels of these companies grew over this period, especially during the 1990s, and they were highly profitable (see Lazonick, 2006a). It was their innovative successes that resulted in increases in their stock prices. By creating new value, innovation boosted a company's stock price. Redistribution, in contrast, transferred value from labour incomes to capital incomes, raising the stock price even when no new value was created.

Third, sophisticated stock market investors saw that the combination of redistribution and innovation provided a solid foundation for sustained stock price increases, and speculated on further upward movements. Over certain periods (from the fourth quarter of 1985 to third quarter of 1987, and from the first quarter of 1995 to the third quarter of 2000) speculation became an increasingly important factor in the rise of stock prices. Professional insiders, within corporations and on Wall Street, encouraged and generally gained from this speculation because of the existence of a long queue of unprofessional outsiders who bought shares at inflated prices, implicitly assuming that 'greater fools' than themselves remained ready to buy the over-priced shares on the market. At some point, however, the 'greatest fools' were left holding these shares, as happened in the fourth quarter of 1987 and, more profoundly, from the fourth quarter of 2000 when the longest 'bull run' in US stock market history was (for the time being) put to rest.

During the 1980s and 1990s ever larger numbers of employees acquired a direct interest in stock price increases as corporate stock became increasingly important as a mode of compensation. From the late 1930s US corporations had granted stock options to top executives, primarily to give them access to a form of compensation that would be taxed at the low capital gains rate (Lazonick, 2003a). From the 1960s, however, high-tech startups based in Silicon Valley began to use stock options to lure technical and administrative personnel away from secure careers with established companies, and subsequently to compete for these employees among themselves. By the 1980s and 1990s broad-based employee stock options had become widespread among newer technology companies, and in the late 1990s migrated to many older corporations, not only in the United States but also abroad, that competed for this highly mobile labour (Carpenter et al. 2003; Glimstedt et al. 2006).

But did this financial behaviour lead to a more efficient allocation of resources, as the shareholder-value proponents claim? There are a number of flaws in agency theory's analysis of the relation between corporate governance and economic performance. These flaws have to do with a) a failure to explain how corporations came to control the allocation of significant amounts of the economy's resources; b) the measure of 'free cash flow'; and c) the claim that only shareholders have 'residual claimant' status. These flaws stem from the fact that agency theory, like the neoclassical theory of the market economy in which it is rooted, lacks a theory of innovative enterprise. These flaws are, moreover, amply exposed by the history of the industrial corporation in the United States, the national context in which agency theory evolved and in which it is thought to be most applicable.

First, agency theory makes an argument for taking resources out of the control of inefficient managers without explaining how, historically, these corporations came to possess the vast amounts of resources over which these managers could exercise allocative control. From the first decades of the twentieth century, the separation of share ownership from managerial control characterized US industrial corporations (Berle and Means, 1932). Innovative managerial corporations emerged as dominant during the first decades of the century (Chandler, 1977 and 1990). During the post-Second World War decades, however, many of them grew to be too big, especially during the 1960s conglomerate movement. Top managers responsible for corporate resource allocation became segmented, cognitively and behaviourally, from the organizations that would have to implement these strategies. In the 1970s and 1980s, moreover, many of these US corporations faced intense foreign competition, especially from innovative Japanese corporations, also characterized by a separation of share ownership from managerial control. An innovative response required governance institutions that would reintegrate US strategic decision-makers with the business organizations over which they exercised allocative control. Instead, guided by the ideology of 'maximizing shareholder value' and rewarded with stock options, what these established corporations got were managers whose prime objective was to boost stock prices, even if it was accomplished by a redistribution of corporate revenues from labour incomes to capital incomes and even if the quest for stock price increases undermined the productive capabilities that these companies had accumulated (Lazonick and O'Sullivan, 2000b).

Second, agency theory does not address how, at the point in time when innovative investments are being made, one can judge that managers are allocating resources inefficiently. Any strategic manager who allocates resources to an innovative strategy faces technological, market, and competitive uncertainty. Technological uncertainty exists because the firm may be incapable of developing the higher quality processes and products envisaged in its innovative investment strategy. Market uncertainty exists because, even if the firm succeeds in its development effort, future reductions in product prices and increases in factor prices may lower the returns from the investments. Finally, even if a firm overcomes technological and market uncertainty, it still faces competitive uncertainty: The possibility that an innovative competitor will have invested in a strategy that generates an even higher quality, lower cost product that enables it to win market share and drive down product prices. One can state formulaically, as Jensen does, that the firm should only invest in 'projects that have positive net present values when discounted at the relevant cost of capital'. But anyone who contends that, when committing resources to an innovative investment strategy, one can foresee the stream of future earnings that are required for the calculation of net present value knows nothing about the innovation process. It is far more plausible to argue that if corporate managers really sought to 'maximize shareholder value' according to this formula, they would never contemplate investing in innovative projects with their highly uncertain returns (Baldwin and Clark, 1992).

Third, it is simply not the case, as agency theory assumes, that all the firm's participants other than shareholders receive contractually guaranteed returns according to the productive contributions that they make. The argument that shareholders are the sole 'residual claimants' is a deduction from the theory of the market economy. It does not, however, accord with reality. The argument may hold when, in an open, competitive market, one firm purchases a physical commodity as a productive input from another firm. But one cannot assume contractually guaranteed returns when the inputs are made available to business enterprises by the state. Nor can one make the assumption when the inputs are made available to the business enterprise in the form of the labour services of employees. Finally, once one recognizes that the innovative enterprise cannot be understood as a 'nexus of contracts', one can ask whether public shareholders actually perform the risk-bearing function that the agency theory claims.

Given its investments in productive resources, the state has 'residual claimant' status. Any realistic account of economic development must take into account the role of the state in a) making infrastructural investments that business enterprises would not have made on their own; and b) providing business enterprises with subsidies that encourage investment in innovation. In terms of investment in new knowledge with applications to industry, the United States may well have been the world's foremost developmental state over the course of the twentieth century. As a prime example, it is impossible to explain US dominance in computers, microelectronics, software, and data communications without recognizing the role of government in making seminal investments that developed new knowledge and infrastructural investments that facilitated the diffusion of that knowledge (see, e.g., National Research Council, 1999; Abbate, 2000).

The US government made investments to augment the productive power of the nation through government, corporate, and university research labs that generated new knowledge as well as through educational institutions that developed the capabilities of the future labour force. Business enterprises made ample use of this knowledge and capability. While they may have paid fees for these services – for example, the salary of an engineer whose education was supported in whole or in part by state funds – one would be hard put to show that there existed a nexus of contracts that guaranteed the state a return on these investments. In effect, in funding these investments, the state (or more correctly, its body of taxpayers) bore the risk that the nation's business enterprises would further develop and utilize these productive capabilities in ways that would ultimately redound to the benefit of the nation, but with the 'return' to the nation in no way contractually guaranteed.

In addition, in the name of national economic development, the US government often provided cash subsidies to business enterprises to develop new products and processes, or even to start new firms. Sometimes these subsidies were built into the rates that firms could charge as regulated monopolies. For selected industries, tariff protection permitted firms the time to develop higher quality, lower cost products. The public funded these subsidies through current taxes, borrowing against the future, or by paying higher product prices than would have otherwise prevailed. By definition, a 'subsidy' lies beyond the realm of a market-mediated contract; one dictionary defines 'subsidy' as 'a grant paid by a government to an enterprise that benefits the public'.[3]

Like the government, workers can also find themselves in the position of having made investments in their own productive capabilities that they supply to firms without a guaranteed contractual return. In an important contribution to the corporate governance debate, Margaret Blair (1995) argued that, alongside a firm's shareholders, workers should be accorded 'residual claimant' status because they make investments in 'firm-specific' human capital with the expectation – but without a contractual guarantee – of reaping returns on those investments over the course of their careers. Moreover, insofar as their human capital is indeed 'firm-specific', these workers are dependent on their current employer for generating returns on their investments. A lack of interfirm labour mobility means that the worker bears some of the risk of the return on the firm's productive investments, and hence can be considered a 'residual claimant'. Blair goes on to argue that if one assumes that only shareholders bear risk and 'residual claimant' status, there will be an underinvestment in human capital to the detriment of not only workers but also the economy as a whole.

For those who were concerned about the propensity of US corporations in the 1980s and 1990s to 'downsize-and-distribute', Blair's focus on investments on firm-specific human capital provided a 'stakeholder' theory of the firm in which workers as well as shareholders should be viewed as 'principals' for whose benefit the firm should be run. While fully accepting Blair's 'stakeholder' amendment to the shareholder argument, however, a corporate executive who is intent on downsizing his labour force could logically argue that the productive capabilities of workers in, say, their 50s who had made investments in 'firm-specific' human capital earlier in their careers have now become *old* because of competition from equally adept but more energetic younger workers or, alternatively, *obsolete* because of technological change. The executive could then argue that, in making investments in 'firm-specific' human capital in the past, these (now) older workers had taken on the risk-bearing function, and like any risk-bearing investor had to accept the possibility that their investments would at some point lose their market value.

The workers could respond by arguing that the corporate executive is wrong; that their accumulated capabilities are not old and obsolete, but rather, given a correct understanding of technological, market, and competitive conditions in the industry, remain critical to the innovation process. They might even, as 'principals', accuse the executive, as their 'agent', of acting opportunistically, perhaps because he has stock options that align his interests with shareholders. They might claim that the proposed downsizing actually entails a redistribution of value from labour to capital rather than a restructuring of the workforce for the purpose of innovation. Clearly, even from the workers' point of view, agency theory's concerns with hidden information and hidden action on the part of managers are relevant. The problem is that agency theory provides no guide to analyzing whether or not the executive is in fact acting innovatively or opportunistically because agency theory has no theory of innovative enterprise.

Investment in innovation is a direct investment that involves, first and foremost, a strategic confrontation with technological, market, and competitive uncertainty. Those who have the abilities and incentives to allocate resources to innovation must decide, in the face of uncertainty, what types of investments have the potential to generate higher quality, lower cost products. Then they must mobilize committed finance to sustain the innovation process until it generates the higher quality, lower cost products that permit financial returns.

What role do public shareholders play in this process? Do they confront uncertainty by strategically allocating resources to innovative investments? No. As portfolio investors, they diversify their financial holdings across the outstanding shares of existing firms in order to minimize risk. They do so, moreover, with limited liability, which means that they need not necessarily spend any time or effort in actually analyzing the innovative capabilities of the firms whose shares they hold. To be sure, they can rely on someone else whose job it is to do such an analysis, but in doing so open themselves up to manipulation by insiders; that is, they simply shift the locus of the agency problem from managers to analysts. But even if shareholders are able to evaluate with confidence the innovative investment strategy of any given firm in their financial portfolio, as public shareholders their only practical recourse if they do not like what they see is to sell their shares (what has long been called the 'Wall Street walk'), which is precisely what the existence of a highly liquid stock market allows them to do.

But for this ability to exit an investment easily, public shareholders would not be willing to hold shares of companies over whose assets they exercise no direct control. It is the liquidity of a public shareholder's portfolio investment that differentiates it from a direct investment, and indeed distinguishes the public shareholder from a private shareholder who, for lack of liquidity of his or her shares, must remain committed to his or her direct investment until it generates financial returns. The modern corporation entails a fundamental transformation in the character of private property, as Berle and Means (1932) recognized. As property owners, public shareholders own tradable shares in a company that has invested in real assets; they do not own the assets themselves.

Indeed, it can be argued, certainly on the basis of US experience (see O'Sullivan, 2003a), that the fundamental role of the stock market in the twentieth century has been to transform illiquid claims into liquid claims on *the basis of investments that have already been made*, and thereby separate share ownership from managerial control. Business corporations sometimes do use the stock market as a source of finance for new investments (O'Sullivan, 2003a), but this has been most common in periods of stock market speculation when the lure for public shareholders to allocate resources to new issues may have been the prospect of quickly 'flipping' their shares to make a rapid, speculative return. Public shareholders want financial liquidity; investments in innovation require financial commitment. It is only by ignoring the role of innovation in the economy, and the *necessary* role of insider control in the strategic allocation of corporate resources to innovation, that agency theory can argue that superior economic performance can be achieved by maximizing the value of those actors in the corporate economy who are the ultimate outsiders to the innovation process.

4.   Social conditions of innovative enterprise[4]

A business enterprise seeks to transform productive resources into goods and services that can be sold to generate revenues. A theory of the firm, therefore, must, at a minimum, provide explanations for how this productive transformation occurs and how revenues are obtained. Further, it must explain how, in competing for the same product markets, some firms are able to gain sustained competitive advantage over others. For a perspective on corporate governance to have any claim to relevance for understanding how a firm achieves superior economic performance, it must be rooted in a theory of innovative enterprise (for elaborations, see O'Sullivan, 2000b; Lazonick and O'Sullivan, 2000b; Lazonick, 2006b).

The innovation process is *uncertain, cumulative,* and *collective.* As a result, innovative enterprise requires *strategy, finance,* and *organization* (O'Sullivan, 2000b; Lazonick, 2006b). In the theory of innovative enterprise, the role of strategy is to confront uncertainty by allocating resources to investments in developing human and physical capabilities that can enable the firm to compete for specific product markets. The role of finance is to sustain the productive process from the time at which investments in productive resources are made to the time at which financial returns are generated through the sale of products. The role of organization is to transform technologies and access markets, and thereby develop and utilize the value-creating capabilities of the firm's resources to generate products that buyers want at prices that they are willing to pay.

From this perspective, innovation is a social process, supported in certain times and places by 'social conditions of innovative enterprise'. Three distinct but interrelated social conditions – *strategic control, financial commitment,* and *organizational integration* – can transform strategy, finance, and organization into innovation. The social conditions of innovative enterprise manifest themselves in social relations that, embedded in the business enterprise, are central to the performance of the firm and the development of the economy. The need for these social relations to generate innovation has direct implications for understanding the relation between corporate governance and economic performance.

The social condition that can transform strategy into innovation is *strategic control*: a set of relations that gives decision-makers the power to allocate the firm's resources to confront the technological, market, and competitive uncertainties inherent in the innovation process. For innovation to occur, those who occupy strategic decision-making positions must have both the abilities and the incentives to allocate resources to innovative investment strategies. Their abilities to do so will depend on their knowledge of how the current innovative capabilities of their organization can be enhanced by strategic investments in new, typically complementary, capabilities. Their incentives to do so will depend on the alignment of their personal interests with the interests of the organization in attaining and sustaining its competitive advantage.

To generate innovation, corporate governance must therefore concern itself with who exercises strategic control and how they are motivated. Those who exercise strategic control must be capable of understanding the technological, market, and competitive characteristics of the industries in which their firms are competing as well as the capabilities for learning of the business organizations upon which they rely to implement their innovative investment strategies. This integration of strategic decision-makers into the business organization can break down because the firm overextends itself by expanding into too many lines of business, as in the 1960s US conglomerate movement. Those who exercise strategic control may no longer understand the organizational and technological requirements of the innovation process. The corporate governance challenge is to find ways of reintegrating strategic decision-making with the learning organization. To do so, rewards to strategic decision-makers must be based on the success of the organization as a whole. This organizational success is not necessarily well-measured by stock price, since stock prices can be driven by redistribution and speculation as well as innovation. Indeed, as recent business history has shown (Lazonick and O'Sullivan, 2000a; Carpenter et al. 2003), for the sake of their own stock-based rewards, corporate executives may take actions that result in redistribution and foster speculation, both of which can undermine the innovative capabilities of the organizations.

The social condition that can transform finance into innovation is *financial commitment*: A set of relations that ensures the allocation of funds to sustain the cumulative innovation process until it can generate financial returns. What is often called 'patient' capital enables the capabilities that derive from organizational learning to cumulate over time, notwithstanding the inherent uncertainty that the innovation process entails. Strategic control over internal revenues is the foundation of financial commitment. The size and duration of investments in innovation required, however, may demand that such 'inside capital' be supplemented by external sources of finance such as stock issues, bond issues, or bank debt. In different times and places, depending on varying institutional arrangements, different types of external finance may be more or less committed to sustaining the innovation process.

Control over internal funds, leveraged if need be by external funds, enables corporate executives to commit to innovative investment strategies of large size and long duration. There will be cases in which corporate executives squander corporate resources on ill-conceived investment strategies, as agency theorists contend. Given the cumulative character of the innovation process, however, an investment strategy that absorbs costs without generating returns at one point in time may turn out to be successful later. Given the uncertain character of the innovation process, the full extent of financial commitment required to generate higher quality, lower cost products is not known at the outset of an investment strategy, but only unfolds over time. The corporate governance challenge is to evaluate the often-escalating demands of corporate executives for financial commitment so that innovation is not nipped in the bud, while good money is not thrown after bad.

The social condition that can transform organization into innovation is *organizational integration*: A set of relations that creates incentives for people to apply their skills and efforts to organizational objectives. The need for organizational integration derives from the developmental complexity of the innovation process – that is, the need for organizational learning – combined with the imperative to secure high levels of utilization of innovative investments if the high fixed costs of these investments are to be transformed into low unit costs. Modes of compensation (in the forms of promotion, remuneration, and benefits) are important instruments for integrating individuals into the organization. To generate innovation, however, a mode of compensation cannot simply manage the labour market by attracting and retaining employees. It must be part of a reward system that manages the productive processes that are the essence of innovation. Most importantly, the compensation system must motivate employees as individuals to engage in collective learning. This collective learning, moreover, cumulates over time, thus necessitating financial commitment to keep the learning organization intact.

Of central importance to the accumulation and transformation of capabilities in knowledge-intensive industries is the *skill base* in which the firm invests in pursuing its innovative strategy. Within the firm, the division of labour consists of different functional specialties and hierarchical responsibilities. A firm's functional and hierarchical division of labour defines its skill base. In the effort to generate collective and cumulative learning, those who exercise strategic control can choose how to structure the skill base, including how employees move around and up the enterprise's functional and hierarchical division of labour over the course of their careers. At the same time, however, the organization of the skill base will be constrained by both the particular learning requirements of their industrial activities and the alternative employment opportunities of the potential employees.

The innovative enterprise requires that those who exercise strategic control be able to recognize the competitive strengths and weaknesses of their firm's existing skill base and, hence, the changes in that skill base that will be necessary for an innovative response to competitive challenges. These strategic decision-makers must also be able to mobilize committed finance to sustain investment in the skill base until it can generate higher quality, lower cost products than were previously available. To build the types of organizations that can generate innovation, corporate governance institutions must concern themselves with financial commitment and strategic control.

5.   Corporate governance and economic development

Innovation is a necessary but not sufficient condition for economic development. In the United States at least, corporate governance institutions that invoke the ideology of 'maximizing shareholder value' have, if anything, undermined stable and equitable economic growth by permitting corporate resource allocation to be driven by redistribution and speculation. One might argue that, given the widespread use of non-executive stock option plans and stock-based pension plans, workers have become shareholders, and hence a mode of corporate governance that maximizes shareholder value is in effect run for workers' benefit. It is much more plausible to argue, however, for the case of the United States at least, that the shareholder-value perspective has provided corporate executives with an ideology that has enabled them to justify enriching themselves, even when their firms fail to innovate, employees are laid off, and corporate stock prices are volatile. 'Maximizing shareholder value' has not yielded stable and equitable economic growth.[5]

To achieve stable and equitable economic growth, the power of corporate executives needs to be regulated, monitored, and controlled. Corporate governance bodies, most notably boards of directors, must include participation by representatives of government and labour as well as business. Such participation would manifest a recognition that the corporate enterprise operates in the public domain, with responsibilities for generating returns to the governments and employees, as well as financiers, who have made investments in the corporation's productive resources. Business corporations often have to restructure in response to changes in technologies, markets, and competitors (Lazonick, 2004a). The corporate governance challenge is to restructure in ways that regenerate the innovation process – in some cases within existing firms and in other cases through the creation of new firms – but with the costs of restructuring equitably shared and with instability in employment incomes mitigated.

Corporate revenues contribute to the support of not only the current workforce but also those who have retired from the labour force. In influencing the allocation of corporate resources and returns, corporate governance institutions in the advanced economies must deal with the problem of supporting an aging population, itself one of the outcomes of successful economic development. Over the course of the twentieth century, many US corporations took responsibility for retired employees through defined-benefit company-sponsored pension plans that especially rewarded people who stayed with the same company over the course of their careers. Over the last decades of the century, however, and continuing into the 2000s, corporations have been moving toward defined-contribution pension plans, portable from one employer to another, based on individual employee accounts and highly dependent on returns on corporate securities, and particularly corporate stock. The long stock-market boom of the 1980s and 1990s encouraged the belief among US households that stock yields could only rise, a belief that was shattered by the stock-market crash of the early 2000s.

For national economic development to be sustained, business corporations and their trade associations have to be willing to support public spending to educate the next generation of workers. Public funding of education cannot be understood in abstraction from the needs of major US business corporations for a highly educated labour supply. In recent decades, the emergence of large supplies of highly educated labour in developing economies has combined with the globalization of both corporate activities and labour market to reduce dramatically the dependence of developed countries like the United States on a 'home-grown' higher-end labour supply. As a result corporate interests in these countries have been far less willing than in the past to pay taxes and support government programme designed to educate the next generation (see Lazonick, 2006a).

In making these investments in the next generation of workers, developing economies have recognized, implicitly at least, the centrality of the 'developmental state' to the wealth of nations. Indeed, they are following the experience, if not the official ideology, of the developed nations, which would not have become wealthy without the active involvement of the government in subsidizing and investing in the process of economic development (Chang, 2002). For that process to succeed, however, the developmental state must be joined with innovative enterprise. Of particular importance for understanding the role of the developmental state, a theory of innovative enterprise provides the rationale for government subsidies (as, for example, in the infant industry argument). An innovative firm invests in the development of productive resources, but is at a competitive disadvantage because of both the size and duration – and hence high fixed costs – of the investment required. Government subsidies support firms as they attempt to transform the high-fixed costs of innovative investments into low units costs, and in doing so transform competitive disadvantage into competitive advantage (see Lazonick, 2006b).

In effect, government subsidy provides firms that constitute a national industry with a source of *financial commitment* while they are engaging in 'indigenous innovation' (see Lazonick, 2004a). But financial commitment in and of itself does not, and cannot, ensure the success of an innovative investment strategy. Given the financial commitment provided by tariff protection or other types of subsidies, it matters *who exercises strategic control and what types of investments in organizational learning they make.* Arguments for the efficacy of state subsidy for developing economies need to specify the 'business model' that will combine strategic control, organizational integration and financial commitment to generate innovation as a foundation for economic development. The theory of innovative enterprise does not 'explain' economic development. That explanation must be sought in the social conditions of innovative enterprise in a particular time and place. The theory of innovative enterprise provides a coherent analytical framework for researching the existence of those conditions and for devising policies that, for the sake of economic development, can help put the social conditions of innovative enterprise in place.

Notes

1. I would like to acknowledge helpful comments on a much longer version of this paper from Ha-Joon Chang, Thomas David, and Ajit Singh. Research on this paper has been supported by UNU-WIDER, the European Commission project on European Socio-Economic Models of a Knowledge-Based Society (ESEMK), and the Work Foundation. This paper reflects my intellectual collaboration with Mary O'Sullivan, for whose insights I am grateful.
2. This section draws upon O'Sullivan (2000b; 2002), Lazonick and O'Sullivan (2000a; 2000b), and Lazonick (2002).
3. http://dictionary.reference.com/search?q=subsidy
4. See Lazonick (2006b) for a formal presentation of the theory of innovative enterprise.
5. For an elaboration of this argument see Lazonick and O'Sullivan (2000b); O'Sullivan (2000a; 2003b); Lazonick (2004a; 2004c), as well as Lazonick (2006c).

References

Abbate, J. 2000. *Inventing the Internet*, Cambridge MA: MIT Press.

Baldwin, C. and Clark, K. 1992. 'Capabilities, and Capital Investment: New Perspectives on Capital Budgeting', *Journal of Applied Corporate Finance*, 5, 2: 67–87.

Berle, A. and Means, G. 1932. *Private Property and the Modern Corporation*, London: Macmillan.

Blair, M. (ed.), 1993. *The Deal Decade: What Takeovers and Leveraged Buyouts Mean for Corporate Governance*, Brookings Institution Press.

Blair, M. (ed.) 1995. *Ownership and Control: Rethinking Corporate Governance for the Twenty-First Century*, Brookings Institution.

Carpenter, M., Lazonick, W. and O'Sullivan, M. 2003. 'The Stock Market and Innovative Capability in the New Economy: The Optical Networking Industry', *Industrial and Corporate Change*, 12, 5: 963–1034.

Chandler, A. 1977. *The Visible Hand: The Managerial Revolution in American Business*, Cambridge MA: Harvard University Press.

Chandler, A. 1990. *Scale and Scope: The Dynamics of Industrial Enterprise*, Cambridge MA: Harvard University Press.

Chang, H. 2002. *Kicking Away the Ladder – Development Strategy in Historical Perspective*, London: Anthem Press.

Dittmar, A. and Dittmar, R. 2004. 'Stock Repurchase Waves: An Explanation of the Trends in Aggregate Corporate Payout Policy', Working Paper, University of Michigan Business School, February.

Glimstedt, H., Lazonick, W. and Xie, H. 2006. 'The Diffusion and Functions of Stock Options: US-Style Compensation for Swedish High-Tech Employees', INSEAD working paper, January.

Hall, B. and Leibman, J. 1998. 'Are CEOs Really Paid Like Bureaucrats?' *Quarterly Journal of Economics*, 113, 3: 653–91.

Jensen, M. 1986. 'Agency Costs of Free Cash Flow, Corporate Finance, and Takeovers', *American Economic Review*, 76, 2: 323–29.

Jensen, M. and Murphy, K. 1990. 'Performance Pay and Top Management Incentives', *Journal of Political Economy*, 98, 2: 225–64.

Lazonick, W. 2002. 'Innovative Enterprise and Historical Transformation', *Enterprise and Society*, 3, 1: 35–54.

Lazonick, W. 2003a. 'Stock Options and Innovative Enterprise: The Evolution of a Mode of High-Tech Compensation', UMass Lowell and INSEAD, working paper, August.

Lazonick, W. 2003b. 'The Theory of the Market Economy and the Social Foundations of Innovative Enterprise', *Economic and Industrial Democracy*, 24, 1: 9–44.

Lazonick, W. 2004a. 'Corporate Restructuring', in S. Ackroyd, R. Batt, P. Thompson, and P. Tolbert (eds), *The Oxford Handbook of Work and Organization*, Oxford: Oxford University Press: 577–601.

Lazonick, W. 2004b. 'Indigenous Innovation and Economic Development: Lessons from *China's Leap into the Information Age*', *Industry and Innovation*, 11, 4: 273–298.

Lazonick, W. 2004c. 'The Innovative Firm', in J. Fagerberg, D. Mowery, and R. Nelson (eds), *The Oxford Handbook of Innovation*, Oxford: Oxford University Press: 29–55.

Lazonick, W. 2006a. 'Evolution of the New Economy Business Model', in E. Brousseau and N. Curien (eds), *Internet and Digital Economics*, Cambridge: Cambridge University Press.

Lazonick, W. 2006b. 'Innovative Enterprise and Economic Development', in Y. Cassis and A. Colli (eds), *Business Performance in the Twentieth Century*, Cambridge: Cambridge University Press.

Lazonick, W. 2006c. 'Corporate Governance, Innovative Enterprise, and Economic Development', WIDER Research Paper 2006–71, Helsinki: UNU-WIDER.

Lazonick, W. and O'Sullivan, M. 2000a. 'Maximizing Shareholder Value: A New Ideology for Corporate Governance', *Economy and Society*, 29, 1: 13–35.

Lazonick, W. and O'Sullivan, M. 2000b. 'Perspectives on Corporate Governance, Innovation, and Economic Performance', Report to the European Commission (DGXII) under the TSER Programme (http://www.insead.edu/cgep).

National Research Council. 1999. *Funding a Revolution: Government Support for Computing Research*, National Academy Press.

O'Sullivan, M. 2000a. *Contests for Corporate Control: Corporate Governance and Economic Performance in the United States and Germany*, Oxford: Oxford University Press.

O'Sullivan, M. 2000b. 'The Innovative Enterprise and Corporate Governance', *Cambridge Journal of Economics*, 24, 4: 393–416.

O'Sullivan, M. 2002. 'Corporate Control', in W. Lazonick (ed.) *The IEBM Handbook of Economics*, Thomson: 129–155.

O'Sullivan, M. 2003a. 'The Financing Role of the US Stock Market in the 20th Century', INSEAD working paper, November.

O'Sullivan, M. 2003b. 'The Political Economy of Comparative Corporate Governance', *Review of International Political Economy*, 10, 1, 23–72.

Pearl Meyer and Partners 2001. 'Trends 2001: Looking Forward and Back' at http://www.execpay.com/trends2001.htm.

Shleifer, A. and Summers, L. 1988. 'Breach of Trust in Hostile Takeovers', in A. Auerbach (ed.) *Corporate Takeovers: Causes and Consequences*. National Bureau of Economic Research: 33–56.

US Congress, 2005. *Economic Report of the President*, Washington, DC: US Government Printing Office.

Williamson, O. 1985. *The Economic Institutions of Capitalism*, Free Press.

Williamson, O. 1996. *The Mechanisms of Governance*, Oxford: Oxford University Press.

CHAPTER 8
THE POLITICAL ECONOMY OF TAXATION AND TAX REFORM IN DEVELOPING COUNTRIES

Jonathan di John

'Revenue is the chief preoccupation of the state. Nay more it is the state'
Edmund Burke[1]

1.   Introduction: The problem of state capacity and taxation in less developed countries

Resource mobilization lies at the heart of economic development. And among various means of resource mobilization (e.g., forced savings, inflation tax, manipulation of terms of trade, etc.), tax is most closely related to the questions of state formation and capability. Tax also provides one of the principal lenses in measuring state capacity, power and political settlements in a society. In the wake of fiscal crises of the state in sub-Saharan Africa and Latin America, designing tax systems that can provide incentives for growth, can meet distributional demands and can increase revenue collection is central to state viability and effectiveness (Toye, 2000). In post-war economies, reconstruction of the revenue base is essential for the reconstruction of a viable state and sustained peace (Addison et al. 2002).

Surprisingly, taxation is not explicitly listed as a separate 'fundamental' task of a state (as spelled out in the World Bank Development Report 1997)[2] This error of omission is indeed remarkable given the centrality of revenue production and resource mobilization in the historical process of state formation (Schumpeter [1918] 1954; Tilly, 1990). As Schumpeter notes: 'the fiscal history of a people is above all an essential part of its general history' (quoted in Levi, 1988: 6).[3] The neglect of making tax central to understanding state capacity and governance reflects the decline in the political economy of resource mobilization as a focal point of development theory and policy.

This is not to say that tax reform has not been a central part of World Bank and IMF operations in structural adjustment reform. However, tax reform has been largely couched in technical, non-political terms. This is part of the larger reform agenda where state capacity-building has been viewed largely as a 'technical' exercise in administrative reform (raising wages of civil servants, more training, greater meritocracy). According to the diagnosis of the capacity approach, 'poor governance' is the result of an over-extended state relative to its institutional capacity at a given moment in time (see World Bank 1997: 61–75). The analysis of governance crucially assumes that *inherited* capacity constrains and that this constraint is what should orient the shape of administrative, institutional and policy reform. The policy advice, therefore, for poorly performing economies generally advocates reducing the state's role in resource allocation decisions. The main message of the capacity approach is 'don't try difficult interventions and reforms at home'. The technical and apolitical nature of the good governance agenda, however, limits an understanding of the political and institutional processes underlying the power and legitimacy a state requires to *enforce and change rights and institutions and extract and mobilize the resources* required to sustain development and growth.

Fiscal crises confronting many LDC's in Latin America and sub-Saharan Africa have necessitated bringing fiscal reform to the centre of macroeconomic stabilization processes (Moore and Schneider, 2004). However, the tax component of the Washington Consensus follows along the lines of the capacity approach. The main policy proposals have been to simplify and broaden tax bases, lower income and corporate tax rates (that is, make taxes more pro-business), promote reduction in trade tax rates through trade liberalization, and emphasize the widening and simplification of value-added taxes (VAT). Importantly, the latter is promoted on the grounds not only that it is less distortionary, but also that it is *administratively and politically easier* to implement than income and property taxes.[4] Because property and, particularly, income taxes are generally the most progressive taxes, equity concerns have been downplayed, which may have important implications for political stability in countries with very unequal levels of asset and income distribution.

The order of the rest of the paper is as follows. Section 2 considers the economic, administrative, and political economy approaches to analysing tax and the policy implications derived from the insights of each approach. Based on the theoretical and historical insights developed in the critical examination of different approaches to tax, I argue that it is essential to consider the historical, political and institutional factors that have established durable tax collection capacity in some cases and not others. Section 3 provides an examination of the political economy underlying the extraordinary success of tax collection and, in particular, income tax capacity collection in South Africa. A brief comparison with the Brazilian experience is presented to highlight the importance of historical political economy analysis in understanding variations in income tax capacity across countries. Section 4 complements the Brazil-South Africa comparison by presenting a comparison of the structure of tax collection in East Asia, Eastern Europe, and Latin America. The evidence suggests that the Latin American state relies to a much greater extent on indirect taxes, revealing both policy choices and a weakness of the state to extract resources from upper income groups. The Conclusion presents policy implications.

2.   Approaches to analysing taxation

The determinants of tax collection and tax reform have been the subject of extensive analysis. Several theoretical approaches inform debates on two main issues: Firstly, why tax collection increases over time and, secondly, what should be the main concern when designing tax systems. There are three main approaches to these issues: The economic approach, the administrative approach, and the political economy approach. While the first two approaches have dominated theoretical and policy debates on tax in developing countries, the incorporation of political economy factors such as the role of threat, the perception of threat, and interest group formation and balances is essential to understanding the evolution of tax capacity.

2.1.   *The economic analysis of tax*

Traditional tax analysis has focused on the design of tax systems that makes possible financing the 'necessary' level of public spending in the most efficient and equitable way (Stern, 1987; Tanzi and Zee, 2000). The neoclassical theory of public finance proceeds by describing the effects of taxation and then applying criteria (normally a social welfare function) to evaluate those effects (Stern, 1987: 24). This approach divides taxation into a logically-prior positive side and a subsequent normative side on which value judgements are introduced. Following Stern (1987), examples of positive issues include: a) the consequences of income or wealth taxation on risk-taking; b) the effects of corporate taxes on investment and distribution of profits; c) the effects of national debt and taxation on savings; and d) how different households or groups are affected or burdened by tax changes (the problem of incidence of tax). The basic problem in such a model is that the government wishes to raise revenue to distribute income without sufficient information on the preferences and endowments of citizens to do so by means of lump-sum taxes. Therefore, governments can achieve its goals only by raising taxes in some distortionary way. This gives rise to the standard neoclassical concern of the tension (or costs and benefits) between achieving equity and efficiency in a general equilibrium framework.

An important component of the applied literature on tax concentrates on why the level and composition of taxes in less developed countries differs from that of more advanced countries.[5] With respect to developing countries, the focus of the analysis centres on why their tax capacity is limited relative to more advanced countries. One set of factors concerns the economic structure of developing countries. For instance, developing countries are characterized by a large share of agriculture in total output and employment, large informal sectors and occupations; many small establishments, a small share of wages in total national income, a small share of total consumer spending made in large, modern establishments, and so on (*ibid.*: 3). These characteristics, it is argued, reduce the possibility of depending on certain types of taxes, such as personal income tax, and make them more dependent on indirect taxes such as foreign trade taxes and, overall, a lower level of tax collection.

The mainstream economic literature on tax, however, does not consider the wider resource mobilization question, which was a concern of earlier development economists (e.g., Lewis, 1954). As indicated in Table 8.1, while tax revenues in sub-Saharan African and Latin American countries from the mid-1980s to 2000 were collected at a similar proportion to GDP as in East Asia, there were dramatic differences in the savings rates between the regions.

The East Asian savings rate average is more than double as a percentage of GDP compared with South Asia and sub-Saharan Africa and two-thirds higher than in Latin America.[6]

The state's capacity to mobilize resources beyond taxation is one important feature of developmental success stories that the economic literature misses. In particular, high levels of gross domestic savings have supported robust investment rates. The East Asian economies were in a class of their own in terms of savings rates. This was largely achieved through the coercive power of the state, which was deployed to mobilize resources through various forms of forced savings.[7] Among the coercive elements in East Asian economies were restrictions on consumer credit, financial restraint, mandatory provident pension contributions (used in Singapore and Malaysia) and encouragement of postal savings. Although state actions to increase savings are clear in East Asia, the high and sustained *growth* rates may have also had an important feedback effect on income growth and therefore in sustaining savings.

Table 8.1 Resource mobilization and poverty in developing countries: Regional comparisons

Regions	GDP p.c. growth (1) (1985–2002)	Tax revenues (% GDP) (2) 1985–88	1997–2000	Gross savings (%GDP) (3) 1980–90	1990–2000	1990–2002
Sub-Saharan Africa	-0.4	21.7	16.3	13.9	12.5	12.7
South Asia	3.3	12.8	12.2	13.5	16.7	16.8
East Asia and Pacific	6.1	15	15.6	**30.8**	**31.6**	**31.2**
Latin America	0.8	15.2	15.9	21.7	18.9	18.9

Sources: (1) World Bank, *World Development Indicators*. (2) IMF *Government Financial Statistics* and calculations by the author. (3) World Bank (2004).

In sum, the economic approach to tax examines the trade-offs between efficiency and equity in a general equilibrium framework, and in the applied literature, examines the effects of levels of development and economic structure on tax takes and tax structure. The economic approach to tax does not consider the wider role of developmental states in mobilising savings. Also, this approach does not do explain why tax structures differ in otherwise similar economies. Moreover, the economic approach abstracts from the political and institutional processes that determine the ability of the state to create tax policies and enforce them.

2.2. *The administrative approach to tax*

The administrative approach focuses on the role institutional design and policy plays in enhancing the prospects of efficiency and effectiveness of the tax system. Efficiency refers to administrative costs in collecting different types of taxes, enforcing tax laws, and the costs of tax payers in complying with those laws (Lledo et al. 2004: 6). Effectiveness refers to the extent to which taxes are predictable, transparent, and enforced by a fair judicial system (*ibid.*).

In line with the 'technical' view of institutions inherent in the above-mentioned capacity approach, administrative constraints are identified as the main constraint to the ability of states to collect revenues overall and direct taxes such as income tax in particular.[8] The detrimental factors commonly identified in developing country tax systems are: Insufficient staff with appropriate skills, low public-sector wages, lack of up-to-date equipment and facilities, ill-defined and complex tax and related laws; poor enforcement of penalties for evasion and corruption; poor information collection and identification of taxpayers and so on (see Kaldor, 1955; Bird, 1989: 315–46).[9] Based on this approach, the policy advice is to simplify tax rates and laws, make revenue authorities as autonomous from political pressure as possible, and form tax policy based on the implementation capacity of the tax administration.

There are many shortcomings to the administrative approach. First, the conception of capacity is static. There is no attempt to explain why and how administrative capacities *change*. Second, there is no explanation as to why tax capacities *differ* across countries. While the much of the applied literature acknowledges the political obstacles as the root cause of low tax collection (Bird and Oldman, 1964; Gillis, 1989; Burgess and Stern, 1993; Tanzi and Zee, 2000), there is no attempt to map which types of political obstacles matter more in some contexts as opposed to others. Thirdly, there is little analysis as to why sound tax policies are not *enforced*. Although not often emphasised, low levels of state legitimacy are often behind a state's inability to ensure compliance (Levi, 1988) and the genesis and variation in this legitimacy is not analysed in the applied literature. Finally, as in the case of the capacity approach, the emphasis on discouraging the collection of taxes with high information requirements (like income tax) does not provide the impetus for countries to *improve* administrative tax collection capacity for such taxes.

Interestingly, the technical requirements of information collection and enforcement generally seem to be much *more* stringent in taxation than managing industrial policy, which is often dismissed on the ground that it is too demanding for most developing countries. However, as seen in the case of East Asia, the conduct of industrial policy involves deliberative councils of a relatively small number of government bureaucrats and a relatively small number of medium and large firms or business conglomerates (see World Bank, 1993), and therefore has a much lower informational requirement than tax policy. The apparently sophisticated technical requirements of tax policy may be one of the principal reasons why the WDR 1997 neglects and explicit discussion of the political economy of taxation.

One recent development within the administrative approach has been the advocacy of autonomous revenues authorities (ARAs). International financial institutions have developed the proposition that, in weak states, revenue collection authorities are more effective when they operate *autonomously* from the state (and particularly the finance ministry), as a commercial entity at arms length from the government rather than as a department within the government administration (Taliciero, 2004). According to this line of thinking, autonomy protects revenue authorities from political interference and allows directors to circumvent the institutional obstacles of weak public sectors such as cumbersome regulations, low pay, antagonistic unions and so on (Therkilsden, 2003: 2). As a result, the creation of parallel agencies is favoured over the restructuring of existing tax institutions.

While there is some evidence in Africa and Latin America that autonomous revenue authorities may have been instrumental in *initiating* reforms, it is less clear that such arrangements are *sustainable*. Typically, where there have been initial successes in the efficiency and legitimacy of tax collection, these gains have proved ephemeral.[10] The Ugandan and Peruvian experiment with ARAs were directed by Presidents who governed on a political strategy of anti-party politics, which made the revenue authority vulnerable to shifting policies and electoral calculations of the President. In each case, Museveni in Uganda and Fujimori in Peru ceased to support their respective ARAs when the introduction of necessary taxes became unpopular.

Such a technical approach to tax policy abstracts from politics in at least three ways. First, the reasons why such reforms were politically feasible in the first place are not addressed. Second, there is little analysis of why such autonomy is acceptable to relevant political coalitions over time. Third, there is no accepted definition of autonomy. Since tax policy, which the domain of finance ministries, can not practically be divorced from tax collection, which the domain of newly created ARAs, it is not ultimately possible for the latter in purely autonomous ways. In effect, autonomy can never be complete where there are inter-dependencies among agencies and thus is always a contested notion (*ibid.*).

While the theoretical and applied literature has identified many common problems among developing countries, the focus on tax collection in technical terms abstracts from an analysis of where and how the power of the state originates. As importantly, the economic literature is unable to explain the wide variation and growth in the capacity of states to extract, mobilize and re-distribute assets for developmental and other aims. Simply put, the historically specific political coalitions underlying state support and particularly, the important roles of internal and external threat to political order and stability are not incorporated.

2.3.   *Political economy approach to tax*

The diversity of patterns of taxation and resource mobilization among states is clearly a product of history. A brief look at the history of today's developed countries demonstrates why an assessment of taxation, good governance and institutional formation needs to incorporate an understanding of processes of conflict and bargaining. The institutional capacity of states to mobilize resources had to be *created*. War played a particular role in that process, not least because it created a context in which the wealthy in society felt threatened enough to allow the creation of capability and the centralization of authority at the level of the state.[11]

Standard histories of European state formation underline the crucial contribution of external threat and war. Tilly (1990: 54) argues that 'war made the state and the state made war'. War caused states to be more efficient in revenue collection by forcing them to dramatically improve administrative capabilities (allowing states to fund administrations and economic systems). Most importantly, the effort to finance war and the military led to varying patterns of *bargains* between the state and interest groups, particularly merchants, landlords and in some cases, directly with the peasantry. In general, the distributional struggles between the state and societal actors (and between competing groups within civil society) led to uneven but mutually recognised rights: Rights of citizens with respect to states as well as the rights of state officials (and corporate entities) with respect to citizens.

Of course, while Heraclitus argued that 'war is the father of all things', understanding the role of war in the history of institutional formation has its limits as a guide to policy. But it does allow us to ask whether there are conditions today that can replicate some of the incentives that historically emerged in times of warfare. Threat, which can provide 'windows of opportunity' for tax reform, may today be derived from domestic social movements, fiscal crises or the 'global economy' rather than imminent prospects of war.

This historical perspective also allows us to demonstrate that 'capability' is not simply an inheritance of history – entirely 'path dependent' – but has always been created by actors who are making history all the time. The formation of the state and its capacity to grow and survive was intimately related to its ability to tax. In turn, rights and institutions formed as bargains – or settlements of conflict in the course of struggle. This is consistent with some theoretical work on institutions that view institutional formation as a by-product of distributional struggles and power balances.[12]

A second important political economy factor in understanding taxation is the role played by political organizations that mediate the conflicts between interest groups, classes, and coalitions. Political parties are particularly important as they operate in the milieu that links state and civil society and they can provide political support necessary to legitimate state tax policies as well as organise demands on the state for social expenditure and tax breaks. That tax struggles are among the oldest types of class struggles (Goldscheid, 1958: 202) suggests that the power of classes and other interest groups are a key determinant of taxation (Campbell, 1993: 168). The historical evidence in the now advanced countries suggests that governments run by leftist parties mobilize and support higher tax levels (Cameron, 1978) and more progressive tax systems (Heidenheimer et al., 1983: 178–9) than those run by conservative parties. The well developed welfare states in Scandinavian countries in the second half of the twentieth century were controlled by social democratic coalitions. In less developed countries, countries with relatively historically high tax collection as a percentage of GDP, such as South Africa, Brazil, and Malaysia, are characterized by strong (though not always leftist or competitive) political party systems.

Third, the literature on the 'resource curse' in mineral abundant economies has made important contribution to the political economy of tax. The main premise of this model is that when states gain a large proportion of their revenues from external sources, such as oil rents, the reduced necessity of state decision-makers to levy domestic taxes causes leaders to be less accountable to individuals and groups within civil society; more prone to engage in and accommodate rent-seeking and corruption; and less able to formulate growth-enhancing policies (Mahdavy, 1970; Karl, 1997). Although the literature has been an inadequate guide in explaining differential growth performance among oil states, and changes in growth rates in particular oil states over time (Di John, 2004), it has drawn attention to an important issue, namely that the type of taxes (and not just the level) and the manner in which the state appropriates resources is central to understanding the historical development of state capacity.

Finally, a historical perspective highlights the differential impact colonial legacies have had on tax structures. For instance, different patterns of English and Spanish colonialism and the institutions they left behind have influenced differences in tax policy between the Caribbean and Latin America. (Thirsk, 1997). In particular, the British Caribbean countries inherited legal institutions that enabled the development of more *formal* labour markets which can explain, in part, the higher capacity of this to collect income tax compared to Central and South American economies

(Stotsky and WoldeMariam, 2002). Additionally, Caribbean countries generally inherited parliamentary systems of governance, which may offer more feasible mechanisms of institutionalising pacts with elites to pay taxes than in the generally more presidential systems in Latin America (*ibid.*).

The differential impact of colonial economic development (and in particular the structure of labour markets and the historical process of the integration of indigenous populations into the colonial order) appears to have had an impact on the tax collection capacities in sub-Saharan Africa too.[13] One striking feature of African economies is the regional differences in the share of tax revenue in GDP, with countries of Southern African (South Africa, Zimbabwe, Botswana, Namibia) generally having higher tax takes and tax effort indicators than would be predicted on the basis of the per capita incomes.[14] The reason for this difference owes to the greater formalization of labour in the colonial period in the Southern African economies and Kenya compared with the rest of sub-Saharan Africa. Patterns of colonization have turned out to have produced institutional arrangements and practices that have proved remarkably resilient.

In sum, the political economy approach offers an important complement to the economic and administrative frameworks to understanding taxation. In particular, such an approach, in providing historical and comparative analyses, can contribute to an understanding of why tax capacity differs across countries and changes over time. As importantly, this approach not only integrates economic and political processes, but also specifically examines the interaction of taxation and state formation.

3.   Political settlements and tax capacity in South Africa and Brazil

The highly successful income and overall tax collection capacity of the South African state since the 1960s is particularly instructive of the need to incorporate political analysis in an understanding of institutional and administrative reforms. In the period 1960–2000, the tax collection as a percentage of GDP has consistently been the highest among middle-income countries. In the period 1997–2002, the tax take as a percentage of GDP in South Africa averaged over 25 per cent compared with the middle-income country average of 15 per cent of GDP. The South African state has been particularly successful in collecting direct taxes in the form of corporate and personal income taxes, which are generally the most progressive types of tax. In the period 1975–78, income tax collection averaged 12.9 per cent of GDP compared with the Latin American average of 5.0 per cent and the East Asian average of 5.7 per cent. In the more recent period 1997–2002, income tax collection averaged 14.6 per cent of GDP compared with the Latin American average of 3.9 per cent and the East Asian average of 6.9 per cent.

The factors that permitted this high level of income tax collection capacity have been the subject of considerable analysis (Lieberman, 2001; Friedman and Smith, 2004). First, there has been a high degree of cooperation between the state and upper-income white groups which supported state-led reforms. This challenges the idea that simply instituting an autonomous revenue agency is central to effective tax collection. Second, the introduction of computerization in the 1960s greatly enhanced the ability of the Department of Inland Revenue to calculate and issue assessments, to record payments, and to register and monitor large tax payers, and maintain controls on tax payments more generally. Third, the introduction of a withholding pay-as-you-earn (PAYE) system also greatly enhanced tax collection. This system made employees responsible for withholding taxes on a monthly basis. The willingness of business owners to cooperate greatly reduced the transaction costs of implementing the PAYE system.

In the post-apartheid state, there have been several further reforms that followed from the Katz Commission which included representatives from the state, political parties, business chambers, labour unions, and national and international tax and legal experts. The Inland Revenue and Customs and Excise departments were integrated in 1995 and granted administrative autonomy under the new name South African Revenue Service (SARS) in 1997. The high degree of consultation within the state and between the state and interest groups were crucial to enhancing the legitimacy of the reforms. The key feature that marked the continued success of SARS in tax collection capacity was the high degree of administrative cooperation within the state, particularly between SARS, the Finance Ministry and the Central Bank. Such cooperation allowed for exchange in information that improved budget planning and tracking tax evasion. In sum, the mutually supportive ministerial relationships improved the resource mobilization capacity of the state.

While the above discussion examined the technical means through which tax capacity developed in South Africa, such dynamic capacity-building can not be understood without examining politics, which is the terrain upon which these technical capacities are legitimated and rules of the game enforced. Historical political analysis contributes greatly to explaining *why* the tax capacity in general, and the income tax collection capacity of the South African state was high *relative to that in other middle-income countries.*

For Lieberman (2001), the historical process in which the national political community was constructed in the early 1900s contributes greatly in explaining the evolution of income tax capacity in South Africa. The 1909 Constitution defined the South African polity along two main lines. First, it created an exclusionary racial state that eventually manifested itself in the form of apartheid. Secondly, it created a unified central state. In terms of the first factor, the white supremacy that was embodied in the state's laws and codes legitimated the state for white-owned firms and white upper-income groups. The apartheid state influenced the calculations of upper income groups, who became assured that their income tax would benefit 'their own' group, and not 'the other'. At the same time, a racially defined project allowed lower income whites to demand progressive taxation by drawing on the shared identity of a cross-class white project. Importantly, the *centralized and national* structure of white-based unions and political parties helped lower the transaction costs of collective action that are more prevalent in decentralized and regionally-based party systems and unions.

The contrast of the South African experience with the Brazilian tax state in the twentieth century is instructive of the value of comparative historical political economy analysis in understanding *variations* in income tax capacity. The Brazilian state has indeed achieved among the highest tax takes as a percentage of GDP in Latin America (and indeed among all less developed countries) in the twentieth century, and in the period 1990–2004, has increased its take from 22 per cent of GDP to over 30 per cent of GDP. However, in comparison with South Africa, the Brazilian state tax system is much more regressive and is characterized by a more *adversarial* as opposed to cooperative relationship between the state and upper-income groups (Lieberman, 2001). As such, the Brazilian state collects less than one-third the South African rate of income tax and relies on a series of inefficient and regressive indirect taxes such as multi-tiered value-added taxes, and financial transaction taxes (Schneider, 2005).

The comparison of South Africa and Brazil is interesting since both share many common features. Both economies are upper middle-income, semi-industrialized economies that have followed a largely inward-looking state-led import-substitution regime for most of the second half of the twentieth century Both also have the most unequal income distributions in the world. The main difference, according to Lieberman, is that, in Brazil, the polity was defined as a non-racial federation where *regional* interests were much more salient than in the South African state, which developed more centralized state along racial lines. As a result, race did not become an idiom along which upper-income white groups in Brazil could develop cross-class alliances and solidarity. The regional nature of the polity meant that both firms and white upper-income groups were less willing to cooperate with state as they were not confident that direct taxes would be used to benefit 'their' region. As a result, elites continued to challenge state efforts to increase income tax in the course of the twentieth century. Moreover, regionalism bred greater polarization and fragmentation of political parties and labour unions which weakened the collective capacity of lower income groups to demand more progressive taxation.[15]

This comparative analysis highlights why focusing on technical capacity or structural economic factors (e.g., income distribution, per capita income) is insufficient in explaining the differential income tax collection capacity of South Africa and Brazil. Rather, this comparative analysis highlights the importance of considering the structure of political institutions and settlements, and the way in which the national political community is defined as critical to understanding the evolution of tax capacity of states.[16] As such, the political economy approach provides a lens of analysis that probes issues raised by the economic and administrative approaches.

4.   Tax compositions in Latin America, East Asia, Eastern Europe, and South Africa

There have been very little systematic comparisons of the *composition* of tax across developing regions. As Lieberman's study comparing South Africa and Brazil suggests, overall take collection figures can mask important differences in developmental capacities of states. The capacity of states to collect direct taxes (income and property taxes) provides an important window into their power and legitimacy vis-à-vis upper income and middle-class groups. The aim will be to underscore differences in the types of taxes collected between the two regions.

Consider the differences between Latin American and East Asian economies during the 1997–2002 period in terms of the share of direct taxes collected as a percentage of GDP. In this period, personal income and property tax collection in East Asia was, on average, 4 times higher as a proportion of national income as indicated in Table 8.2.

Table 8.2 Personal income and property tax burden: Latin America, East Asia, and Eastern Europe compared

(Ratio of personal income and property tax as a per cent of GDP)

	1975–78	1985–88	1997–2002	2000 GDP per capita
Latin America				**(2000 US$)**
Average	**1.7**	**1.2**	**1.0**	**$4,399**
Argentina	0.4	0.8	1.1	7,726
Brazil	0.2	0.2	1.4	3,537
Chile	3.3	1.1	na	4,964
Colombia	1.8	1.6	0.6	1,979
Costa Rica	2.9	2.2	0.7	4,185
Mexico	2.7	2.0	na	5,935
Peru	1.5	na	1.5	2,046
Venezuela	1.0	1.0	1.0	4,818
East Asia				
Average	**1.8**	**2.3**	**3.9**	**3,716**
Indonesia	0.8	0.9	3.5	800
Korea	1.9	2.8	3.6	10,890
Malaysia	2.1	2.4	6.1	3,881
Philippines	1.6	1.1	2.6	990
Thailand	1.1	1.9	2.2	2,020
Taiwan	3.4	4.5	5.2	
Eastern Europe				
Average			**6.8**	**4,327**
Average			**6.8**	**4,327**
Latvia			6.5	3,259
Estonia			7.7	3,987
Poland			6.7	4,309
Hungary			7.8	4,656
Czech Republic			5.2	5,422

Source: IMF *Government Finance Statistics*; Statistical Yearbook of the Republic of China 2002 for Taiwan.

Moreover, the share of personal income and property tax as a percentage of GDP was six times higher in Eastern Europe compared with Latin America's average. This significant difference in personal income tax collection in 1997 is not due to any substantial differences in income per capita between the regions.

The very low personal income tax burden in Latin America is due to several factors all of which point to states in the region with weak leverage over the elite economic classes. First, the average maximum personal income rate has fallen from an average of 50 per cent in 1985–86 to 38 per cent in 1991, and 34 per cent in 1997, rate of decline 'that is considerably more rapid than in the OECD, where the top rates declined from 52.8 per cent in 1985–86 to 43.6 per cent by 1997 (Shome, 1999: 3–4). Second, poor administrative capacity and high level of tax evasion limit the productivity of tax collection (Shome, 1999). Third, while the top marginal personal income tax rate has been reduced in the 1990s, the top personal exemption level in terms of GDP per capita has risen from 1.29 in 1991 to 1.36 in 1997 (*ibid.*: 6). If one were to add that the significant levels of foreign savings held by Latin Americans (the result of several episodes of massive capital flight) are not taxed, it would not be unreasonable to argue that the economic elite in the region are the group least preyed on by their respective states.[17] These trends obviously imply that the tax burden of the upper income groups is negligible.

When one expands the category of direct taxes to include corporate income tax, East Asia still collects over 75 per cent more as a percentage of GDP as indicated in Table 8.3. The Eastern European economies in the sample had more than double the income tax collection as a share of GDP compared with Latin America. It is again worth highlighting the extraordinarily high income tax capacity of South Africa, which was discussed earlier.

Table 8.3 Income, profit, and capital gains burden: East Asia, Latin America, South Africa, and Eastern Europe compared

(Tax on income profits and capital gains as a per cent of GDP)

	Income, profit, and capital gains burden		
	1975–78	**1985–88**	**1997–2002**
Latin America			
Average	**5.0**	**4.1**	**3.9**
Average (excluding Venezuela)	**3.2**	**3.0**	**3.8**
Argentina	0.7	0.8	2.2
Brazil	3.2	4.4	4.5
Chile	3.8	4.0	4.2
Colombia	3.7	3.1	4.7
Costa Rica	2.8	2.4	2.8
Mexico	5.6	4.4	4.9
Peru	2.7	2.0	3.5
Venezuela	17.6	12.0	4.7
East Asia			
Average	**5.7**	**6.0**	**6.9**
Average (excluding Indonesia)	**4.4**	**5.2**	**6.3**
Korea	4.2	4.8	5.5

	Income, profit, and capital gains burden		
	1975–78	1985–88	1997–2002
Malaysia	8.3	9.6	8.4
Philippines	2.8	3.2	6.3
Indonesia	12.6	10.3	9.5
Thailand	2.1	3.2	5.0
Taiwan	4.0	4.8	6.6
South Africa	**12.9**	**13.1**	**14.6**
Eastern Europe			
Average			**8.3**
Latvia			7.5
Estonia			8.5
Poland			7.9
Hungary			9.3
Czech Republic			8.4

Source: IMF *Government Finance Statistics*, and *International Financial Statistics*; Statistical Yearbook of the Republic of China 2002 for Taiwan data.

The lower levels of income tax collection has meant that the burden of structural change in tax falls relatively more on indirect taxes in Latin America than in East Asia. As seen in Table 8.4, ratio of value-added taxes to GDP is significantly higher in Latin America compared to East Asia in the period 1997–2002.[18]

In the period 1997–2002, VAT-to-GDP ratios averaged 5.6 per cent in Latin America compared to 2.9 per cent in East Asia. While it is true that South Africa has a higher VAT-to-GDP ratio than both regions, VAT in South Africa represents a lower percentage of *total* taxes than in either region since income tax collection is, at 14.6 per cent of GDP, a much more significant component of total tax collection. The same story applies to Eastern Europe though to a lesser extent.

These patterns have several important implications. First, the indirect consumption taxes, and in particular, VAT, which is generally one of the more regressive taxes, is occupying a relatively substantial place within the overall tax burden in Latin America.[19] Second, as a result of the low levels of income tax collection, the region's tax collection is only 16 per cent of GDP when the international norm, given the average income per capita should be 24 per cent of GDP (IADB, 1998:6). Thirdly, the poor tax effort and the reliance on generally regressive indirect taxes in Latin America is reflective of the weakness of the state vis-à-vis upper income groups. Finally, in comparison with East Asia, the tax effort in Latin America is further from achieving re-distributive goals. This is because the challenges of re-distribution

Table 8.4 Value-added taxes in Latin America, East Asia, South Africa, and Eastern Europe compared

(VAT as a percentage of GDP)

	VAT		
	1975–78	**1985–88**	**1997–2002**
Latin America			
Average	**2.5**	**3.6**	**5.6**
Argentina	1.1	1.8	3.8
Brazil	0.0	8.7	12.1
Chile	6.5	8.1	8.2
Colombia	1.8	2.8	4.8
Costa Rica	1.6	2.8	4.8
Mexico	2.5	3.1	3.2
Peru	4.4	1.8	6.4
Venezuela	na	0.0	4.3
East Asia			
Average	**2.0**	**2.3**	**2.9**
Indonesia	1.6	2.8	3.5
Korea	2.6	3.5	4.1
Malaysia	1.2	1.5	2.0
Philippines	1.9	1.1	1.7
Thailand	2.7	2.8	3.4
Taiwan	na	na	na
South Africa	**1.2**	**6.1**	**6.1**
Eastern Europe			
Average			**7.4**
Latvia			7.4
Estonia			8.2
Poland			7.3
Hungary			9.0
Czech Republic			6.5

Source: IMF *Government Finance Statistics* and *International Financial Statistics*. Statistical Yearbook of the Republic of China 2002 for Taiwan data.

are much greater in Latin America because income distribution is, on average, much more unequal (IADB 1998). Without an explicit political programme to redesign and enforce personal income tax collection, the level and progressiveness of taxation and hence poverty reduction strategies in Latin America would appear limited, particularly in the context of persistently high income and asset inequality.

5.   Conclusion

The main theme emerging from a historical perspective on taxation is that while technical aspects of tax reform are crucial, an understanding of the sustainability of reforms is not possible without understanding how reforms become legitimate. Because taxation affects incentives and distribution simultaneously, tax reform requires either a degree of social consensus that such policies are in the collective interest and/or it requires a state with the ability to coerce those who challenge its allocations. The focus on institutional designs (such as the degree of autonomy) and other technical issues of tax is incomplete since it ignores the political nature of taxation.

While the current focus on value-added taxes and tax simplification have been useful to initiating tax revenue collection reforms, the more difficult administrative tasks of tax collection require further attention. The capacity approach of the World Bank and the IMF has been pragmatic in focusing attention on feasible revenue generation in the short and medium run. However, the long-run consolidation of tax states requires a diversification toward more direct and progressive income and property taxes. This is particularly the case in countries with very unequal income distributions.

The stakes of deepening the tax capacity in late developers are great. Tax contributes to making operational the social contract, and in particular, to creating the mutual obligations between state decision-makers and relevant political actors. Of critical importance to poor late developers is the development of bargaining mechanisms between the state and elite groups, who generally control much of the production and export sections of the economy. Because direct taxes are more challenging to collect in both administrative and political terms, apolitical and ahistorical approaches to state capacity are inadequate. A major challenge of research for the development community is to develop a more strategic, historical, and politically informed basis to promote the more difficult tax reforms.

Notes

1. Quoted in O'Brien (2001: 25).
2. According to the World Bank (1997: 41–60), the five 'fundamentals' that lie at the core of good governance for a state are: a) establishing a foundation of law, b) maintaining a non-distortionary policy environment, including macroeconomic stability, c) investing in basic social services and infrastructure, d) protecting the vulnerable, and e) protecting the environment. While tax is not explicitly mentioned as a core function of governance, tax capacity is implicitly behind items c) and d).
3. Or as Rudolph Goldscheid notes: 'the budget is the skeleton of a state stripped of all misleading ideologies' (quoted in Levi, 1988: 6).
4. The advocacy for tax simplifications and tax neutrality have been the result of disillusionment with progressive tax structures in enhancing vertical equity in the 1970s and 1980s (Tanzi, 1992); and the influence of neo-liberal ideas such as supply-side economics, which views state intervention, and direct taxes in particular, as providing disincentives for productive investment. Moreover, as a

result of globalization, the desire to attract foreign investment has created intense tax competition among states, which has created pressure to keep income taxes low.

5. For reviews of economic theories of tax and the applied literature on developing countries, see Gillis (1989); Burgess and Stern (1993); and Tanzi and Zee (2000).

6. Kriekhaus (2002) argues that higher *public* savings is correlated with growth rates in less developed countries.

7. See Wade (1990); Chang (1994); Kohli (1999); and Huff (1995).

8. As Bird and Casanegra (1992) argue: 'In developing countries, tax administration *is* tax policy'.

9. Because of these deficiencies Bird (1989: 329), for instance, notes that 'there is no place for an income (or other general direct) tax in any developing country'.

10. On the Peruvian and Ugandan cases respectively, see Durand and Thorp (1998), and Therkildsen (2003).

11. For an early and influential analysis of the relationship between war and state formation, and between state formation and taxation, see Schumpeter ([1918] 1954). In Schumpeter's analysis, the 'most important cause of financial difficulties consisted in the growing expenses of warfare (*ibid*: 13) and that 'without financial need the immediate cause for the creating of the modern state would have been absent' (*ibid*.). However, see Centeno (1997) and López-Alves (2001) for analysis of why the potential stimulus of war did not transform Latin American states in the nineteenth century in ways similar to Western Europe.

12. See Knight (1992), Moore (1966), and Brenner (1976).

13. This paragraph draws on a personal note from Thandika Mkandwire (2005).

14. Tax effort measures the relationship between actual and potential levels of taxation, the latter being the predicted value derived from the statistical relationship between the tax share in GDP and various combinations of explanatory variables, usually including levels of per capita income and the shares of agriculture, industry, and manufacturing in GDP, import shares and levels of urbanization. Tax effort is the residual of each country's equation. If it exceeds zero, then a country's actual level of taxation exceeds the predicted one while if it falls below then the country tax level is below its potential.

15. Even in Lula da Silva's administration, income tax has remained off the agenda despite the fact that the Worker's Party (PT) has risen on a social democratic platform.

16. However, in a larger comparative perspective, the focus on ethnicity/race and regionalism does not why tax capacities differ within Latin America and differ across middle-income countries more generally.

17. Tanzi and Zee (2000: 30) note that Latin American countries have virtually stopped taxing financial income to avoid chronic capital flight.

18. It is important to note here that standard analysis of tax incidence indicates that who bears the ultimate burden of the tax may be substantially different from who pays the tax in the first instance. For example, a corporation may not pay the full amount of a corporate tax if it can shift some of that burden to consumers via higher prices or if it can force workers to accept a lower wage (see Stiglitz, 1986: 411–55).

19. In theory, the overall impact of VAT need not be regressive. This would be the case if luxury items are taxed at a higher rate than basic goods, and if public expenditure that is financed by VAT is targeted to lower-income groups.

References

Addison, T., Chowdhury, A. and Murshed, S. M. 2002. 'Taxation and Reform in Conflict-Affected Countries', paper presented at the conference on Taxing Perspectives: A Democratic Approach to Public Finance in Developing Countries, Institute of Development Studies, Sussex, 28–29 October.

Bird, R. 1989. The Administrative Dimension of Tax Reform in Developing Countries, in M. Gillis (ed.) 1989. *Tax Reform in Developing Countries*. Durham: Duke University Press.

Bird, R. and Casanegra, M. (eds) 1992. *Improving Tax Administration in Developing Countries*, IMF, Washington, DC.

Brenner, R. 1976. 'Agrarian Class Structure and Economic Development in pre-Industrial Europe', *Past and Present*, 70.

Burgess, R. and Stern, N. 1993. 'Taxation and Development'. *Journal of Economic Literature*, 31, 2.

Campbell, J. L. 1993. 'The State and Fiscal Sociology', *Annual Review of Sociology*, 19.

Cameron, D. R. 1978. 'The Expansion of the Public Economy: A Comparative Analysis', *American Political Science Review*, 72.

Centeno, M. A. 1997. 'Blood and Debt: War and Taxation in Nineteenth-Century Latin America', *American Journal of Sociology*, 102, 6.

Chang, H-J. 1994. *The Political Economy of Industrial Policy*, London: Macmillan.

Di John, J. 2004. 'The Political Economy of Industrial Policy in Venezuela, 1920–1998', PhD dissertation, Faculty of Economics, University of Cambridge.

Durand, F. and Thorp, R. 1998. 'Reforming the State: A Study of the Peruvian Tax Reform', *Oxford Development Studies*, 26, 2.

Friedman, S. and Smith, L. 2004. 'Tax and Society in South Africa', in V. Lledo, A. Schneider and M. Moore. Governance, Taxes, and Tax Reform in Latin America, IDS Working Paper 221, March.

Gillis, M. (ed.) 1989. *Tax Reform in Developing Countries*. Durham: Duke University Press.

Goldscheid, R. [1925] 1958. 'A sociological approach to problems of public finance', in R. Musgrave and A. T. Peacock (eds) *Classics in the Theory of Public Finance*. New York: Macmillan.

Heidenheimer, A. J., Heclo, H. and Adams, C. 1983. *Comparative Public Policy: The Politics of Social Choice in Europe and America*. New York: St Martins Press.

Huff, W. G. 1995. 'What is the Singapore Model of Economic Development?', *Cambridge Journal of Economics*, 19.

Inter-American Development Bank. 1998. *Economic and Social Progress in Latin America 1998–99 Report*, Washington DC, Johns Hopkins University Press.

IMF, *Government Financial Statistics*, Washington DC.

Kaldor, N. 1955. *An Expenditure Tax*. London: George Allen and Unwin.

Karl, T. L. 1997. *The Paradox of Plenty: Oil Booms and Petro States*. Berkeley: University of California Press.

Kohli, A. 1999. 'Where Do High Growth Political Economies Come From? The Japanese Lineage of Korea's Developmental State', in M. Woo-Cummings (ed.) *The Developmental State*. Ithaca: Cornell University Press.

Knight, J. 1992. *Institutions and Social Conflict*. Cambridge: Cambridge University Press.

Kriekhaus, J. 2002. 'Reconceptualizing the Developmental State: Public Savings and Economic Growth', *World Development*, 30(10).

Levi, M. 1988. *Of Revenue and Rule*. Berkeley: University of California Press.

Lewis, A. 1954. 'Economic Development with Unlimited Supplies of Labour', *The Manchester School*, 22(2).

Lieberman, E. 2001. 'National Political Community and the Politics of Taxation in Brazil and South Africa in the Twentieth Century', *Politics and Society*, 29(4).

Lledo, V., Schneider, A. and Moore, M. 2004. Governance, Taxes, and Tax Reform in Latin America, IDS Working Paper 221, March.

Lopez-Alves 2001. 'The Transatlantic Bridge: Mirrors, Charles Tilly, State Formation in the River Plate', in M. A. Centeno and López-Alves (eds) *The Other Mirror: Grand Theory through the Lens of Latin America*. Princeton: Princeton University Press.

Mahdavy, H. 1970. 'Patterns and Problems of Economic Development in Rentier States: The Case of Iran', in M. A. Cook (ed.) *Studies in the Economic History of the Middle East*. Oxford: Oxford University Press.

Mkandwire, T. 2005. 'On Tax Efforts and Colonial Heritage: A Note'. Mimeo, Geneva: UNRISD.

Moore, B. 1966. *The Social Origins of Democracy and Dictatorship: Lord and Peasant in the Making of the Modern World*. Boston: Beacon Press.

Newberry, D. and Stern, N. (eds) 1987. *The Theory of Taxation for Developing Countries*. World Bank, Washington, DC: Oxford University Press.

O'Brien, P. 2001. Fiscal Exceptionalism: 'Great Britain and Its European Rivals', Working Paper 65/01, Department of Economic History, LSE.

Schneider, A. 2005. 'Wholesale versus Within Institutional Change: Pacting Governance Reform in Brazil for Fiscal Responsibility and Tax', paper presented at Crisis States Programme Research Seminar, February.

Schumpeter, J. [1918] 1954. 'The Crisis of the Tax State', International Economic Papers, No. 4.

Shome, P. 1999. 'Taxation in Latin America: Structural Trends and Impact of Administration', *IMF Working Paper*, WP/99/19.

Statistical Yearbook of the Republic of China 2002

Stern, N. 1987. 'Aspects of the General Theory of Taxation', in N. Stern and D. Newberry (eds). *The Theory of Taxation for Developing Countries*. World Bank, Washington, DC: Oxford University Press

Stiglitz, J. 1986. *Economics of the Public Sector*. New York: W. W. Norton and Company.

Stotsky, J. and WoldeMariam, A. 1997. 'Tax Effort in Sub-Saharan Africa', IMF Working Paper WP/97/101, Washington, DC: IMF.

Taliceiro, R. 2004. 'Designing Performance: The Semi-Autonomous Revenue Authority Model in Africa and Latin America', *Policy Research Working Paper* 3423. World Bank: Washington, DC.

Tanzi, V. 1992. 'Fiscal Policy and Economic Reconstruction in Latin America', *World Development*, 20, 5.

Tanzi, V. 2000. 'Taxation in Latin America in the Last Decade', Working Paper 76, Stanford: Center for Research on Economic Development and Policy Reform, Stanford University.

Tanzi, V. and Zee, H. H. 2000. 'Tax Policy for Emerging Markets: Developing Countries', *IMF Working Paper*, WP/00/35.

Therkilsden, O. 2003. 'Revenue authority autonomy in sub-Saharan Africa: the case of Uganda', draft paper for NFU conference on 'Poverty and Politics', Oslo, 23–24 October.

Thirsk, W. 1997. *Tax Reform in Developing Countries*, Washington, DC: World Bank.

Tilly, C. 1990. *Coercion, Capital and European States: AD 990–1992*. Oxford: Blackwell.

Toye, J. 2000. 'Fiscal Crisis and Reform in Developing Countries', *Cambridge Journal of Economics*, 24(1).

Wade, R. 1990. *Governing the Market*. Princeton: Princeton University Press.

World Bank. 1993. *The East Asian Miracle*. New York: Oxford University Press.

World Bank. 1997. *World Development Report: The State in a Changing World*, Oxford: Oxford University Press.

World Bank 2004. *Partnerships in Development*. Washington, DC.
World Bank. *World Development Indicators*: Washington, DC.

CHAPTER 9
THE RULE OF LAW, LEGAL TRADITIONS, AND ECONOMIC GROWTH: THE EAST ASIAN EXAMPLE

Meredith Jung-En Woo

This chapter is concerned with the rule of law, types of law, and economic development. While the rule of law is widely thought to go hand in hand with economic development, international financial institutions (barred through their charters from any political interference in member countries) have largely eschewed exploring the relationship between law and politics – until quite recently. But economic theorists who write on law have always had their eyes cocked on the state and its power. F.A. Hayek defined the rule of law as an understanding that government in all its actions is bound by the rules fixed and announced beforehand, preventing it from stultifying the individual efforts by *ad hoc* action (1944, 1972: 72).

This Hayekian insight has not been lost to a group of economists who have taken the argument about the rule of law to an extreme: Different legal traditions have different thumb prints of the state, and the legal tradition that bears the least imprint is the one most likely to promote economic growth. More specifically, the argument was that a common law tradition, which arose at arms-length to the state, was more likely to promote economic development. By the same token, the civil law tradition, which abets the power of the state, was more likely to privilege state intervention in economic processes, and hence less growth-promoting.

In this chapter I will argue that however compelling this argument may be, legal traditions and institutions do not determine the nature of the state (although they may be reflected in it), nor its likely role in the economy – nor do they critically determine the course of economic development.

Instead of common law leading to a minimal state and the broadest extension of the market, or civil law leading to state intervention in the economy and corresponding shrinkage of market activity, there may be no relationship at all between forms of law and the role of the state.

I will begin by reviewing the core literature on the rule of law and economic growth; the influential arguments of some institutional economists on the relationship between law, finance, and government. In particular, I will examine the influential argument by La Porta et al., on the superiority of the Anglo-American common law system (as versus the civil law tradition of continental Europe, Latin America, and East Asia) in fostering financial development (often understood to be synonymous with economic development). I will seek to demonstrate the inadequacy of these arguments on the rule of law and economic development, by flashing them against the backdrop of East Asia.

I will first argue that these mechanisms of state intervention in the economy (*Gyosei shido* in Japanese and its direct transliteration, *Haengjŏng Chido* in Korea) were highly *informal* mechanisms which had at best a tangential relationship to formal law or law traditions, and thus this experience contradicts the argument that it is the structure of formal law that determines the nature of the relationship between the state, economy, and society. Administrative guidance developed both in the 'civil law' countries like Japan and Korea, but also in a 'common law' country like Malaysia − in the latter case an elaborate and sophisticated common law system still posed no barrier to arbitrary decisions by the chief executive.

Second, I will also show that the process of *reform* itself has developed out of the same pre-existing patterns of state intervention, in particular in the Republic of Korea, one of the success stories of reform since 1997. I will argue that the Korean government has used administrative guidance as an effective policy tool to restructure the corporate sector and to bring about neoliberal reforms − precisely in the direction of accountability and transparency. This experience of state action that was simultaneously heavy-handed and successful, may therefore illustrate that rapid economic reform in a developing society will bear fruit most quickly and effectively in countries already having a more centralized and powerful government, with the trick being to direct that state toward a commitment to economic growth.

1.   Common law and civil law

Douglass North has been a prolific advocate of the idea that states throughout history have more often been inimical to economic growth than conducive of it, and that the key to economic development is to get states to behave as 'impartial third parties', or to adapt a role sometimes called that of a 'night watchman state' (North, 1981; 1990). A good system of impersonal exchange combined with third-party enforcement of the rules of the game, has been 'the critical underpinning of successful modern economies involved in the complex contracting necessary for modern economic growth' (North, 1990: 35). By and large, the most effective of those modern economies have been ones that sprang from the common law tradition.

A more detailed argument for the virtues of a common law tradition comes from La Porta, Lopez-de-Silanes, Shleifer and Vishney (hereafter LLSV). Through an empirical study of the determinants of quality government in a large cross-section of countries, the authors assess state performance using various measures of government intervention, public sector efficiency, public good provision, size of government, and political freedom (LLSV 1999). 'Good government' is what is good for 'economic development', and 'economic development' is really about the security of property rights – lack of intervention by the government, benign regulation, and low taxation (1999: 225). Because common law developed in England as a defence of Parliament and property owners against the attempts by the sovereign to regulate and expropriate them, and because it is made by judges who put their emphasis on the private rights of individuals and especially on their property rights, the LLSV authors see it as the best legal system for economic development, as they define it.

Civil law, on the other hand, is seen as an instrument of the state in expanding its power – as illustrated by the fact that the greatest codes were introduced by Napoleon and Bismarck – and this type of law focuses on discovering a just solution to a dispute (often from the point of view of the state) rather than on following a just procedure that protects individuals against the state. Not surprising, the LLSV authors find that the use of a more interventionist legal system, such as the French civil law, predict inferior economic performance (1999: 224).

Investor protection, which is interchangeably used as economic development, is also interchangeable with good corporate governance, which they define as 'a set of mechanisms through which outside investors protect themselves against expropriation by the insiders' (LLSV 2000:1). This expropriation may take the form of transfer pricing, asset stripping, investor dilution, and outright stealing, with the authors finding several practices which may be legal (like investor dilution) having the same effect as stealing. Once again they argue that common law countries offer the strongest protections for outside investors, having judges who base themselves on precedents 'inspired by principles such as fiduciary duty or fairness'. Effective investor protection, according to the LLSV authors, enhances savings and also channels these savings 'into real investment'; the development of strong financial protection 'allows capital to flow toward the more productive uses, and thus improve the efficiency of resource allocation'. Civil law countries, on the other hand, offer much weaker protection to outside investors, with laws made by legislatures rather than judges looking at precedent.

History, however, does not support the contention of the LLSV authors. The path of financial market development have not been as linear, but instead show many fluctuations and departures in countries like the US, France, Germany, and Britain. For instance in 1913, France's stock market capitalization as a fraction of GDP was almost twice that of the US, but then decreased to almost one-fourth of the US by 1980, and in 1999, the two countries seem to have converged (Rajan and Zingales, 2000: 4). In the beginning of the twentieth century, Germany (a civil law country) also outpaced England (a common law country) both in the volume of total market issues, and in the proportion of issuance consisting of equity. Thus it was not legal or cultural factors that determined the level of financial system development, but political factors such as the support by government and interest groups for financial institution growth that determined the course of development.

In fact, whereas it took over a century and a half for the English common law system to work out something like the limited liability form to its satisfaction, a mere ten years were required for the French civil code to emulate it. The almost instant success of continental European governments in promoting financial development seems to indicate that what is critical is the will of the government to develop the financial market, and furthermore, that financial reform may bear fruit more quickly in the more centralized governments of the civil law tradition than in the weaker governments associated with the common law tradition.

Another example along these lines would be the fairly remarkable experience in Latin America, a region made up almost entirely of civil law tradition countries, of governments moving quickly toward market-oriented policies. Indeed, market-oriented policies do not require changes in the legal traditions of given countries, so much as the emergence of new political leadership committed to change; effective leaders can not only implement new market-oriented measures, but can also change public opinion and, over time, the nature of legal practice itself.

The concern with the origins of the legal system also has the effect of putting the cart before the horse. Investor protection tended to develop in most countries only after the period of transplanting major legal systems, and much of that transplantation involved civil law countries adopting Anglo-American law. This was particularly true for Japan, Korea, and Taiwan. In other words, the historical sequence of events defies a simple categorization of countries according to the origin of their legal systems for laws governing investor protection, in light of the fact that different economies use different combinations of substantive and procedural protection in their laws. These combinations are the result of repeated legal change that can hardly be traced to the origins of an economy's legal system (Pistor and Wellons, 1999: 139–141).

Most tellingly, Davis and Trebilcock (1999), in a study conducted for the World Bank, argued that there is little evidence of a causal relationship between law and economic development; empirical studies of the relationship between growth and law do not point to causality. They scrutinized the economic impact of property rights, including 'titling', 'privatization', 'alienability', 'land redistribution', concluding that it is difficult to say that clear property rights lead to positive economic benefits. They obtained the same inconclusive results in examining the economic impact of contract laws, taxation law, criminal law, social welfare legislation, human rights, family law, and the like. The more daunting challenge, they think, is to enhance 'the quality of institutions charged with the responsibility of enacting laws and regulations', and that exclusive or predominant occupation with the court system inappropriately discounts the important role played by government departments and agencies.

Much of my previous work has been concerned with identifying the specificities of 'late' industrial development. How do the requirements of industrial strategy, finance, and the role of the state differ, depending on when a country begins to industrialize? (Woo, 1991). Without putting too fine a point on it, from this perspective it seems clear that a common law tradition is consonant with early industrial development, in which the private sector is much more active than the state in promoting industrialization, the time frame for industrialization is much more lengthy, and leaders do not have to worry so much about competition from countries that have already arrived at an advanced industrial status. This sequencing would also suggest that judges have the luxury of time to develop precedents on a case-by-case basis. The civil law tradition, to the contrary, is much more identified with 'late' industrializers like Germany and Japan, in which the state became a resource to be deployed to hasten the process of development and to make up or substitute for various disadvantages, like the modest nature of private sector business or the middle class.

One of the 'advantages of backwardness', in the words of Alexander Gerschenkron, was the ability of late industrializers to copy the earlier industrializers, and often the state was the key institution engaged in doing that. But copying a machine is much easier than copying the theory and practice of a law tradition that evolved over centuries, through the establishment and subsequent citation of precedent. It was thus far easier to write a code authorizing desired economic behaviour, than splice a common law tradition based on long historical evolution into effective day-to-day practice in the hot-house conditions of the twentieth century development.

2.   Japan: Informality, administrative guidance, and 'rule-by-law'

It is a curiosity that Japan endured, first an unconditional surrender and then a seven-year occupation by the standard-bearer of the rule of law, the United States, and yet law was more important in Japan before 1945 than it was in the long period of rapid growth that ensued after the Occupation ended. A civil law code modelled on German examples played a significant role in the eighty years of Imperial Japan after the Meiji Restoration in 1868, but with the advent of the post-war democracy came a relative shrinkage of the legal sector. As Japan became a model of post-war industrial growth, formal legal institutions played at best a back-up role to informal mechanisms, especially the well-known state practice of administrative guidance. Instead, economic policy was formed and implemented largely through informal mechanisms, consciously shielded from the interference of the formal legal system. The courts were relatively inactive, citizens rarely brought actions to them on behalf of individual rights or privileges, and consumer protection was minimal, at least through lawsuits brought to the courts. Intervention by the courts in the implementation of economic policy on behalf of private parties was rare to the point of non-existence. Foreign firms were on the outside looking in on policy formation, of course, and had little recourse to the courts to protect their interests (Upham, 2000).

During the American occupation a new constitution replaced the Meiji Constitution with its continental notion of the *Reichstaatsprinzip*, and one of the major advances of the new constitution was to abolish the Administrative court and introduce the Anglo-American system of judicial review. Did that eventuate in grafting a system of common law onto the Japanese experience of civil law? Some scholars argue that the predictable did indeed happen: That Japanese law thereafter developed in the direction of American law, and that in spite of the vast differences in historical, political, economic, and social backgrounds of Japan and the US, the post-war system has steadily been 'proving its fitness', with case law and precedent developing rapidly (Hashimoto, 1963: 271). Or as another scholar puts it, the old practice of 'rule by law' (*hochishugi*) gave way after 1945 to the 'rule *of* law' (*ho no shihai*) (Takayanagi, 1963: 13).

Most others, however, do not think that post-war Japanese legal practice has ever come very close to resembling the Anglo-American system. Indeed, the translation of the above terms is quite revealing. In Japan *hochishugi* (*pŏpch'ijuŭi* in Korean) is used without carrying the negative connotation that in the West would be attributed to the phrase 'rule by law', and this is not a matter of poor translation. Instead the phrase bespeaks the difficulty of translating or conveying liberal conceptions in a statist society; even the term 'liberal' developed the connotation in Japan and Korea of conservatism, so the distinction may also be lost between the (liberal) 'rule of law' and the (illiberal) 'rule by law'. Or as a legal scholar puts this point,

> [In] the introduction of rules and principles of common-law origin ... it is quite natural that those rules and principles were interpreted by Japanese jurists according to the civilian [i.e., civil law] methods in which they were experts. If one compares commentaries on the Philippine constitution with those on the new Japanese constitution, he will be surprised at the striking difference in the mode of exposition and interpretation, even in cases in which the constitutional text is exactly the same... (Takayanagi, 1963: 37)

Nor did the Japanese adoption of American-inspired law make people more litigious, as one might expect; instead they were far less litigious than citizens in any other advanced-industrial country, and even less litigious than they had been before 1945. The average civil litigation rate for 1892–1940 was 146,683 (or 26.8 per million people), whereas the average for 1950–90 was 176,211 (or 16.6 per million people); in 1962, litigation per million people had not yet come back to the level achieved in 1916 (Pistor and Wellons, 1999: 230). Thus the ubiquitous lawyer jokes that Americans love are inexplicable in Japan ('What do you call 10,000 lawyers found on the bottom of the ocean? A good start', etc.). This experience speaks quite soberly to the travelability of the arguments made by the LLSV scholars and others of the law-and-economics school. That is: Have law (but), won't travel.

Instead post-war Japan preferred administrative action to litigious reaction, and even though the 1946 Constitution required that administration be based on legislation coming out of the Diet, in fact the Diet merely set general guidelines and then authorized the bureaucracy to flesh out the rules, which gave bureaucrats substantial discretion in practice. Constitutional legality receded as administrative guidance (AG) proceeded, a practice that we can usefully define as giving broad discretion to the bureaucracy to make, interpret, and enforce detailed rule of economic behaviour. Or as the most famous analyst of this practice put it, administrative guidance

> refers to the authority of the government, contained in the laws establishing the various ministries, to issue directives (*shiji*), requests (*yodo*), warnings (*keikoku*), suggestions (*kankoku*), and encouragements (*kansho*) to the enterprises or clients within a particular ministry's jurisdiction. Administrative guidance is constrained only by the requirement that the 'guidees' must come under a given governmental organ's jurisdiction, and although it is not based on any explicit law, it cannot violate the law (for example, it is not supposed to violate the Antimonopoly Law). (Johnson, 1982: 265)

Not only was administrative discretion very broad, but powerful ministries, pre-eminently the Ministry of Finance (MOF), got away with dusting off interwar laws dealing with financial regulation (especially control of foreign exchange and cross-border financial flows), thus allowing the MOF to change policy by prewar ordinance if not by fiat. The MOF thus based its control over the financial sector on the Banking Act of 1928 and the Foreign Exchange Control Act of 1933 (Pistor and Wellons, 1999: 92–3, 98). South Korea likewise often based post-war economic regulation on prewar (Japanese) law. Administrative guidance also effectively reflected the needs and demands of those being 'guided'. It was a regulatory form for government intervention in the economy that has helped to preserve a competitive market economy by maximizing the freedom of individual firms over economic decisions although behind the veil of pervasive government direction (Haley, 1986: 108).

If the role of the MOF, MITI, and the reliance on prewar laws was mitigated by the atmosphere of reform and deregulation in the 1980s, and if administrative guidance seems at best vestigial in the twenty-first century, that probably happened because of the disutility of state direction in an era of information-age industries and technologies, not because someone in Tokyo finally saw the common-law light. Indeed, substantial legal scholarship by Michael Young has shown how, even in the atmosphere of change and deregulation in the 1980s, when procedures of judicial review were used to confine AG to carefully-defined purposes, judges did not seek to eliminate AG in favour of an ideal vision of the rule of law; instead they sought a balance between the good that came from administrative flexibility, and the bad that came from excessive bureaucratic intrusion. Courts refused to determine the priority of competing claims of rights, as an American judge would do, in order to protect individual rights without sacrificing the flexibility that AG provided. They were more concerned with bringing AG into line with an informal social consensus than with conforming to legal procedure or abstract legal principle, as might have happened in a common law system. Rather than giving a priority to one side's view, as in an adversarial legal system, the courts have been reluctant to state their position and preferred to rely on societal consensus and informal agreement between the involved parties (Young, 1984: 923–25, 965–67, 977). Of course AG was itself an informal system, and so the remedies for the abuses of administrative guidance also had to be informal.

3.   Have law, will travel: Korea learns from Japan

One clear case of dramatic international or cross-border learning is the Republic of Korea (ROK), where administrative guidance remains the primary tool used by the state to intervene in the economy, something that Koreans learned under Japanese imperial tutelage before 1945, but also through emulation of Japan's post-war industrial prowess.

In Korea, however, there may have been a kind of *over*-learning, since the use of administrative guidance is far more pervasive than in Japan, and in two important ways goes to unheard of lengths: First, administrative guidance is not just the province of the state ministries, but can be issued directly by the president through the relevant ministries and agencies, in an executive-dominant political system where the president has far more power than in Japan's parliamentary democracy. Second, the informalities of AG in Japan, limited by formal mechanisms of judicial review and shaped by a prior consensus, give way in Korea to AG almost by fiat; extensive consultations do not necessarily precede administrative guidance, and judicial review was non-existent during the decades of dictatorship and remains weak under the democratic governments of the past decade. Befitting Korea's long authoritarian legacy and its extraordinary history of centralizing everything in the capital (far more so than in Japan) and then concentrating that authority in the hands of the chief executive, administrative guidance is more uneven and less consensual, resembling a coercive demand more than an informal guidance.

For much of the period of authoritarian rule and world-beating economic growth Korea's judges were not so much as august interpreters of constitutional intent as dependent factotums; at best 'distinguished bureaucrats' and at worst 'expert clerks' (Song, 1996a). They were essentially civil servants, and given that the administration of justice had little bearing on governmental and political life, their real sphere of influence and action was in civil and commercial matters where their expertise was needed to adjudicate conflicts among private parties and to rule upon the application of criminal laws. Here the power brokers felt no need or interest in interference, so the judges could have their realm of autonomy. Given the bureaucratic nature of the judicial system, which exercised its own effect on the basic lack of judicial creativity that all observers noted, and given the judges' lack of power even to interpret (let alone create) the law, the basic requirements for a judge were to be technically competent, inveterately apolitical, risk averse, and preternaturally quiet (Song, 1996a: 300–2).

What is the legal basis for administrative guidance in Korea? When the president or other executive organs of the state intervene into the private sphere of civil society and commerce, the legal basis of such intervention must be knowable in advance by the subjects of such regulation. In a constitutional order, such state action is subject to public scrutiny and if necessary, to legal challenge. It is stated in Article 119(2) of the ROK Constitution:

> The state may regulate and coordinate economic affairs in order to maintain the balanced growth and stability of the national economy, to ensure proper distribution of income, to prevent the domination of the market and the abuse of economic power, and to democratize the economy through harmony among the economic agents.

In truth, however, administrative guidance was complex, opaque and often legally irregular. Discipline was imposed through explicit regulations, tacit threats of unfavourable treatment in the future, by intimidating use of punitive tax audits, and sometimes by cynical abuse of the criminal justice system (West, 1998: 328).

Administrative guidance had been ubiquitous in Korea going back to the 1960s, of course, but its very breadth of activity made defining it quite difficult. Thus one of Korea's leading legal authorities, Sang-Hyun Song, wrote that there is

> … no clear definition of administrative guidance. It is generally understood that the Korean government will exert its authority under

regulatory and criminal laws to provide protection or to prevent violations …. The Korean government has exercised and still exercises wide regulation over the Korean business community. Such control is possible as a result of the government's authority to grant business licenses, and its direct or indirect influence on financing [with respect to] the specific industry. Furthermore, suggestions or requests from the government that a company act or refrain from acting in a particular way are generally honored by businesses. Therefore, administrative guidance may be effective…. (Song, 1996b: 1,249)

Real change can come – and has come – to Korea's judiciary only from outside forces. Since the national protest mobilization of June 1987, civil society has advanced rapidly and a proliferation of new laws has done much to democratize the judicial sphere: Reform of government fiat under the Administrative Procedure Act (APA), opening of politics through the Freedom of Information Act and the Information Protection Act, devolution of power from the centre under the Local Autonomy Law, and the development of case law through the (finally) vitalized law-finding activities of the courts. Like Lazarus the Supreme Court and the Constitutional Court sprang to life, trading *rigor mortis* for *habeas corpus* and discovering an utterly unaccustomed penchant for judicial review and a theretofore invisible activism in examining the constitutionality of laws.

This new-found judicial determination is attributable to the demands and pressures from an invigorated popular sphere, especially for good governance having both a better quality of performance and clear adherence to the principle of the rule of law. Citizen pressures, often in the form of suits filed against public authorities demanding that they do what the letter of the law long authorized them to do (something unheard of under the dictators, even though all Korean constitutions going back to 1948 look liberal on paper), brought about the court reorganization of 1994, established the Administrative Court in 1998, along with more recent reform measures that add up to a newly-invigorated judicial function in Korea. The significance of these gains cannot be underestimated, since for forty years Korean judges and government officials themselves often felt unconstrained by the very laws that they were are called upon to implement, there having been so little force in the concept of 'legal right' in Korean law practice; even when there was evidence of good judicial intervention – or justice in the best sense – it rested upon 'common sense', 'good will', or the judge's 'benevolence' – but not the 'rights' of the individual (Song, 1996b: 1,246).

The revitalization of the judiciary, however, has not meant an end of the era of administrative guidance. Under a democratic government, administrative guidance can be invoked, even if its uses today are often to correct the abuses of yesterday. Kim Dae Jung came to power in February 1998 as a result of the first truly important political and democratic transition in Korean history, and proceeded to use this informal mechanism of state interventionism to bring about the rule of law, Korean-style. The 'rules of law' that Kim wanted to champion in the economic sphere were: Creating transparency in corporate governance, reducing excessive reliance on the banking system for capital, improving the financial structure of the conglomerates, separating ownership from management, giving labour a voice at the bargaining table, and improving minority shareholder rights.

The best symbol of how administrative guidance went from stoking the Korean industrial economy to reforming it is the industrial reorganization of 1998 which proposed to find the comparative industrial advantage of each conglomerate and then demand that the firms stick to it. The end goal was to reduce over-investment by shrinking the number of firms in a given industry, thus forcing firms to focus on their 'core competence' after years of excess, redundant diversification. Kim's reforms sought both to preserve the perceived comparative advantage of Korea's chaebol in world markets, and to break the nexus of state and corporate power, which had gained its sustenance through capital provisioned by the government to the big firms in the form of huge state-mediated, preferentially-priced loans, something that had long been the distinguishing characteristic of the Korean model of development.

In the worst of times Korean administrative guidance has been destructive of the rule of law, involving outright expropriation of property in the name of industrial reorganization; in ordinary times it has been the mundane, informal instrument of an intrusive executive power. But does that necessarily negate the value of administrative guidance, which in the best of times was the core architectonic force behind Korea's rapid industrialization?

In the empyrean of the Hayekian rule of law, administrative guidance should be (at best) no more than the handmaiden of an arm's-length, disinterested third-party justice, and even then it would be better if it simply did the right thing and abolished itself. But perhaps the Japanese precedents we surveyed earlier provide a more realistic roadmap toward how real-world AG can morph into a useful practice constrained by an evolving and ever-stronger form of judicial review or, as in the Korean case, an energized populace. The alternative of a delayed and dilated euthanasia for Korean administrative guidance looks even better when we grasp that in the aftermath of the 1997 crisis it did in fact become an effective mechanism of reform, the intrusive arm of government that propelled financial restructuring, cleaned up corporate governance, and got economic growth back on track. Perhaps now we can look forward to administrative guidance finding a way to prepare its own deathbed.

4. More like them: Common law 'looks East'

Malaysia is a fascinating case to compare with Korea and Japan, given that it long had a more liberal market and a state based in a common law background that was less interventionist than Japan's (let alone Korea's), yet under Mahathir it developed the aspiration to be more like Japan and Korea (during the so-called 'Look East' strategy), and even though it failed in that effort, it succeeded in destroying its own common-law based constitution. How did it do so, and what happened to its British common law tradition? The simple answer is that Mahathir expanded the power of the executive and used it first to hamstring and then to demolish the judiciary. Law did not appear to be the 'proxy' for the state or the determinant of the state-market nexus as the LLSV scholars would claim, but quickly fell away before the advance of a powerful state.

The legal basis of pre-colonial Malaya was customary and Islamic law, but it had a far longer period of exposure to British or common law than did many colonies, as British control lasted from 1874 to 1957. The post-independence legal system consisted basically of British law and some elements of Islamic law, which reflected the ethnic balance between Chinese businessmen and other non-Islamic groups, and the majority Malays who believe in Islam. Existing laws and statutory and judicial precedents bear the indelible marks of English common law and equity and what the colonial judges thought was just, fair, reasonable, and equitable. The 1957 Federal constitution was drafted by the British Parliamentary draftsmen, broadly based on the Westminster Parliamentary model.

The judiciary and the entire judicial process operated and is still operating under the profound influence of the English common law and equity, judicial precedents, principles, ideas, and concepts. The polity had a number of major democratic features, such as regular elections contested by independent parties, a parliament to which the government is responsive, and a constitutionally independent judiciary (Biddle and Milor, 1999: 11). If the organized bar was small, countervailing legal efforts to control the government's growing power were rule-based. Administrative law, as interpreted by the courts, provided rudimentary controls over the government; judicial independence was high; and judges were as career appointees and not at that time part of the political majority.

Despite the trappings of democracy, though, the actual limitations on democratic process were many. When a twelve-year state of emergency, originally announced to fight a communist insurgency, ended in 1960, the government implemented an Internal Security Act (ISA) allowing detention without trial. Following racial riots in 1969, and a temporary suspension of

Parliament, authoritarian controls were expanded. The ISA and other government measures, such as the Sedition Act and Official Secrets Act, continued to hamper the exercise of democratic political rights, especially free expression. But these limitations on Malaysia's democracy were not fatal, and until the 1980s most observers applauded the functioning of its democratic system. The same was true of the economic system, formed in a common-law incubator.

As the Malaysian economy began to take off in the 1960s laws and legal procedures were 'market-allocative' and rule-based. In this period the procedures reflected a rights-based approach to internal government controls, and laws provided for the regulation of various professions (accounting, architecture, engineering, and so on). There was also a mix of state and market-allocative laws to support the government's economic strategy. Concomitant with the 'Look East' policy in 1981, however, abuses of public office grew, and the legal system was used extensively to implement policy. More laws conferring discretionary power to the executive were adopted than in any previous time since Malaysian independence. A common feature of these legislations was the confiding of exclusive discretionary power upon the minister to make decisions, coupled with a right to enact subsidiary legislation to better administer the statute; it also carried the ubiquitous finality clause that made his decisions final and conclusive with no right of review (Das, 1981: 2).

The Malaysian state frankly adopted the Japanese and Korean model, claiming that there was a trade-off between economic growth and democracy. The policy was anti-Western, and more especially, anti-British. Prime Minister Mahathir pursued an interventionist strategy partially modelled on South Korea's Heavy and Chemical Industries industrial policy of the early 1970s, involving close collaboration between the government and big business. What was 'Malaysia Inc.' supposed to look like?

The Malaysian government established HICOM (Heavy Industries Corporation of Malaysia) to diversify manufacturing activity, increase local linkages, and generate local technological capacity. HICOM, however, suffered significant financial losses, and these, combined with a deterioration in the terms of trade (fuelled by drops in world prices for major commodities such as petroleum and palm oil) and increasing external debt, alongside a slump in external demand in primary commodities and electronics and curtailed demand for steel, cement and cars, occasioned a recession lasting from late 1984 until 1987. As a consequence, Malaysia experienced negative growth rates and investments, both public and private, dropped precipitously. In other words, Malaysia tried to be Korea and it all ended in an embarrassing and massive failure, a fortunate outcome for rule-of-law believers attributable, among other things, to crashingly bad timing. Many of the firms the state has sponsored proved to be inefficient, usually due to cronyism, but also because there were simply too many competing firms in the region (Pillay, 2000: 209).

But the economic failure did not stop Mahathir from decisively defeating judicial activism, at the hands of the executive; basically the independence of the judiciary was destroyed in a few years in the late 1980s. Let us trace this a little bit. Previously Article 4(1) of the Constitution had proclaimed the Constitution to be supreme, and borrowing from the US model, allocated certain powers, including judicial review, to the Malaysian courts. Judicial review was also one of the five pillars of the national ideology, called the *Rukunegara*:

> The year preceding the crippling of the judiciary saw a great deal of judicial activism, with a number of important decisions going against the government, but the upshot of this judicial activism (or resistance) was that Mahathir, who had encountered no resistance in the cabinet or the Parliament, felt that he faced resistance only from the judiciary – and so judicial independence had to go. Mahathir got much assistance from the Parliament, which passed the Federal Constitution (Amendment) Act of 1988, removing the powers of the judiciary from the Constitution, deeming instead that they would be conferred by parliament through statutory decree. By this Act, the Courts were summarily stripped of the power of judicial review previously granted in the Constitution. (Milne and Mauzy, 1999: 47)

Observers were understandably shocked that the whole judicial system could so easily be transformed, but Mahathir claimed that he was merely guarding the prerogatives of the legislature to 'develop the law' (Khoo, 1995: 288). In general, laws which at first blush seemed to undergird the power of the judiciary and various checks and balances, over time were used to entrench the executive's power. Rule-making in the executive expanded as its economic activism spread, despite the significant growth of lawyers in the economy (almost 6,000 advocates and solicitors in the country by the end of 1995) (Pistor and Wellons, 1999: 91).

In short, there is precious little in the Malaysian case to suggest that the heritage of common law, a carefully-crafted democratic constitution, or several decades of human experience with the workings of the rule of law, offered much of an obstacle to an authoritarian reworking of the system. It seems more likely that Korea, moving out of its authoritarian path even as it uses the mechanisms of state intervention to do so, comes much closer to democracy and to an effective form of the rule of law than does Malaysia, going in the opposite direction. In any event neither the Korean nor the Malaysian case offers much support for the idea that learning how to act according to the ideal of disinterested third-party rule enforcement will ever be a simple or easy process of hearkening to the scholars and then acting accordingly.

5.   Conclusion: The right institutions

The concern with law and economic governance is part and parcel of the 'second generation reform', which in the words of the former President of the World Bank, James Wolfensohn (1999), refers to 'the structure of the right institutions, of the improvement of the administrative, legal, and regulatory functions of the state, addressing the incentives and actions that are required to have private sector development and to develop the institutional capacity for reforms...' First generation reform had focused on economic policies designed to make markets work more efficiently – 'pricing, exchange rate and interest rate reforms, tax and expenditure reforms and the establishment of rudimentary market institutions' (Camdessus, 1999) – but with the second wave the very structure of law and government, that is, *politics* came to the fore.

I have argued that this new emphasis on law, conceived as an elixir for developing and transitional countries, cannot solve the vexing problems of politics and development. However admirable in its intentions, the new World Bank perspective draws on a peculiarly Anglo-American discourse and experience, generalizing on the basis of a set of governmental institutions that are themselves anomalous survivors in the twentieth century – this state form that Samuel Huntington once called the 'Tudor polity' (Huntington, 1968). As the *Federalist Papers* long ago noted, the point of this state form was to disperse and confine political power, to divide it into three branches of government that would check and balance each other, to have the legislators keep an eye on the executive, the local states corral and confine the central government, and the judges watch them all. It was a form of politics suitable to an agrarian economy of yeoman farmers, and as that economy slowly became urban and industrial, no less than Thomas Jefferson condemned this transformation in the name of the pastoral ideals that underlay his conception of American governance. That was more than 200 years ago, of course, and for the past 150 years the central problem was not how to *restrain* power, but how to *create* it in the first place. Ever since, the problem of good governance has been how to comprehend and deal with the large bureaucratic central states that emerged in the context of industrialization – either to further the growth of industry, as in Germany and Japan, or to reign in the excesses of industrial capitalism, as in the American New Deal.

I think the real problem – the actually-existing practical conundrum of good *policy* – is how to find effective tools to realize the substance of arm's-length, third-party governance in the existing context of strong states that may not be 'the right institutions', but happen to be the ones we have to work with in the real world. We have to find ways to achieve the admirable goals of transparency, accountability, and disinterested justice without expecting to mimic a set of institutions developed in the tranquil, bucolic ambience of the eighteenth century; often this will be a matter of creatively utilizing those 'wrong institutions' that were the sources of past developmental success, like the heritage of administrative guidance that I focused on in this chapter.

References

Biddle, J. and Milor, V. 1999. 'Consultative Mechanisms and Economic Governance in Malaysia', Occasional Paper 38, Private Sector Development Department, World Bank.

Camdessus, M. 1999. 'Second Generation Reforms: Reflections and New Challenges'. Opening remarks to IMF Conference on Second Generation Reforms, Washington DC, 8 November.

Das, C. V. 1981. 'Administrative Law and the Citizen', *Malaysian Current Law Journal*, 1(23): 65–72, 114–117.

Davis, K. and Trebilcock, M. J. 1999. 'What Role Do Legal Institutions Play in Development?' Paper prepared for the IMF Conference on Second Generation Reforms, Washington DC, 8–9 November.

Haley, J. O. 1986. 'Administrative Guidance versus Formal Regulation: Resolving the Paradox of Industrial Policy', in G. R. Saxonhouse and K. Yamamura (eds), *Law and Trade Issues of the Japanese Economy: American and Japanese Perspectives*, Seattle: University of Washington Press.

Hashimoto, K. 1963. 'The Rule of Law: Some Aspects of Judicial Review of Administrative Action', in A. T. von Mehren (ed.), *Law in Japan*. Cambridge MA: Harvard University Press.

Hayek, F. A. von (1944, 1972) *The Road to Serfdom*, Chicago: University of Chicago Press.

Hong, J-H. 1999. 'The Rule of Law and Its Acceptance in Asia: A View from Korea', *Asia Perspectives*, 2(2): 11–18.

Huntington, S. P. 1968. *Political Order in Changing Societies*. New Haven: Yale University Press.

Johnson, C. 1982. *MITI and the Japanese Miracle: the Growth of Industrial Policy, 1925–1975*, Stanford: Stanford University Press.

Khoo, B. T. 1995. *Paradoxes of Mahathirism*. Kuala Lumpur: Oxford University Press.

La Porta, R., Lopez-de-Silanes, F., Shleifer, A. and Vishny, R. W. 1998. 'Law and Finance', *Journal of Political Economy*, 106: 1113–55.

La Porta, R., Lopez-de-Silanes, F., Shleifer, A. and Vishny, R. W. 1999. 'The Quality of Government', *Journal of Law, Economics, and Organization*, 15(1): 222–79.

La Porta, R., Lopez-de-Silanes, F., Shleifer, A. and Vishny, R. W. 2000. 'Investor Protection and Corporate Governance', *Journal of Financial Economics*, 58(2000): 3–27.

Mahoney, P. G. 1999. 'The Common Law and Economic Growth: Hayek Might be Right', *Transition*, 10(6): 28–9.

Milne, R. S. and Mauzy, D. 1999. *Malaysian Politics under Mahathir*, London and New York: Routledge.

North, D. C. (1981). *Structure and Change in Economic History*, New York: Norton.

North, D. C. (1990). *Institutions, Institutional Change and Economic Performance*, New York: Cambridge University Press.

Pillay, S. S. 2000. 'The Malay Model: Governance, Economic Management and the Future of the Development State', in F-J. Richter (ed.), *The East Asian Development Model: Economic Growth, Institutional Failure and the Aftermath of the Crisis*, New York: St Martin's Press.

Pistor, K. and Wellons, P. A. 1999. *The Role of Law and Legal Institutions in Asian Economic Development: 1960–1995*, Hong Kong: Oxford University Press and the Asian Development Bank.

Rajan, R. G. and Zingales, L. 2000. 'The Great Reversals: The Politics of Financial Development in the 20th Century'. Working Paper, University of Chicago.

Song, S. H. 1996a. 'Role of Judges in Korea', in Sang-Hyun Song (ed.), *Korean Law in the Global Economy*, Seoul: Bak Yong Sa.

Song, S. H. 1996b. 'Administrative Action, Guidance and Discretion', in Sang-Hyun Song (ed.), *Korean Law in the Global Economy*, Seoul: Bak Yong Sa.

Takayanagi, K. 1963. 'A Century of Innovation: The Development of Japanese Law, 1868–1961', in A. T. von Mehren (ed), *Law in Japan*. Cambridge MA: Harvard University Press.

Upham, F. K. 2000. 'Ideology, Experience, and the Rule of Law in Developing Societies', in M. J-E. Woo (ed.), *Neoliberalism and Institutional Reform in East Asia*, Ithaca: Cornell University Press.

West, J. M. 1998. 'Kukje and Beyond: Constitutionalism and the Market', *Seggye hŏnbŏp yŏngu (World Constitutional Law Review)* 3: 321–51.

Wolfensohn, J. 1999. Keynote Address at the IMF Conference on Second Generation Reforms, Washington DC, 8 November.

Woo, M. J-E. 1991. *Race to the Swift: State and Finance in Korean Industrialization*. New York: Colombia University Press.

Young, M. 1984. 'Judicial Review of Administrative Guidance: Governmentally Encouraged Consensual Dispute Resolution in Japan', *Colombia Law Review*, 84: 923–83.

PART III

COUNTRY EXPERIENCES

CHAPTER 10
STATE FORMATION AND THE CONSTRUCTION OF INSTITUTIONS FOR THE FIRST INDUSTRIAL NATION[1]

Patrick Karl O'Brien

'It is upon the Navy under the Providence of God that the safety, honour and welfare of this realm do chiefly attend.'
(Preamble to articles for the First Anglo-Dutch War, 1652–54)

1. Cursory remarks on the formation of states and the construction of institutions

In recent years modern economics has expanded its remit to include problems that Cunningham recommended to Marshal and is fruitfully engaged in a programme of classifying, theorizing and occasionally attempting to measure how a range of institutional variables conditions both the flow and the productivity of the inputs of land, labour, capital, technology and other more proximate determinants of economic growth (Menard and Shirley, 2005).

Perhaps economic historians, engaged with traditions of enquiry going back to the German historical school, had less need to be reminded that production and exchange across early modern Eurasia were embedded in diverse but less than enabling frameworks of law, institutions and cultures (Hodgson, 2001). Although the taxonomies and insights derived from this promising branch of economics are certainly enlightening to contemplate, there is one foundational premise where its agenda for research seems ill-informed and under-specified. Ships adrift on uncharted waters certainly deserve credit for every mile travelled in the right direction, but the 'new' economic theory of institutions has not left harbour when it comes to analysing and explaining the formation and behaviour of states (Field, 1981).

That represents a serious lacuna because throughout history states created and sustained the legal frameworks and institutions within which productive and counter-productive activities occurred. States defined and enforced property rights. States solved or failed to solve the contractual, infra-structural and coordination problems involved in extending and integrating markets. States reordered or neglected to reform ideologies, religions and cultures of behaviour in order to reduce shirking, cheating, free-riding moral hazards and transaction costs and sought ways to encourage thrift, work and innovation. Above all, states supplied economies, bounded by vulnerable frontiers but engaged in hazardous 'foreign' trade with those vitally important public goods: External security, protection at sea and internal order without which investment, innovation, production and exchange could only have remained at levels that produced stasis rather than growth (Field, 1991).

Unless economic historians opt (like many economists) to 'endogenize' their role and thereby support convenient retrodictions that the constitutions of states and frameworks of rules for the operation of economic activity altered as and when it became 'sufficiently profitable' for 'rulers', 'innovators' or 'revolutionaries' to bring about profitable transformation, they must conclude that new institutional economics, lacks a theory of state formation and *mutatis mutandis* a comprehensive theory that also includes institution building and institutional innovation (North, 1990).

So does history! Even though the preoccupations of historians have always been with the evolution of states, laws, rules, religions, ideologies and cultures conditioning personal and group behaviour. The subject's libraries are dominated by enormous volumes of research into these problems for particular places at particular times. Most of this literature does not however recognize that the formation of states took place in arenas that can be simulated to marketplaces. Historians do not find modern attempts to model the actions, inactions or failures of rulers and their servants with reference to 'trade-offs', and 'rent seeking' or even the 'revenue maximizing' behaviour of rulers particularly illuminating. Perhaps there is too much violence, path dependence, vested interest, custom, inertia, and unavoidable bargaining recorded for national and local histories of political change? Apart from the maintenance and augmentation of power they find no overriding and persistent objective that rulers attempted to maximize, which disables prospects for modelling and econometric tests, based upon assumptions of rational choice (Hall and Schroeder, 2005).

Superior insights might be derived from theories formulated to model the evolution of advantages embodies in a plurality of incentive systems established by large scale, hierarchically organized firms, producing a multiplicity of goods and services for sale to consumers. Economics begins to extend theories of industrial organization to explore conditions for efficiency among complex organizations with less clear cut objectives but charged to deliver amorphous packages of public goods, such as security, good order, health, education, environmental protection etc. (Prendergast, 1999). Unfortunately too much of the current generation of neo-classical literature has been a historical and ideologically concerned to expose bureaucratic failures; anachronistically explained as: Corruption, rent seeking, inertia, rigidities and other theoretically plausible attributes of organizations designed and run by Europe's ancient regimes to serve a multiplicity of purposes (Menard, 2003).

Until very late in the nineteenth century moral hazards and every conceivable kind of principle agent problem continued to be the omnipresent and daily concerns of states attempting to manage their armies, navies and fiscal systems and other branches of administration. The political constraints on developing departments and institutions nominally under the control of rulers and their advisers, to deliver public goods at acceptable 'fiscal' and 'political' costs were then and continue, in many third world countries today, to be formidable. Historians of European state formation recognize that the modes and scale of public and quasi-public organizations, the systems in place for the recruitment of personnel, levels of corruption, degrees of rigidity and prevalence rent seeking exemplify the multiple objectives and structural constraints restraining the operation's ancient regimes regardless of their political forms (Ertman, 1997). Historically European states made 'unavoidable' bargains with powerful vested interests required to secure compliance and stability by supplying external security, victories in war, and internal order and other public goods and rents on terms that did not threaten their own rights, legitimacy, dynastic succession, and prospects for compliance (Zmera, 2001).

During the long transition to 'Weberian' degrees of sovereignty, chains of command and bureaucratic efficiency which provided conditions for functional (not optimal) levels of efficiency, the organizational capacities at the disposal of every conceivable kind of constitutional regime (imperial, parliamentary, monarchical, oligarchical, republican and absolutist alike) remained severely constrained by evolving technologies for communication and control, as well as the omnipresent political difficulties of establishing organizations that might without stimulating undue resistance implement policies, however benign for growth (Epstein, 2002).

To achieve anything approaching successful outcomes for their policies states invariably resorted to markets and franchising. Private firms networked in tandem with politically appointed hierarchies and Crown servants to deliver even such overwhelmingly important public goods as security and internal order. Regardless of their pretensions to rule by dynastic authority (with or without divine rights) or claims to legitimacy bestowed by unrepresentative assemblies of notables, nothing serious could be accomplished without the services of private firms and individuals and above all without command over resources. That is why generations of Europe's historians have analysed the political economy of taxation as the entrée and key to the comprehension of state formation. How different states constructed and sustained complex fiscal policies and how well their trusted advisers, franchised administrations or appointed bureaucracies charged to assess and collect an astonishing variety of direct and indirect taxed performed has been under investigation since Jean Bodin (Bonney, 1995).

2.   Liberal and mercantilist narratives of state formation in the United Kingdom

2.1.   *Liberal myths and mercantilist realities*

This chapter is a contribution to a programme for the construction of a general theory of state formation, elite behaviour and institution building by governments. Historically-based studies of this kind might expose the geographical and political, as well as the economic, conditions that favoured the emergence of ideal type 'Weberian' states in some polities before others.[2] It will, moreover, be my aim to restore in brief compass a representation of state formation and institution building in the United Kingdom that degrades an established 'Whig' view of Britain's famous economic transition to an industrial market economy as *a*, if not *the*, 'paradigm case', supporting a Washington Consensus for *laissez-faire*, free trade, democratic governance, and the triumph of private enterprises virtually unassisted by help from the state (North and Weingast, 1989). There may even be some lessons here for developing economies but I will confine them to my conclusion.

Unfortunately (and as a liberal myth that is all to congenial to modern economics) by default something approximating to a Washington Consensus has also dominated the writing of British economic history since Ashton published his classic text on the Industrial Revolution in 1948. As a scion of the Manchester school Ashton almost ignores central government because he wrote history from below and saw entrepreneurs and artisans as the prime movers behind economic change and observed that 'the instinct of the industrialists was to eschew politics. It was not by the arts of lobbying or propaganda, but by unremitting attention to their concerns they became a power – perhaps the greatest power – in the state' (Ashton, 1950: 132). His neglect of metropolitan government (followed by almost all writers of textbooks on this famous conjuncture in British history) emanates not only from ideological representations (derived from Adam Smith) concerning the nature of the kingdom's pre-industrial ancient regime as one of corrupt, aristocratic and expensive governance; but more significantly of from preconceptions that flow from a shortened chronology for any serious historical analysis of Britain's precocious transition to an industrial market economy. Unfortunately, with agendas of their own and carrying from their schoolbooks recollections of the 'Whig' tradition in England's political history, the 'new' political economy of its Glorious Revolution continues to represent that Dutch *coup d'état* in 1688 as a triumph for democratic rule over royal tyranny; a victory for private enterprise over public monopolies, a felicitous substitution of science for religion, and more recently as a crucial commitment by way of the triumph of 'Parliamentary' governance to secure property rights and the rule law. It is no surprise that institutional economists rely upon anachronistic history. They find it easier to reach for the First Industrial Revolution as the paradigm, a historical case study of political commitments maturing teleologically into an optimally designed set of 'liberal' institutions for Britain's long term economic growth (Goldstone, 2002).

Braudel insisted, however, that the formation of states which accompanied the growth of economies can only be comprehended by studying very long time spans, which might expose underlying and enduring geographical, geopolitical and political structures conditioning economic performance, not as waves or tides, but as the sea and the sea bed (Braudel, 1984). By focussing on *la longue durée*, historians might locate structural parameters as well as significant conjunctures which, looked at retrospectively, from some vantage or end point could help social scientists to mobilize and reconfigure historical evidence in order to shape more plausible narratives and to endow histories with theoretical, statistical, and rhetorically persuasive power.

Alas, only a précis of the long and complex history of English state formation (1453–1815) as a necessary perspective and basis for the comprehension of the institutions constructed and sustained through to a first industrial revolution could possibly be presented here (but see Mann, 1986). My concentration for purposes of brevity upon the fiscal and budgetary 'architecture' of the state behind the construction of English institutions might however expose conjunctures in its evolution, which did not occur as an outcome of the Glorious Revolution of 1688, in the wake of the publication of the Wealth of Nations in 1776, or even follow the passage of the first Parliamentary reform bill of 1832, but rather 'came to pass' with the final defeat (1805–15) of Iberian, Dutch, American and above all, French pretensions to countervail the realm's 'mercantilist and maritime strategy' for: The provision of those pervasively important public goods for the security of the realm, for internal stability, for British commerce overseas and for the acquisition and protection of the largest occidental empire since Rome (Ferguson, 2002).

2.2.   *The formation of a fiscal state*

Economically Britain did exceptionally well during a long upswing in trans-continental trade that succeeded the consolidation of the Qing dynasty (1644–83) and which coincided with the break-up of the Mughal empire in India (1761–1818) (Pomeranz, 2000). Was that (as some famous global economic historians maintain) because the country's Parliamentary system of governance, institutions and its cultures of behaviour and enterprise had become clearly more hospitable to private investment and innovation than comparable responses from its rivals on the mainland or located in those rich maritime regions of China and Tokugawa Japan (Landes, 1998)? Comparative research into the histories of European economies has left us more agnostic about the superiorities of the realm's institutions and cultures. A recently rediscovered 'world of surprising resemblances' across a range of advanced economic regions of Eurasia undergoing Smithian growth for centuries before the First Industrial Revolution has effectively degraded both Marxian and Weberian perceptions that only certain countries of North Western Europe (particularly England), had proceeded far along trajectories of institution building or up learning curves towards cultures promotional for modern economic growth (Frank, 1998).

Nevertheless one significant contrast between Britain and all other pre-modern candidates for a First Industrial Revolution remains heuristic to study. Under restoration here that salient contrast will be located in the kingdom's geographically conditioned process of state formation which became inseparable from a sustained commitment by Crown, Parliament and its elites to a maritime strategy for the defence of the realm, which, over time, turned out to carry unintended but benign consequences for the protection of foreign trade, internal stability and the expansion of a leading maritime sector for the development of the economy.

Not long after the First Hundred Years War (1337–1453) when England's feudal armies had ignominiously retreated from centuries of dynastic and imperialistic warfare on the mainland, the Island's kings, aristocrats and merchants began to conceive of naval power as the first line of defence against external threats to the security of their Island realm and as the force required to back conquest and commerce with continents other than mainland Europe (Rodger, 1997). For several reasons that conception took nearly two centuries (1453–1649) to mature into a political and fiscal commitment by its elites for the defence of a vulnerable and unstable kingdom and for the realization of its potential as a maritime power and economy. First, internal colonization, the expropriation of ecclesiastical property and free riding upon the research development and investments undertaken by Iberians to support commerce with Asia and colonization in the Americas continued to be more attractive and easier options for Tudor and Stuart monarchs (1485–1642) and their coteries of courtiers and predatory territorial magnates to pursue (Lenman, 2001). Second, and despite the vulnerability of the Tudor dynasty and the kingdom to threats of invasion and takeover, initially by France in the reign of Henry VIII and then more seriously by Spanish Armadas, despatched by Philip II, the aristocracies and the propertied elites assembled periodically in the Houses of Lords and Commons to discuss taxes (and very little else except religion) successfully resisted all attempts by the Crown to deepen and widen its fiscal base in order to fund the resources required to establish standing forces (navies as well as armies) of sufficient scale, scope, and technological capability to defend the realm, maintain internal order and protect private investment in commerce and colonization overseas (Braddick, 1996).

Eventually nearly two centuries of fiscal stasis, economically malign disputes over religion and persistent acrimony over the crown's rights to taxation, culminated in an 'interregnum' (1642–60) of highly destructive civil war, republican rule, and the restoration of monarchy and aristocracy, which in outcome (replete with unintended consequences) led to the formation of a modern and effective state (Hirst, 1999).

As well as truly massive destruction of life and capital, this famous conjuncture witnessed: The most serious threats to hierarchy and property rights in English history, the appreciation by wealthy elites (represented in Parliament) of the advantages attending the establishment of a standing fleet of warships under centralized control of the Crown, for the defence of an island realm, as well as the externalities generated by a Royal Navy for the maintenance of that other and equally significant public good – internal order. Above all, the majority of stakeholders in the wealth of the realm recognized the inter-related needs for the reconstruction of a fiscal and financial system that could provide the funds required for its security, for the stability of the regime and for the protection of an established and highly inegalitarian system of property rights, to assets and capital located within the kingdom, to merchant ships on the high seas and to capital invested in bases, plantations and colonies in England's expanding empire in the Americas, Africa, and Asia (Russell, 1971).

Following on from a series of republican and royalist experiments with the political principles, methods of assessment and collection of taxes, a reconstructed fiscal base came into place under a restored Stuart king. Constitutionally that base rested, first and foremost, upon his reaffirmation of the tradition that English monarchs could not levy taxes without formal consent from the House of Commons (Hutton, 1990).

Thereafter, Parliament only presumed to control royal expenditures but hardly ever withheld consent for supply; particularly in wartime, when the loyalty of honourable members to the protestant succession and national ideology could be called into question by their aristocratic patrons or arraigned before the xenophobic and loyal public opinion of Britons (Colley, 1992). Predictable degrees of compliance with demands from the restored state depended upon three major and quasi-constitutional reforms that were effectively institutionalized before the Dutch *coup d'état* removed all traces of the taint of Catholicism from the English monarchy in 1688.

Figure 10.1 Total taxes collected for the state, 1490–1820

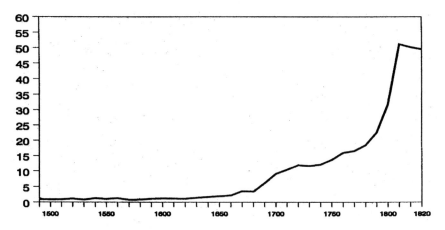

Notes: The points plotted are 9-year moving averages for every tenth year 1490–1820, measured in constant prices of 1451-75. Unit: millions of £ sterling

Source: http://www.le.ac.uk./hi/bon/.ESFD/tax.html, see also Bonney (1999).

First (and before Pitt introduced a wartime income tax act in 1799) the restored state reluctantly abandoned a long history of futile attempts, going back to Domesday of 1086, to assess direct taxes on the income and wealth of households according to some pre-specified, transparent and centrally monitored criteria to pay. Instead it settled (with no serious resistance from Parliament) for an extension of royal powers over indirect taxes and for control of their administrations (which replaced franchised tax farming). Customs and tariffs, which had been part of England's fiscal constitution since the Middle Ages, were supplemented and complemented and eventually dominated by excise and stamp 'duties' (long established on the mainland) to form an integrated and productive system of indirect taxation (Tomlinson, 1979).

Coherence in fiscal policy then came into operation because the selected and carefully calibrated range of products and services subjected to these novel internal duties in effect received virtually complete protection from imports and exemptions (in some cases bounties) when exported or re-exported overseas (Ashworth, 2003). Following the Interregnum an accelerated and radical shift from direct to indirect forms of taxation occurred and the system became outstandingly successful in supplying the English state with the revenues required to fund the provision of external security and internal stability with commercial and imperial expansion overseas. Between 1670 and 1810 total revenues from taxes rose around 16 times in real terms, while national income increased by a multiplier of 3 (O'Brien, 1988).

More significantly the augmented and predictable inflows of indirect taxes provided the state with the means to borrow ever increasing amounts of money from the sale of redeemable, irredeemable, short and long-term bills and bonds on London, Amsterdam and other European capital markets. Loans (also subject to formal but never withheld Parliamentary approval) serviced by hypothecated receipts from indirect taxes can be represented as an English innovation copied from the Dutch that introduced flexibility into the capacities of the Island state to fund defence, with internal order and support altogether more aggressive and expansionist, mercantilist, and geopolitical strategies against rival European (and eventually Asian) economies which were designed to reap gains from trade and colonization overseas (Dickson, 1993).

Between 1652 and 1815 the English state engaged in eleven wars against its leading economic competitors (mainly conflicts with France and Spain, but including four wars against the Netherlands). After 1689 something like 80 per cent of all the incremental revenues required to mobilize its forces emanated from loans and the nominal capital of the national debt grew from less than £2 million in the reign of James II to the astronomical sum of £854 million or 2.7 times the national income for 1819 and the share of taxes devoted to servicing government debt jumped from modal ratios of 2–3 per cent before the Glorious Revolution to 60 per cent after the Napoleonic War. When Castlereagh signed the Treaty of Vienna in 1815 (which, for global commerce, effectively marks the end of the era of mercantilism) the, by then, United Kingdom possessed unchallengeable hegemony at sea, controlled the largest occidental empire since Rome, enjoyed extraordinary shares of world trade and income from servicing international commerce and its integrated domestic economy stood half way through an Industrial Revolution (O'Brien, 2002).

One of the major reasons why Britain found itself in such an envied and feared position at that conjuncture in European and global geopolitical history, is because the reconstructed Stuart state (taken over by William of Orange and his German successors) allocated very high and rising proportions (85 per cent is the modal ratio) of all the rapidly increased flows of revenue and by British and foreign investors to sustain much larger (and potentially more efficient) navies and armies than had been possible for two centuries before and for some decades after the Republic interregnum.

Figure 10.2 Debt servicing ratios as a percentage of total taxes, 1688–1814

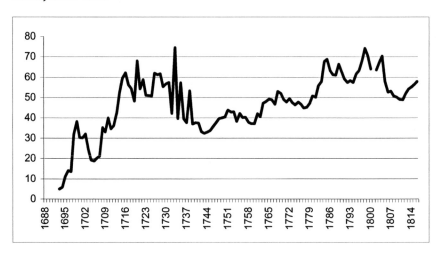

Source: Parliamentary papers (1868–69).

Apart from contemporary and recently repeated Whig spin, about the foundations of Parliamentary sovereignty the really significant outcomes that flowed from the Glorious Revolution of 1688 resided in profound changes to the realm's foreign and strategic policies exemplified by and sustained by an immediate uplift and sharp rise in real expenditures on the armed forces. That uplift was sustained over a Second Hundred Years War with France, increased erratically from war to war to reach a very high ratio of around 15 per cent of gross domestic product by the closing years of an era of mercantilism during the final conflict with Napoleon (Prados de la Escosura, 2004).

3. A maritime strategy for the security, stability, and economic growth of the realm 1688–1815

In an international economic order riven with dynastic and imperial rivalries, the Island state's allocations of resources to preclude invasion, preserve internal stability and retain advantages over its competitors in armed

Figure 10.3 Total tax revenues expressed as shares of conjectures for national income, 1490s to 1810s

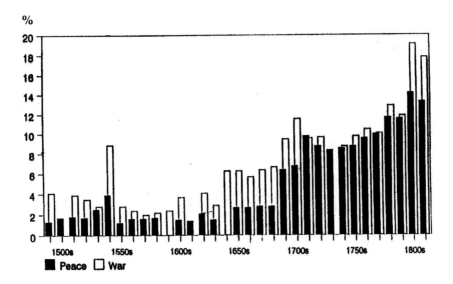

Notes: The ratios, measured in current prices, refer to the lowest percentage for a given peace time year and the highest percentage for a war year within each decade. In the 1490s the king collected a low of 1.3 per cent in peacetime and a high of 4.1 per cent in wartime.

struggles for gains from global commerce and colonization formed the inescapable geopolitical parameters within which institution-building for sustained macro economic growth occurred (Magnusson, 1993). In that mercantilist international economic order, analyses concerned with the distortions from competitive equilibria wrought by taxation or counterfactual scenarios concerned with unmeasured 'crowding out' effects that flowed from high levels of government borrowing are interesting, but anachronistic exercises for economists to pursue (Digby, 1992). In that sense they are largely irrelevant to questions of how the English state raised and allocated the resources that carried the kingdom and its economy to a plateau of safety, political stability and potential for future development envied at the Congress of Vienna, and whether governments of the day proceeded in ways that could be plausibly represented as functional for the building of institutions and the growth of the economy. Since nobody then or now elaborated alternative strategies which combined security for the realm with the growth for the economy, predictable advice from historians to study what was done, compare English strategies with those pursued by other European and Asian powers and perhaps conclude (with Voltaire) that virtually everything that was done was done for the best in the *worst* of all possible worlds looks sensible (O'Brien, 1998).

With hindsight that appears to be the appropriate Panglossian stance to take on the maritime strategy pursued for the defence of the Isles, (a persuasive notion floating under the Tudors and early Stuarts) but taken forward during the Commonwealth to mature into a well-funded and binding commitment by the restored monarchical state to a standing navy of the size and technical capability required to preclude invasions by sea. That commitment which has continued to our own era of airpower made sense to Cromwell's isolated Republic in possession of funds (expropriated from Charles I and his treasonable supporters) to invest heavily in the building of warships, in order to protect overseas trade and countervail royalist inspired invasions supported by outraged kings from the mainland. Ironically the Republic's large 'model fleet' escorted Charles II back to his kingdom (Seaward, 1991). The restored state (stimulated by widespread anxiety aroused by Colbert's programme to build a modern and superior French Navy) responded to its 'natural and necessary enemy' by constructing and maintaining the largest and most powerful navy in Europe. Thereafter (with occasional lapses) the Royal Navy defended the realm, won a string of famous victories at sea and (through a range of benign interconnexions) helped, in no small way, to carry an expanding maritime and leading sector of the British economy towards levels of integration, competitive efficiency and potential for precocious industrialization (Black and Woodfine, 1988).

Between 1700 and 1815 persistently high levels of public expenditure on the Royal Navy probably exceeded private allocations for gross domestic capital formation and in times of war amounted to around half of the value of Britain's exports, plus re-exports. This commitment provided the kingdom with the world's largest fleet of battleships, cruisers and frigates, manned by a coerced workforce of able seamen, managed by a well motivated corps of upwardly mobile officers. Britain's huge fleet was constructed and maintained in readiness for multiple missions at sea by a skilled workforce of shipwrights, carpenters and other artisans and serviced by an infra-structure of ports, harbours, dockyards, stores for victuals and spare parts, ordnance depots and other onshore facilities in both public and private ownership and control (Rodger, 2004).

Figure 10.4 Numbers of warships in the service of the Royal and rival navies, 1650–1810

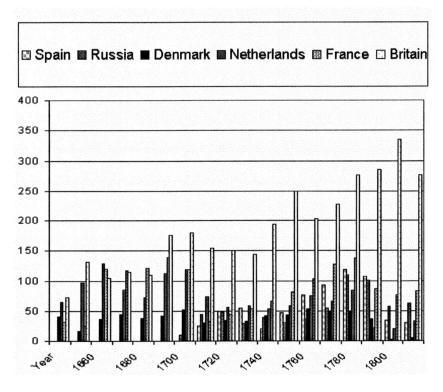

Source: Glete (1993).

The Royal Navy and its onshore infra-structure of human and physical capital accorded top priority to maintaining ships of the line strategically placed at sea as the first bastion of defence for the realm. At declining average cost the Navy also sustained cruisers, frigates and other well armed ships for 'mercantilist missions' designed for the protection of British trade and its colonies; for predation on all 'hostile' and potentially hostile merchant marines; for the bombardment of the enemy's maritime cities and colonies, for the interdiction of competitive trade, and finally for gunboat diplomacy (Ormrod, 2003).

In addition the state's strategy for defence turned out to include all kinds of unanticipated advantages for internal stability, for protection of property rights and the growth of Britain's home and colonial economies. First, a huge fleet of durable, strategically placed and proficient ships of the line (floating fortresses) provided external security at a relatively high level of efficiency compared to the logistical costs per joule of force delivered larger European armies (Anders, 2003).

Paradoxically, this relatively low cost, and in outcome, highly successful and economically significant offshore strategy for defence allowed the British state to spend more upon its armed forces and to allocate greater proportions of its already elastic fiscal and financial resources not only to complementary mercantilist and imperial missions pursued at sea, but to sustain surprisingly high levels of expenditure upon hiring and equipping soldiers. Throughout the period 1688–1815, the military share of expenditures on armed force by the European state most committed to naval defence and aggression fluctuated but amounted to a modal 60 per cent. Part of that allocation included the costs of hiring of mercenary regiments of Hanoverian, Hessian and other soldiers for combat outside the kingdom; part consisted of subsidies and subventions to European allies willing to field troops to thwart the designs of France and its allies on the mainland, or in India and the Americas; and finally, part consisted of the commitment of serious numbers of British troops to theatres of war on the continent, notably in 1702–12 and again in 1808–15 (Parliamentary Papers, 1868–69). Expenditures on military forces engaged directly or indirectly with rival armies prevented Bourbon states (France and Spain) and their European allies from allocating funds to construct fleets of a size and capability required to mount more serious challenges to the Royal Navy's defence of the realm and its increasingly effective protection and aggressive promotion of British interests overseas (Baugh, 1988).

The largest proportion of military expenditure was allocated, however, to British regiments, militias, volunteers and yeomanry on stations in the realm. This force formed a less than credible second line of defence against invasions, but was utilized consistently, successfully, and economically over a period of population growth and rapid urbanization to preserve the stability of the regime against subversion and to protect hierarchy and property rights against periodic but serious challenges to internal law and order

(Palmer, 1978). Prospects for trade across a less than United Kingdom came, from time to time, under serious threat from within its potentially seditious Celtic provinces of Scotland and Ireland; particularly the latter where a colonized Catholic population resented 'English' property rights and the metropole's discriminatory regulation of local commerce and industry. With external security taken as given, stability, good order, respect for an established inegalitarian system of property rights and the maintenance of hierarchy over their potentially unruly employees became a key political-cum-economic interest for landowners, merchants, farmers, industrialists, and other businessmen of Hanoverian Britain. On the whole, their 'monarchical and aristocratic' state met concerns for the protection of property and for the maintenance of social control. When necessary Parliament redefined the legal rights enjoyed by propertied elites by promulgating statutes for the realm which superseded common laws that might otherwise be interpreted by the judiciary as providing protection for the interests of the majority of the nation's workforce without assets, status and political power.

Modern social historians (less impressed than their Whig predecessors with Parliament's rhetorical antipathies to standing armies in times of peace) have made us aware that the actual numbers of troops, embodied militiamen and patriotic volunteers on station in Britain and Ireland year after year and (particularly in wartime) were more than adequate to deter and repress disturbances to the peace (Emsley, 1983). For purposes of political stability, maintaining internal order, the protection of property and upholding hierarchies of all kinds, it is not at all obvious that on a per capita basis, the political and legal authorities of constitutional Britain commanded less effective coercive force than those despotisms on the mainland of Europe. Indeed in 1808 the numbers of soldiers mobilized to combat Luddites in the Midlands and North of England exceeded troops under Wellington's command in the Peninsular (Townsend, 1982).

4.   Conclusions: Public goods, security, stability, internal order, and the growth of the economy

Somehow through eleven wars (which included three, perhaps four, occasions when French and Spanish admirals failed to take advantage of openings in the kingdom's first line of defence) the Royal Navy retained command of the Channel and the North Sea. Throughout the period which witnessed Britain's combined geopolitical and economic rise, the Navy's guard over Western and Eastern approaches to the Isles, blockades of enemy naval bases, the interdiction of their supplies of strategic raw materials and weapons and occasional pre-emptive strikes effectively prevented any rival fleet from clearing a viable sea route for the landing of armies on the kingdom's shores (Rodger, 1997). In wartime the proportions of the British workforce (particularly skilled artisans) drafted into the army (the country's secondary line of defence) remained low. Troops (and embodied militias) required for defence and service overseas could, moreover, be recruited overwhelmingly from among the unskilled under employed fringes (often Celtic and Colonial) of an expanding imperial workforce or, when necessary, hired as mercenary soldiers from more labour abundant societies on the mainland. While the Navy operated as the realm's main relatively cheap but highly effective first line of defence, the state purchased foreign troops and funded a home army which (together with local militias) remained on call for the preservation of the internal order necessary for investment, innovation and the integration of the kingdom's markets and economic growth. With virtually no civil police at their command, the Navy allowed the political authorities (central and local) of Hanoverian Britain to allocate less of their revenues, to give smaller weight to external security and to afford more for the provision of an effective military presence and exemplary displays of the armed and flexible force required to maintain good order, protect property and preserve authority over a potentially 'ungovernable population' becoming urban and industrial, but eventually more orderly and deferential by the year (Emsley, 1983).

Although the significance of an expanding fiscal base and the direct benefits and externalities from the state's unswerving commitment to a maritime strategy became clear enough after the Republic, naval historians could be dissatisfied with any narrative which accounted for the long term superiority for 'their' Royal Navy in terms of geographical advantages, along with the creation of institutions that delivered the taxes and loans required for high and sustained levels of investment in warships and their on-shore infra-structural support systems. They prefer to discuss: Technological and economic leads and lags in the costs and designs of European warships and their guns; the quality of British, compared to enemy crews of seamen; the recruitment, promotion and incentive systems surrounding officers in charge of battleships, cruisers and frigates. Furthermore, (but only latterly) they have started to investigate the relative efficiencies of centrally coordinated organizations, firms and networks on shore that constructed, repaired and maintained armed ships for service at sea. They are looking across Europe into the admiralties, boards and commissions that recruited and motivated officers and their coerced or conscripted crews to achieve an evolving plurality of objectives selected by states for their standing navies (Morris, 2004).

Repeated assertions (written in the glow of its victories at sea) that the long-run success of the Royal Navy is clearly imputable to British technology, better seamanship, bravery in battle, effective tactics, carefully designed incentives, more efficient logistical support systems, the Nelson factor and, above all, to the inherent superiorities of Parliamentary systems of governance in formulating policies and constructing complex organizations for their implementation and coordination will be very difficult to demonstrate without an extensive research programme in comparative political and institutional histories. Research for systematic comparisons of navies as national institutions is not out there and it is not clear that economic theory will be that helpful (Dixit, 2002). Meanwhile most patriotic claims by British naval historians are simply not proven.

In any case economists will be more interested in a specified and quantified elaboration of long-run economic outcomes connected to Britain's maritime strategy for the defence of the realm, combined with successful mercantilism and colonialism (Chang, 2002). In an essay designed to adumbrate upon connexions between state formation and the construction of institutions that provided for effective external security, regime stability, internal order and the protection of established property rights, that elaboration must await another paper. Meanwhile major and familiar, backward and forward linkages that configure the Royal Navy at the *hub* of an evolving, integrating and progressive maritime sector of an Island economy in process of securing an inordinate share of the gains from global commerce by sea between 1660 and 1846, can be mentioned simply as headings for discussion and future research. For example, several obvious backward linkages run from naval expenditures upon ships, canvas, ropes, timber, ordnance, small arms, bar iron, pitch, tar, and other raw materials, as well as the preserved foodstuffs required to feed sailors at sea. Naval demands for ships and seamen during frequent interludes of warfare imparted a measure of stability that reduced risks for merchants and investors engaged in overseas as well as coastal trades.

Forward linkages and spinoffs may well, however, prove virtually impossible to quantify because they appear across such an extensive range of industries and services connected with cheap transportation by sea. For example, the economic benefits that Britain's mercantile marine, fisheries, coastal shipping, and related industries derived in the form of subsidized and relatively effective protection against predation by enemy powers and piracy – as well as two centuries of fairly effective enforcement of Navigation Acts (promulgated to reserve metropolitan and imperial trade by sea for British shipping and mercantile services) have so far defied measurement.

Furthermore, and if an implied counterfactual specified to quantify the costs and benefits of high and sustained investment in naval power is conceived more broadly to encompass externalities from networking and gains from agglomeration that accrued from the concentration of industry and commerce within the island's array of favourably located and well defended maritime towns and cities, then investment in sea power begins to look like a substantial (if not indispensable component) of any comprehensive narrative (or analysis) about the First Industrial Nation. At the time the Royal Navy certainly occupied a position of the very highest esteem in public opinion; contributed in no small way to the trust and deference that all classes reposed in their ancient monarchical and aristocratic constitution and helped the state secure a greater degree of compliance for its ever increasing demands for taxation than was ever accorded to Britain's rivals on the mainland (Lincoln, 2002).

If and when economic historians begin to analyse connexions between state formation and the construction of institutions and turn to that most enduringly efficient of British institutions, and consider the Royal Navy at the hub of a leading maritime sector for an Island economy, they could well conclude that British naval power was an indispensable protective shield of an engine for trade with growth, pressed forward along learning curves and cumulating mechanisms for reinforcement by the combined investments of the kingdom's private and public sectors in a rather coherent strategy for security, stability, good order and precocious structural change. That representation could never be a comprehensive narrative of the First Industrial Revolution, but even as restored history from above, it makes for more plausible chapters in a story than Whiggish rhetoric that highlights Parliamentary government, private enterprise, liberalism and *laissez-faire*. To some significant degree (and despite bowdlerized versions of Adam Smith) an Industrial Revolution emerged on the Isles as the outcome of aggressive and successful mercantilism. In the beginning was a fiscal state with its Royal Navy.

Lessons for today from this exceptional and precocious case will, however, be difficult to draw simply because the economic gains and spin-offs that an ancien regime derived from geopolitical aggression are no longer available. Some rather obvious points do however stand out.

State formation conditions the construction of institutions. States cannot implement strategies and build institutions to promote development unless they obtain the fiscal resources and degrees of autonomy to provide external security, internal stability, and good order. It may take something like a regime change followed by an interregnum of autocratic rule for powerful elites of stakeholders in established property rights to unite around the consensus required to form a Weberian state and comply with demands for the taxes it needed to support national development with internal stability.

Notes

1. I am very grateful to Ha-Joon Chang, Bill Lazonick, and Eric Rauchway for helping me to clarify and sharpen the argument.
2. Some states (England, Holland, and possibly Prussia) constructed and managed the bureaucracies, departments and complex organizations required to raise revenues, investigate and solve problems, preserve stability and delivery arrays of public goods that promoted rather than restrained economic growth sooner and more effectively than others, including France, Spain, and Austria (Tilly, 1990). It seems that political pre-requisites for the formation and integration of markets emerged in the Chinese empire long before Europe, the Americas, and Africa (Wong, 1997).

References

Ashton, T. S. 1950. *The Industrial Revolution 1760–1830*. Oxford: Oxford University Press.

Ashworth, W. 2003. *Customs and Excise: Trade Production and Consumption in England, 1640–1845*. Oxford: Oxford University Press.

Baugh, D. 1988. 'Great Britain's Blue Water Policy 1689–1815', *International Historical Review*, X, 38–58.

Black, J. and Woodfine, P. (eds) 1988. *The British Navy and Use of Naval Power in the Eighteenth Century*, Leicester: Leicester University Press.

Blockmans, W. and Genet, J-P. (eds) 1995–99. *The Origins of the Modern State in Europe*, 7 volumes, Oxford: Oxford University Press.

Bonney, R. 1995. 'Early Modern Theories of State Finance', in R. Bonney (ed.) *Economic Systems and State Finance*, Oxford: Oxford University Press.

Bonney, R. 1999. 'Introduction', in R. Bonney (ed.) *The Rise of the Fiscal State in Europe c. 1200–1815*, Oxford: Oxford University Press.

Braddick, M. 1996. *The Nerves of State: Taxation and the Financing of the English State 1558–1714*, Manchester: Manchester University Press.

Braudel, F. 1984. *Civilization and Capitalism*, 3: 71–85, London: Collins.

Chang, H. J. 2002. *Kicking Away the Ladder – Development Strategy in Historical Perspective*. London: Anthem Press.

Colley, L. 1992. *Britons: Forging the Nation*. New Haven, Yale.

Dickson, P. M. G. 1993. *The Financial Revolution in England. A Study in the Development of Public Credit 1688–1756*, Aldershot: Gregg.

Digby, A. et al. (eds) 1992. *New Directions in Economic and Social History*, Basingstoke: Macmillan.

Dixit, A. 2002. 'Incentives and Organizations in the Public Sector. An Interpretative Review', *Journal of Human Resources*, XXXVII: 696–713.

Emsley, C. 1983. 'Military and Popular Disorder in England 1790–1801', *Journal of the Society for Army Historical Research*, LXI: 10–21 and 97–111

Emsley, C. 1987. *Crime and Society in England 1750–1900*, Basingstoke: Macmillan.

Epstein, S. R. 2002. *Freedom and Growth. The Rise of States and Markets in Europe* 1300–1750, London: Routledge.

Ertman, T. 1997. *Birth of the Leviathan, Building States and Regimes in Medieval and Early Modern Europe*, Cambridge: Cambridge University Press.

Ferguson, N. 2002. *The Cash Nexus. Money and Power in the Modern World 1700–2000*. London: Allen Lane.

Field, A. 1981. 'The Problem with Neoclassical Institutional Economics', *Explorations in Economic History*, 18:174–98.

Field, A. 1991. 'Do Legal Systems Matter?' *Explorations in Economic History*, 28: 1–35.

Frank, A. G. 1998. *Reorient. Global Economy in the Asian Age*, Berkeley: University of California Press.

Glete, J. 1993. *Navies and Nations: Warships, Navies and State Building in Europe and America 1500–1860*, 2 vols. Stockholm: AWI.

Goldstone, J. 2002. 'Europe's Peculiar Path: Would the World be Modern if William III's Invasion of England in 1688 had Failed?', in W. Lebow et al. (eds) *Counterfactual History*, New York: Norton, pp. 26–38

Hall, J. and Schroeder, R. (eds). 2005. *The Anatomy of Power*, Cambridge: Cambridge University Press.

Hirst, D. 1999. *England in Conflict 1603–60*. London: Arnold.

Hodgson, G. M. 2001. *How Economics Forgot History*. London: Routledge.

Hutton, R. 1990. *The British Republic 1649–60*. London: Arnold.

Landers, J. 2003. *The Field and the Forge. Population, Production and Power in the Pre-industrial West*. Oxford: Oxford University Press.

Landes, D. 1998. *The Wealth and Poverty of Nations*. New York: Little Brown.

Lenman, B. 2001. *England's Colonial Wars 1550–1688*. Basingstoke: Palgrave.

Lincoln, M. 2002. *Representing the Royal Navy. British Sea Power, 1750–1815*. Aldershot: Ashgate.

Magnusson, L. (ed.) 1993. *Mercantilist Economics*. London, Routledge.

Mann, M. 1986. *The Sources of Social Power, Vol. 1 A History of Power from the Beginning to AD 1760*. Cambridge: Cambridge University Press.

Menard, C. 2003. 'The New Institutional Approach to Institutions: Concepts, Methods and Results', *Social Science Tribune*, 3: 5–25.

Menard, C. and Shirley, M. N. (eds) 2005. *Handbook for New Institutional Economics*. Boston: Kluwer.

Morris, R. 2004. *Naval Power and British Culture, Public Trust and Government Ideology*. Aldershot: Ashgate.

North, D. C. and Weingast, B. 1989. 'Constitutions and Commitment: Evolution of Institutions Governing Public Choice in Seventeenth Century England', *Journal of Economic History*, 49: 11–24.

North, D. 1990. *Institutions, Institutional Change and Economic Performance*, Cambridge: Cambridge University Press.

O'Brien, P. K. 1988. 'The Political Economy of British Taxation, 1660–1815', *Economic History Review*, 41: 1–32.

O'Brien, P. K. 1998, 'Inseparable Connexions. Trade, Economy, Fiscal State and the Expansion of Empire', in P. J. Marshall (ed.) *The Oxford History of the British Empire. The Eighteenth Century*, Oxford: Oxford University Press, pp. 53–78.

O'Brien, P. K. 2002. 'Fiscal Exceptionalism: Great Britain and its European Rivals from Civil War to Triumph at Trafalgar and Waterloo' in Winch, D. (ed.) *The Political Economy of British Historical Experience*, Oxford: Oxford University Press, pp. 245–66.

Ormrod, D. 2003. *The Rise of Commercial Empires. England and the Netherlands in the Age of Mercantilism 1650–1770*. Cambridge: Cambridge University Press.

Parliamentary Paper (1868–69) 'Accounts of the public income and expenditure', pp. 1868–69 (XXXV).

Palmer, S. H. 1978. 'Calling out the Troops. The Military, the Law and Public Order in England 1650–1850', *Journal of the Society for Army Historical Research*, 56: 198–214.

Pomeranz, K. 2000. 'The Great Divergence. China, Europe and the Making of the Modern World Economy', Princeton: Princeton University Press.

Prados de la Escosura, L. (ed.) 2004. *Exceptionalism and Industrialization. Britain and its European Rivals, 1688–1815*, Cambridge: Cambridge University Press.

Prendergast, C. 1999. 'The Provision of Incentives in Firms', *Journal of Economic Literature*, 37: 7–63.

Rodger, N. A. M. 1997. *The Safeguard of the Sea. A Naval History of Britain, vol. 1, 660–1649*, London: Allen Lane.

Rodger, N. A. M. 2004. *The Command of the Ocean. A Naval History of Britain, 1649–1815*. London: Allen Lane.

Russell, C. 1971. *The Crisis of Parliaments: English History 1509–1660*. Oxford: Oxford University Press

Seaward, P. 1991. *The Restoration*. London: Longman.

Sylla, R. and Toniolo, G. (eds) 1991. *Patterns of European Industrialization*. London: Routledge.

Tilly, C. 1990. *Coercion, Capital and European States 990–1990*. Oxford: Oxford University Press.

Tomlinson, H. L. 1979. 'Financial and Administrative Developments', in J. R. Jones (ed.) *The Restored Monarch 1660–88*. London: Longman.

Townsend, C. 1982. 'Martial law, Legal and Political Problems of Civil Emergency in Britain and the Empire', *Historical Journal*, 1:167–95.

Wong, R. B. 1997. *China Transformed: Historical Change and the Limits of European Experience*. Ithaca: Cornell.

Zmera, H. 2001. *Monarchy, Aristocracy and the State in Europe 1300–1800*. London: Routledge.

CHAPTER 11
THE ROLE OF FEDERALISM IN DEVELOPING THE US DURING NINETEENTH-CENTURY GLOBALIZATION

Eric Rauchway

Despite disputes over the inputs to globalization in the long nineteenth century, the major outcome has been generally agreed since at least the publication of Sellar and Yeatman's assessment of the world at 1918: 'America was thus clearly top nation, and History came to a .'[1] Later refinements in this view stress the United States of America's position as principal beneficiary of the free movement of both labour and capital in the 'first great globalization boom', but the essential point remains the same: The US received the lion's share of internationally mobile capital and labour (O'Rourke and Williamson, 1999: 4), and the Americans made such profitable use of these additions to their already prodigious factor endowment that they transformed their nation from the world's great debtor to its great creditor and stood ready, at least economically, to assume the role of 'top nation', as recently vacated by Great Britain.

We might therefore suppose that, as an outlier in the pool of developing nations, the US would not provide usable lessons in the role of institutions on the course of development. But this is true only if we consider national economies as impervious black boxes – if we think in Sellar-and-Yeatmanesque terms of top *nations*. If we consider that regions within the US developed unevenly, we should learn a set of lessons from the American *regional* pattern of development that might have a broader application (Good, 1986).

The dispositive governmental institution in determining the unevenness of American development was federalism, by which we mean the relative autonomy of geographic regions within the nation, which were also represented, as regions, in the national legislature. This institution not only abetted the disparity of development among the Northern, Southern, and Western sections of the US, but also ensured that the emergent 'top nation' in 1918 had a state possessing few central powers, but considerable economic regulations. The distinguishing characteristic of American federalism, as we shall consider it here, is its tendency to give representation and a measure of self-government (including the ability to borrow, develop infrastructure, and set social policy) to regions for essentially arbitrary reasons, irrespective either of their population or of their cultural integrity.

Scholars generally regard federalism as one of three defining features of American constitutionalism, the others being presidentialism and judicialism. All three institutions provide that parts of the political structure enjoy a significant degree of independence from the national legislature – presidentialism entails an executive independent of the legislature and judicialism a judiciary independent of the legislature; federalism entails semi-sovereign local entities, principally the states, independent of the national legislature.

Federalism has attracted a great deal of international interest for its ability to defuse political differences within a large polity. In turn American federalists had borrowed extensively from David Hume, and the political functions of federal union have a long transatlantic history. But federalism played an underappreciated role in allowing Americans to adapt to the conditions of nineteenth-century globalization.[2]

Federalism had three principal consequences in American development.

1. Local autonomy meant that different regions established institutions conducive to economic development at different rates; it also meant that the nation developed such institutions more swiftly than it would have under a non-federal regime.
2. Local autonomy under a national umbrella encouraged the establishment of a layer of private intermediaries that helped direct overseas investment in the US economy.
3. Local autonomy combined with the foregoing factors channelled regional politics of protest against industrialization into national politics, shaping the modern American state.

To draw conclusions for the present day from this history, we should consider the role played by federalism both in determining US success at attracting investment and also in distributing the benefits of investment within the United States.

First we should consider the role of institutions in the phenomenon of American divergence. Kenneth L. Sokoloff and Stanley L. Engerman note that the divergence between the US and Canada and the rest of the Western hemisphere does not appear until the era of industrialization, in the early 1800s (Sokoloff and Engerman, 2000). Before that the Caribbean islands were richer. Thus the literature on differential development within the New World emphasizes variation in habits and institutions associated with growth of industry – 'security of property rights, prevalence of corruption, structures of the financial sector, investment in public infrastructure and social capital, and the inclination to work hard or be entrepreneurial' (Sokoloff and Engerman, 2000: 218). But as Sokoloff and Engerman remark it is difficult to identify the encouraging factors in the establishment of such institutions. National heritage – i.e., the legacy of colonization by Britain as opposed to colonization by Spain – does not explain much of the international divergence in development. And initial factor endowments look similar across New World nations, with their relatively high availability of land and other natural resources and low supplies of labour. What differed was inequality, which was higher in the richer Southerly countries, which subsequently established institutions encouraging the persistence of inequality, and inhibited growth. The US and Canada instead promoted the rapid settlement of their interiors, extended the suffrage, and promoted education. Sokoloff and Engerman hypothesize these institutions reinforced early patterns of lower inequality in the North American nations and encouraged sustained growth through investment in productive capacity (2000: 230).

So far we stand on familiar ground. Even if we abandon theories of cultural heritage (which amount to racial inheritance by another name) we face the same point – an institutional mix favouring economic development (maybe because it did not favour inequality) prevailed in the United States. We get stuck here because we think in terms of national economies – of the United States as a whole – rather than of constituent components. Yet we know both that economic development occurred unevenly within the United States and also that the institutions favouring it developed unevenly as well. This uneven development created pockets of economic backwardness within an otherwise forward country. It also shaped the overall national process of development.

1.   Regional representation and institutions favouring economic development

If it is true that the US established institutions, like widespread education, that promoted development of its interior, it is also true that these institutions did not appear throughout the country but were concentrated in particular regions. Research on the determinants of international variation in developing these institutions indicates that regional representation and local autonomy played a key role in allowing the creation of backward pockets within the United States and also in pushing the US to the forefront of nations encouraging economic development. Peter H. Lindert (2004) finds that the forward position of the US in developing primary schooling owed to the nation's decentralized character, which allowed the pro-schooling North to establish an educational system in the early nineteenth century while the South, less enthusiastic about learning, remained behind (see Table 11.1). Lindert shows that the decentralization of representation allowed the whole country to move ahead faster than it would have with a central, national government that would have required a national majority to set schooling policy. And it allowed the South to remain backward. Despite a momentary shift in Southern opinion in the era of Reconstruction that followed the Civil War – when Southern states had some degree of black voting and a viable Republican Party – the subsequent era of segregation in the 1880s and 1890s saw Southerners reaffirm their determination to underfund schools (2004: 126–27).

Table 11.1 Lindert's model showing how regional autonomy encourages the establishment of schools*

	Share of voters in favour of taxes and public schools (%)			Whose children get public schools?	
Era	North	South	Both	with decentralization	with centralization
Backward era	30	10	20	none	none
Early rise	55	25	40	North only	none
Middle era	70	40	55	North only	all
Advanced era	85	55	70	all	all

Note: *The hypothesis is two regions, North and South, with differential desires for better schooling that advance as economic development in the region advances.

Source: From Lindert (2004: Table 5.4).

The nineteenth century thus established the pattern of a Northern US willing to invest in institutions like widespread public education that encouraged economic development while the Southern US resisted this use of public funds. The same pattern applied to investment in infrastructure: Northern politicians tended to favour spending public monies on roads, canals, and railways while Southern politicians did not. This regional disparity had an expected outcome both in the proliferation of such transport links in the North and, if Lindert's model of education funding applies here too, in the country overall to a greater degree than would have been the case had Americans relied solely on their national government to fund such improvements. It had an unexpected outcome in contributing to the growth of another institution critical to the pattern of American development.

As Joel Silbey notes, the partisan division within the US over the use of federal money for internal improvements in infrastructure complemented and cut across a sectional division over the same issue. Democrats strongly opposed the use of federal dollars to pay for such improvements, leaving their opponents, the Whigs, to favour it. But even within the Whig party, Southerners remained ambivalent about the use of national power to promote such expansion. The Whigs thus failed to present a unified front on this issue. The funding of infrastructure fell to local authorities including, principally, state governments who sold bonds to pay for them (Silbey, 1991).

This borrowing, followed by the economic downturns of the late 1830s and early 1840s, led eight states and the territory of Florida to default on their debt, much of which had found its way into the hands of British investors. At the time the British writer and investor Sydney Smith railed against the Americans for refusing to raise taxes sufficiently to honour their obligations, condemning them as 'a nation with whom no contract can be made, because none will be kept; unstable in the very foundations of social life, deficient in the elements of good faith, men who prefer any load of infamy however great, to any pressure of taxation, however light' (1843: 9). Wallis et al. (2004: 23) find that at least in the case of Pennsylvania Smith was correct; the state should have been able to avoid default if it had 'imposed a realistic property tax'.

The case of Mississippi presented a different picture, inasmuch as bigotry, which would keep the South underdeveloped for generations, played some role in its default and because the reasons for its default differed. Wallis et al. (2004) point out that Mississippi borrowed heavily to establish a state bank for development purposes. When this bank failed, Mississippi defaulted. The Magnolia State might have devoted its tax revenues to covering its debts but instead repudiated. Governor Alexander McNutt explained that this was because the debt would enrich one of the Rothschilds:

> [Rothschild] has advanced money to the Sublime Porte [i.e., the Ottoman Empire, and Islamic kingdom; this was not true], and taken as security a mortgage upon the Holy City of Jerusalem, and the Sepulchre of our Saviour. [This was not true either, though it helped inflame anti-Semitic prejudice.] It is for the people to say whether he shall have a mortgage on our cotton fields, and make serfs of our children. Let the Baron [Rothschild] exact his pound of flesh of ... the Bank of the United States... (Veto Message of Governor McNutt, of Mississippi, 1841: 276)[3]

Such anti-foreign sentiment, coupled with racism and religious bigotry, helped isolate the South from internationally mobile capital and also from internationally mobile labour. Despite the hopes of New South boosters that immigration might reinvigorate the Southern economy after the end of slavery, few immigrants went to the South and those that did go soon left, unimpressed by wages and little interested in being 'treated just as the black race used to be' (Berthoff, 1951: 331).

So we have seen that the institution of federalism, so central to the United States constitution, allowed Northerners to indulge their preferences for schooling and thus to lift the educational level of the nation as a whole, and also to allow the South to exercise its preference for slavery, plantation agriculture, and their cultural consequences over economic modernization. These developments both kept the United States *per se* an attractive investment and also ensured that global investment went chiefly into the Northeast of the country, the Great Lakes region and, as rail lines extended, the further West.[4] The Northeast and the West became more developed sooner than the South, comprising an increasingly integrated market from which the South remained measurably excluded.

2.   Regional representation and private financial intermediaries

Within the world of nineteenth-century capital investment, the United States stands out as a peculiar case. It received the largest single share of capital invested in developing countries – but that is a question of quantity, and not an interestingly large quantity; relative to the size of its economy, foreign investment in the United States did not amount to much. But in terms of the distribution of investment, foreign investment in the United States differed from foreign investment in other large borrowers. Particularly, while foreign investment in other developing countries went often into government securities, in the United States government borrowing accounted for a small share of foreign investment, the largest chunk of which went into private railway securities (see Table 11.2).

As Wilkins (1989) and Davis and Gallman (2001) indicate, the reasons for this have partly to do with the American states' defaults, not only in the 1840s but again in the 1870s. As Davis and Gallman write,

> [g]overnments with good reputations, Australia and Canada for example, did not have to draw on the services of international financial syndicates to underwrite and market their bonds. In the case of the United States such syndicates were required. Although costly, they generated collateral economic benefits in terms of the evolution of the domestic financial structure. The American syndicates included not only well-established British and continental merchant banks, but also young US investment banks; and syndicate membership improved the reputations of those American bankers both at home and abroad...
> The better the reputation of the government issues, the less need there was for specific private institutions designed to link foreign savers to domestic investors, institutions that could, at a later date, be modified to channel domestic savings into domestic investment.[5]

In countries like Argentina, with less capital of their own, where British investors could place their money directly, the import of poor reputation was less perverse than in the United States. But the US had not only a history of bad credit, but also a peculiar political structure within which to distribute responsibility for it.

In the wake of the defaults of the 1840s, 'United States' security' became a by-word for worthless paper, as Charles Dickens had Ebenezer Scrooge exclaim in *A Christmas Carol* (1857: 1–47). Sydney Smith claimed that the United States 'cannot draw the sword because the have not money to buy it', and could not support 'a long, tedious ... war of four or five year's duration' (1843: Letters 9, 14, and 20). Smith proved wrong. The United States was able to finance its Civil War, by any standard a major war of four years' duration. Banker Jay Cooke recruited thousands of salesmen to sell government debt (Carosso, 1970: 15–17). Cooke wanted to finance the war without going to the global markets – '[w]e ... had better not put a whip into the hands of foreigners to punish us', he wrote. His success on the market and the US Army's success in the field re-established America's viability as an investment proposition and also established the role of private investment banks as central to that viability.

Table 11.2 Capital called on British market by economic sector, 1865–1914

	US	Canada	Argentina	Australia	India
Government	6	34	22	66	46
Railways	62	40	58	1	40
Public utilities	9	6	9	4	3
Financial	6	6	5	12	2
Raw materials	5	4	0	13	6
Industrial	11	10	5	4	2
Shipping	1	0	1	1	1
Total private	94	66	78	34	54
Total %	100	100	100	100	100

Note: Numbers rounded and so may not add exactly to 100.

Source: Stone (1999).

The panic of 1873 cemented the lesson that American states could not be relied upon. Ironically, Cooke's firm touched off the panic when the failure of the Northern Pacific railroad caused its own failure. Afterward 11 states, ten of them in the South, defaulted on debt amounting to perhaps $130 million (converted to today's dollars, as a relative share of US GDP, this would amount to about $159 thousand million) (Lewis and Schlotterbeck, 1938: 59). In consequence, as Wilkins notes, the 1870s and 1880s saw relatively little foreign capital go into US government bonds (1989: 111). Instead it went through private intermediaries, such as investment banks with offices on both sides of the Atlantic: J. S. Morgan and Co. and Drexel Morgan; Brown Shipley and Brown Brothers; Seligman Brothers and J.W. Seligman, and so forth.

As Davis and Gallman (2001) establish, this history of public defaults and the rise of a private substitute for the unreliable public financial intermediary made the United States unusual among frontier nations of the late nineteenth century. Argentina, Australia, and Canada all used public debt to fund the development of their rich interiors. Even though Australia and Canada enjoyed political independence from Britain, the British saver tended to view their securities as backed by the British Treasury, and ultimately the law backed this view. US securities not only were not so soundly supported but bespoke a worryingly careless history, and so American government issues paid 1.8 per cent points more than Canadian ones on average and 2.3 per cent points more than Australian issues. Argentina did not enjoy such a favourable position, but lacking so much capital of its own saw its railroads controlled by British investors (Davis and Gallman, 2001: 759–63).

On this interpretation what makes the US experience distinctive is not, or not only, the canny behaviour of the early Federalists, but the careless behaviour of the subsequent Democrats, and the dispersal of financial responsibility among the various American states (Bordo and Vegh, 1998). Despite the success of the 1790 reorganization of US debt under Alexander Hamilton and the subsequent good behaviour of the US federal government as debtor, the ability of Americans to borrow through their government suffered from the bad behaviour of the individual American states. US government debt remained relatively small, and domestic savers tended to buy it. The financing of major projects like the construction of Western railroads encouraged the establishment of a relatively responsible private investment market devoted in part to channelling foreign capital into the United States.

To the extent that the United States' national government did finance and direct internal development it did so fitfully and with an eye often to partisan advantage rather than any particular economic theory. The first transcontinental railroad was indeed financed from public wealth, mainly by land-grants. Analysts have wrangled, at least since this effort imploded in scandal in the early 1870s, whether the decision to use public wealth to finance the railroad was wise. Few have disagreed that the distribution of resources benefited a few key figures with close ties to Republican politicians. Later historians have noted, though without quite reaching complete consensus, that the public subsidy of the railroads did not achieve significant developmental advantages. As Atack and Passell summarize the debate,

> Federal land grant subsidies, then, were a proposition of dubious value. They were unnecessary incentives for some of the railroads since claims of market failure were unfounded. They were an unnecessarily expensive incentive for others because the actual form of mitigating market failure was inefficient. The only possible saving grace of federal land grant subsidies was their value as a deterrent to inefficient monopoly pricing by the carriers. But the practical impact of that deterrent has yet to be demonstrated empirically (1994: 443–4).

And while it is true that beyond the railroad grants, the Republican Party established a national policy for economic development in the 1860s that had some important effects, it is also true that the party departed from that policy when its political costs became too heavy. The railway subsidies went along with a protective tariff, an act to distribute homesteads, an act to encourage immigration, and the Morrill Land Grant Act, which created public institutions of higher education in American states, with the idea of promoting the development of scientific agriculture and mining. The encouragement and subsidy of immigration proved both unpopular and unnecessary. The tariff quickly lost whatever theoretical integrity it had in the chaos of intra-regional bargaining, and by the 1890s had become a compromise brokered between Western and Eastern elements of the Republican coalition, tied to the purchase of voter loyalty through the pension system. The Morrill Land Grant institutions, perhaps alone among the elements of the Republicans' national plan of the 1860s, lasted and contributed to American economic development. But the Republican Party had by the early 1870s backed off the commitment to a national developmental policy.[6]

We can then say that the institution of regional representation and the federal structure entailed at least two major consequences for the pattern of US development. First, regional representation allowed the expression, protection, and implementation of local preferences for the establishment of institutions conducive to economic development. This meant not only that certain sections of the US became more developed earlier than others, but also that the whole nation became more developed than it otherwise would. Thus the US became an attractive investment for overseas capital, but some parts of it became more attractive than others. Second, regional representation allowed the expression, protection, and implementation of local preferences for financial responsibility. This meant that certain sections of the US were better able to borrow than others, and that Americans had to develop a national institution devoted to serving the role of information aggregator and arbiter, a role otherwise and elsewhere served by governments. Thus the US remained an attractive investment for overseas capital, but that capital tended to come through private investment banks rather than through public coffers. Taking these developments together we can move to a consideration of the third, and perhaps most important, consequence of federalism for the US as a developing nation.

3. Regional representation and the reaction to globalization

As we have seen, federalism allowed the US South to effectively exempt itself from the process of globalization, opting out of the international movement of capital and labour. Southern states resisted investment in institutions that increased the value of their workforce, resisted immigration, and accounted for the majority of defaults. This isolated the South economically, and contributed to its historic sense of alienation from nationalizing projects. Federalism also meant that the relatively under-populated Western part of the country, especially when allied with the perennially discontented South, could determine national policy with respect to the movement of global capital and labour.[7]

Foreign investment in the United States, going as it did into railways, mining, and other frontier activities, sped the development of the West. Between the US Civil War and the Great War, twelve new Western states entered the American union. Even though these states often had few people living in them, owing to the US Constitution they enjoyed equal representation in the United States Senate.[8] The new states thus contributed one-quarter of the nation's Senators by 1913.

An economically colonial connection bound the new states to the Northeastern portion of the country, such that Westerners and subsequent historians alike identified the relationship between the sections as imperial (see Figure 11.1). Developing the American West, much like the process of colonizing Africa or Southeast Asia, was undertaken by 'an expanding metropolitan economy creating ever more elaborate and intimate linkages' to a hinterland rich in natural resources (Cronon, 1991). The people of the West nursed resentment at their 'essentially "colonial" relationship' to the capital-rich East (Meinig, 1972: 181).

Westerners protesting this relationship saw private bankers with foreign connections as the source of their trouble.[9] They identified houses such as J.P. Morgan and Co. as playing a semi-sovereign role in American development, a role that in other countries was played by government. They complained about the authority thus given to unelected men responsive to their clientele and not to political constituents.[10] They objected to immigration, which affected the wages of less-skilled workers and which, Hatton and Williamson (1998) confirm, pushed native-born workers out of their home cities and into the West.[11] They blamed foreign investors for laws protecting high interest rates and monopoly prices: 'Englishmen now own a majority of the stock of our railroads [not true of the industry overall though true of some major lines… [O]ur fields and factories are being stripped to pay interest to the money lenders of England... In Egypt and India she has placed her soldiers to protect her bondholders... The money lenders of America, who are advocating our present financial laws, are the soldiers of England on the soil of the United States' (Harvey, 1975: 80–2).

Figure 11.1 The path of the Union Pacific railway, one of the great successes and scandals of post-Civil War railway construction, showing the railroad passing through seven of the twelve post-Civil War states

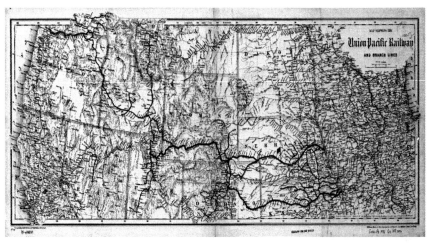

Source: Library of Congress Railroad Map no. 596; call number G4051.P3 1888 .G15 RR 596.

As Wallis et al. (2004) suggest, we might thus view the United States as 'less a nation or country in the usual sense, and more akin to an empire of different geographic and economic regions at different stages of development. Like the British Empire of that era, the United States had its commercial-industrial centre (similar to Great Britain) in the northeast, its semi-tropical cash-crop exporting area (its India) in the South, and its temperate region of recent settlement (its Canada, Australia, and New Zealand) in the old northwest' (Wallis et al. 2004: 26). Unlike the British Empire, the United States gave its colonial regions representation in its metropolitan parliament. India had no MPs at Westminster, but Wyoming had two Senators and a Congressman at Washington.

In consequence, protest against the colonial relationship found an outlet in the national politics of the United States. During the period from the 1880s through the First World War, when other rich industrial countries were busily establishing welfare-state policies, the United States focused instead on regulating commerce and banking within the internal empire of continental America. And although support for such measures was not confined to peripheral regions, it was characteristic of the American federal institution that, as Sanders (1999: 164) argues, in the US Congress the farmers of the South and West together 'had the incentive and provided the muscle' to create such a regulatory state.[12]

By 1917, American politics of sectional protest funnelled through its institutions of regional representation provided the US with a regime of economic regulation. Its Interstate Commerce Commission, established in 1887 and strengthened by subsequent legislation, regulated railway and other shipping within the continental empire. Its Federal Trade Commission, established in 1914, investigated, weighed, and judged accusations of unfair trade practices. An Employee's Compensation and an Eight-hour Commission, established in 1916, enforced labour law. Bureaus of Immigration and Naturalization, established in 1891 and 1906, enforced restrictive immigration legislation that included a literacy test in the migrant's native language. All these measures enjoyed their strongest support from the regions within the United States that were peripheral to its economy – which is to say, from the South and the West.

The adoption of such a regulatory regime increased the power of the national government in the United States, and so it may appear paradoxical that the South, which had only recently fought a Civil War over its asserted right to keep the federal government out of its affairs, should have supported such an agenda. But as Sanders (1999) points out, the South and West supported a particular kind of increase in state power: 'guarantees, benefits, or prohibitions [that] might require judicial suits and, ultimately, the exercise of federal police power', but 'little, if any, bureaucratic discretion'. The eight-hour day or the bar on monopolies had, Sanders writes, 'an automatic, relatively self-enforcing quality' and so Southerners or other libertarians might back them in the hope they would not increase the permanent bureaucratic structures of the state (p. 388). Even the most bluntly redistributive policies supported by this coalition – the taxes on income, inheritance, and excess profits – partook of this generally rule-based, ostensibly self-enforcing character (Weisman, 2002).

Indeed even in policy areas that would normally require centralization and expertise, the politics of reaction against globalization, funnelled through the institutions of regional representation, created decentralized, purportedly rule-based systems. The major example of such an institution is the US Federal Reserve, created in 1913. After early experiments, the United States abandoned its central banks and did not seriously consider establishing one again until after the panic of 1907. The US adopted central banking late and indeed at an awkward time; the first Federal Reserve Board took office in the week after the First World War began. And its makers did not intend the Federal Reserve System to operate as a central bank – it was not central but, with its twelve districts, obviously decentralized; nor was it a bank, but a banking system supervised by a politically appointed board.[13] Whatever it was, there is general agreement that it was ill-suited in its infancy to guide the US through the challenges of the World War and the crises that followed.[14] But perhaps this failure is a matter of timing rather than of the Federal Reserve System's intrinsic nature; had not the mantle of 'top nation' fallen on American shoulders so soon after the Fed's creation, it might not have made such a mess of its work. Following the logic of historians who see the US as a federated empire, we might consider it a well-integrated and well-regulated empire, successful at managing the openness of internal and external markets, because its central legislature allowed representation of its colonized regions, and thus of economic interests within the empire, irrespective of their population or their colonial status.

4.   Lessons for today

In 1948 the political scientist and historian Charles Austin Beard argued that 'with the world just emerging from one global war and trembling on the verge of another, federalism is now offered as the best pledge that mankind, tormented by wars for countless generations, may at last establish tranquillity throughout the earth' (1948: 4). The institution of federalism offered a solution to the creation of a large republic: Divide it into semi-autonomous parts (Adair, 1974: 103). In the late 1940s, the institution of federalism appeared to offer a mechanism whereby nation-states could shed pool their sovereignty in international councils and defuse interstate conflict.

As we have seen there is some reason to argue that the institution of federalism also helped the United States adapt to the influence of overseas capital and labour coming into the country. Federalism encouraged the regional establishment of widespread public education and other institutions, including flexible labour markets, which underwrote economic growth. It allowed those regions wishing to establish such institutions to do so without waiting for the assent of other areas. The ability of the South to opt out of such processes while the rest of the country went ahead also contributed, albeit by indirect methods, to the establishment of the generally successful private investment intermediaries that distinguished foreign investment in the US from that in otherwise comparable developing countries of the era. Finally, federalism defused the backlash from America's internal colonized regions, channelling it into regulatory policies. Because these regions enjoyed representation at Washington, they played an outsized role in shaping the American regulatory state.

Yet American federalism does not much appeal to other countries, apart from some exceptions. Federal nations like Belgium, Germany, and Switzerland, embracing distinct principalities, regard American federalism kindly.[15] But otherwise countries ignored federalism or subsumed it under parliamentary supremacy. Federalism sometimes failed (as in Yugoslavia) or led to uncomfortable success (as in Canada).[16] The problems in such cases appear to be that, as James C. MacPherson writes, 'ethnic configurations did not follow clear territorial boundaries' (1994: 11).

But we have found American federalism played an important part in the US response to globalization. The story we know suggests, however perversely, that the arbitrary drawing of regional lines can succeed as well, provided the lines correspond to catchments of economic interest. The key to Wyoming's role in the development of the American state lay not in the mystical tie of Wyomingers to their land, nor to their ethnic homogeneity, but to their shared experience of annoyance at railroads, to their interest in the prosperity of commodity producers, and to their absolute entitlement, however ungrounded in a theory of representation, to two Senators and a minimum of one Congressman at Washington.[17]

It also appears that semi-sovereign localities may fail in their fiscal responsibility, provided that some umbrella protections allow private-sector institutions to take their place. The defaults of American states contributed to the successful emergence of private investment institutions to play a part governments would not.[18]

We cannot let these qualified comments about the unintended successes of US federalism blind us to the failures of the system. One of its great successes, as we have seen, was its ability to let some sections of the country forge ahead while others remained behind. The Northern states abandoned slavery while the Southern states kept and strengthened it. And so the Civil War came. Even afterward, the South deprived freedmen of their civil rights and kept the region backward (Ransom and Sutch, 2001). Only the internal colonialism of the New Deal and the Warren Court came near to ending this Southern backwardness.[19] We note also the war on and resettlement of aboriginal populations in the US West, which if it to occurred today would qualify as ethnic cleansing.[20]

We see three lessons. First, the institution of regional representation, preserving some local autonomy under a national umbrella, allowed the US to adapt to globalization. Second, this institution did not protect minority rights. Third, its failures required forms of colonial intervention.

We can hazard some speculative analysis. Proselytizers for the US Constitution expected a world federation and perhaps one will someday come. But it looks unlikely. Even proper unification of Europe seems far off.

But the US model might work within developing countries or developing regions. One can imagine a confederation of Asian, Latin American, or African nations whose federal government enjoyed regulatory authority over the movement of capital and labour while its constituent polities retained jurisdiction over schooling and infrastructural improvements. One can imagine regional trade federations evolving in this direction. One can imagine a newly established developing country adopting a federal structure specifically to encourage the flexibility that the late nineteenth-century US showed.

But newly established nations appeal to the unity of the Westphalian nation-state to pull the country out of crisis, as for example Ayad Allawi did after the Iraqi elections of 2005: 'If the objective of national unity is missed, if the objective of national reconciliation is overlooked, then this will definitely spell out disaster' (Shadid, 2005). It is hard to imagine such a leader appealing instead to the idea of consciously dividing his nation into bits, especially when the history of federalism in the United States suggests that under such a system bad social features will survive and tensions persist, and intervention from outside – whether from the IMF or some military coalition – might prove necessary anyway.

Notes

1. Which is to say, 'full stop'. Sellar and Yeatman (1993: 115).
2. On elements of American constitutionalism and their influence abroad, see Billias, (1990); and Blaustein (1986). On Hume and American federalism, see Adair (1974), and Livingston (1998: 318–24).
3. The Rothschilds did not establish a lending relationship with Turkey until 1854; the rumour that they had or wished to acquire Jerusalem was an anti-Semitic myth of long standing in the US press (Ferguson, 1998).
4. On the isolation of the Southern market, see Wright (1982; 1986). Also see Rosenbloom (1990).
5. Davis and Gallman (2001: 763); and Wilkins (1989: 111).
6. On the national plan of the 1860s, see Richardson (1997). On the demise of that plan, see Richardson (2001). On the tariff as part of a bargaining chip in the Republicans' sectional coalition, see Bensel (2000). On the Land Grant College Act, see Ferleger and Lazonick (1994). Again, because of federalism, this act had highly varying sectional impact, and in the South often supported the developmentally counter-indicated tradition of segregation; see Lee (1963).
7. On Western and Southern roles in resisting globalization and establishing legislation in Congress, see Rauchway (2004).

8. On the order of admission of new states, see also Stewart and Weingast (1992).
9. For a discussion of the real or illusory origins of farm protest, see Mayhew (1972).
10. e.g., Harvey 1963, (1975); Loucks (1975).
11. See Hatton and Williamson (1998: 164–9), also see Eldridge and Thomas (1964); and Goodrich et al. (1936).
12. On other sources of protest, see Chang (2004: 687–715).
13. See Meltzer (2003) and Timberlake (1993). Also Sanders (1999: 236–59).
14. See Eichengreen (1992a, 1992b) and Temin (1989).
15. e.g., Blaustein (1986: 18).
16. The convention of referring to the discomforts of Canadian federalism owes to the occasional recurrence of Quebecois separatism, but unless it should someday succeed in the global scheme of things Canadian federalism looks a considerable success. See essays in Randall and Gibbins (1994).
17. On the political role of the new states, see McCarty et al. (2002); Stewart and Weingast (1992).
18. See Hovenkamp (1991) and Kens (1991). Also more recent Novak (1993).
19. See Powe (2000) and Schulman (1994).
20. On the military campaigns, see Utley (1984). On resettlement and expropriation, see Hoxie (2001).

References

Adair, D. 1974. 'That Politics May Be Reduced to a Science: David Hume, James Madison, and the Tenth Federalist', in T. Colbourn (ed.) Fame and the Founding Fathers: Essays by Douglass Adair, pp. 93–106. New York: W.W. Norton.

Beard, C. A. 1948. *The Enduring Federalist*. Garden City NY: Doubleday.

Bensel, R. F. 2000. *The Political Economy of American Industrialization, 1877–1900*. Cambridge: Cambridge University Press.

Berthoff, R. T. 1951. 'Southern Attitudes toward Immigration, 1865–1914'. *Journal of Southern History*, 17: 328–60.

Billias, G. A. (ed.) 1990. *American Constitutionalism Abroad: Selected Essays in Comparative Constitutional History*. New York: Greenwood.

Blaustein, A. P. 1986. 'The Influence of the United States Constitution Abroad'. Washington DC: Washington Institute.

Bordo, M. D. and Vegh, C. A. 1998. 'What If Alexander Hamilton Had Been Argentinean? A Comparison of the Early Monetary Experiences of Argentina and the United States'. NBER Working Paper 6862, 1–56: National Bureau of Economic Research.

Carosso, V. P. 1970. *Investment Banking in America*. Cambridge MA: Harvard University Press.

Chang, H-J. 2004. 'Regulation of Foreign Investment in Historical Perspective'. *European Journal of Development Research*, 16(3): 687–715.

Cronon, W. 1991. *Nature's Metropolis: Chicago and the Great West*. New York: W.W. Norton and Co.

Davis, L. E and Gallman, R. E. 2001. *Evolving Financial Markets and International Capital Flows: Britain, the Americas, and Australia, 1870–1914*. Cambridge: Cambridge University Press.

Dickens, C. 1857. *Christmas Stories*. 2 vols. Philadelphia: T.B. Peterson.

Eichengreen, B. 1992. *Golden Fetters: The Gold Standard and the Great Depression, 1919–1939*. New York: Oxford University Press.

Eichengreen, B. 1992. 'The Origins and Nature of the Great Slump Revisited'. *Economic History Review* 45, 2: 213–39.

Eldridge, H. T. and Thomas, D. S. 1964. 'Demographic Analyses and Interrelations', in S. Kuznets (ed.), *Population Redistribution and Economic Growth*, Vol. 3. Philadelphia: American Philosophical Society.

Ferguson, N. 1998. *The World's Banker: The History of the House of Rothschild*. London: Weidenfeld & Nicolson.

Ferleger, L. and Lazonick, W. 1994. 'Higher Education for an Innovative Economy: Land-Grant Colleges and the Managerial Revolution in America'. *Business and Economic History*, 23(1): 116–28.

Good, D. F. 1986. 'Uneven Development in the Nineteenth Century: A Comparison of the Habsburg Empire and the United States'. *Journal of Economic History*, 46(1): 137–51.

Goodrich, C., Allin, B. W., Thornthwaite, C. W., Brunck, H. K., Tryon, F. G., Creamer, D. B., Vance, R. B. and Hayes, M. 1936. *Migration and Economic Opportunity: The Report of the Study of Population Redistribution*. Philadelphia: University of Pennsylvania Press.

Harvey, W. H. 1975. *Coin on Money, Trusts, and Imperialism, 1899*. Reprint, Westport, CT: Hyperion Press.

Harvey, W. H. 1963. *Coin's Financial School*. Cambridge MA: Belknap Press of Harvard University Press.

Hatton, T. J. and Williamson, J. G. 1998. *The Age of Mass Migration: Causes and Economic Impact*. New York: Oxford University Press.

Hovenkamp, H. 1991. *Enterprise and American Law, 1836–1937*. Cambridge MA: Harvard University Press.

Hoxie, F. E. 2001. *A Final Promise: The Campaign to Assimilate the Indians, 1880–1920*. Bison Books edn. Lincoln: University of Nebraska Press.

Kens, P. 1991. 'The Source of a Myth: Police Powers of the States and Laissez Faire Constitutionalism, 1900–1937'. *American Journal of Legal History*, 35(1): 70–98.

Lee, G. C. 1963. 'The Morrill Act and Education'. *British Journal of Educational Studies*, 12(1): 19–40.

Lewis, C. and Schlotterbeck, K. T. 1938. 'America's Stake in International Investments'. Washington DC: Brookings Institution.

Lindert, P. H. 2004. *Growing Public: Social Spending and Economic Growth since the Eighteenth Century*. Cambridge: Cambridge University Press.

Livingston, D. W. 1998. *Philosophical Melancholy and Delirium: Hume's Pathology of Philosophy*. Chicago: University of Chicago Press.

Loucks, H. L. 1975. *The Great Conspiracy of the House of Morgan, and How to Defeat It*. New York: Arno.

MacPherson, J. C. 1994. 'The Future of Federalism', in S. Randall and R. Gibbins (eds) *Federalism and the New World Order*. Calgary: University of Calgary Press, pp. 9–13.

Mayhew, A. 1972. 'A Reappraisal of the Causes of Farm Protest in the United States, 1870–1900'. *Journal of Economic History*, 32(2): 464–75.

McCarty, N., Poole K. T. and Rosenthal, H. 2002. 'Congress and the Territorial Expansion of the United States', in D. W. Brady and M. D. McCubbins (eds) *Party, Process, and Political Change in Congress: New Perspectives on the History of Congress*. Stanford: Stanford University Press, pp. 392–451.

Meinig, D. 1972. 'American Wests: Preface to a Geographical Interpretation'. *Annals of the Association of American Geographers*, 62(2): 159–84.

Meltzer, A. H. 2003. *A History of the Federal Reserve, 1913–1951*. Chicago: University of Chicago Press.

Novak, W. J. 1993. 'Public Economy and the Well-Ordered Market: Law and Economic Regulation in 19th-Century America'. *Law and Social Inquiry*, 18(1): 1–32.

O'Rourke, K. H. and Williamson, J. G. 1999. *Globalization and History: The Evolution of a Nineteenth-Century Atlantic Economy.* Cambridge MA: MIT Press.

Powe, L. A. Scot. 2000. *The Warren Court and American Politics.* Cambridge MA: Belknap Press.

Randall, S. and Gibbins, R. (eds) 1994. *Federalism and the New World Order.* Calgary: University of Calgary Press.

Ransom, R. L. and Sutch, R. 2001. *One Kind of Freedom: The Economic Consequences of Emancipation.* 2nd edn. Cambridge: Cambridge University Press.

Rauchway, E. 2006. *Blessed among Nations.* New York: Hill and Wang.

Rauchway, E. 2004. 'The Transformation of the Congressional Experience', in J. E. Zelizer (ed.) *The American Congress: The Building of Democracy.* Boston: Houghton Mifflin, pp. 319–34.

Richardson, H. C. 2001. *The Death of Reconstruction: Race, Labor, and Politics in the Post-Civil War North, 1865–1901.* Cambridge MA: Harvard University Press.

Richardson, H. C. 1997. *The Greatest Nation of the Earth: Republican Economic Policies During the Civil War.* Cambridge MA: Harvard University Press.

Rosenbloom, J. L. 1990. 'One Market or Many? Labor Market Integration in the Late Nineteenth-Century United States'. *Journal of Economic History*, 50(1): 85–107.

Sanders, E. 1999. *Roots of Reform: Farmers, Workers, and the American State, 1877–1917.* Chicago: University of Chicago Press.

Schulman, B. J. 1994. *From Cotton Belt to Sunbelt: Federal Policy, Economic Development, and the Transformation of the South, 1938–1980.* Durham: Duke University Press.

Sellar, W. C. and Yeatman, R. J. 1993 [1931]. *1066 and All That.* New York: Barnes & Noble.

Shadid, A. 2005. 'Iraq Must Unify or Face 'Disaster', Premier Warns'. Washington Post, 18 February, A16.

Silbey, J. H. 1991. *The American Political Nation, 1838–1893.* Stanford: Stanford University Press.

Smith, S. 1843. *Letters on American Debts.* London: Longman, Brown, Green & Longmans.

Sokoloff, K. L. and Engerman, S. L. 2000. 'History Lessons: Institutions, Factor Endowments, and Paths of Development in the New World'. *Journal of Economic Perspectives*, 14(3): 217–32.

Stewart, C., III and Weingast, B. R. 1992. 'Stacking the Senate, Changing the Nation: Republican Rotten Boroughs, Statehood Politics, and American Political Development'. *Studies in American Political Development*, 6: 223–71.

Stone, I. 1999. *The Global Export of Capital from Great Britain, 1865–1914: A Statistical Survey.* New York: St Martin's.

Temin, P. 1989. *Lessons from the Great Depression.* Cambridge MA: MIT Press.

Timberlake, R. H. 1993. *Monetary Policy in the United States: An Intellectual and Institutional History.* Chicago: University of Chicago Press.

Utley, R. M. 1984. *Frontier Regulars: The United States Army and the Indian, 1866–1891.* Bison Books edn. Lincoln: University of Nebraska Press.

'Veto Message of Governor M'nutt, of Mississippi'. 1841. US Commercial and Statistical Register, 5 May, 273–77.

Wallis, J. J., Sylla, R. E. and Grinath, A., III. 2004. 'Sovereign Debt and Repudiation: The Emerging-Market Debt Crisis in the US States, 1839–1843'. NBER Working Paper 10753, 1–50: National Bureau of Economic Research.

Weisman, S. R. 2002. *The Great Tax Wars: Lincoln to Wilson.* New York: Simon & Schuster.

Wilkins, M. T. 1989. *The History of Foreign Investment in the United States to 1914.* Cambridge MA: Harvard University Press.

Wright, G. 1986. *Old South, New South: Revolutions in the Southern Economy since the Civil War.* New York: Basic.

Wright, G. 1982. 'The Strange Career of the New Southern Economic History'. *Reviews in American History*, 10(4): 164–80.

CHAPTER 12
INSTITUTIONS AND ECONOMIC GROWTH: THE SUCCESSFUL EXPERIENCE OF SWITZERLAND, 1870–1950

Thomas David and André Mach[1]

Despite the absence of natural resources and no sea access, Switzerland became one of the wealthiest countries in the world between 1870 and 1940. For most scholars, this 'Swiss success story' resulted from a combination of a privileged position at the heart of Europe, a neutrality status that preserved the country from the World Wars, and a successful integration in the international economy, combined with liberal economic policies. Even if it has largely been classified as a stereotypical example of a 'liberal success', the high performance of the Swiss economy did not solely rely on these precepts. On the contrary, notwithstanding its overall liberal trade policy, the Swiss economy also developed core institutions that largely departed from neo-classical recipes.

In this chapter, we focus on the impact of institutions in the economic growth of Switzerland. Few scholars have taken into account the role of political and economic institutions in analyzing the Swiss growth experience; they have only integrated this dimension when dealing with the impact of political institutions, in particular the political freedom and stability of the Swiss democracy, on economic development.

We can distinguish two categories of political institutions, that were important in the economic development of Switzerland: First, the 'institutions of conflict management' among economic and political elites that promoted consensual problem solving among them; second, partly linked to these institutions, close public-private partnerships also played a crucial role in the promotion of growth enhancing economic institutions.

These political institutions contributed decisively to the adoption of two types of economic institutions. First, what we called 'institutions of domestic compensation' – that compensated the social groups that fell behind in the developmental process (e.g., agricultural subsidies, high tolerance for domestic cartels, tariffs for some industries, institutions for labour disputes resolution). Second, the political institutions also determined the adoption of growth-enhancing institutions, such as patent law and central banking, which, according to the IMF or the World Bank, favour growth by establishing an incentive structure that reduces uncertainty and promotes efficiency. However, the Swiss historical experience demonstrates that these 'good institutions', which are generally considered as important for economic growth, did not play a central role in the first phase of the 'Swiss success story' (see Chang, 2002 for other historical experiences). Until 1907, these two types of institutions did not exist (or barely existed) in Switzerland; and despite their absence, the Swiss economy nonetheless witnessed a very fast growth during the preceding decades.

Our chapter has four parts. In the first section, we present a model of the links between institutions and economic growth in small European countries. In subsequent sections, we examine the Swiss case. In the second part, we briefly present the 'Swiss success story', the fast economic growth of this country between 1870 and 1950. In the third part, we explore the importance of political institutions in Switzerland during this period. Finally, we analyse the impact of economic institutions on Swiss growth.

1.   Institutions and economic growth in small European countries

Growth-stimulating political and economic institutions were not specific to Switzerland. Other small European countries shared similar institutional characteristics. Menzel (1988) published an important book on the successful industrialization of four similar countries (Switzerland, Denmark, Sweden and Canada). The industrialization process was first and foremost based on the following factors: A mix of technology transfer and endogenous invention; trade policies that coupled greater world economic integration through free trade with selective protectionist measures for some domestic sectors; a niche strategy based first on low wages, then on a very flexible marketing strategy oriented towards the quality of export goods; a policy of liberalization of trade and policy associated with growing state intervention (see also Menzel, 1992).

As a second step, these countries were able to link the export sectors with the whole economy and to avoid a too strong concentration of wealth. This transition was made possible by economic, social and political preconditions. Economic preconditions included among others a relatively equal distribution of income in the export sectors and an intervening state (selective protectionist measures, nationalization of natural resources) in order to diminish foreign competition but also to support import substitution. An equal distribution in landownership, a homogenous social structure, a generally high level of education were essential social preconditions for the spread and maintenance of flexibility and readiness to innovate. Finally, Menzel emphasized the political preconditions, in particular democratic institutions 'in which forces favoring development can articulate themselves and patterns have to be established which make conflict resolution in an institutionalised manner possible' (1992: 80). These political institutions gave way to a far-reaching participation of the whole population (bourgeoisie, middle class, farmers, workers) and allowed them to gain sufficient political influence to limit the resistance of the old elites.

Following Menzel (1988) and Katzenstein (1985), who both insist on the importance of political institutions in the economic development of small European countries, we argue that small countries present a particular framework for the interaction of institutions and economic growth (see Figure 12.1). First, the small size of their domestic markets provides an explanation for the early economic openness of these countries. On the eve of the First World War, Belgium, the Netherlands and Switzerland were the developed countries with the highest export per capita and with very high stock of foreign direct investment per capita (David, 2003). However, none of these countries simply developed by opening itself up to foreign trade and investment. On the contrary, export dependence and the general liberal orientation of their trade policy was 'embedded' in domestic institutions that were far from liberal, but favourable for economic growth.

In addition to a similar structural position in relation to international markets, small European countries also shared common political institutions, particularly ones that dealt with conflict management and public-private cooperation (see Figure 12.1). The vulnerability of these countries to changes in the international environment favoured the establishment of peaceful conflict-resolution institutions that would invite the participation of the major political and economic representatives of the various strata of society. Consensual political systems (based on a proportional electoral system and coalitions governments) and democratic corporatist institutions (where the major employers associations, trade unions and public officials negotiate economic and social policies) were particularly frequent in small European countries (Katzenstein, 1985). In addition, these institutions of conflict management were often completed or enlarged through the consolidation of public-private cooperative institutions designed to promote efficient social and economic policies, where the interest of the national economy overrode the interests of one special social category or interests groups.

These political institutions were, in turn, decisive in the adoption of some specific economic institutions in small countries.[2] Indeed, various elements of domestic compensation and 'selective protectionism' complemented the globally liberal orientation of their trade policies. In the words of Menzel (1988), their strategy towards international markets was 'associative-dissociative': Associative because of their dependence on international markets for exports and imports, and dissociative because these countries also introduced different measures to reduce the pressures of world markets on specific economic sectors or actors, such measures as import-substitution policies, state intervention or other forms of protectionism and public subsidies for some economic sectors (agriculture or industries producing for the domestic market, see Katzenstein, 1985, Schröter, 1999).

This argument has often been advanced to explain the 'dualist structure' of small European economies, having, on the one hand, export-oriented sectors that were very competitive on international markets and, on the other hand, sectors producing mainly for the domestic market and largely sheltered from international competitive pressures. However, these forms of 'selective protectionism' also existed in export-oriented sectors and their larger companies through the establishment of specific regulations concerning company law and financial markets. These regulations, such as complex voting rights structures or 'pyramidal' forms of control, allowed small European economies to maintain control over their large companies and to avoid the risk of foreign takeovers (see David and Mach, 2004).

Besides these institutions of domestic compensation, the political institutions also favoured the adoption of economic institutions that enhanced productivity and favoured growth, such as strong protection of property rights, vocational training system, and the presence of stable (financial) markets, which influenced the structure of economic incentives in society.

Figure 12.1 Institutions and economic growth in small European countries: A simple model

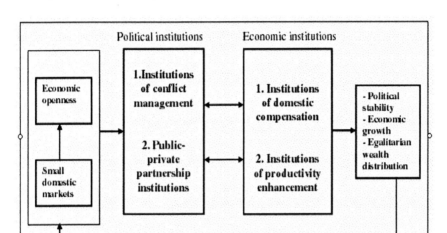

These political and economic institutions were beneficial to economic growth in several ways. First, the political institutions favoured the establishment of peaceful conflict-resolutions mechanisms, in other words, of a consensual political order (on this issue, see North et al. 2000). By protecting the 'losers' from international recessions or shocks (farmers, workers, etc.) through domestic compensation, they contributed to political stability, thereby creating an investment- and growth-friendly environment. Second, these distributive policies also promoted a rather egalitarian wealth distribution, which stimulated the economic development of these countries (Alesina and Rodrik, 1994). Third, by preventing social fragmentation, these institutions created structures and opportunities for cooperative problem-solving and increased society's potential for productive investment, innovation and human resource development (Bardhan, 2000). Finally, they influenced the structure of economic incentives in society and provided a structure for everyday transactions that reduced uncertainty and allowed groups and individuals to enlarge the set of possible fruitful exchanges (North, 1991).

In the small European countries, the national elites learned to adjust to the pressures of their international environment on which they had no influence. This fact is an important reason why national institutions were rather flexible. Katzenstein (1985) thus emphasized the capacity of small European countries for 'flexible adjustment' to the fluctuations of international markets. This institutional flexibility is important because 'the most important elements of institutional structures are those that ensure an ability to adapt to different conditions and to adjust to new circumstances as seems necessary, rather than those that entail the retention and maintenance of any specific set of policies. The capability for adaptation, based in part on the population's education and their political liberties, may ultimately be more significant for economic growth than the continuation of any particular set of beliefs, rules, or behavior' (Engerman and Sokoloff, 2003: 13).

2.   The Swiss success story (1870–1950): General characteristics

Before turning our attention to the emergence, functioning and consequences of particular institutions that helped Switzerland develop economically, we will first present some general facts and evidence on the growth path followed by the Swiss economy between 1870 and 1950.

During this period, Switzerland exhibited the highest growth rate of all European countries. Table 12.1 reports estimates of growth rates and income levels of real GDP per capita for Western Europe in the period 1870–1950. It shows that in terms of income per head Switzerland progressively overtook all the other European countries between 1870 and 1950.

Table 12.1 Rates of growth and levels of real GDP per capita, 1870–1950

	Rates of growth (% per year)			Levels of GDP (UK=100)		
	1870–1913	1913–50	1870–1950	1870	1913	1950
Belgium	1.1	0.7	0.9	84.4	85.8	78.7
Denmark	1.6	1.6	1.6	62.8	79.5	100.1
Finland	1.4	1.9	1.7	35.7	42.9	61.3
France	1.5	1.1	1.3	58.8	70.8	76.0
Germany	1.6	0.2	0.9	57.6	74.1	55.9
Italy	1.3	0.8	1.1	47.0	52.1	50.5
Netherlands	0.9	1.1	1.0	86.4	82.3	86.4
Norway	1.3	2.1	1.7	44.9	50.8	78.7
Sweden	1.5	2.1	1.8	52.1	62.9	97.1
Switzerland	1.7	2.1	1.8	65.9	86.7	130.6
United Kingdom	1.0	0.9	1.0	100.0	100.0	100.0

Source: Maddison (2003).

During the first period (1870–1913), Switzerland went through the fastest growth among the developed countries (Table 12.1). This growth is even more striking when the Swiss performance is compared to those of the United Kingdom and Belgium, two other countries that became industrialized at an early stage. In fact, Switzerland had a rate of growth comparable to the late industrializers (Germany or Sweden). It had a strong position in the sectors of the First Industrial Revolution (textile, watch-making), but also in the sectors, which emerged at the end of the nineteenth century (chemical, machine and electrical industries) (Siegenthaler, 1985).

For the period 1870–1913, Swiss economic growth benefited from two other factors. The first is linked to the use of electricity. Switzerland was a pioneer in the development of the hydro-electrical industry and became the second largest producer of electricity per capita after Norway in 1914. The replacement of other forms of energy with electricity led companies to increase the number of motors and thus their motive power (Paquier, 1998).

Second, during the three decades preceding the First World War, the financial sector played an important role in Swiss industrial growth. By providing more or less long-term operating credits, by facilitating investment operations on capital markets and by creating financial companies, banks backed the activities and the growth of certain industrial branches, in particular the electrical industry. Big banks also profited from the industrial development during this period (Mazbouri, 2005).

Profound structural changes in the industrial sector marked the second period (1914–50). The textile industry, which until 1870 had played a leading role in the industrialization process of Switzerland and which had been able to maintain its dominant position until about 1918, started to decline rapidly. At the same time, the growth of the metal and machine industry, which had begun during the previous period continued, turning it into the leading industry during the first half of the twentieth century. The success of this sector can be explained partly by its capacity to integrate foreign technologies and to adapt them to the Swiss particularities (such as predominance of hydraulic resources; see Paquier, 1998). Furthermore, Swiss companies were able to benefit from the backing of financial companies created between 1890 and 1913 by German and Swiss banks in order to respond to the long-term investment needs generated by the enormous infrastructure expenditure (mainly electrification of lighting and transport, see Hertner, 1987). Lastly, the public authorities played a non-negligible role in this growth. Indeed, from the 1890s onwards, the municipal and cantonal authorities controlled the production and distribution of gas and electricity. These authorities would systematically give preference to Swiss companies.

From 1910 to 1950, the service sector represented also an important pillar for the Swiss growth, contributing to almost 60 per cent of the growth of

Swiss GDP (David and Ritzmann, 2002: Table 9). This element is closely linked to Switzerland's growing eminence as a financial centre in the international arena. The First World War and the 1920s marked Swiss finance's emergence as a leading actor on the world stage. A comparison illustrates this evolution: Whereas before the First World War, the assets of the seven major Swiss banks accounted for only 26 per cent of those of German banks, the proportion doubled in 1928; the cumulated assets of the eight major Swiss banks amounted to 52 per cent of that of the five largest German banks.

The Swiss banking centre had three major trump cards. First of all, the Swiss franc's stability played a crucial role at a time characterized by the marked instability of the international financial order. Secondly, Swiss banks benefited from political stability and neutrality, circumstances that favoured the inflow of foreign capital. Lastly, capital was attracted by rather non-constraining circumstances, such as a tax system in favour of the holders of capital and bank secrecy, which was codified into a banking law in 1934 (Perrenoud et al. 2002; Guex, 2002).

Switzerland clearly benefited from its neutrality during the two World Wars. Research concerning the 'Swiss success story' has also stressed the significance of external markets; some have insisted on the leading role of export industries, others (less numerous) on the importance of the sectors linked to the domestic markets (agriculture, handicrafts; see David, 2003). However, very few scholars have taken into consideration the role of institutions in supporting growth. The next part will try to fill this gap.

3.   Emergence and consolidation of political institutions (1870–1950)

Some economists have already underlined the central importance of political stability in the economic success of the Swiss economy (Knöpfel, 1988; Brunetti, 1992). These studies have especially highlighted the decisive role of the referendum in promoting political and social stability in this country, which in turn created an environment favourable to investment and growth. These studies have, however, only broached the subject superficially without exploring in any thorough or detailed manner the link between political institutions and economic growth. We will first present the general historical context of the second half of the nineteenth century, which was a decisive period in terms of institutional innovation and political integration, and then analyse the creation and consolidation of these political institutions.

The second half of the nineteenth century was a crucial period in the establishment of stable political institutions that later played a central role in the growth path followed by the Swiss economy. The creation of the Swiss Confederation in 1848 by the Protestant radical-democratic movement against the opposition of the Catholic cantons was combined with the maintenance of a federalist structure with large power in the hands of the cantons. The strong federalist structure of the new Confederation was a concession for the Catholic cantons that had lost the Sonderbund war against the Protestant cantons in 1847. The maintenance of an important power structure at the cantonal level largely allowed the peaceful cohabitation of the Protestant elites, organized in the radical democratic movement, and the Catholics organized in the Christian-Democratic Party.

After two decades of rapid growth until the mid-1870s, the long depression also hit Switzerland during the last third of the century. It was during this period that some decisive political institutions were established. Following the early democratization of the country in 1848, the total reform of the Constitution in 1874 enlarged the scope of Swiss democracy with the introduction of the most important direct democratic instrument: The facultative referendum, which allowed voters to challenge any act passed by Parliament if they succeed to gather 50,000 signatures. According to several authors, the referendum was the key institution behind the development of a consensus-based political system (see Neidhart, 1970; Knöpfel, 1988; Brunetti, 1992). The government, dominated by the Radical-Democratic Party, learned to share its power with the opposition in order to prevent its bills from being challenged through the referendum. The government introduced an inclusive policy-making strategy by allowing the relevant actors, especially the major economic peak associations, to co-draft legislation in what was now called the pre-parliamentary phase.

While the Radical Democratic Party (founder of the Confederation) was by far the dominant political force, it progressively integrated all the major economic and political actors in order to reduce the potential threat of the referendum: The major peak economic associations at the end of the nineteenth century (the trade unions only later during the 1920s and 1930s) and the other major political parties from the last decade of the nineteenth up to the 1950s.[3]

In his analysis of the impact of Swiss political institutions on economic growth, Brunetti (1992: 108ff) advanced the following causal argument: By favouring the integration of all major political actors in the decision-making process, the referendum facilitated political power sharing and prevented brutal political changes. Power sharing induced by the referendum at the federal level (in addition to the federalist structure of the state) reinforced the strong pro-status-quo bias and the low capacity for rapid change of the Swiss political system. This slowness had however an important advantage: It reinforced the predictability and legal security of the country, promoting an environment favourable to investment and thus growth during the first half of the twentieth century.

Besides this general impact of the referendum (political stability, predictability, and reduction of uncertainty), other institutions, related to the existence of the referendum, had a strong positive impact on economic growth. We can distinguish two sets of political institutions that were decisive in the strong growth of the Swiss economy. First, institutions of conflict resolution were very important in supporting social and political stability of the Swiss economy. Second, the weakness of the central state and the early organization of encompassing peak level economic associations promoted the institutionalization of efficient public-private partnerships providing different types of public goods at the federal and cantonal levels.

3.1.   *Conflict resolution institutions and social peace*

The early political integration of all the major economic and political forces in the decision-making process helps to understand the political and social stability that largely prevailed during the first half of the twentieth century. First, the 'pre-parliamentary institutions' of inclusive policymaking provided strong incentives for peaceful conflict resolution at the political level. In order to prevent the risk of a rejection in a popular referendum, the dominant political actors could not ignore the position of any important economic or political actor. These institutions were decisive for cooperation among the economic and political elites of all the major social groups (business interests, farmers representatives, and trade unions),[4] and it led to the adoption of public policies and regulations aimed at satisfying all the major actors involved in policy decision-making.

Second, at the turn of the century, we could see the progressive formation of a 'bourgeois bloc', comprising all the major economic associations[5] and the two major political parties (the Radical Democratic and Christian Democratic parties), which learned to cooperate in order to counteract the pressures from the rising labour movement (Humair, 2004). The institutions of pre-parliamentary negotiations were largely limited to the major peak economic associations, while the trade unions and the political left remained largely excluded from this new political configuration emerging at the end of the nineteenth century. However, the early democratization of the Swiss political system and the subsidization of the Swiss federation of trade unions (USS), beginning at the time of its creation in 1880, helped to weaken the polarization at the political and economic level. Moreover, the gravity of social conflicts was reduced by the absence of large urban and industrial concentrations or large landownership (Jost, 2001). Even though numerous labour disputes took place during the beginning of the twentieth century, reaching a peak with the general strike of 1918, the political left and the trade unions were progressively integrated in the political decision-making process during the 1920s and 1930s.

The importance of consensus in Switzerland should not obscure two important facts (Jost, 2001). First, this country went through important conflicts. The creation of the Swiss Confederation was the result of a civil war. In a comparative perspective, labour disputes and strikes were in Switzerland as numerous as in other European countries during the decades preceding the First World War. The formation of a 'bourgeois bloc' at the end of the nineteenth century was dictated as much by the will to fight the rise of the labour movement as by the political institutions of conflict resolution.

Second, this consensus was often dominated by right-wing political parties and by peak business associations. Katzenstein (1985) defined Switzerland as a liberal variant of democratic corporatism (as opposed to the social variant), characterized by a strong and centralized business community and a relatively decentralized and weak labour movement (see also Mach, 2006)[6].

3.2. Public-private partnership institutions: Weak central state and powerful encompassing associations

Although partly linked to the institutions designed to facilitate conflict resolution, the public-private partnership institutions were not directed toward conflict management but toward the coordination of public and private actors in the resolution of social and economic problems (Hotz, 1979). Even though pre-parliamentary institutions, composed of representatives of economic associations and civil servants, already represented public-private partnership institutions, their function was very different. Whereas the former were mainly designed to produce widely supported political decisions, the function of public-private partnership institutions was mainly to produce collective goods, designed to provide services for the whole society.

It is important to stress the central role of the major peak economic associations in Switzerland, not only in the political decision-making process (as shown above), but also in the proper functioning of the economy. All the peak economic associations were created very early, and they were all subsidized by the federal government from 1870 onwards in an effort at achieving public duties, such as statistics gathering, vocational training, technical norms, or the self-discipline of the sector (Lehmbruch, 1991; Mach, 2006). It was easier for the government to financially support these encompassing associations instead of hiring new civil servants or of enlarging the bureaucracy of the central state. But, it is necessary to underline the fact that the government imposed the establishment of one peak association per major social group (workers, industry, farmers, and artisan sector), which had to be representative of its members. This favoured the creation of encompassing associations (by contrast to specialized interests, see Olson, 1982), which were responsible for a large proportion of the whole population and the economy. For example, they were very often obliged to self-discipline themselves and create self-regulating rules that applied to all their members.[7] In addition, the importance of private regulation left ample room for manoeuvre and allowed for the flexible adoption of economic and social rules.

The representatives of all these encompassing peak associations were absolutely decisive in the development and implementation of all important social and economic policies. This meant that economic associations and the state administration established very close ties and worked together on all economic and social issues. This facilitated the build up of the trust between political and economic actors and the diffusion of information among them.

4.   Economic institutions: Domestic compensation and growth supporting institutions

The creation and consolidation of the above-mentioned political institutions were the results of both international factors, related to the 'perceived vulnerability' toward their international environment (dependence on foreign markets; political and military threat of powerful surrounding states) by economic and political elites, and domestic factors, such as the fragmentation of society. As a consequence, they promoted policies that encouraged social cohesion and stability, but also economic institutions that were particularly favourable to economic growth. We can distinguish between two distinct sets of economic institutions. First, the institutions of domestic compensation provided the 'losers' of economic openness with protection, that strengthened political stability. Second, there were economic institutions that fostered exchange by lowering transaction costs and structured economic incentives.

4.1. *Institutions of domestic compensation*

The Swiss political institutions favoured the adoption of 'institutions of domestic compensation' that were very important during the long economic depression of the late nineteenth century. These institutions were adopted in order to protect some sectors (workers, farmers, and industrialists) from global competition and to stabilize the domestic economy: Agricultural subsidies and protectionist barriers against imports, creation of public cantonal banks, the regional consolidation of the railways network, and the formation of the first cartels. Without going into a detailed analysis of each economic institution, we can provide some general comments on these economic institutions.

Trade barriers and agricultural subsidies were introduced in response to the economic depression of the late nineteenth century during the course of the numerous negotiations on bilateral trade agreements between Switzerland and its major commercial partners. From a very liberal stance, Switzerland moved to a much more protectionist country, especially with regards to its agriculture, but also some industrial sectors (Humair, 2004).

The early organization of economic interests went hand in hand with the formation of the first cartels, which were created during the world depression of the last decades of the nineteenth century. During the beginning of the twentieth century, cartels were even more tolerated and consolidated because of some decisions of the Swiss Federal Court. The timing for the creation of cartels was particularly important during economic crises and wars.

These measures of domestic compensation were the result of the inclusion of different social groups in the decision-making processes, both at the federal and the cantonal level. They transformed the Swiss political economy in a fundamental way. Although still open to goods and international capital, it ceased to be liberal in a strict sense. It reinforced the dualist structure of the Swiss economy which now featured, on the one hand, sheltered domestic sectors (agriculture, construction and more generally sectors linked to local markets) and, on the other hand, competitive sectors oriented toward international markets (textiles, mechanical engineering, watches, chemicals, banks, and insurance companies).

Selective protectionist measures were reinforced during the first half of the twentieth century, particularly during the World Wars and during the economic crisis of the 1930s. For example, the reform of company law allowed Swiss companies to issue different categories of share in order to protect them against the threat of foreign takeovers. Thus, selective protectionism not only concerned the domestic sectors of the economy, but also the sectors active on international markets. After the Second World War, the adoption of the new economic articles of the Constitution included the recognition of the legal character of cartels.

In addition to these policies of 'selective protectionism', we can also point to the first labour law (*Fabrikengesetz*) adopted as early as 1877 to protect workers, because of the pressure from the left wing of the Radical Democratic Party. This law was among the most advanced labour legislation of the time despite the relative weakness of the trade unions. The mechanisms of conflict resolution at the political level presented above also spread to the economic sphere, especially to industrial relations between trade unions and employers associations. In 1937, the very important 'labour peace' agreements in the two major industrial branches (machine and watch-making industry) were concluded. They contributed decisively to the pacification of industrial relations and to the consolidation of social partnership institutions.

4.2.   *Growth supporting economic institutions*

We now focus our analysis on economic institutions that, according to the IMF or the World Bank, support growth. We selected two case-studies: Patent law and central banking. These institutions resulted from conflict management among elites and intensive public-private cooperation, and are therefore particularly illustrative.

The creation of a central bank illustrates the influence of the main Swiss political institutions. In 1896, a referendum was launched against the proposition of a national bank adopted by the Parliament after several years of deliberation. This project was contested by a coalition of conservative federalists, and by the main peak economic association, who was opposed to a state central bank and militated for a mixed or private institution. This project was finally rejected in a popular vote in 1897. In reaction, the government created a pre-parliamentary commission in which numerous opponents were represented. This commission was finally able to reach a compromise so that in 1907, the Swiss National Bank finally opened its doors. It was, as required by the Swiss Federation of Commerce and Industry, a mixed institution, a joint-stock company with public and private shareholders, the majority of the shares being held by the cantons. The creation of a central bank illustrated the importance of conflict resolutions institutions (referendum, pre-parliamentary commissions) and the close interaction of the state and private interests (see Zimmermann, 1987).

The foundation of this financial establishment, as well as other fundamental reforms at the institutional and organizational levels, such as the progressive cartelization of the Swiss banking sector and the creation of the Swiss Banker's Association in 1912 gave a new impulse to the emergence of the Swiss financial centre.

The introduction of a patent law was also made possible by cooperation among the economic elites and by the close interaction of the state and private interests. In 1882, the Swiss population rejected a constitutional reform, which would have allowed the government to legislate in the field of intellectual property rights. Six years later, after a new vote, the first patent law was enacted. It was 'the most incomplete and selective patent law ever enacted in modern times' (Schiff, 1971: 93). It excluded from patentability all inventions in the chemical field, but also inventions of new procedures in any industry whatsoever. The limits of this law can be explained by the fact that it was the result of a compromise between industrial elites.

For some sectors, in particular the watch making industry, a patent law was considered a necessity to protect intellectual property rights and to encourage investments in new technology (Veyrassat, 2001). Other industrial sectors were fiercely opposed to a patent law. The chemical industry played a leading role in this opposition (Tanner, 1996). In the 1870s, the young Swiss chemical industry was in a difficult position, unable to compete with German firms with a big scale advantage. The Basle companies were confronted with two alternatives: Either give up in the face of German competition or adopt a new strategy (Straumann, 1997). The Swiss chemical industry followed the latter path. This new strategy, which explains the impressive growth of the Swiss chemical industry until the First World War, was based on two pillars: Innovation and imitation/variation (Tanner, 1996; Straumann, 1997; Moser, 2003). The Swiss chemical industry abandoned mass production in order to focus on products with high value added, especially medicines. This specialization was linked very closely to a rise in research and development activities within companies. This strategy of innovation was backed by a policy of imitation. The absence of regulation concerning patents for the Swiss chemical industry allowed the Basle firms to concentrate its resources on imitating the products and processes developed abroad (particularly in Germany and France).

By excluding from patentability all invention in the chemical field, the patent law of 1888 was thus able to conciliate the antagonist interests of Swiss industrialists. It was only in 1907 that a patent law worth its name came into being, even if a number of exclusions from patentability still existed. This new law was introduced for several reasons. Germany placed a great amount of political and economic pressure on its successful Swiss chemical competitor. The German chemical industry claimed that the latter's success was largely due to imitation – some spoke of 'practices of robber barons'. The changing attitude of the large chemical firms was also responsible for the introduction of the 1907 patent law. Their development made them more and more dependent on innovations through their own activities of R&D and less on imitation, on learning by doing. In these conditions, a patent law became important for the Basle industry. In a few decades, the accusations of piracy were forgotten, and the Swiss chemical industry became known for the quality of its products (Tanner, 1996).

5.   Conclusions

As argued above, political institutions were particularly decisive in the long-term growth of the Swiss economy between 1870 and 1950 by providing social stability, legal security and efficient coordination for economic actors. These characteristics led to the adoption of economic institutions that were far removed from the liberal orthodoxy adopted by the IMF and the World Bank during the 1980s and 1990s. The positive effects of these economic institutions have not profoundly changed during the last period, and political stability is still very high.

The Swiss economy exhibited very good performance in terms of growth and economic development during most of the twentieth century. However, during the last two decades, especially during the 1990s, the average growth of the Swiss economy has been among the lowest of OECD countries since the beginning of the 1990s, several (neo-)liberal economists as well as business representatives, especially from the largest multinational companies, have been complaining about this weak growth and particularly pointed to the negative impact of political institutions (especially the facultative referendum, but also federalism) on the growth of the Swiss economy (Borner et al. 1990). In a very 'Olsonian' perspective, these economists stress that the referendum is unilaterally favouring specialized interest groups opposed to change, the referendum being the privileged instrument of 'conservative' forces of both the left and the right opposed to any political and economic reforms. It has thus become an obstacle for the 'necessary' economic and social reforms in a period of globalization and fierce international competition.

Without going into an analysis of the recent slow growth period, which gave rise to a highly politicized debate[8], this changing interpretation of the impact of Swiss institutions is interesting. It first stresses that the role of institutions in one country can change over time, and, second, lessons from one country should not be considered as universal. If we want to understand the influence of institutions, we should take into account the specific social and economic context of each nations, in which institutions operate.

Having mentioned this, we can nevertheless try to draw some lessons from the role of political and economic institutions for the Swiss growth between 1870 and 1950.

First, by reinforcing political stability and by creating opportunities for cooperative problem-solving mechanisms among major economic and political actors, political institutions provided positive structure to adopt economic institutions that were favourable for growth.

Second, institutions of domestic compensation, besides their role in terms of political and social stability, also had an economic function. Domestic compensation and 'associative-dissociative' development strategy adopted by Switzerland helped the country to abandon an export-led growth path (dominated by the major industrial exports) to a more 'autocentric' economic development at the end of the nineteenth century and the first half of the twentieth century.

Third, the absence of certain economic institutions, such as patent law and central banking, generally considered as very important for economic growth by the IMF or the World Bank, was not detrimental to the rapid development of the Swiss economy during the second half of the nineteenth century. The Swiss historical experience showed that these 'good institutions', seen today as necessary for economic development, did not play a central role in the first phase of the 'Swiss success story'. However, they were replaced by other mechanisms that supported the economic development of the industrial and financial sectors.

Notes

1. We would like to thank the participants of the project for their helpful comments, in particular Ha-Joon Chang, Patrick O'Brien, and Eric Rauchway. Elisabeth Spilman, Béatrice Veyrassat, Tobias Straumann, and Matthieu Leimgruber also made very interesting comments. For a more detailed argument, refer to David and Mach (2006).
2. For a distinction between economic and political institutions, see Acemoglu et al. (2004).
3. In 1891, the Christian-Democratic Party joined the government, the Swiss people's Party in 1929 and finally the Social-Democratic Party in 1943. This led to the formation of the so-called 'magic formula' of the Swiss government coalition in 1959, composed of the four most important parties.
4. While Katzenstein (1985) mainly focuses his analysis on the 1930s because of the creation of democratic corporatist institutions in small European countries, the

cooperation between economic and political actors was already institutionalized in Switzerland during the end of the nineteenth century.

5. The Swiss Federation of Commerce and Industry, the Swiss Association of Small Business (USAM), representing the interests of artisans and crafts, and the Swiss Farmers' Union (USP).

6. Moreover, this consensus did not include certain social groups. Women had to wait until 1971 to get universal suffrage at the federal level, and foreigners, who have represented close to 10–20 per cent of the Swiss population throughout the course of the twentieth century, have also had very restricted political and economic rights.

7. Lehner (1983) tried to explain why the Swiss case did not fit Olson's theory on the rise and decline of nations. His argument was different from the one developed here. His major argument was to stress the role of the openness of the Swiss decision-making process, which reduces the power of specialized interests groups and prevents the adoption of rent-seeking institutions (for a critic, see Mach, 2006).

8. These institutions might have contributed in some ways to slow the growth of the last decades; in particular, by overemphasizing stability and incremental changes, Swiss political institutions tend to prevent innovation and new initiatives, which can be detrimental to growth. However, other factors, such as very restrictive macroeconomic policies (especially the monetary policy since the breakdown of the Bretton Woods system, which led to a steady appreciation of the Swiss franc and represented a handicap for exports) and more stringent credit policy of the banking sector, have also contributed to the stagnation of the 1990s.

References

Acemoglu, D. et al. 2004. *Institutions as the Fundamental Cause of Long-Run Growth*. Documento CEDE.

Alesina, A. and Rodrik, D. 1994. 'Distributive Politics and Economic Growth'. *Quarterly Journal of Economics*, 109: 465–90.

Borner, S. et al. 1990. *Schweiz AG. Vom Sonderfall zum Sanierungsfall?* Zurich: Verlag NZZ.

Bardhan, P. 2000. 'The Nature of Institutional Impediments to Economic Development', in M. Olson and S. Kähkönen (eds) *A Not-so-Dismal Science. A Broader View of Economies and Societies*. Oxford: Oxford University Press, pp. 245–67.

Brunetti, A. 1992. *Politisches System and Wirtschaftswachstum*. Chur: Rüegger.

Chang, H-J. 2002. *Kicking Away the Ladder – Development Strategy in Historical Perspective*. London: Anthem Press.

David, T. and Ritzmann-Blickenstorfer, H. 2002. 'Gross Domestic Product in Switzerland, 1891–1950. A New Estimation'. *Working Paper*, University of Lausanne.

David, T. 2003. 'Croissance économique et mondialisation: le cas de la Suisse (1870–1914)', in H-J. Gilomen et al. (eds), *Globalisierung. Voraussetzungen, Chancen und Risiken aus historischer Sicht (1700–2000)*. Zurich: Chronos, pp. 145–69.

David, T. and Mach, A. 2004. 'The Specificity of Corporate Governance in Small States: Institutionalisation and Questioning of Ownership Restrictions in Switzerland and Sweden', in R. Aguilera and M. Federowicz (eds), *Corporate Governance in a Changing Economic and Political Environment*. London: Palgrave, pp. 220–46.

David, T. and Mach, A. 2006. 'Institutions and Economic Growth: The Successful Experience of Switzerland, 1870–1950'. WIDER Research Paper 2006–101. Helsinki: UNU-WIDER.

Engerman, S. and Sokoloff, K. 2003. 'Institutional and Non-Institutional Explanations of Economic Differences'. *NBER Working Paper* 9989.

Guex, S. 2002. 'La politique de la Banque nationale suisse (1907–1939): modèles, références, spécificités', in O. Feiertag and M. Margairaz (eds). *Politiques et pratiques des banques d'émission en Europe (XVIIe-XXe siècles)*. Paris: Albin Michel, 526–47.

Hertner, P. 1987. 'Les sociétés financières suisses et le développement de l'industrie électrique jusqu'à la Première Guerre mondiale', in F. Cardot (ed.). *Un siècle d'électricité dans le monde*. Paris: PUF, pp. 341–55.

Hotz, B. 1979. *Politik zwischen Staat und Wirtschaft*. Diessenhofen: Ruegger.

Humair, C. 2004. *Développement économique et Etat central (1815–1914)*. Bern: Lang.

Jost, H-U. 2001. 'Critique historique du consensus helvétique'. *Traverse* 3: 57–80.

Katzenstein, P. 1985. *Small States in World Markets. Industrial Policy in Europe*. Ithaca: Cornell University Press.

Knöpfel, C. 1988. *Der Einfluss der politischen Stabilität auf die internationale Wettbewerbsfähigkeit der Schweiz*. Grüsch: Rüegger.

Lehmbruch, G. 1991. 'The Organization of Society, Administrative Strategies and Policy Networks', in R. Czada et al. (eds). *Political Choice, Institutions, Rules and the Limits of Rationality*. Francfort: Campus, pp. 121–58.

Lehner, F. 1983. 'Pressure Politics and Economic Growth: Olson's Theory and the Swiss Experience', in D. Müller (ed.). *The Political Economy of Growth*. New Haven: Yale University Press, pp. 203–14.

Mach, A. 2006. *La Suisse entre internationalisation et changements politiques internes: législation sur les cartels et relations industrielles dans les années 1990*. Chur: Rüegger.

Maddison, A. 2003. *The World Economy. Historical Statistics*. Paris: OCDE.

Mazbouri, M. 2005. *L'émergence de la place financière Suisse, 1890–1913. Itinéraire d'un grand banquier*. Lausanne: Antipodes.

Menzel, U. 1988. *Auswege aus der Abhängigkeit. Die entwicklungspolitische Aktualität Europas*. Francfort: Suhrkamp.

Menzel, U. 1992. 'The Experience of Small European Countries with late Development. Lessons from History', in L. Mjoset (ed.). *Contributions to the Comparative Study of Development*. Oslo: Institute for Social Research, pp. 44–95.

Moser, P. 2003. 'How do Patent Laws Influence Innovation? Evidence from Nineteenth Century World Fairs'. *NBER Working Paper* 9909.

Neidhart, L. 1970. *Plebiszit und pluralitäre Demokratie*. Bern: Francke.

North, D. 1991. *Institutions, Institutional Change and Economic Performance*, Cambridge: Cambridge University Press.

North, D. et al. 2000. 'Order, Disorder, and Economic Change: Latin America vs. North America', in B. Bueno de Mesquita and R. Hilton (eds). *Governing for Prosperity*. New Haven: Yale University Press, 17–58.

Olson, M. 1982. *The Rise and Decline of Nations. Economic Growth, Stagflation and Social Rigidies*. Yale University Press.

Paquier, S. 1998. *Histoire de l'électricité en Suisse. La dynamique d'un petit pays européen (1875–1939)*. Genève: Passé Présent.

Perrenoud, M. et al. 2002. *La place financière et les banques suisses à l'époque du national-socialisme. Les relations des grandes banques avec l'Allemagne (1931–1946)*. Zurich: Chronos.

Schiff, E. 1971. *Industrialization without National Patents. The Netherlands, 1869–1912 and Switzerland, 1850–1907*. Princeton: Princeton University Press.

Schröter, H. 1999. 'Small European Nations: Cooperative Capitalism in the Twentieth Century', in A. Chandler et al. (eds). *Big Business and the Wealth of Nations*. Cambridge: Cambridge University Press, pp. 176–204.

Siegenthaler, H. 1985. 'Die Schweiz, 1850–1914', in W. Fischer (ed.), *Handbuch der europäischen Wirtschafts- und Sozialgeschichte.* Stuttgart: Klett-Cotta: vol. 5, pp. 443–73.

Straumann, T. 1997. 'Die Wissenschaft ist der goldene Leistern der Praxis. Das deutsche Modell und die Entstehung der Basler Chemie (1860–1920)', in T. Busset et al. (eds). *Chemie in der Schweiz. Geschichte der Forschung und der Industrie.* Basel: Merian, pp. 77–99.

Tanner, J. 1996. 'Property rights, Innovationsdynamik und Marktmacht', in A. Ernst and E. Wigger (eds). *Die neue Schweiz? Eine Gesellschaft zwischen Integration und Polarisierung (1910–1930).* Zurich: Chronos, pp. 273–303.

Veyrassat, B. 2001. 'De la protection de l'inventeur à l'industrialisation de l'invention', in H-J. Gilomen et al. (eds). *Innovations. Incitations et résistances – des sources de l'innovation à ses effets.* Zurich: Chronos, pp. 367–84.

Zimmermann, R. 1987. *Volksbank oder Aktionsbank?* Zurich: Chronos.

CHAPTER 13
THE RISE AND HALT OF ECONOMIC DEVELOPMENT IN BRAZIL, 1945–2004: INDUSTRIAL CATCHING-UP, INSTITUTIONAL INNOVATION, AND FINANCIAL FRAGILITY

Leonardo Burlamaqui, José A. P. de Souza, and Nelson H. Barbosa-Filho

1.   Introduction

In the 35 years following the Second World War, Brazilian GDP doubled every decade. This extraordinary economic performance came to a halt in the last 25 years. This chapter seeks to explain that experience in terms of the country's institutional dynamics, where waves of institutional innovation were followed by periods of institutional inefficiency and/or inertia, showing how these waves of institutional change affected state capacity, policy-making, long-term expectations concerning investment decisions, and the overall macroeconomic performance.

The chapter covers the period from the end of the first Vargas Government in the mid-1940s to the end of the second Cardoso administration. Our analytical framework is structured around the concepts of technological and institutional innovation (Schumpeter), the relationship between long-term expectations, investment and growth (Keynes), financial fragility and destabilizing stability (Minsky) and the critical importance of the presence of a Developmental State (Gerschenkron, 1961; Johnson, 1982).

Our analysis of the crucial relationship between institutional change and economic growth will be organized around four main questions. First, what was the role of the State in general, and the government bureaucracy in particular, as an agent of institutional innovation and change? Second, how did the institutional structure channelled resources to capital accumulation and cope with the bottlenecks common to late-late industrialization? Third, how did the existing institutions manage the economic and social conflicts in each period? Fourth, how was the institutional landscape, especially government procedures, affected by the dominant ideology of the time?

The chapter is in five sections. Section 2 analyses the economic conditions at the end of the 1940s and discusses how the institutional innovations introduced under Vargas and Kubitschek gave birth to the Brazilian version of the Developmental State, releasing the growth potential of the economy during the 1950s. Section 3 discusses the inflationary crisis and the institutional inertia of the early and mid-1960s, and the subsequent wave of institutional innovations, especially the new conflict management devices introduced between 1964 and 1967, and their impacts on long-term expectations and growth during 'the Brazilian growth miracle' (that is, from 1968 until 1980). Section 4 covers the institutional changes following the debt crisis of early 1980s and the cluster of ineffective institutional innovations during various unsuccessful macroeconomic stabilization plans from the mid-1980s through the mid-1990s, the period usually known as the Brazilian inflationary trap. We then proceed to analyse another wave of institutional innovations associated with the pro-market reforms of the 1990s and their consequences up to the present. Section 5 concludes the chapter.

2.   Building state capacity and forging the catch-up system: 1945–60

During 15 years in office (1930–1945),[1] Getulio Vargas promoted a fundamental institutional change in the Brazilian economy.[2] After 1937 especially, Vargas began to transform the country's administrative, legal and productive structure in a pragmatic but increasingly authoritarian way. In the period, the state delimited workers rights and organized professional and political representation from above, using coercion in no small way. The bureaucracy was improved through the creation of a specific department to select and train public servants (DASP – Departamento da Administração do Serviço Público – Department of Public Services Administration), accountable only to the president. As a result, the state's capacity to monitor and support development was greatly improved.

The proclaimed objective of Vargas was development through the restructuring of the forces of the nation and the establishment of fundamental industries (Castro, 1994: 186). Financial resources and entrepreneurship skills were transferred from the production and export of coffee (the then hegemonic economic activity) to the manufacturing industries, and the frequent devaluation of the currency created the conditions for the internal production of industrial goods. The state progressively centralized finance, coordinated investment projects, built infrastructure and produced basic goods. Those were the years when the basis of the Brazilian Developmental State was crafted.[3]

Eurico Dutra's democratic government (1946–50) discontinued Vargas's policies, lowering the competence of the civil service and cutting short the industrializing plans. Due to over-valued exchange rate, imports rose swiftly and international reserves disappeared. When it had to incur short-term debts, the government introduced a system of quantitative import control without devaluating the currency, in order to protect coffee interests (Furtado, 1965). Imports of raw materials, intermediate goods, and equipment were privileged, with the (unintended) consequence that the industry was protected from import competition.

Vargas returned to power in 1951, this time as a democratically-elected president, and increased his commitment to state-led development, which greatly diminished the political support from the elites. Investments in infrastructure, especially in energy and transportation, were emphasized. For the first time, the main agrarian, industrial, urban, and institutional questions were identified and tackled in an integrated, explicit and purposeful way.

During this period, the seeds of some fundamental public institutions for an industrial society were sown. The emerging scientific community was organized through the Brazilian Society for the Progress of Science (SBPC 1948), and the National Council of Research (CNPq) was formed in 1951. Universities were organized, while some elite military engineering schools reflected the increasing professionalization of the armed forces.

Two main restrictions put pressure on Vargas's strategy: Inflation was rising quickly (see Table 13.1) and external and public-finance deficits were mounting. Sustainable economic growth, therefore, required foreign capital. As official loans were favoured, this gave the government discretionary power over the uses of foreign capital. Public enterprises were to become the main economic actors of the period. The BNDES (Banco Nacional de Desenvolvimento Econômico e Social – National Bank for Economic and Social Development)[4] was created in 1952 with the manifest intention of rationalizing the use of public resources by selecting projects by technical, rather than political, criteria (Castro, 1994: 187).[5]

Table 13.1 Basic macroeconomic indicators of Brazil

	Real GDP growth (%)	Annual inflation rate (%) Consumer price index-IPC/FIPE	Trade balance as % of GDP
1950	6.80	3.72	2.7
1951	4.90	11.27	0.2
1952	7.30	27.16	-1.4
1953	4.70	19.23	3.2
1954	7.80	22.57	1.3
1955	8.80	18.44	2.8
1956	2.90	26.46	3.0
1957	7.70	13.74	0.5
1958	10.80	23.36	0.5
1959	9.80	42.70	0.5
1960	9.40	32.20	-0.1
1961	8.60	43.51	0.6
1962	6.60	61.73	-0.5
1963	0.60	80.53	0.5
1964	3.40	85.60	1.6
1965	2.40	41.20	2.9
1966	6.70	46.29	1.5
1967	4.20	25.33	0.7
1968	9.80	25.22	0.1
1969	9.50	22.58	0.9
1970	6.70	17.46	0.5
1971	11.30	20.60	-0.7
1972	11.94	17.46	-0.4
1973	13.97	13.97	0
1974	8.15	33.05	-4.2
1975	5.15	29.26	-2.7
1976	10.26	38.07	-1.5
1977	4.93	41.10	0.1
1978	4.97	39.91	-0.5
1979	6.76	67.19	-1.3
1980	9.20	84.77	-1.2
1981	-4.25	90.87	0.5
1982	0.83	94.63	0.3
1983	-2.93	164.09	3.4
1984	5.40	178.56	6.9
1985	7.85	228.22	5.9
1986	7.49	68.08	3.2
1987	3.53	367.12	4.0
1988	-0.06	891.67	6.3
1989	3.16	1,635.85	3.9
1990	-4.35	1,639.08	2.3

	Real GDP growth (%)	Annual inflation rate (%) Consumer price index-IPC/FIPE	Trade balance as % of GDP
1991	1.03	458.61	2.6
1992	-0.54	1,129.45	3.9
1993	4.92	2,490.99	3.1
1994	5.85	1,172.96	1.9
1995	4.22	23.17	-0.5
1996	2.66	10.04	-0.7
1997	3.27	4.83	-0.8
1998	0.13	-1.79	-0.8
1999	0.79	8.64	-0.2
2000	4.36	4.38	-0.1
2001	1.31	7.13	0.5
2002	1.93	9.90	2.9
2003	0.54	8.18	4.9
2004	4.9	6.56	5.5

A currency crisis in 1952 led to a dual exchange rate system, whereupon some imports and the main exports followed an official rate, with a free market rate for the rest. The result was a fall in exports, with the public debt mounting without monetary flexibility or credit expansion. In October 1953, Vargas re-established the currency monopoly of Banco do Brasil and created a system of multiple exchange rates, eliminating direct quantitative controls and establishing foreign currency auctions.[6] Imports were classified according to its 'essentiality' character, and SUMOC (Money and Credit Bureau) allocated foreign reserves accordingly. This arrangement favoured capital goods imports, bringing about a much-needed technological upgrade, but did not stimulate an exports drive. Accordingly, a sizable market for domestically-produced goods was created, first through the higher relative costs of imports included in the 'non-essential' categories, and second through the subsidies to the imports of capital goods and raw materials (Vianna, 1987). The resulting industrialization was neither self-sustainable nor particularly intensive: Light durable consumer goods were the main items.

In 1954, political tensions and pressures had become so unmanageable that Vargas committed suicide. This dramatic gesture unleashed a period of turmoil until the election of a new President, Juscelino Kubitschek (1956–60), under whose leadership Brazil experienced something of a golden age. In a deliberate effort to advance beyond conjunctural responses, long-range targets (Plano de Metas, Development Targets Plan) were proposed to install an integrated industrial structure, with a growth of productive capacity far ahead of any expected expansion of the markets in the capital and durable goods sectors. Its slogan was 'Fifty years in Five'.

The new president created an impressive climate for development. The 'Plano de Metas' had a considerable success in its four main areas (transportation, energy, intermediate goods, and capital goods), as well as in the fifth, the building of the new capital, Brasilia. However, Kubitschek's main solution to the problems of funding development projects was an inflationary one of allocating funds for specific areas, using special surtaxes amounting to 22 per cent of federal revenue in 1957. These surtaxes were not included in the federal budget and were collected and deposited directly with the BNDES. During this time, the BNDES came into its own, providing more than investments and performing and important screening function (Geddes, 1990: 227).

Reversing a trend from the previous period, between 1955 and 1959 Brazil actively invited multinational companies. The public sector increased its direct participation in domestic capital formation, financing it through inflationary funding (inflation more than doubled – see Table 13.1) and external credit. From 1957 onwards the exchange rate system was simplified (Lessa, 1982) and a monetary stabilization plan was attempt, although it did not go very far, especially after Kubitschek fell out with the IMF.

In the administrative sphere, new kinds of insulated agencies was created by presidential decree, the 'Grupos de Trabalho' (Working Groups) and the 'Grupos Executivos' (Executive Groups). The Working Groups were consultative organs which brought together representatives of the public and the private sectors, conducting sectoral studies in order to increase policy efficiency. The Executive Groups worked as forums of consultation, exchange of information, and negotiation between the government and the business class. Both played a key role in the task of implementing sectoral goals, with enough autonomy concerning budgets and personnel recruitment. There were five main Working Groups, of which the electric energy and steel ones were the most successful. Of the Executive Groups, those related to the auto, naval, and mechanical industries were the most effective. Using Chalmers Johnson's perspective, we can think of the Executive Groups as the Pilot Agency in charge of the development strategy (Johnson, 1982).

Before closing this section, it is worth underlying Hirschman's point that at least one experience in Latin America, of which Brazil during the 1950s, came fairly close to the picture drawn by Gerschenkron: Sustained and rapid progress of steel, chemical and capital goods industries, financed by inflation, and the flowering of a 'developmentalist' ideology (Hirschman, 1971: 95). The Brazilian experience of the 1950s, however, could not be replicated easily: It was very dependent on exogenous conditions and lacked conflict management institutions. In this sense, questions raised by Furtado (1965) still holds: Can a system of power oriented to the preservation of the *status quo* formulate and carry out a development policy in a country where development necessarily means modifications in the social structure? Will this system of power hold, or will it evolve towards a rupture?

Jânio Quadros, elected the President in 1960, took office in the new capital in a country with a much more robust industrial structure, although with serious political tensions and a growing inflationary pressure. However, in the next few years, the country was thrown into disarray by the political, economic and social disturbances of the early sixties to which we now turn.

3.   Institutional creative destruction, rapid growth, and increasing financial fragility: 1964–84

Although the catch-up strategy of Kubitschek was a huge success in terms of upgrading the industrial structure, it nonetheless had very shaky finance-funding mechanisms and virtually no 'conflict management' institutions. The soaring inflation coupled with the deceleration of growth and the defeat of the ruling coalition in the 1960 presidential election signalled a *politics-policy watershed*.

Among the episodes which constituted that watershed, apart from the deterioration in macroeconomic fundamentals, were Quadros's strident discourse against inflation and corruption, his ambiguous external policy, and especially his enigmatic resignation only eight months after taking office. The military, foreign capital, and the new-born native entrepreneurs were worried about the 'dangerous' proximity to the working class of the Vice President, João Goulart (nicknamed Jango), who would succeed Quadros (Skidmore, 1972), and changed the system of government into a parliamentary one, in order to weaken the presidency – an act that, in retrospect, could be seen as a rehearsal for 1964's *coup d'état*.

The parliamentarian episode lasted until the beginning of 1963 when a plebiscite brought back the presidential system, but by then inflation had jumped to 62 per cent and the trade balance had turned negative for the second time since 1953 (see Table 13.1). Institutionally and in terms of macroeconomic conditions, the country had clearly deteriorated. The investment/GDP rate declined from 18 per cent in 1959 to 13 per cent in 1961, and the annual growth rate fell from 9.8 per cent in 1961 to 6.6 per cent in 1962 and 0.6 per cent in 1963.[7]

Politically, the situation was also dismal. Jango was a weak President who could not govern. His actions alienated the military, businessmen and a sizeable part of civil society. A new profit remittance law was approved in September, 1961 (limiting the profit repatriation to 10 per cent of the invested capital), and by the end of 1963, with inflation reaching 80 per cent, Jango himself raised the wages of all public employees by 60 per cent and the minimum wage by 56 per cent (Viella, 2004: 63). His promises for nationalistic and *socialistic* reforms (such as the Foreign Capital Law and the Land Reform) and his appeals to the rank and file inside the military only aggravated the political tensions and triggered the military *coup d'état*.

On 31 March 1964, the military seized power, backed by the business elite, foreign capital, the middle class, and the US government. A period of political and institutional changes followed (Skidmore, 1972; Belluzzo and Melo, 1982). The military government asked two leading conservative economists, Octávio Gouveia de Bulhões and Roberto Campos (appointed finance and planning ministers, respectively) to undertake the necessary reforms to put the economy back on the growth track while getting rid of inflation and fixing the balance of payments. The Campos-Bulhões plan, mainly authored by Campos, contained a robust institutional reform to tackle government deficits and wage pressures, which were identified as the *causa causans* of the inflationary process (Campos, 1964, and chapter 12 of Campos, 1994, his monumental autobiography). Its main elements included: (a) a programme of fiscal adjustment increasing fiscal revenue by means of tax rise; (b) a monetary programme, reducing rates of expansion of the means of payment; (c) a financial policy controlling credit, by tying its expansion to the monetary budget; and (d) a wage indexation mechanism through which the *average real wage would be kept constant* except for the partial incorporation of productivity increases (Hermann, 2004).

Indexation was rapidly extended from wage contracts to almost all contracts, being removed completely only after the hyperinflation of 1988–94.[8] Wage indexation was introduced as an authoritarian, but clever, 'conflict management' institutional device, keeping wages and prices relatively aligned. The problem with the device was that its short-term and long-term effects are conflicting ones. While in the short term it stabilizes expectations by producing some degree of predictability on future wage negotiations, it also introduces an element of inertia in the inflationary dynamics that prevents it from being effectively controlled, while amplifying the inflationary consequences of any sort of supply shock.

As a stabilization plan, the PAEG (Plano de Ação Econômica do Governo – Government Plan for Economic Action) was not very successful. However, as an institutional reform, it was a success. The fiscal and financial reforms re-equipped the state to lead the development process. They improved considerably the 'fundamentals' of the Developmental State forged under Vargas and Kubitschek and launched the era of extremely rapid growth during 1968–80.

The fiscal reform aimed explicitly at raising fiscal revenue as well as rationalizing the tax structure (see Hermann, 2004, and Resende 1990, for details). The results showed up quickly: The tax/GDP rate went from 16 per cent in 1963 to 21 per cent in 1967 and escalated to 26 per cent in 1970.[9] The financial reform included the following elements: (a) the creation of the Central Bank[10] and of the National Monetary Council as its main regulatory institution (1964); (b) the creation of a National System of Real Estate Funding in order to promote the construction industry (1964); (c) the creation of indexed bonds, which created what would later become a massive market for public debt (1964); (d) a capital market law which extended indexation to financial products issued by private financial institutions (1965); (e) several incentives for private investors, mainly in the form of tax exemptions, to acquire stocks; (f) a new foreign investment law liberalizing financial transfers abroad and profit repatriation; (g) a Central Bank Resolution that regulated foreign borrowing by native banks and its conversion to domestic credit to private firms; and h) the extension of foreign borrowing directly to private firms. Financial deepening and openness combined to produce an *institutional creative destruction*. The result was, to use a Schumpeterian analogy, synchronization between the capitalist – economic – *system* and the capitalist – institutional – *order* (Schumpeter, 1928, 1942).

Besides also rationalizing the country's financial system, the financial reform created a private capital market. By doing that, the reform, while keeping the *visible hand* of the State in the core of the development process, gave Business the means to privately finance its own growth. The result was the conversion of the vast amount of industrial idle capacity inherited from Kubitschek into an extremely rapid growth.

The growth spurt began in 1968 with the GDP growing 9.8 per cent, and accelerating to 11.3 per cent in 1971, 11.9 per cent in 1972 and topping 14 per cent in 1973. For the period 1968–73, the average was 11 per cent and for the 1968–80 period, 8.23 per cent. The impact of the first oil-shock in 1973 on growth was, as in South Korea, merely to *decrease the growth rate*.[11] This massive growth was, surprisingly, accompanied by decreasing inflation between 1968 and 1973 and stable inflation between 1974 and 1978 (see Table 13.1). Moreover, the balance of payments situation improved with surpluses showing up from 1967 to 1973 and again in 1976–78.[12] That was Brazil's *miracle*.

The political basis of the *miracle* was, of course, the military whose rule acted as a powerful (and authoritarian) 'conflict management institution'. Nevertheless, the civil elites and the upper middle class were also 'recruited' to support the new regime by financial gains and the diffusion of consumer durable goods (Cardoso, 1977). Economically, the miracle was the heir to Kubitschek's 'Fifty years in Five' catch-up strategy, but its institutional architecture was clearly crafted by the Campos-Bulhões plan. Ironically it was Antonio Delfim Neto, finance minister from 1967 to 1974 (dubbed the 'czar of the economy') who took credit for the 'miracle', despite simply 'cruising' an economy already prepared for a new boom.

Delfim's 1968s Plan, called the Strategic Development Plan, was openly 'developmental', exhorting: (a) the consolidation of private enterprise; (b) expansion of the domestic market (especially for durable goods); (c) infrastructure development (by means of public enterprise investment); (d) price stabilization *but* with no explicit inflation targets; (e) incentives to increase foreign borrowing; and (f) the extension of indexation to the exchange rate (what became known as the 'mini-devaluations'). Of the elements mentioned above, the last three were the *Achilles heel* of the plan and causes of both the soaring inflation and the financial fragilization of the eighties. They helped to create a classic Minskyan situation of 'destabilizing stability'.

Two factors were crucial in sustaining growth from 1974 to 1980 in spite of the oil shock and the international recession that followed it.

The *first* was the industrial strategy, which was structural adjustment by means of industrial deepening. The Second National Development Plan (II PND) launched in 1974, under General Ernesto Geisel's Presidency, diagnosed that a recessionary (orthodox) response to the external shocks would only worsen the domestic situation both through impeding the completion of the heavy phase of import-substitution strategy and by eroding an export-led response to the balance of payments deterioration.[13] The Plan was Brazil's own version of South Korea's 1973 Heavy and Chemical Push (Burlamaqui, 1989), also with 'national self-sufficiency' as its main target. The main sectors to be promoted were oil production and substitution (the alcohol-as-fuel programme), steel, petrochemicals, telecommunications, electric energy (especially the giant hydroelectric plant in Itaipu), highways, and the nuclear programme (Castro and Souza, 1985 and Castro, 2003). The projected GDP growth for the period 1974–1979 was 10 per cent per year![14] Those were the years of the '*marcha forçada*' ('forced march') of the Brazilian economy, to quote Castro and Souza's classic book (Castro and Souza, 1985).

The *second* enabling condition for that '*marcha forçada*' was (reckless) finance. Skyrocketing external debt provided by the huge liquidity pool created by the *petrodollars*. Brazilian external debt, which was already increasing very fast since 1967, reached US$38 billion in 1977, US$64 billion in 1980 and escalated to US$102 billion in 1984 (Brazilian Central Bank statistics). Both the terms and interest rates attached to these debt contracts were floating. Therefore, the 'forced march' years can be seen as a classic case of *destabilizing stability*, which unfolded as a double process of financial fragilization: Rapidly raising domestic inflation and external vulnerability.

The second oil shock in 1979, followed by the Volcker interest-rate shock pushed the Brazilian government's debt structure from a speculative position into a Ponzi one (Minsky, 1982, 1986).[15] In 1981, a huge recession occurred, and in 1982 Mexico declared moratorium. From then on, external financing completely dried up. Although GDP still increased 7.8 per cent and 7.5 per cent in 1985 and 1986, the growth era was clearly coming to an end. On the ideological front, big changes were also taking place. With stagflation and financial liberalization, both Keynesianism and national developmental-*ism* were, as economic ideologies, fading away.

4.   Stabilization, institutional reforms, and stagnation – the 'lost decades': 1985–2004

The mid-1980s marked the return to a civilian government. Reducing inflation quickly became the main priority of the new government led by José Sarney (1985–90), since the annual inflation rate rose from 90 per cent in 1980 to 202 per cent in 1984. The high degree of price indexation meant that devaluation was quickly transmitted to domestic prices, which in turn led to currency appreciation, in a continuing loop. In other words, because of widespread indexation, Brazilian inflation had a strong persistence. From an institutional perspective, the conflict-management rules instituted by indexation were clearly counterproductive because, as each group tried to defend itself against changes in relative prices, the only result was more inflation and increasing macroeconomic instability.

Between 1985 and 1994, Brazil was subject to six heterodox stabilization plans, namely: The *Cruzado* plan of 1986 (named after the new currency); the *Bresser* plan of 1987 (named after the finance minister at the time); the 'Summer' plan of 1989 (implemented in January); the *Collor* I plan of 1990 and the *Collor* II plan of 1991 (named after the President at the time); and the *Real* plan of 1994 (named after the new currency). Their common element was the use of price controls and a currency reform to reduce inertial inflation abruptly. The consensus at the time was that an orthodox (IMF-style) stabilization strategy would be useless because inflation was mostly inertial and, therefore, independent of the level of economic activity. The main difference among these plans concerned the method of price control and macroeconomic management.[16]

The first five plans failed mostly because of a mix of poorly-designed price controls and a chronic inability to control the exchange rate. In the late 1980s and early 1990s capital inflows were minimal and trade surpluses were insufficient to sustain an exchange-rate peg, which was a vital part of any stabilization strategy. Thus, after an initial success in reducing inflation, each of the first five plans failed because of the circumvention of the price controls and exchange-rate pressures.[17] The most dramatic episode occurred in 1987, when the government declared a moratorium on foreign debts (Batista Jr., 1988).

The late 1980s and early 1990s were also marked by major political and institutional changes. In 1989 Brazil had its first direct presidential election since 1960. In a highly competitive and turbulent process, Fernando Collor de Mello defeated the left-wing candidate, Lula, and took office in 1990.

Collor's economic policy was based on a mix of a heterodox stabilization strategy and liberal institutional reforms. The basic idea was that it would be possible to reduce and stabilize inflation only if capital flows returned, which in turn required liberalized capital markets. In the early 1990s, a world-wide increase of capital flows to emerging markets, combined with the failure of the *Collor* stabilization plans, led the government to intensify the liberal part of its strategy. In fact, in parallel with institutional reforms geared towards financial and trade liberalization, the government adopted a high-real-interest rate policy, to which financial markets responded quickly.

The surge in capital inflows was temporarily halted in 1992, with a massive popular movement to impeach Collor, who was impeached in October 1982 and replaced by his vice president, Itamar Franco. Franco started with a more nationalist and interventionist economic strategy, but quickly toned down his position in face of the risk of a major economic crisis. After three finance ministers in his seven months, Franco gave in to Business ('the markets') and, in May 1993, appointed Fernando Henrique Cardoso to the position.

In response to the high real interest rates and Cardoso's market-friendly approach to economic policy, capital flows returned *en masse* and the country was able to accumulate the foreign reserves necessary to make another stabilization attempt, this time with the aid of an exchange-rate peg. Cardoso also renegotiated Brazil's foreign debt, normalizing the country's international financial position.

The *Real* plan was implemented in 1994. The basic idea was to simulate a hyperinflation by creating two official currencies: One to serve as the unit of accounting, and the other to serve as means of payment. Prices had to be quoted in a government index, but transactions had to be settled in the official currency. The government adjusted the value of its unit of account on a daily basis to keep it stable in terms of US dollars and, after private agents had four months to adjust their prices to the new unit of account, a new currency, the *real*, was introduced, at par with the US dollar. Inflation fell abruptly to a one-digit level and the economy boomed because of the reduction of the inflation tax and currency appreciation.

To keep inflation down after the currency reform, high real interest rates were maintained in order to attract foreign capital and sustain the appreciated exchange rate, anchoring the prices of tradable goods to international prices. Moreover, to intensify the competitive pressure on domestic producers, the government also reduced import tariffs unilaterally, which together with currency appreciation and a consumption boom, quickly led the economy to high current-account deficits (see Table 13.1). However, despite the increase in foreign indebtedness-based financial fragility, the stabilization strategy worked well as long as there were enough foreign capital inflows. The unfavourable domestic counterpart was an increase in the ratio of public debt to GDP, since government bonds were the main instruments for attracting foreign capital. In terms of Minsky's analysis, the *Real* plan brought the country to a highly speculative position, which could only be reversed by a huge increase in net exports which was *expected* to happen after the stabilization and liberal reforms increased the international competitiveness of the economy.

Cardoso was elected president in 1994, and re-elected in 1998. Contrary to the liberal expectations, the recovery of net exports did not materialize during his first term (1995–98). In fact, the balance-of-payments problems worsened after the 1997 East Asian crisis, and became unsustainable after the Russian 1998 crisis. Because of the reduction in foreign finance and the high current-account deficits, the inevitable currency crisis came in 1999. However, because it had been predicted, when the crisis actually occurred, almost all firms and wealthy individuals were hedged and the effects in the banking system were extremely mild. Inflation rose, but due to the now lower degree of indexation and the restrictive macroeconomic policy, it did not get out of control. On the monetary side, the Central Bank adopted an inflation-targeting policy and a floating exchange-rate regime. On the fiscal side, because of the crisis and as a condition to obtain liquidity assistance from the IMF, the government increased its primary surplus substantially.[18]

Despite the change in exchange-rate policy, macroeconomic policy continued to be characterized by high real interest rates after 1999, but this time with high primary fiscal surpluses. Officially, the Central Bank had no exchange-rate target, but because of liberalized capital flows and the importance of the exchange rate for domestic prices, monetary policy had to follow international conditions and investors' expectations – otherwise a sharp devaluation of the *real* would have driven inflation well above the pre-specified ceilings.

Despite restrictive macroeconomic policy and investor-friendly approach of Cardoso, the economy was hit hard again in 2001, because of the Argentine crisis, and in 2002, because of the expectation of Lula's victory in that year's presidential elections. The two events led investors to anticipate a default by Brazil, which resulted in a substantial reduction in capital inflows. The exchange rate shot up, inflation accelerated, and growth decelerated.

Despite the expectations of a major change in macroeconomic policy after Lula's victory, the new administration quickly announced that it would adhere to Cardoso's policies, if anything with greater intensity. It raised interest rates, increased government primary surplus, and assured investors that the country would not default on its debt.[19] Financial markets responded quickly and enthusiastically. Capital poured in, the currency strengthened, inflation decelerated and, after a short recession in 2003, the economy boomed in 2004, although it is not clear whether such an expansion is sustainable.

In short, since 1999 Brazil has a dirty floating regime with high real interest rates and high primary surpluses to avoid an acceleration of inflation and an explosive increase of public debt. However, during most of the period, interest rates have been so high that even large primary surpluses could not stop the increase in the public debt-GDP ratio. Because of this fiscal-monetary inconsistency, and because of the low inflation targets, the Central Bank has been tolerating exchange-rate appreciations, which can lead to balance-of-payments problems. So far the increase in commodity prices and worldwide expansion of 2003–04 have countered the effects of currency appreciation, but such a speculative growth strategy can quickly turn bad in face of adverse external financial shocks. The other important consequences of the macroeconomic policy of Cardoso and Lula have been an increase in the tax burden and a reduction of government investment in terms of GDP, especially in infrastructure. The immediate result has been a slowing-down in the growth rate of productivity, hurting the competitiveness of domestic production, and increasing financial risks.

Between 1985 and 2004, a series of institutional changes were made. The first round of institutional changes in 1985–86 was aimed at reducing inflation. Monetary policy was centralized at the Central Bank by eliminating the overdraft credit lines that it had offered to *Banco do Brasil*. On the fiscal side, the National Treasury Department was created within the Ministry of Finance to centralize federal budget and debt managements. Initially, these changes had little impact, but since the creation of the *real* in 1995, the Central Bank and the National Treasury Department have become the most important centres of power within the federal government. They turned to be the new pilot agency – with a new diagnosis and a new policy agenda.

The second and major round of institutional changes stemmed from the 1988 Constitution. The main institutional innovations were an increase in the control by state and local governments over tax revenues, and an increase in public resource allocation to education and to unemployment and social-security benefits. The main result was to channel public resources to specific ends, which subsequently led the federal government to circumvent part of the legislation by special and temporary decrees, while creating new taxes to recover part of its tax revenue. The other major institutional change of the period was the creation of *Mercosul*, a tariff union of Brazil, Argentina, Uruguay and Paraguay.

The third round of changes happened in the early- and mid-1990s and consisted of reinforcing financial liberalization, foreign-debt securitization, and privatization. Collor started the privatization programme and Cardoso intensified it, especially in the mining, telecommunications, finance, and energy sectors. The neoliberal expectation was that this would improve efficiency, substitute private for public investment, and free resources for social expenditures. Unfortunately, much of the privatization was done in 1997–98 after the East Asian crisis, and therefore many concessions had to be made to private investors, such as special funding by BNDES (which became *the* agent of privatization) and the indexation of energy and telecommunication tariffs to a exchange-rate-sensitive price index (in order to attract foreign capital). The reinstitution of indexation to public-utility prices has made inflation targeting more difficult and costly in terms of output and employment.

The final round of institutional changes happened in the wake of the 1999 crisis and consisted of the introduction of inflation targeting, the increase in the tax burden, and the adoption of strict fiscal guidelines. In 1996 the Central Bank created the Monetary Policy Committee (*Copom*) to set its base interest rate. With the adoption of inflation targeting, the Central Bank became very important and, in the Lula administration, it has been acting pretty independently of the federal government, despite the lack of formal independence. A council formed by the Ministry of Finance, the Ministry of

Planning, and the President of the Central Bank sets the inflation target, and then the *Copom*, made up of the President and the eight directors of the Central Bank, manages interest rates, exchange rates and reserve requirements to meet such targets. Following the 1999 crisis, the government instituted the Fiscal Responsibility Law in 2000, which imposed strict limitations on the expenditures of local and state governments, as well as creating a set of austere budgeting rules for the federal government. Most importantly, a target for primary surplus was set for the whole public sector.

Altogether, the institutional changes of 1985–2004 had two main objectives: To control inflation and to reduce state intervention. On the one hand, because of the high inflation tax on the poor during the high-inflation years, reducing inflation became crucial for every civil President to obtain political support from the population. On the other hand, given the financial fragility crisis and the overextension of the military development strategy in the early 1980s, reducing the economic role of the state was perceived as a natural complement to the return to democracy. Most importantly, reducing the economic role of the state was also crucial to implement a liberal stabilization strategy based on foreign capital inflows, as well as to gather political and financial supports from the Brazilian elite. Consequently, since 1985 and especially during the 1990s, economic policy has been dominated by *rentier* interests, with growth, employment and income distribution occupying subsidiary roles.

Despite the praise by financial markets and the IMF, so far the record of ten years of the neoliberal strategy has been, from the developmental perspective, poor.[20] The average GDP growth rate was 2.8 per cent in the high-inflation years (1985–94), and 2.3 since stabilization (1995–2004). The corresponding per capita numbers are 1.1 per cent and 0.9 per cent. Inflation has been reduced, but unemployment rose to double-digit levels in the late 1990s. Informal jobs grew relatively to formal jobs, and the average real wage stagnated. Public debt rose substantially in relation to GDP, despite the increase in the tax burden and the cut in government investments (especially in infrastructure) – interest payments account for most of the increase. The economy became more open to foreign trade and finance, but it has neither increased its share in world exports, nor reduced its fragility to sudden stops in foreign capital inflows.

The main progress happened in agricultural production (agribusiness), with substantial increases in production and productivity of export products, and in oil production, where the still state-controlled company, Petrobrás, increased its share of the domestic market substantially.[21] Also noticeable were the changes in social policy brought by the 1988 constitution. Since then, the average schooling of the population has been increasing slowly, while poverty has been falling gradually. However, income distribution has remained practically the same, with a reduction in the income-share of the middle class.

5.   Conclusion

For those who are interested in the study of the relationships between institutions and economic development, the Brazilian experience in the last half century is a crucial one. And the causality runs *from* institutional change/innovations *to* economic development. *Institutional origins for economic outcomes* would be a good way to characterize it.

Obviously, the relationship is not unidirectional. There is a feedback: Institutional change is usually followed by institutional inertia, which brings, *because of its stabilizing effects*, what Schumpeter termed a constant tension between the capitalist order and the capitalist system (Schumpeter: 1928 and 1942 part 2) or, in Minsky's terms, a destabilizing stability.

Why did Brazil's growth, which was one of the fastest in the world between the 1930 and the mid-1980s, suddenly stop? We have outlined an answer to this question within a Schumpeterian-Minskyan framework, with an important reference to the dynamics of the Developmental State.

From the Schumpeterian angle, the Vargas period was one of intensive institutional innovation (and state building), when the basis of the Brazilian developmental state as well as an appropriate institutional landscape for industrial creative destruction were forged. A wave of (imported) creative destruction happened under Kubitschek. The period of 1956–61 was that of both a robust gale of institutional innovation and creative destruction, combined with a successful catching-up development strategy. The monetary and financial problems and the institutional mismatch of the early sixties were endogenously created by the previous boom. The subsequent stagnation was a 'therapeutic' one and the wave of institutional innovation under the first military government was a necessary pre-condition for reinstating growth.

The development plans of the late 1960s and early 1970s, which propelled the 'Brazilian miracle', were more 'industrial capacity–intensive' than 'innovation-intensive', and therefore failed to allow the country to fully participate in the emerging third technological revolution. From the mid-eighties onwards, successive waves of ineffective institutional innovation and policy shifts (including the partially successful attempt to destroy the already financially-damaged Developmental State), together with the technological 'falling behind', should be seen as the hard core causes of the *lost decades*. This characterization, however, leaves an extremely important element out of the picture: Finance. It is here that the Minskyan approach enters.

From a Minskyan perspective, the whole financial architecture enabling the Brazilian growth spurt was always a shaky one. From Kubitschek's inflationary finance-funding scheme (and balance of payments problems), through Campos's ingenious (but ultimately self-defeating) indexation scheme, to the reckless management of the country's' increasing financial fragility (both internal and external) by Delfim Netto and the crowd of finance ministers from 1985 to 1995, and culminating in the fixed exchange rate policy of Central Bank president Gustavo Franco between 1995 and 1999, the financial structure has always had the propensity towards financial fragility. The simultaneous emergence of intractable problems on both fronts since the mid-1980s turned the endemic, and ever increasing, financial fragility into financial vulnerability and finally into financial crises, leading to the *lost decades*.

When will the Brazilian economy finally recover from its long-term prostration? It's an open question. From the point of view of 'enabling' institutional innovations, we can say that important positive changes were made in the last few years and some are still in the making. Those include a new (and much more modern) Civil Code, an innovation law, an industrial policy agenda to be implemented under the supervision and financial assistance of the BNDES, and the restructuring of the Brazilian Patent office (currently underway). But in answering it, finance – debt structures, financial regulation and interest rates – will surely have the final word.

Notes

1. At first as a revolutionary leader (1930–34), then as a democratically elected president (1934–37), and finally as a dictator (1937–45).
2. For a short account of Brazilian economic history until 1930, see Dean (1989). See Wirth (1970) and Levine (1998) for the Vargas era.
3. Jonhson (1982) coined the concept. See Woo (1999) for its discussion.
4. Initially the institution was named BNDE and aimed only to economic development. In the 1980s the bank's operations were extended to social areas and its name was changed to BNDES. For simplicity, we will refer to it as BNDES in this chapter.
5. The BNDES was set apart from the traditional bureaucracy, and its staff was known for its technical competence and strong sense of public mission. Nevertheless, it was subordinated to the president and lacked autonomy in funding, which was provided by a 15 per cent surtax on loans and individual and corporate income taxes. Only under Kubitschek BNDES became a major player in the Brazilian economy (Geddes, 1990: 226).

6. During this period, Brazil did not have a central bank. The government main financial institution was Banco do Brasil, and monetary and currency policies were implemented by SUMOC (Money and Credit Bureau).

7. Giambiaggi et al. (2004: Appendix A14). Also see FIPE statistics for the Brazilian economy (www.fipe.org).

8. However, in 1998, indexation, now to the exchange rate, was re-established for some (newly-privatized) public utilities. See section 4.

9. Today, it is around 36 per cent. See Giambiagi et al. (2004).

10. As mentioned earlier, until then the Central Bank functions were divided between the SUMOC and Banco do Brasil, which was an ambiguous institutional creature mixing commercial lending and other functions of a public commercial bank with policy-making and implementation.

11. In fact, there are striking similarities between the Park regime in South Korea and the military rule in Brazil, especially regarding industrial policy. There are also important differences, such as rates of inflation, treatment of foreign capital, social policy, and especially educational policy. Some of these similarities and contrasts are explored in Canuto: 1994 and Amsden: 2001.

12. See Giambiaggi et al. (2004: Table A4, p. 407).

13. See Velloso (1986), and Castro and Souza (1985). For a more critical account, see Suzigan and Villela (1997). The recessionary orthodox response to an external shock, which intends to increase export by switching expenditure from domestic to the external sector, would only work (a) if the economy was fully employing its productive capacity, which was clearly not the case, and (b) if (global) imports demand was infinitely elastic with respect to (increasing) national exports, which obviously is never the case.

14. The actual rates were, 8.15, 5.15, 10.26, 4.93, 4.97, and 6.76 per cent respectively.

15. Minsky's analysis, based on the relationship between debt structures and investment expending, defines three balance sheet configurations: Hedge, speculative and Ponzi. The Ponzi structure is one where economic units need to increase their borrowing just to 'stay in business', but to which bankers should not lend under any circumstances (also see Kregel, 1997).

16. For further details, see Arida and Resende (1984), Lopes (1986), Bresser-Pereira and Nakano (1986), Modiano (1988), Pastore (1990) and Franco (1995)

17. See Solnik (1987) on the Cruzado plan. Castro (2005a and 2005b) discusses all stabilization attempts.

18. The average primary surplus was 0.5 per cent of GDP during Cardoso's first term, and 3.2 per cent in during his second term.

19. The primary-surplus target has been raised to 4.25 per cent of GDP and the annual base real interest rate has been fluctuating between 9 per cent and 12 per cent.

20. The neoliberal strategy did not contain institutional innovation. It mostly involved an institutional *dejà-vu*, since all the reforms were about turning the clock fifty years back. The big exception here is the de-indexation strategy by means of an indexed *currency* (the opposite of the overwhelming indexation of *prices*). This was a major, and successful, *policy innovation.*

21. It is worth noting that the agricultural sector benefited from a subsidized credit from BNDES under Cardoso, whereas Petrobrás increased its production through the investment of retained earnings and the discovery of new oil fields. Interestingly enough, both measures were clearly running against the neoliberal textbook agenda.

References

Amsden, A. 2001. *The Rise of the Rest*. Oxford: Oxford University Press.

Arida, P. and Resende, A. L. 1984. 'Inflação Inercial e Reforma Monetária', in P. Arida (ed.), *Brasil, Argentina, e Israel: Inflação Zero*, Rio de Janeiro: Paz e Terra.

Batista Jr, P. N. 1988. *Da crise internacional à moratória brasileira*, Rio e Janeiro: Paz e Terra.

Belluzzo, L. and Melo, J. M. C. 1982. 'Reflexões sobre a Crise Atual' in L. Belluzzo and L. Coutinho (eds.) *Desenvolvimento Capitalista no Brasil – Ensaios sobre a crise*. São Paulo, Brasiliense.

Benevides, M. V. M. 1976. *O Governo Kubitschek – Desenvolvimento Econômico e Estabilidade Política – 1956-1961*; 2nd edn, Rio e Janeiro: Paz e Terra.

Bielschowsky, R. 1995. *Pensamento Econômico Brasileiro – o ciclo ideológico do desenvolvimentismo*. 2nd edn, Rio e Janeiro: Contraponto.

Brazil's Central Bank statistics (www.bcb.gov.br)

Bresser-Pereira, L. C. and Nakano, Y. 1986. 'Inflação inercial e choque heterodoxo no Brasil' in J. M. Rego (ed.), *Inflação Inercial, Teorias sobre Inflação e o Plano Cruzado*, Rio de Janeiro: Paz e Terra.

Burlamaqui, L. 1989. 'Condicionantes Sócio-políticos e Política Industrial na Coréia do Sul'; *Contexto Internacional*, 10, July-December.

Campos, R. 1994. *A lanterna na popa – memórias*, Rio: Topbooks

Canuto, O. 1994. *Brasil e Coréia do Sul – Os (des) caminhos da Industrialização Tardia*; São Paulo, Nobel.

Cardoso, F. H. 1977. *O Modelo Político Brasileiro*. Difel.

Castro, A. 1994. 'Renegade Development: Rise and Demise of State-Led Development in Brazil' in W. C. Smith, C. H. Acuña and E. A. Gamarra (eds) *Democracy, Markets and Structural Reform in Latin America: Argentina, Bolivia, Brasil, Chile and Mexico*, Transaction Publishers.

Castro, A. B. and Souza, F. E. P. 1985. *A Economia Brasileira em Marcha Forçada*; Rio, Paz e Terra.

Castro, A. B. and Proença, A. 2001. 'Novas Estrat´egias Industriais: Sobreida ou Inflexão?' in J. P. Velloso (ed.) *Fórum Nacional*. São Paulo, Nobel.

Dean, W. 1989. 'Economy' in L. Bethell (ed.) *Brazil – Empire and Republic 1822-1930*, Cambridge: Cambridge University Press.

Franco, G. 1995. *O Plano Real e Outros Ensaios*, Rio de Janeiro: Francisco Alves.

Fundação Instituto de Pesquisas Econômicas – FIPE/USP Statistics. (www.fipe.org)

Furtado, C. 1965. 'Political Obstacles to Economic Growth in Brazil', *International Affairs*, April.

Geddes, B. 1990. 'Building "State" Autonomy in Brazil, 1930-1964'; *Comparative Politics*, 22, 2 (January).

Gerschenkron 1961. *Economic Backwardness in Historical Perspective*. Harvard: Harvard University Press.

Giambiaggi. F, Villela, A., Castro, L. and Hermann, J. (eds) 2004. *Economia Brasileira. Contemporânea* (1945-2004). Rio de Janeiro, Campus.

Hermann. 2004. Reformas, Endividamento Externo e o 'Milagre Econômico' (1964-1973) in F. Giambiaggi et al. (2004).

Hirschman, A. O. 1971. 'The Political Economy of Import Substituting Industrialization in Latin America' in *A Bias For Hope – Essays on Development and Latin America*, Yale University Press.

Johnson, C. 1982. *MITI and the Japanese Miracle*. Stanford: Stanford University Press.

Lessa, C. 1982. *Quinze Anos de Política Econômica*; São Paulo, Brasiliense.

Levine, R. M. 1998. *Father of the Poor? Vargas and His Era*. Cambridge: Cambridge University Press.

Lopes, F. 1986. *O Choque Heterodoxo - Combate à Inflação e Reforma Monetária*, Rio de Janeiro: Campus.

Kregel, J. 1997. 'Margins of Safety and Weight of the Argument in Generating Financial Fragility', *Journal of Economic Issues*, June: 543–8

Malan, P. S., Bonelli, R., Abreu, M. P. and Pereira, J. E. C. 1980. *Política Econômica Externa e Industrialização no Brazil (1939/52)*; Rio de Janeiro, IPEA/INPES.

Minsky, H. 1982. *Can 'It' Happen Again? Essays on Instability and Finance*. New York: Sharpe Books.

Minsky, H. 1986. *Stabilizing an Unstable Economy*; Yale University Press

Modiano, E. 1988. *Inércia, Inflação e Conflito*, Rio de Janeiro: Campus.

Pastore, A. C. 1990. 'A Reforma Monetária do Plano Collor' in C. Faro, *O Plano Collor - Avaliação e Perspectiva*, Rio de Janeiro: Livros Técnicos e Científicos.

Resende, 1990. 'Estabilização e Reforma – 1964–1967', in Abreu, M. P. (ed.) *A Ordem do Progresso – Cem anos de Política Econômica Republicana – 1889–1989*; Rio de Janeiro, Campus.

Schumpeter, J. A. 1951 [1928]. 'The Instability of Capitalism' in *Essays of J. A. Schumpeter*. New York: Addison-Wesley Press.

Schumpeter, J. A. 1994 [1952]. *Capitalism, Socialism and Democracy*. London: Routledge.

Skidmore, T. 1972. *Politics in Brazil, 1930–1964: An Experiment in Democracy*. Oxford: Oxford University Press.

Solnik, A. 1987. *Os pais do Cruzado contam por que não deu certo*; Porto Alegre, LPM.

Suzigan, W. and Villela, A. 1997. *Industrial Policy in Brasil*. Unicamp Press.

Velloso, J. P. 1986. *O Ultimo Trem para Paris – De Getúlio a Sarney: milagres, choques e crises do Brasil moderno*. Nova Fronteira.

Vianna, S. B. 1987. *A Política Econômica no Segundo Governo Vargas (1951–1954)*. Rio de Janeiro, BNDES.

Villela. 2004. *Dos Anos Dourados de JK à Crise não Resolvida (1956–1963)* in Giambiaggi et al. (2004).

Wirth, J. D. 1970. *The Politics of Brazilian Development 1930–1954*; Stanford, Stanford University Press.

Woo, M. J-E. (ed.) 1999. *The Developmental State*. Cornell University Press.

CHAPTER 14
RETHINKING IMPORT-SUBSTITUTING INDUSTRIALIZATION: DEVELOPMENT STRATEGIES AND INSTITUTIONS IN TAIWAN AND CHINA

Tianbiao Zhu

1.   Introduction

There is little dispute about the economic miracles created by Taiwan in the 1960s and 1970s and China in the 1980s and 1990s; average double-digit growth figures in both cases were recorded for almost twenty years, which only a few economies have achieved in history. However, how the miracles were created has been subject to various debates. A conventional argument points to the shift from import-substituting industrialization (ISI) strategy, emphasizing infant industry protection, to export-oriented industrialization (EOI) strategy, which stresses exports and upgrading one's industrial structure from labour-intensive to capita-intensive industries gradually, in both Taiwan and China as the key to their economic success.

This chapter argues that the development strategies in Taiwan and China have always been a combination of ISI and EOI strategies during their entire miracle-creating period; far from the shift from ISI to EOI strategies, export promotion was used in both cases to sustain ISI, which has always been the central focus of development. The chapter also shows that in both Taiwan and China there is a set of institutions which has played a key role in supporting ISI, in particular, the government, the bank sector, public enterprises, and their relationship.

The differences between Taiwan and China are obvious. China has a much larger internal market. China is also a regional power if not a world power, while Taiwan is without much political and military power. In a small economy like Taiwan, import-substituting industries can quickly saturate the markets, making further expansion of such industries difficult. Due to a large domestic market, it is relatively easy for a large economy to engage in ISI. Moreover, China's status as a regional power put ISI on top of the agenda right from the beginning and sustained the development of heavy industries even after the opening-up in the early 1980s.

However, the two cases also share some striking similarities, which are often ignored. Taiwan of the 1960s and 1970s was firmly ruled by Kuomintang party (the KMT or the nationalist party), which actually shares some fundamental similarities with its counterpart on the mainland. The KMT is also a radical leftist party. Its organizational structure is still much like that of a Leninist party. The party's principle was described by its founding father – Sun Yat-Sen – as 'socialism' (Li, 1968: 2). So it is no surprise to see that Taiwan has had one of the largest public sectors in the non-communist world. Many KMT leaders, most notably Chiang Ching-Kuo who became the premier of Taiwan in the early 1970s and the president later, were trained in the Soviet Communist party school.

The above discussion suggests that, despite the differences in size and international positions, it is not so absurd as it may appear to compare Taiwan and China, especially during their respective 'miracle' periods, that is, Taiwan of the 1960s and 1970s and China of the 1980s and 1990s.

2.   ISI in Taiwan's policy transition

2.1.   *The conventional view and its problems*

In standard economic analyses, Taiwan's post-1949 industrialization is often divided into four phases. In the first phase, from 1949 to the late 1950s, Taiwan engaged in primary ISI in basic consumer goods, such as textile, food, and other labour-intensive industries. The second phase, from the late 1950s to the late 1960s, was an era of EOI focusing on labour-intensive products. In this period, Taiwan's economy began to take off, and rapid industrial growth was maintained for more than two decades. The third phase extends from the early 1970s to the early 1980s. Exports continued to be promoted, and began to move from labour-intensive products to higher value-added and skill-intensive ones. At the same time, Taiwan engaged in so-called secondary ISI, which involved import substitution in a variety of intermediate goods and capital goods. Heavy and chemical industries were promoted, along with several big public infrastructure projects. Finally, the fourth phase from the early 1980s onwards involved major government focus on the development of technology-intensive products.

It has been argued that, since the early 1960s, export promotion was a major feature of Taiwan's economic policy. Various studies (e.g., Gereffi and Wyman, 1990) compare Taiwan's shift to EOI with continued ISI in other developing economies, which led to inefficiency in domestic industries and balance of payment problems. Taiwan's ISI in the 1950s has also been seen as having those problems. Neoclassical economists in particular see this break as the key to Taiwan's economic success (Woronoff, 1986; World Bank 1993).

The conventional explanation of this policy shift, usually put forward by mainstream economists (such as Ho, 1978; Kuo et al. 1981; and Kuo, 1983) but also by some others (such as Gold, 1988), points to two factors. The first involves economic needs. It is argued that, due to its small size, the Taiwanese market was saturated by the end of the 1950s. Thus, it became necessary to develop the export market. The second factor points toward American influence (e.g., Cumings, 1987). It is argued that, towards the late 1950s, the US government began to encourage Taiwan to develop through economic liberalization with the aim of reducing and eventually terminating economic aid. In 1959, US official Wesley Haraldson offered the Taiwan government an eight-point economic programme that called for a reduction in military spending, non-inflationary fiscal and monetary policies, tax reform, a uniform and realistic exchange rate, liberalized exchange control, efficient public utility management, an efficient banking system, and the sale of public enterprises to the private sector.

However, the evidence does not match the story of sharp policy break. For example, it is not true that Taiwan dramatically reduced its import controls from the early 1960s; in fact, they simply became highly selective. As Wade (1988:139) explains, 'Taiwan's tariff structure is minutely differentiated by product, with tariffs ranging from zero to well over 100%'. A number of Taiwan scholars went further to argue that the ISI strategy as a whole was pursued in parallel to the EOI strategy from the early 1960s, and export promotion was essentially supplementary to ISI (Hsing, 1993, Ma, 1994, and Ch'en, 1994).

A review of policy over the 1960s supports this observation. In the book, *An Introduction to Our Economic Development Strategy* (1987: 147), Li and Ch'en clearly state that between 1961 and 1972 the aim of industrial development strategy was to continue pushing the development of import-substituting industries, and in particular to give more support to the development of heavy and chemical industries. In the 1960s, the first two four-year economic plans (1961–68) emphasized the need to develop heavy and chemical industries. Clearly, not only did Taiwan continue ISI in the 1960s but also went further to enter the secondary phase of ISI by developing heavy and chemical industries.

Actual growth trend figures of heavy and chemical industries in the 1960s reflect both the continuation of ISI and further switch to a secondary ISI. Sasaki (1992: 30) shows that the increase in the growth rate of heavy and chemical industries in the period from 1961 to 1968 was the highest of any period between 1950 and 1985, and argues that in Taiwan the move from developing domestic markets to exploring external markets and the move from developing light industries to assisting heavy and chemical industries took place not in sequence, but at the same time. Figure 14.1 shows that the weight of heavy industry in Taiwan's manufacturing sector increased 9 per cent from 1961 to 1971. This is a higher increase than in the following ten years, when secondary ISI is conventionally believed to have taken place.

This point is crucial if we are to understand Taiwan's industrial development. The conventional view focuses on export promotion because secondary ISI is thought to have taken place after EOI of the 1960s. However, if the development of heavy and chemical industries actually took place ten years earlier, then both ISI and EOI strategies laid a solid foundation for further industrial growth in Taiwan. Chu (1995: 62) argues that people trying to prove the superiority of EOI use Taiwan as an example often ignore the continuation of ISI after the 1950s.

Figure 14.1 Relative weight of heavy industry and light industry in manufacturing production in Taiwan, 1961–91

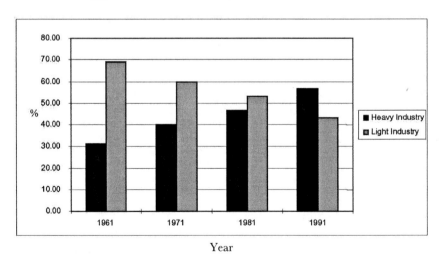

Source: Hsiao (1994: 35).

If the conventional description of the policy shift of the 1960s is problematic, its explanations in terms economic necessity and American influence fare no better.

The argument that there was an excess supply of domestic goods is often overstated. Hsiao (1997: 65) argues that, while the prices of some domestic products dropped between 1957 and 1958, the annual rate of reduction for most goods was within 5 per cent. Furthermore, prices for some goods, such as textiles, did not fall in 1957 or 1958. Hsiao notes that the price reductions could be related to a general recession in world markets around 1957, since some of the domestically-produced goods were exported (though in small amounts).

The argument of American influence does not survive a close examination. The key piece of evidence for American influence is Haraldson's eight-point programme of 1959. However, Li Kuo-ting, a key technocrat at the time, points out that, while Haraldson's eight points were concerned with economic liberalization, none of them emphasized export promotion (Wang, 1993: 119). In fact, although the government took most suggestions of the eight-point programme, many have still not been effectively carried out (Wang, 1993: 141 and Hsing, 1993: 78). What happened in the end was almost the opposite of the eight-point programme; its suggestions were not put into effect and what it did not emphasize – export promotion – has been consistently enforced since the early 1960s.

2.2. *Explaining policy change and continuity*

An explanation of both change and continuity in Taiwan's economic policy begins with the basic need of ISI. In order to substitute imports with domestic products, ISI requires foreign exchange to buy technology and equipment (i.e., intermediate and capital goods). In the 1950s, having difficulty raising revenue domestically, the Taiwan government relied on US aid to finance ISI (US economic aid to Taiwan constituted 40 per cent of its total investment in the 1950s.) However, after a re-examination of its global aid policy, the US government in 1959 hinted that it would soon cut economic aid to Taiwan (Li and Ch'en, 1987: 137). Even with massive aid, the Taiwan government was running budget and balance of payments deficits. The termination of the aid would have made the situation much worse. In fact, it can be argued that, without US aid, Taiwan could never have successfully pursued ISI.

Hsiao (1997: 65) argues that the real reason for the policy change (in the early 1960s) is that the Taiwan government anticipated a possible reduction in US aid, after the US government re-examined its global aid policy in

1957. This is confirmed by Wei Yung-ning, who as an economic bureaucrat personally experienced the policy shift in the early 1960s, in his reminiscences (1994:93). But, given Taiwan's small market size, why did it want to keep the expensive ISI and why not completely switch to EOI?

The extra push for keeping ISI and EOI together came from Taiwan's security concern. Facing a constant military threat from Mainland China, the Taiwan government had to build an economy that would strengthen its defence capacity in the long-term. Not any kind of economy would do; it must be one capable of sustaining a strong and autonomous defence industry. For this, Taiwan had to develop heavy and chemical industries.

There was no way that EOI could produce an immediate growth of heavy and chemical industries when the exports of the 1960s were basically primary labour-intensive products.[1] Although export earnings gradually replaced US aid as a source of foreign exchange, such EOI could not support economic independence. Independence required ISI, but with a focus on secondary ISI promoting heavy and chemical industrialization. This was the precise course the Taiwan government followed from the early 1960s, resulting in the rapid growth of heavy and chemical industries during the 1960s, as Figure 14.1 shows.

In fact, EOI and ISI strategies worked hand in hand in the 1960s and 1970s. Exports provided foreign exchange to import-substituting industries, which developed Taiwan's economic independence. Thus both policy change and continuity were simultaneously promoted by the desire for economic independence. In the early 1970s, the weakening of the US commitment to East Asian security, Taiwan's loss of its seat in the United Nations (UN), and Nixon's visit to Beijing further strengthened the Taiwan government's determination to seek economic independence. In 1973, Premier Chiang Ching-kuo announced ten big development projects, including several major public infrastructure projects and industrial projects to construct steel, petrochemical, and ship-building plants.[2]

As a response to the changing security environment, '[t]he decision to allocate investment resources to the development of defense industries in the early 1970s formed a central part of overall industrial strategy' (Nolan, 1986: 110). In order to establish a solid base for the defence sector, the government promoted the development of infrastructural facilities such as roads and highways, while enhancing the development of heavy and chemical industries. Despite a small domestic market and a lack of comparative advantage in capital-intensive industries, the Taiwan government pushed its defence-related industrial strategy and used public enterprises to lead the way in developing those industries.

The government, the banking sector and public enterprises were the key institutions supporting Taiwan's ISI. Taiwan has had one of the largest public sectors in the non-communist world. From 1952 to 1995, state capital consistently amounted to around 45 per cent of gross national capital formation (CEPD 1996: 47). Up to 1990, public enterprises contributed 10–25 per cent of total government revenues (Wu, 1992: 7). During Taiwan's high growth period (in the 1960s and 1970s), the growth of public enterprises exceeded that of the whole economy. It should be especially noted that large public enterprises exceeded large private ones in size. According to Wade (1990: 178), '[i]n 1980 the six biggest industrial public enterprises had sales equal to the fifty biggest private industrial concerns. Of the ten largest industrial enterprises seven are public enterprises; of the largest fifty, nineteen are public enterprises'. In 1981, 98 per cent of the enterprises in Taiwan were privately-owned enterprises that each employed fewer than 50 employees (Chen, 1995: 86).

The importance of state capital was not only a matter of size. The state also controlled the vital parts of Taiwan's economy. State capital monopolized the electricity, gas, water, railway, and telephone utilities. It also controlled strategic or 'upstream' industries, like petroleum refining, petrochemicals, steel and other basic metals, shipbuilding, heavy machinery, transport equipment and fertilizer. According to Liu and Huang (1993: 47), in the 1980s state capital comprised 90 per cent of the energy industry, 80 per cent of metals, 95 per cent of petrochemicals and 80 per cent of shipbuilding. Private business and especially the small and medium-sized enterprises tended to be located in downstream industries. Taiwan, thus, had a distinct industrial structure in which public enterprises dominated the upstream of production processes, while most private businesses occupied the downstream of production process.

The government in Taiwan had almost complete control over the banking sector before the 1980s. 'The four private banks had only 5 per cent of deposits and branches of all the commercial banks in 1980, and the biggest of the four is only nominally private' (Wade, 1990: 161). Since the 1960s, financial institutions were also influenced by the capital accumulated by the ruling party (Ch'en and Chang, 1991: 12). So, the banking sector in Taiwan was under double control – by the government and by the ruling party.

Industrial policies were carried out through the allocation of financial resources by the government. The focus of credit allocation was on public enterprises. This should not be surprising since, as mentioned earlier, public enterprises were the main vehicle for government industrial policy. Wu (1992: 141) notes that between 1965 and 1975, among 32 enterprises receiving direct investment from the economy's largest bank (the Taiwan Bank), 19 were public enterprises. The most important bodies of the government involved in industrial policy-making had little contact with the private sector, and the industrial plans they made were basically public sector plans requiring 'little knowledge of the intentions of the private sector, not even investment intentions' (Wade, 1990: 277).

The government bureaucracy is also a subject of study (Tung, 1996; Cheng et al. 1998; Evans, 1998). Although the key economic institution (or the 'pilot agency') took various names and even forms over the years,[3] the key personnel were always there. The KMT leaders also made the pilot agency independent from the rest of the bureaucracy, and its power of policy making and implementing was therefore enhanced (Cheng et al. 1998). The pilot agency linked the banking sector and public enterprises, and played the key role in promoting industrial development.

It should be noted that, public enterprises, the banks and the bureaucracy are institutions as well as organizations and even political actors. To emphasize their institutional features is to understand the ways they operated and the ways in which they were linked together.

The government, in particular the pilot bureaucracy, is clearly at the centre of the connection. Given the socialist orientation in the KMT's founding economic thought, the pilot agency favoured public enterprises as the key instrument in promoting industrial development, directing the financial resources from the banking sector to them. The experience of hyper-inflation in the last few years of the KMT's rule over the mainland made Taiwan's banking sector conservative about the money it lends out[4]. Thus, the key institutional features of the KMT state in the 1960s and 1970s are the linkages between the government, the public enterprises, and the banking sector, where the government was at the centre of the linkages, the public enterprises as the key instruments of government's industrial policy dominated the upstream of the production process, and were supported by a conservative but obliging banking sector.

3.   ISI in China's policy transition

3.1.   *The origin of the combined strategy of ISI and EOI*

The nature of the transformation of China's development strategy in the early 1980s is no less controversial than Taiwan's in the early 1960s. The conventional view is that China made the switch from ISI to EOI in the late 1970s and early 1980s. China is seen following the footsteps of Taiwan – between the 1950s and 1970s China was engaged in ISI (just like Taiwan in the 1950s), and from the early 1980s China's development strategy changed to EOI (just like Taiwan from the early 1960s). One commentator further argues that China's open-door policy was induced by international markets forces (Moore, 1996 and 2002). I argue that, like Taiwan's policy transition in the early 1960s, China's policy transition was also born out of a moment of crisis of ISI, the solution to which was not to give up ISI but to combine it with EOI.

The problem began with China's adoption of 'extreme' ISI strategy in the 1950s. Unlike Taiwan, where even in the height of its ISI private sector was still a significant part of the economy, in China ISI was the key part of central planning system copied from the Soviet model, which made its ISI measures extreme – instead of infant industry protection, it protected all industries; instead of putting tariffs on the imports similar to what the infant industries produce, it put tariffs on all imports. More importantly, ISI was financed in a particular way – following the Soviet model, agricultural production was collectivized in order to transfer all surplus to industry, all industries and banks were nationalized in order to ensure that the government could re-invest all possible resources into industrial development. The 'extreme ISI' thus aimed at achieving the goal of rapid industrial growth by mobilizing all domestic resources rather than relying on foreign assistance, which clearly reflected the international isolation and the urge for quick industrialization the Soviets had in the 1930s. Ironically, it did not take long for China to enter a similar situation. After the 1950s, during which the Soviet Union supported China's ISI, China was isolated and had no support from neither the Soviet nor American camps in the 1960s and much of the 1970s.

Although the extreme ISI created an industrial foundation for China's modernization, it alone clearly had its limitations. First, China seriously lacked modern technology and equipment. Taiwan's ISI in the 1950s was supported by the US with relatively advanced technology and equipment, while China's extreme ISI was founded on domestic resources. Thus, '[a]n ISI could not be effective simply because there was no hard currency to buy the goods which were so urgently needed by China to produce import products' (Li and Vinten, 1997: 188). Second, in order to mobilize all available resources, China's extreme ISI had to suppress domestic consumption, which in the long run damaged people's incentive to work. The incentive problem was also worsened by political turmoil during the Cultural Revolution between 1966 and 1976.

In retrospect, the solution to these two problems seems obvious. By promoting exports, foreign exchange can be earned to pay for the imported technology and equipment, while the suppression of domestic consumption can be relaxed (at least to a certain extent), providing people with more incentive to work. However, extreme ISI had been going on in China for three decades, and the old institutions of the Soviet model had become a way of life and had also created special interests to support it (extreme ISI has survived in North Korea until today). It is difficult to change without a major crisis which could make people more open to alternative thinking.

For Taiwan, the crisis was the withdrawal of US aid; for China, it was the campaign of so-called 'leap forward by foreign means' (*yang yue jin*). In 1976 Mao passed away and the new leadership under Hua Guofeng effectively ended the Cultural Revolution by putting the extreme leftists (the 'gang of four') into jail. The welcome political change temporarily pushed up economic growth, in 1977 and 1978 total output of agricultural and industrial production grew at 11.5 per cent annually and government revenue increased 44 per cent (Jin, 1990: 140). Hua went on to campaign for even higher growth rate and advocated for a 'new leap forward in national economy'. The Ten Year Plan of 1978 called for the construction and completion of 120 large development projects, including ten large iron and steel establishments, ten large oil fields, eight large coal establishments, six new rail roads, five large ports, and 30 large electricity stations (Gao, 1993: 91). In order to meet the targets, investment in basic construction grew by 50 per cent in 1978, the number of heavy trucks imported by 50 per cent, and steel materials by 64 per cent (Gao, 1993: 92).

With those large investments and imports, finance became a key problem. Oil sales were the main export for China in the 1970s. However, towards the late 1970s few new oil fields were found, and worse, a rapid expansion of petroleum output even damaged the long-term productivity of the existing fields. Since the government was unable to fund those large development projects with foreign exchange earned from oil sales, it had to contract a large amount of foreign debt, which is why Hua's campaign for rapid growth is often called 'leap forward by foreign means'. The direct result was the largest balance of payments deficit since People's Republic of China was founded in 1949 (Jin, 1990: 141; Gao, 1993: 93). Large investment also squeezed domestic consumption and therefore delayed people's welfare improvement. By 1980, the government had to put the whole plan on hold.

The economic crisis created an opportunity for reformers like Deng Xiaoping and Chen Yun to change economic strategy, which led to the open-door policy in the early 1980s. However, it is wrong to assume that EOI has replaced ISI after that. Far from it. The open-door policy was born at a particular point of time to deal with the problem of extreme ISI. As mentioned earlier, extreme ISI has key problems of lack of modern technology and equipment and disincentive for people to work. The 'leap forward by foreign means' attempted to solve the first problem by importing modern technology and equipment, only to generate the balance of payment disaster. Thus, China in late 1970s encountered a similar problem that Taiwan did in the early 1960s, i.e., the problem of financing ISI with foreign exchange, and their solutions were the same, i.e., promoting exports in order to continue ISI.

Li and Vinten (1997: 188) argue that 'ISI was vital in order to create the preconditions for a switch to EOI, and without abandoning ISI strategy, China is much closer to integration of the two strategies'. Other scholars go further to argue that China had a combined strategy all the way from the early 1980s (Long, 2004; Dutta, 2005). From the government side, Vice-premier Li Peng argued in 1987 that the open-door policy – learning advanced technology and management experience from the West and obtaining foreign investment – is an important supplement to China's socialist development, and export expansion, export structure improvement, and foreign exchange earning are the key issues in China's foreign economic operations (Zhang et al. 1992: 152). Clearly, the open-door policy was to play a supplementary role to industrial development.

Up to the mid-1990s, average tariff rate was 43 per cent (McKibbin and Tang, 1998: 6). In the mid 1980s, parallel to its effort to promote EOI, the government introduced more import tariffs aimed at inducing domestic firms to buy the products of import-substituting industries. Kueh (1990) argues that during the 1980s the established priority of promoting industrial growth through heavy industry was very much intact. The output share of heavy industry was around 52 per cent of total national industrial output, only marginally lower than its share of 57 per cent in 1978; and expenditure on capital investment in heavy industries as against light industries and agriculture was 45 per cent of the national total, also marginally lower than 49 per cent in 1978 (Kueh, 1990: 110).

Although exports and light industry as the main parts of EOI have been the target for government support since the early 1980s, the above discussion shows that the government continued to promote ISI by maintaining and even raising tariff and by supporting heavy industry, this was particularly true in the 1980s. Moreover, EOI has become a key means for China to solve the main problems of ISI, that is, exports to earn foreign exchange and to relax the repression of domestic consumption.

3.2.   *New challenge and institutional change*

The situation related to China's ISI has become complicated since the early 1990s. China's preparation for and eventual accession to World Trade Organization meant that a few traditional measures associated with ISI had to be abandoned or reduced in significance, including the abolition of import quotas and license and reduction of import tariff. However, the Chinese government has been mobilizing various means, old and new, to protect and support capital- and technology-intensive import-substituting industries.

Officially, the average tariff has been reduced from 43 per cent to under 20 per cent in the 1990s, but according to some foreign exporters, the real tariff was still close to 40 per cent, since local governments could exempt domestic products from value added tax, which has always been levied on imports (Breslin, 1999: 1188). The government also has an active industrial policy to support strategic sectors. For example, by manipulating standard setting in video compact disc (VCD) and digital video disc (DVD) industries, the government has been consistently making effort to reduce royalty payments to overseas patent holders and therefore to help leading Chinese firms to secure technological leverage (Linden, 2004). The government is also believed to give the most favourable treatment to SOEs, which are the foundation of capital-intensive industry, over foreign and domestic private firms. In particular, the government has been channelling foreign capital to set up joint ventures with SOEs, which has led some scholar to believe that China is using foreign capital to preserve, not to dismantle socialism (Huang, 2003: 407–9).

Yu (1998:76) observed that in the 1980s labour-intensive industry expanded more rapidly than the capital-intensive one, but in the 1990s, the situation was reversed, with the capital-intensive industries growing faster. Figure 14.2 shows that in terms of output growth, light industry and heavy industry were neck in neck in the 1990s with the former slightly ahead, but the trend after 1998 points to a stronger growth of heavy industry.

Like Taiwan in the 1960s and 1970s, China's combined strategies of ISI and EOI in the 1980s and 1990s had a strong institutional support. As in Taiwan, the government, the banking sector and SOEs are the major institutions behind ISI. The government controls the banking sector, which provides investments to SOEs. What is different from Taiwan is that in China SOEs plays a larger role. Between 1978 and 1992, the state sectors received about 80 per cent of bank credits (Yu, 1998: 74). Large SOEs on average accounted for more than 40 per cent of industrial sales between 1994 and 1998, and in terms of industrial assets and industrial profits, their shares were 50 per cent and 60 per cent respectively during the period (Lan and Cao, 2000: 49).

Figure 14.2 Growth of heavy and light industries in China, 1990–2004

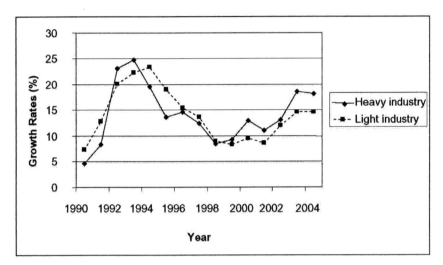

Source: NBS (1991–99) and NBS (2000–05).

Given the dominant role of SOEs in China's economy, the government has been engaging in enterprise reform ever since the beginning of the reform – creating spaces for foreign, collectively-owned and private firms to play greater role in EOI while strengthening and reforming SOEs to lead ISI. The reform has become more urgent since about half of SOEs encountered the problem of non-performing loans in the 1990s.

The solutions are privatization and corporatization with the emphasis of the latter. Between 1994 and 2000, almost 60,000 small to medium-sized SOEs were liquidated, privatized or transferred to employee ownership (Steinfeld, 2004: 1980). At the same time, the government organized large SOEs into large enterprise groups in order to enhance their international competitiveness based on their economies of scale. This is the strategy of so called 'grasping the large while letting go of the small' (*zhuada fangxiao*), which aims at letting the market take over the usually more inefficient small and medium-sized SOEs while focusing on government's effort to support large SOEs.

Between 1991 and 1997, the number of enterprise groups increased from 55 to 120, and between 1996 and 1999 the number of enterprises selected as key enterprises to be supported by the government increased from 300 to 520 (Nolan and Rui: 2004, 97). The re-organization has proceeded well into the twenty-first century and across sectors. Over 120 car manufacturers are to be organized into three large conglomerates, while over 300 electricity suppliers are being organized into five generation and two transmission groups. There are also plans to organize three gigantic media groups. The oil industry and airlines have already been or is being restructured into a few conglomerates (Chung, 2003: 61).

It is important to note that the strategy of 'grasping the large while letting go of the small' is the one of picking the winners. Large SOEs selected are often the best performers among SOEs. The profit rates of large and medium-sized enterprises, among which SOEs and SOE-based joint ventures are the majority, have been consistently higher than SOEs as whole from 1985 to 1997 (Smyth, 2000: 726). In 2000, the profits of the 515 key state enterprises accounted for 98 per cent of total SOEs profits, and in 2002 the profits of the 510 key state enterprises accounted for 104 per cent (Nolan and Rui, 2004: 98).

To support those key state enterprises and enterprise groups, the government employed various measures, in particular the support of the banking sector. The government has been trying to organize the banking sector around selected key SOEs and enterprise groups. For example, in 1996 a banking and enterprise cooperation agreement was signed between a major bank and 279 key enterprises (Smyth, 2000: 722).

In the 1990s, the government also engaged in internal re-organization, one of whose objectives was to help re-organize the SOEs. In 1993 the State Economic and Trade Commission (SETC) was established to modernize the technology and management of SOEs. In 1998, another round of re-organization abolished almost all industrial ministries and associations, and made them state bureaus under SETC, which effectively created a super economic ministry like the Ministry of International Trade and Industry in Japan and the Economic Planning Board in South Korea. In 2003, SETC was transformed into the State Assets Commission and continues to supervise the management of SOEs. At the same time, another long-standing and key economic institution, the State Development and Planning Commission was renamed State Development and Reform Commission, continuing its role in planning and guiding China's development in general and SOEs' development in particular.

As a result of government and SOE re-organizations, the foundation of ISI in China in the 1990s is more like that in Taiwan in the 1970s, that is, SOE-based enterprise groups control the upstream of production processes, which basically consist of petrochemical and heavy industries (Nolan and Wang, 1999), and the banking sector is organized to support those groups, while in the downstream of production processes, privatized small and medium-sized SOEs, together with other private firms, collectively-owned firms, and foreign-owned business, play the dominant role.

4.   Conclusion

ISI and EOI have been present both in Taiwan and China during the eras of their economic success. EOI in both cases began as a means to sustain ISI, which has been the development focus. The government, the banking sector, and the public enterprises are the key institutions supporting ISI in Taiwan and China, and even the way in which those key institutions are linked is similar between the two cases.

This is not to say there are no major differences between Taiwan and China. Market size is a big issue we discussed earlier. Also, China is now facing problems with centralization/decentralization domestically and the challenge of globalization internationally, while Taiwan had none of them 30 to 40 years ago. However, despite those significant differences, this study still has found a parallel experience between Taiwan and China in terms of development strategy and institutions.

One could argue, however, that EOI created the economic miracles in Taiwan and China despite a strong presence of the ISI drive; in other words, the economic success could have been greater without the ISI drive. Perhaps the difference between Taiwan and Southeast Asian tigers can provide part of the answer to this question. Taiwan's economic success is not so much in selling more goods to the world, but to build a solid industrial base for further development, while lack of a solid industrial base was one of the key problems which led to the fall of Southeast Asian economies during the Asian financial crisis of 1997. Now it is China's turn to show the power of combining ISI and EOI.

The present chapter has both theoretical and practical implications. The argument here speaks well to the developmental-state literature. It shows that the state has been the key to economic success of both Taiwan and China. A decade ago, Peter Evans (1995) used the concept of embedded autonomy to explain the successful industrial transformation of Japan, South Korea, and Taiwan. He argued that those developmental states not only had autonomy in terms of economic decision making, but were also embedded in society, which made policy implementation process a smooth and successful one. However, Evans did made a special note of Taiwan's situation by arguing that, compared to Japan and South Korea, the KMT state had a less extensive policy network linking private business, and it compensated the weakness by developing networks between public enterprises and private business (Evans, 1995: 56). The existence of a large public sector and its relation to the government were clearly the main reason for the KMT state to rely less on the private sector in policy implementation.

Compared to Taiwan, China should have more of this problem, given its even larger public sector and much smaller private sector. For now, the Chinese state can get around the problem by exercising direct control over SOEs and indirect control over collectively-owned firms, since they together still represent the main part of China's industrial economy. However, as reform continues, the private sector will become larger and stronger. How much embedded autonomy the Chinese state will obtain is an important future challenge.

What can other developing economies learn from Taiwan and China? Obviously, given different international and domestic situations, it is impossible for other developing economies to copy the development strategies and institutions of Taiwan and China. But they should remember that Taiwan and China are also very different from each other, yet they shared many similarities in their development paths. Other economies can also learn from them, if not the whole, at least the parts of their development strategies and institutions.

First of all, an economy must build its own industrial capacity, and the most direct way of doing it is to engage in ISI. Second, to emphasize ISI is not to overlook the importance of the market, but Taiwan and China show that, export promotion should have a clear aim of supporting ISI. Thus, this study advocates a combined strategy of ISI and EOI. Finally, the government has to control some key institutions. They do not have to be SOEs and/or state-owned banks, but the government has to have an institutional mechanism to exercise a stable influence over key strategic industries and the financial resources, which can be directed to those industries.

Notes

1. It is argued that Taiwan's heavy industrialization was the result of the demand of a rapidly-expanding export sector for intermediate and capital goods in the late 1960s (Ch'en, 1994). This is certainly not what really happened. The Taiwan government pushed for heavy industrialization since the early 1960s, about the same time as the beginning of EOI.
2. Some people believe that the ten projects were a response to the first oil crisis. However, that argument is rejected by former policy-makers such as Li Kuo-ting and Yeh Wan-an (Wang, 1993: 216, Yeh and Ch'iu, 1985: 193), since many of the projects, especially the industrial projects, were already endorsed or planned in the late 1960s.
3. The pilot agency changed from the Economic Stabilization Board established in 1953 to the Council for US Aid in 1958, and to International Economic Cooperation and Development in 1963, and to the Council for Economic Planning and Development in 1977. In addition, the Industrial Development Bureau

established in 1970 under the Ministry of Economic Affairs is also a key economic agency.

4. The autonomy of the central bank was further strengthened by its institutional linkages with the bank community, the Ministry of Finance and the planning agency, and the KMT party organization (Zhang, 2005).

References

Breslin, S. 1999. 'The politics of Chinese trade and the Asian financial crises: Questioning the wisdom of export-led growth' *Third World Quarterly*, 20: 1179–99.

CEPD (Council for Economic Planning and Development, Taiwan). 1996. *Taiwan Statistical Data Book*. Taipei: CEPD.

Chen, M. 1995. *Asian Management Systems: Chinese, Japanese and Korean Styles of Business*. London: Routledge.

Ch'en, Cheng-shun. 1994. 'Chin K'ou Tai T'i Kung Yeh Hua: Chieh Lun Chih T'an T'ao Yu T'ai Wan Chih Shih Cheng Yen Chiu [The ISI: A Conclusive Inquiry and Positivist Research on the Taiwan Case]'. Ma K'ai ed. *T'ai Wan Kung Yeh Fa Chan Lun Wen Chi* [A Collection of Articles on Taiwan's Industrial Development]. Taipei: Ching Lien.

Ch'en, Shih-meng, and Ch'ing-hsi Chang. 1991. '*T'ai Wan Tang Ying Shih Yeh Te Yen Pien Chi Ch'i Cheng Chih Ching Chi Han Yi* [Transformation of Taiwan's Party-Owned Enterprises and Its Political-Economic Implications]'. *Cheng Chih Ching Chi Yen T'ao Hui Lun Wen Chi* [A Collection of Papers for the Conference on Political Economy]. Taipei: China Economics Association.

Cheng, Tun-Jen, Haggard, S. and Kang, D. 1998. 'Institutions and Growth in Korea and Taiwan: The Bureaucracy'. *Journal of Development Studies*, 34(6): 87–112.

Chu, Wan-wen. 1995. 'Chin K'ou T'i Tai Yu Ch'u K'ou Tao Hsiang Ch'eng Chang: T'ai Wan Shih Hua Yeh Chih Yen Chiu [Import-Substitution and Export-Led Growth: A Study of Taiwan's Petrochemical Industry]'. *T'ai Wan She Hui Yen Chiu Chi K'an* [Taiwan: A Radical Quarterly in Social Studies] 18.

Chung, Jae Ho. 2003. 'The Political Economy of Industrial Restructuring in China: The Case of Civil Aviation'. *China Journal*, 50: 61–82.

Cumings, B. 1987. 'The Origins and Development of the Northeast Asian Political Economy: Industrial Sectors, Product Cycles, and Political Consequences', in F.C. Deyo (ed.) *The Political Economy of the New Asian Industrialism*. Ithaca: Cornell University Press.

Dutta, M. 2005. 'China's Industrial Revolution: Challenges for a Macroeconomic Agenda'. *Journal of Asian Economics*, 15: 1169–1202.

Evans, P. 1995. *Embedded Autonomy: States and Industrial Transformation*. Princeton: Princeton University Press.

Evans, P. 1998. 'Transferable Lessons?: Re-examining the Institutional Prerequisites of East Asian Economic Policies'. *Journal of Development Studies*, 34(6).

Gao, B. 1993. *Hong Wenge Shi: Zhongguo Ziyouhua de Chaoliu* [A History of Post-Cultural Revolution: The Trend of China's Liberalization]. Taipei: Lian Jing.

Gereffi, G. and Wyman, D. L. (eds) 1990. *Manufacturing Miracles: Paths of Industrialization in Latin America and East Asia*. Princeton: Princeton University Press.

Gold, T. 1988. 'Entrepreneurs, Multinationals, and the State', in E. A. Winckler and S. Greenhalgh (eds), *Contending Approaches to the Political Economy of Taiwan*. Armonk and London: M. E. Sharpe.

Ho, Ying-ch'in. 1968. 'Kuo Fang Yu Shih Yu [Defence and Petroleum]'. *Tzu Yu Chung Kuo Chih Kung Yeh* [Free China Industry] 30(6).

Hsiao, Ch'uan-cheng. 1997. *T'ai Wan Ti Ch'u Te Chung Shang Chu Yin* [Taiwan's New Mercantilism]. Taipei: Yeh Ch'iang.

Hsiao, Feng-hsiung. 1994. *T'ai Wan Te Ching Yen: Wo Kuo Ch'an Yeh Cheng Ts'e Yu Ch'an Yeh Fa Chan* [Taiwan's Experiences: Our Country's Industrial Policy and Industrial Development]. Taipei: Far Eastern Economic Research Advisory Agency.

Hsing, Mu-huan. 1993. 'T'ai Wan Tso Ts'o Le Shen Mo?: Hui Ku Ching Chi Fa Chan [What Has Taiwan Done Wrong?: Reviewing the Economic Development]'. *Yuan Chien Journal*, 15 September.

Huang, Yasheng. 2003. 'One Country, Two Systems: Foreign-Invested Enterprises and Domestic Firms in China'. *China Economic Review*, 14: 404–16.

Kueh, Y. Y. 1990. 'Growth imperatives, economic recentralization, and China's open-door policy'. *Australian Journal of Chinese Affairs*, 24: 93–119.

Kuo, S. W. Y. 1983. *The Taiwan Economy in Transition*. Boulder CO: Westview Press.

Kuo, S. W. Y., Ranis, G. and Fei, J. C. H. 1981. *The Taiwan Success Story: Rapid Growth with Improved Distribution in the Republic of China, 1952–1979*. Boulder CO: Westview Press.

Lan, Dingxiang and Cao, Bangying. 2000. 'Guoyou qiye de zhangluexing gaizu' [The strategic re-organization of SOEs]. *Jingji Tizhi Gaige* [Reform of economic system] January.

Li, Kuo-ting. 1968. *Ching Chi Cheng Ts'e Yu Ching Chi Fa Chan* [Economic Policy and Economic Development]. Taipei: CIECD.

Li, Kuo-ting, and Mu-tsai Ch'en. 1987. *Wo Kuo Ching Chi Fa Chan Ts'e Lueh Tsung Lun* [An Introduction to Our Economic Development Strategy]. Taipei: Ching Lien.

Li, L. and Vinten, G. 1997. 'An Overview of the Experiences of Chinese Industrialization Strategies and Development'. *Managerial Auditing Journal*, 12(4/5): 183–191.

Linden, G. 2004. 'China standard time: A study in strategic industrial policy'. *Business and Politics*, 6(3).

Liu, Jianxing and Wenzhen Huang. 1993. *Tai Wan Jing Ji Jie Ping* [View and Comments on Taiwan's Economy]. Beijing: Zhong Xin.

Long, Guoqiang. 2004. 'Zhongguo: Yige Jueqi de Maoyi Dago [China: An Emerging Trade Nation]', http://www.people.com.cn/GB/jingji/1040/2410194.html

McKibbin, W. and Tang, K. K 1998. 'The Global Economic Impacts of Trade and Financial Reform in China', Working Papers in Trade and Development No. 8/98, Department of Economics, Research School of Pacific and Asian Studies: Australian National University.

Ma, K'ai. 1994. 'T'ai Wan Kung Yeh Cheng Ts'e Chih Yen Pien [The Transformation of Taiwan's Industrial Policy]'. Ma K'ai ed. *T'ai Wan Kung Yeh Fa Chan Lun Wen Chi* [A Collection of Articles on Taiwan's Industrial Development]. Taipei: Ching Lien.

Moore, T. G. 1996. 'China as a Latecomer: Toward a Global Logic of the Open Policy'. *Journal of Contemporary China*, 5(12): 187–208.

Moore, T. G. 2002. *China in the World Market: Chinese Industry and International Sources of Reform in the Post-Mao Era*. Cambridge: Cambridge University Press.

NBS (National Bureau of Statistics, China). 1991–99. *Zhongguo Tongji* [China Statistics]. Beijing: NBS.

NBS (National Bureau of Statistics, China). 2000–05. *Zhongguo Jingji Jingqi Yuebao* [China Monthly Economic Indicators]. Beijing: NBS.

Nolan, J. E. 1986. *Military Industry in Taiwan and South Korea*. London: Macmillan Press.

Nolan, P. and Huaichuan Rui. 2004. 'Industrial policy and global big business revolution: The case of the Chinese coal industry'. *Journal of Chinese Economic and Business Studies*, 2(2): 97–113.

Nolan, P. and Wang, Xiaoqiang. 1999. 'Beyond Privatisation: Institutional Innovation and Growth in China's Large State-owned Enterprises'. *World Development*, 27(1): 169–200.

Sasaki, T. 1992. 'Kung Yeh Hua Te K'ai Chan Kuo Ch'eng [The Developing Process of Industrialization]'. Taniura Takao ed. *T'ai Wan Te Kung Yeh Hua: Kuo Chi Chia Kung Chi Ti Te Hsing Ch'eng* [Taiwan's Industrialization: the Formation of International Processing Base]. Originally in Japanese, translated by Lei Hui Ying. Taipei: Jen Chien Publisher.

Smyth, R. 2000. 'Should China be promoting large-scale enterprises and enterprise groups?' *World Development*, 28(4): 721–27.

Steinfeld, E. S. 2004. 'China's shallow integration: Networked production and the new challenges for late industrialization'. *World Development*, 32(11): 1971–87.

Tung, An-ch'i. 1996. '*T'ai Wan Ching Chi She Chi Chi Kou Te Pien Ch'ien Yu Cheng Fu Te Chiao Se* [The Role of Government and the Transformation of Economic Planning Organizations in Taiwan]'. The end-year report on the series of research on decisions of Taiwan's economic development. Institute for Economic Research, Academica Sinica.

Wade, R. 1988. 'The Role of Government in Overcoming Market Failure: Taiwan, Republic of Korea and Japan', in H. Hughes (ed.), *Achieving Industrialization in East Asia*. Cambridge: Cambridge University Press.

Wade, R. 1990. *Governing the Market: Economic Theory and the Role of Government in East Asian Industrialization*. Princeton: Princeton University Press.

Wang, L. S. 1993. *Li Kuo Ting K'ou Shu Li Shih: Hua Shuo T'ai Wan Ching Yen* [Oral History by Li Kuo-Ting: About Taiwan Experience]. Taipei: Cho Yueh Wen Hua Shih Yeh.

Wei, Yung-ning. 1994. *Wei Yung-Ning Hsien Sheng Fang T'an Lu* [The Reminiscences of Mr. Wei Yung-ning]. Oral History Series No. 3. Taipei: Academia Historica.

World Bank. 1993. *The East Asian Miracle: Economic Growth and Public Policy*. New York: Oxford University Press.

Woronoff, J. 1983. *Korea's Economy: Man-Made Miracle*. Seoul: Si-sa-yong-o-sa Publishers, and Oregon: Pace International Research.

Wu, Jo-yu. 1992. *Chan Hou T'ai Wan Kung Ying Shih Yeh Chih Cheng Ching Fen Hsi* [A Political-Economic Analysis of Taiwan's Post-war Public Sector]. Taipei: Institute for National Policy Research.

Yeh, Wan-an, and Hsien-ming Ch'iu. 1985. *Chung Kuo Chih Kung Ying Sheng Ch'an Shih Yeh* [China's Public Production Enterprise]. Taipei: Chung Yang Wen Wu Kung Ying She.

Yu, Qiao. 1998. 'Capital Investment, International Trade and Economic Growth in China: Evidence in the 1980–90s'. *China Economic Review*, 9(1): 73–84.

Zhang, Tianrong, Xiao Donglian, and Wang Nianyi, (eds) 1992. *Zhongguo Gaige Dacidian* [The General Dictionary of China's Reform]. Beijing: Zhongguo Guoji Guangbo Chubanshe.

Zhang, Xiaoke. 2005. 'Political Institutions and Central Bank Autonomy in Taiwan'. *European Journal of East Asian Studies*, 4(1): 87–114.

CHAPTER 15
DEVELOPMENTAL NATIONALISM AND ECONOMIC PERFORMANCE IN AFRICA: THE CASE OF THREE 'SUCCESSFUL' AFRICAN ECONOMIES[1]

Julius Kiiza

1.   Introduction

The last few decades have witnessed spirited debates over the role of institutions in fostering or frustrating economic development. The debate appeared, for a time, to be polarized between the orthodox New Institutional Economists (e.g., North, 1990; Hall and Jones, 1999) and a variety of heterodox institutional analysts (Evans, 1995; Chang, 2002). The former camp focused on 'market-enhancing' cum 'enabling' institutions (e.g., World Bank 2001); the latter grappled with institutional development from a context-specific perspective. One group called for democracy, property rights and the rule of law as instruments of capitalist development; the other doubted the effectiveness of these 'best practice' institutions *without* country-specific institutional innovations. One team appeared to address the symptoms of poor economic performance; the other attacked the root cause of the problem.

By the beginning of the new century, some degree of consensus had emerged. That institutions matter in the performance of economies is no longer controversial. That cross-national variations in the performance of economies are shaped by the presence or absence of 'good' institutions is not controversial either. What is controversial is the real meaning of 'good' institutions and in what ways countries with 'bad' institutions may attain 'effective' institutions. That effective institutions (in a developmental sense) are not acquired via the wholesale importation of 'best-practice institutions' is evident from the effectiveness of home grown developmental states in northeast Asia (Johnson, 1982). That effective institutions are not necessarily *Western* is also clear from the superb economic performance of China, which has built capitalism with distinctly *Chinese* (read 'imperfect') institutions (Qian, 2001).

It is the purpose of this chapter to examine the relationship between institution building and economic performance in three 'successful' African economies – Mauritius, Botswana, and Uganda. 'Successful' is used in inverted commas for a simple reason. While all the three have been super-economic stars in their own right, they have achieved substantially different outcomes. Mauritius has achieved Asia-type rapid and sustained growth, backed by the structural transformation of the economy from colonial commodity production (sugar) to postcolonial higher value-added industrial and information outcomes. Botswana has delivered rapid and sustained growth with no structural economic transformation. Uganda has attained rapid growth for a shorter postcolonial period (since 1992) and with no structural transformation.

The central question of this study is: Why, on a developmental continuum, does Mauritius outperform Botswana, which in turn outshines Uganda? What difference did developmentalist institutions make in the economic miracle of Mauritius and Botswana? And in what ways can Uganda-like economies learn from the Mauritius-Botswana experience? This chapter identifies developmental nationalism as a key explanatory factor. A clear understanding of developmental nationalism, however, calls for an outline of the history of mercantilism and institution building.

2.   Mercantile roots of developmental nationalism

Mercantilism has been a controversial term in political economy. Liberal and Marxist political economists conceptualize economic mercantilism in pejorative terms. In the liberal tradition, mercantilism implies the use of protective tariffs, the shielding of inefficient firms from market efficiency and, in short, the distortion of markets (Coleman, 1969: 5–6). This view springs from Adam Smith's (1776 [1937]) *The Wealth of Nations*, in which Smith outlined the 'mercantile' system. The term was not his invention, but the exposition was.

Marxian analysis is also pitted against mercantilism. The Marxian variant of the German historical school describes mercantilism as 'the ideology of the monopoly trading companies' (Coleman, 1969: 7). In Marxist theory, mercantilism is 'a system of State-regulated exploitation through trade ... [it is] essentially the economic policy of an age of primitive accumulation'. Neither Marxism nor liberalism appreciates the *dynamic* character of mercantilism; the fact, that is, that mercantilism changes in character, depending on the contingent needs of the national economy.

My point of departure is that the *contents* of economic mercantilism (or developmental nationalism) are not set in stone. The tools used might involve *direct* state involvement in promoting development or *indirect* approaches such as subsidizing private entrepreneurs. It might involve protectionism at one time and economic openness (or globalization) at another, depending on the concrete demands of the national economy.

Evidence suggests that the countries that are now advanced used nationalistic policies to grow (Chang, 2002). Importation of manufactured or luxurious products was discouraged (via high tariffs or even a total ban). Second, to stimulate domestic industrialization, importation of raw materials was encouraged while the export of raw materials was prohibited. Under the reign of King James I, England for example, banned the export of unfinished cloth to the Netherlands (the economic hegemon of the time). Third, the haemorrhage of gold or silver (a mercantilist measure of wealth) was discouraged. Fourth, imports of skilled artisans and machinery were encouraged; while 'exports' of skilled industrialists and equipment were restricted. Fifth, navigation laws were formulated to promote domestic shipbuilding industries and create business for domestic investors.

These policies of mercantilism – which are central to modern developmental nationalism – historically took roots in countries that acquired an ideology of nationalism, backed by improvements in state bureaucracies. Typical examples are seventeenth-century France under the reign of King Louis XIV and the economic leadership of Jean-Baptiste Colbert (Cole, 1939 [1964]). Another case in point is the reign of the Tudor Monarchs in England (named after Henry Tudor) particularly Queen Elizabeth I (1558–1603). Evidence clearly shows that nationalism as an ideology plays an insignificant developmental role unless it is *institutionalized* in some form of state bureaucracies. According to Chalmers Johnson (1982), the institutionalization of a developmentalist ideology was perfected by Japan's MITI in pursuit of rapid 'late' industrialization.

By implication, therefore, developmental nationalism needs to be embodied in formal institutions or state bureaucracies if it serves the goal of development. The 'developmentalist bureaucracy' documented in this paper, is the institutional embodiment of the ideology of developmental nationalism. According to Chang (2002), the establishment of a meritocratic bureaucracy was a major step in the history of development.

The pioneer in this regard was Prussia. An extensive bureaucratic reform was implemented by Frederick William I from 1713, the year of his accession to the throne. The key measures included: The centralization of authorities scattered over two dozen separate territorial entities (many of them not even physically contiguous)...; the transformation of the status of bureaucrats from private servants of the royal family into servants of the state; regular payments in cash (rather than in kind as before) of adequate salaries; and introduction of a strict supervision system. Thanks to these measures and to the additional measures introduced by his son, Frederick the Great (1740–86), by the early nineteenth century Prussia could be said to have installed the key elements of a modern (Weberian) bureaucracy – an entrance examination, a hierarchical organization, pension systems, a disciplinary procedure, and security of tenure (Chang, 2002: 80).

This chapter grapples with the presence or absence of these essential ingredients of 'Weberian' bureaucracy and how they explain cross-national differences in economic performance. To what degree are the Prussia-like Weberian reforms helpful today? This study does not pretend to develop a new theory of development. I only attempt to explain the association between a developmentalist ideology, Weberianness and the level of economic performance attained in Mauritius, Botswana and Uganda (also see Evans and Rauch, 2005).

3.   Conceptual challenges

Two conceptual challenges persist. First, there is no universally acceptable definition of institutions (although the accent in the literature is placed on institutions as 'rules of the game' and/or as 'organizations' – e.g., van Arkadie 1990). Second, no consensus exists on the role of institutions in promoting or blocking development (Chang, chapter 2, this volume).

Two major species of literature exist, one expounding the 'good bureaucracies' thesis and the other developing the 'institutions first' hypothesis. The 'good bureaucracies' literature (e.g. Rauch and Evans, 1999) argues that replacing patronage systems of state officials with a professional bureaucracy is a necessary (though insufficient) condition for a state to be 'developmental'. This echoes the view that a merit-based, professional system of administration is superior to the spoils system that existed prior to the reforms of the late nineteenth century. Simply stated, (i) having entry requirements for civil service; (ii) paying reasonable salaries; and (iii) a merit-based system of internal promotion all seem to result in 'better quality' bureaucracies – the very antithesis of the spoils system (Rauch and Evans, 1999).

The second species of literature builds on the first. It examines the interface between institutional development and economic growth. This literature argues that institutions matter for explaining cross-country differences in growth. The orthodox discourse, as already hinted, focuses on the minimalist version of institutions. State activism, for example, is restricted to the creation of an 'enabling environment' for private sector-led development. The heterodox variant argues that while the 'enabling' institutions may *influence* economic outcomes, the real *determinants* of the quality and pace of growth are developmentalist institutions whose role is shaped by the concrete contingencies in individual countries.

What seems to be agreeable to both orthodox and heterodox institutionalists is that poor bureaucratic quality (measured by the degree of Weberianness) lowers investment and growth (Knack and Keefer, 1995). Evans and Rauch (2005) emphasize this point in their empirical study of the association between bureaucratic structure and growth. Using an original data set, they examine the characteristics of core state economic agencies and the growth records of a sample of 35 developing countries for the period 1970–90. They use a Weberian scale to measure the degree to which state agencies employ meritocratic recruitment and offer predictable, rewarding and long-term careers. Their main finding is that Weberianness significantly enhances prospects for growth. Their conclusion is twofold. First, Weberianness should be included as a factor in the general models of economic growth. Second, developing countries should build better bureaucracies if they are to promote durable development.

To what degree do the cases of Mauritius, Botswana, and Uganda uphold or falsify the 'good bureaucracies' and the 'institutions first' propositions?

4.   Mauritius: Triumph of hope over endowments?

Mauritius is a tiny island state in the Indian Ocean. With a total area of 1,865 km^2 and a population of 1.2 million people, Mauritius has one of the world's highest population densities – 602 km^2.

Mauritius obtained political independence in 1968 after a unique colonial history. It was first colonized by the Dutch (1638–1710), followed by the French (1715–1810) and the British (1810–1968). French colonialism established sugar estates using slave labour imported from Africa. The colony became so prosperous that it was the object of struggle between the French and the British during the Napoleonic War.

Even when Britain captured the colony from France, several French institutions remained intact. For instance, the Napoleonic code of law was maintained. The French language also remained and is still used more widely than English. More importantly, the Franco-Mauritians (descendants of French planters) remained key players in the economy. While they account for only 2 per cent of the total population – in comparison with Indo-Mauritians (68 per cent), Creoles (27 per cent and Sino-Mauritians (3 per cent) – they constitute the proverbial sugar oligarchy (Meisenhelder, 1997: 280). Today, the Franco-Mauritians dominate banking and other modern businesses.

At the time of independence (1968), the 'initial conditions' of Mauritius were deplorable. The 1961 Royal Commission headed by Professor J. E. Meade documented the hurdles to Mauritian development in no uncertain terms. Mauritius had no mineral or oil deposits. It had a narrow domestic market (about 700,000 people then). The long distance separating Mauritius from European and American markets posed a challenge for industrialization. The Mauritian economy lacked technical skills and capital for investment. Most importantly, the Island was a monocrop (sugar) economy (Meade Report, 1961). By 1967, sugar accounted for 95 per cent of total export earnings, over 30 per cent of GNP and about 35 per cent of total employment. According to Naipul (1972) Mauritius was 'an agricultural colony, created by empire in an empty island and always meant to be part of something larger, now given a thing called independence and set adrift; [it was] an abandoned imperial barracoon, incapable of economic or cultural autonomy'.

By the 1980s, however, the Mauritian economy had experienced *structural* transformation. Sugar exports, which accounted for 95 per cent of export earnings in 1967 declined to about 60 per cent in 1979 and 37 per cent in 1987. The contribution of sugar to total GDP also declined from over 30 per cent in 1967 to 20 per cent in 1979 and less than 14 per cent in the late 1980s (Mauritius, 2004). On the other hand, the share of manufactured exports – coming primarily from the export processing zone (EPZ), a politically constructed developmental institution - increased from 25 per cent in 1979 to 58 per cent in 1989. (The contribution of EPZ manufacturing to total GDP, national employment, and export earnings continued in the 1990s and beyond.) The service sector, which was initially dominated by tourism (a 'commodity service') qualitatively changed in favour of the higher value-added banking and the ICT services. Today, the Mauritian economy is one of the healthiest in Africa. Total GDP stands at US$6 billion while per capita income is US$4,900. The real growth rate is 4.6 per cent, while the average inflation rate is 4.8 per cent.

What institutional variables account for Mauritius' structural transformation into a high value-added industrial and information economy? This question will be addressed once an outline of the economic trend in Botswana and Uganda is given.

5.   Botswana: Possibilities in barren land

Botswana, like Mauritius, is a former colony – of Britain. Like Mauritius, Botswana is a 'small' country (600,370 km²), with about 1.6 million people. The traditional economic activity – cattle rearing – was still dominant at the time of independence in 1966.

However, Botswana had several characteristics that distinguished it from Mauritius. First, is being landlocked. Second, Botswana is larger than Mauritius although over 84 per cent of the landmass is the largely uninhabited Kalahari dessert. In fact, 80 per cent of the Batswana live along the fertile eastern border. Third, British colonialism in Botswana was one of the most ineffective regimes (in a developmental sense).

Bechuanaland was declared a British Protectorate in 1885. From Britain's imperial perspective, the main reason for acquiring Botswana was strategic. With mineral rich South Africa under its control, Britain had no serious economic interest in Bechuanaland (which was deemed to be poor in minerals). But this changed when Germany annexed Namibia in 1884. British strategists feared that Germany would soon acquire Bechuanaland and, thereby, block Britain's major corridor to Northern Africa. As Cecil Rhodes noted, Bechuanaland was the 'Suez Canal into (Africa's) interior' (quoted in Gann et al. 1967: 203).

At the time of independence in 1966, Botswana was the third poorest country in the world (Tregenna, 2003). This was arguably because of *ineffective* British colonialism. The country had just 12 km of paved road and two secondary schools. Only 100 Batswana had completed secondary school and only 22 had graduated from university (Acemoglu et al. 2003: 1). To worsen matters, Botswana was a desert and a primary commodity producer of cattle. Most commentators on Botswana's economic prospects at the time of independence concluded that the country's growth prospects were dismal.

They were wrong. Between 1966 and 1974, Botswana was one of the fastest growing countries in the world. Real GDP growth averaged 16 per cent between 1970 and 1974. Between 1975 and 1989, Botswana maintained its rapid growth rate. With the discovery of diamond deposits at Orapa cattle post (1967) and the subsequent opening of Juaneng diamond mines (1982), mining took the place of agriculture as a leading economic sector. Domestic savings started to exceed investment. Government ran budget and trade surpluses. The ratio of government revenue to GDP was a superb 50 per cent (about double the African average) and peaked at 64 per cent in 1988 (Tregenna, 2003). In 1997, Botswana graduated into middle income category.

Today, Botswana's GDP is a comfortable US$14 billion (2005). Per capita income is US$8,800, while real GDP growth and inflation are 7.6 per cent and 8 per cent respectively. The level of infrastructural development is also high. Botswana now has 888 km of railway and 10,217 km of roads (with 5,619 km paved and the rest unpaved). The country's socio-economic indicators are also impressive, save for the AIDs crisis. Botswana has one of the highest foreign exchange reserves in the world (Jefferis and Kelly, 1999: 212). At a time when most African countries have a huge debt burden, Botswana's foreign debt is only about 14 per cent of GNP. The country has no internal debt and is a net exporter of capital.

How does one explain the superb economic record of Africa's success stories in comparison with economic disasters (e.g., Somalia) and the moderate performers (like Uganda)? This question will be addressed once Uganda's economic record is outlined.

6.   Uganda: Stuck in the Garden of Eden?

Uganda, like Mauritius and Botswana, has a history of colonial occupation. The country was declared a British protectorate in 1894 and remained under British rule for 70 years. With a total area of 236,000 km² and a total population of 25 million people (Uganda 2005) Uganda is a relatively small country – which is, nevertheless, larger than Mauritius. Uganda has some of the best naturally endowed advantages in the world. Blessed with fertile soils, heavy and reliable rainfall in most parts, and temperatures ranging between 18–27°C throughout the year, Uganda is a Garden of Eden. To Sir Winston Churchill, Uganda was the 'Pearl of Africa'. Whether Uganda's Garden-of-Eden status has been a blessing or a 'curse in disguise' will become clearer shortly.

When Uganda obtained political independence in 1962, it had one of the most promising economies in Africa. Between 1963 and 1970, GDP grew by 4.8 per cent a year, while population increased at an estimated rate of 2.6 per cent, implying an annual increase in per capita income of about 2 per cent. Uganda's domestic savings averaged 13 per cent, a level that 'permitted implementation of an ambitious investment programme without undue pressure on domestic prices and the balance of payments' (World Bank 1982: 3). In the 1960s, the terms of trade for Uganda's exports were favourable and export earnings were sufficient to finance imports.

With the rise of Idi Amin to power in 1971, Uganda's rosy economic and institutional credentials were reversed. Real GDP declined at an average rate of 3.8 per cent a year during 1973–79 while inflation skyrocketed to over 40 per cent a year, compared with an average rate of 8.2 per cent during 1967–70 (Collier and Reinikka, 2001). Gross domestic investment declined from 13 per cent in 1963–70 to 8.6 per cent in 1971–78 and the national savings rate fell from 13.4 per cent to 7.7 per cent over the same period (*Uganda Vision 2025*: 3–4). The 'liberation' war of 1979 (which led to the overthrow of Idi Amin) worsened matters. GDP declined by 9.7 per cent, with gross domestic investment falling to as low as 6 per cent of GDP (Uganda 1988).

When the National Resistance Movement (NRM) of President Museveni (1986–to date) came to power, all state institutions had virtually collapsed (Mwenda, 2004). Civil and political upheavals were the order of the day. The civil service, which is the engine of modern governments, had not yet recovered from the underpayment and demoralization of Amin's time.

More importantly, the economy was in bad shape. GDP growth rate declined from 11.7 per cent in 1982 to −1.5 per cent in 1986. Inflation averaged 135.6 per cent in 1986 and rose to 232.6 per cent in 1987. Virtually all other economic indicators (e.g., the balance of payments) had worsened. The attempt by the NRM elites to impose price controls on essential products hit a snag. Donors, who were opposed to state-led development, refused to extend credit to the new government unless it made 'friends' with the IMF. The economic crisis continued unabated. In 1987, state elites abandoned their 'Marxist' experiment and embraced orthodox economic and institutional programmes of the IMF/World Bank fraternity.

Between 1992 and 2000, GDP growth averaged 6.5 per cent and was 5.5 per cent in 2005. Poverty has, on average, also declined from 56 per cent in 1992 to 35 per cent in 2000, although it rose again to 40 per cent in 2005 (Uganda 2005).

In short, Uganda, like Botswana, remains a Ricardian economy, stuck in the Garden of Eden. The services sector, for example, which recently attracted the higher quality telecommunications and information companies, is still dominated by tourism, which, as already hinted, is a 'commodity' service. But unlike Botswana, Uganda's 'impressive' postcolonial growth has taken place for a shorter period of time (the 1990s) and with a poorer record of investment in developmental infrastructure such as roads and railways. How does one explain structural economic transformation in Mauritius, rapid, sustained but commodity-driven growth in Botswana and the rather 'stop-and-go' but fairly high rates of Uganda?

7.   Accounting for the economic miracle in Mauritius and Botswana

Three broad theoretical explanations exist. First is environmental determinism, which emphasizes the role of geography cum natural endowments in growth. Second is the 'enabling institutions' thesis of the orthodox institutionalists. Third is the theory of heterodox institutionalism that puts the accent on a developmentalist ideology and Weberianness (Evans and Rauch, 2005).

Environmental determinism as a theory of economic progress makes two major claims. First, that geography, proximity to the coast and distance from the equator are key determinants of economic growth (Sachs, 2001). (This suggests that coastal countries such as Mozambique should be more developed than landlocked countries such as Botswana and Switzerland.) Second, that tropical countries face insurmountable obstacles to progress. Their wet and humid climate favours a multiplicity of pests/parasites, while the favourable temperatures are a disincentive to innovation. The claim is that nature was too kind to the citizens of the tropics: You don't have to think hard to survive! By contrast, temperate nations had to innovate, develop and survive environmental challenges like winter. 'Necessity', it is asserted, 'is the Mother of Innovation!' What is not explained is why the Eskimos in the cold Tundra have not advanced. Nor does environmental determinism explain why some tropical countries (such as Mauritius and Malaysia) have advanced while others (like Cambodia) have not.

A variant of environmental determinism alleges that Botswana and Libya (which are rich in diamonds and oil deposits respectively) have advanced because of rich resource endowments. The question becomes: Why have some resource rich countries (such as DR Congo, Nigeria, and Uganda) not advanced? Why was colonialism unable to transform Botswana and Libya into strong economies anyway? (Did the resource endowments come with postcolonial regimes?) And why has resource poor Mauritius or Japan been able to advance economically? The answer, it would seem, lies in a developmentalist ideology backed by Weberian institutions.

Orthodox institutionalists such as North (1990) appear to make headway in explaining why some countries grow while others do not. Their central claim is that particular institutions (such as private property legislation) were key determinants of growth in the West. If Botswana and Mauritius are growing, it must be because of 'good' institutions. This view is upheld by Acemoglu et al. (2001) but with a difference. While Acemoglu et al. attribute Botswana's economic progress to 'institutions of private property', their historical analysis focuses on political institutions and the developmentalist ideology of the leadership.

Closely related to the Acemoglu et al. (2001) thesis is the view that Botswana (and Mauritius) made 'good' policy choices. 'The success of Botswana', it is agued, 'is most plausibly due to its adoption of good policy' (Acemoglu et al. 2003). Beaulier (forthcoming), who is critical of the 'enabling' institutions view of Acemoglu et al. (2001; 2003), nevertheless upholds the view that Botswana succeeded because of 'good' policies signified by the adoption of free market capitalism, attraction of foreign investment, use of foreign aid for a short time, and allowing the IMF/World Bank fraternity to play an advisory role, rather than a planning role. Beaulier's conclusion is simple: Botswana's success was the result of good postcolonial policies. If other African countries are to develop, they must also make 'good' policy choices. This begs the question: Where do good policies come from? Virtually all countries have the desire to develop (Evans, 1995). Why are some more effective than others in translating their wish into concrete developmental outcomes? The answer seems to lie in the presence or absence of a developmentalist ideology *plus* Weberian institutions.

8.   Developmentalist ideology and Weberianness in Mauritius and Botswana

In Mauritius, no major ideological differences exist between the major political parties. For example, the Mauritian Labour Party (MLP), which has dominated power since independence, is leftist. The Mauritian Militant Movement (MMM) and the Mauritian Socialist Party (MSP) have a far-leftist ideology. Despite these *formal* differences, Mauritian political parties are at the centre of ideology. More importantly, the major parties are united by their common commitment to national development. Developmental nationalism has been the dominant ideology.

Mauritian developmentalism begins with the colonial administration in the 1960s. Faced with economic hardships in the sugar economy, the colonial state passed laws in 1964 to promote import substitution industrialization. Companies that met the criteria set by state bureaucrats were issued with 'Development Certificates'. The 'DC' companies, as they were coined, were offered a host of incentives. Infant industries were offered protection. Duties on imported capital goods and industrial raw materials were suspended. Tax exemptions for five years and long-term loans from the Mauritius Development Bank (for up to 50 per cent of long-term capital employed) were also put in place.

Mauritian developmental nationalism continued even in the postcolonial period. Faced with the problem of a narrow domestic market, state bureaucrats and developmentalist politicians, established the Mauritian export processing zone (EPZ) in 1970. The EPZ offered several incentives to investors. Companies awarded an EPZ certificate were given the nationally prestigious title of 'Export Enterprises'. They also enjoyed (and largely continue to access) numerous benefits. First is complete exemption from payment of import duty on capital goods. Second is exemption from import and excise duty on raw materials, components and imported intermediate goods (except harmful products such as spirits and tobacco). Third is a tax holiday of 10–20 years, depending on the sector. Fourth is a 5-year exemption from payment of income tax on dividends. Fifth is government provision of developmental infrastructure such as factory buildings for industrialists and subsidized electricity. Sixth is guaranteed access to loans (from commercial banks) at preferential rates for importation of raw materials. Seventh is favourable labour legislation (read 'repressed' minimum wages) to assist export industries. Finally is the exception from crane and other harbour handling dues chargeable by government on imports.

In Botswana, as in Mauritius, the ideology of the dominant party, the Botswana Democratic Party (BDP) was developmentalism. The BDP adopted a pragmatic economic ideology. In the face of limited savings for national development, the BDP invited foreign capital to invest in Botswana. A typical example is De Beers Geologists (a South African Company) which discovered diamonds in 1967 and subsequently played a key role in Botswana's mineral prospecting and development. However, unlike DR Congo and other non-developmentalist states, the BDP state struck a deal with FDI: '70–80% of diamond revenue accrues to the state...' (Tregenna, 2003). More importantly, revenues from mineral wealth have not been stolen. They have been channelled to productive investment, thanks to the developmentalism of both politicians and bureaucrats. It is because of this that some (e.g., Samatar, 1999) attribute the success of Botswana, like that of Mauritius, to 'good leadership'.

Both Mauritius and Botswana *institutionalized* developmental nationalism by building corps of high quality, fairly clean bureaucrats. In Mauritius, it is the prolonged colonial administration that set the pace. Weberianness was allowed to take root via the recruitment of locals into the colonial civil service. The locals were enabled to acquire bureaucratic capacity under colonial tutelage (Goldsmith, 2005). Mauritius had a fairly large public sector, with government employees representing over 1 per cent of the colony's population in 1900 (Lange, 2003: 404) and 1.5 per cent by independence (Goldsmith, 2005). By the end of colonial rule, Mauritians held over 90 per cent of these posts, including most high level positions.

In fact, Mauritius seems to uphold the 'institutions first' thesis. The Mauritian Public Service Commission was set up in 1953 to serve as an agency for meritocratic recruitment of civil servants. A strict Weberian Code of Conduct has since been put in place to enforce public sector ethics. In the eyes of critics, Mauritius is not a pure meritocracy. For instance, political parties are not supposed to use civil servants for patronage purposes; in practice, they sometimes do (Goldsmith, 2005). This however, does not water down the significance of Weberianness. It only demonstrates that an ideal Weberian bureaucracy is *not* what developmentalist institutionalists look for. What we look for are real-world approximations of the Weberian bureaucracy. For all its weakness, the Mauritian bureaucracy approximates the Weberian bureaucracy, particularly in comparison with the poor quality bureaucracies found elsewhere in Africa.

In Botswana, the role of the bureaucracy has not been as effective. For example, no EPZ and no high value-added manufacturing sector exist. The developmentalist ability of the Botswana bureaucratic state is, without a doubt, weaker than that of Mauritius. However, the bureaucracy has been clean, nationalistic and pro-development. Moreover, from the perspective of sustained growth and in comparison with Uganda and other African countries, Botswana has been an impressive performer. Caroll and Caroll (1997) argue that Botswana has had politicians and talented bureaucrats who have 'personal commitment' to economic development.

9.   Dominant ideology and institutional weaknesses in Uganda

Uganda, like Mauritius, adopted a developmentalist ideology in the dying years of colonial administration. ISI, for example, started after the Second World War. In pursuit of industrialization, the colonial state established two strategic institutions in 1952: The Owen Falls Dam and the Uganda Development Corporation (UDC). These 'colonial development companies', as they were called, were meant to promote private British industries in the colony by having the state guarantee the initial risk capital. Specifically, the Dam was meant to provide cost-effective hydroelectric power for industrial development. UDC, for its part, was expected to:

Be able to assist the local investor and be able to enter into partnership with the investor from outside - not with the idea of itself going into industrial businesses and running those businesses permanently, but with the idea of filling this gap, to give enterprise a start, and gradually to be able to pass over to the private investor in the colony both capital burden and the managerial responsibility in the industries. (Colonial Secretary, quoted in *Uganda Herald*, 1 April 1952: 4)

The first postcolonial regime of Dr Milton Obote (1962–71) upheld the developmentalism of the colonial state. Developmental nationalism became the guiding economic ideology of state officials. This comes out clearly in a landmark speech delivered in 1966 by Obote's Vice President, Hon. John Babiiha. According to him,

[T]he achieving of independence by the East African territories has given a new impetus to an even greater revolution, namely, economic revolution. East Africa can no longer be contented with the old colonial maxim of the duty of Government being the maintenance of law and order. The accent must now be on development, more particularly economic development and all other things must serve principally as a medium to facilitate and accelerate this development. It would, therefore, follow that our education, our philosophy, our attitudes and our mental outlook should be re-oriented and geared to this over-all aim. Creation of a new environment to facilitate development revolution becomes an absolute necessity. We cannot afford to take a passive role any longer.

The UDC became the institutional embodiment of Uganda's developmentalism. In the 1960s, UDC was the fulcrum of strategic partnerships between government and foreign capital.

Unfortunately, UDC's ability to steer economic progress in Uganda was compromised by two developments. First was the political instability associated with Amin's regime (1970s) and the post-Amin governments of 1979–86. Second was the death of developmental nationalism and the hegemony of economic liberalism as the official ideology of the Yoweri Museveni regime (1986–to date).

Guided by economic liberalism, President Museveni has driven developmentalist institutions such as UDC to their deathbed. Development banks have been stifled. Strategic public enterprises (such as Uganda Commercial Bank and Uganda Railways) have been privatized, thanks to the dominant view that the 'appropriate' role of government is to create a 'conducive' cum 'enabling' environment for private sector-led development.

It must nevertheless be noted that neoliberal Uganda has registered positive growth rates. The economy has grown by 6.5 per cent a year since 1992 and is now growing at 5.5 per cent. This rapid growth suggests that economic liberalism is not necessarily antithetical to national growth. Uganda's growth, it appears, has happened because of reduced insecurity (which interfered with the rapid growth rates of the 1960s) and *in spite of* the weakened institutional capacities.

The quality of public bureaucracies in Uganda is substantially different from that of Mauritius and Botswana. Uganda started fairly well with the establishment of a Public Service Commission in the run up to independence. But its Weberian credentials were much weaker than those of Mauritius or Botswana. The Civil Service survey of 1962 showed that Uganda had a serious dearth of senior public administrators. Of the 408 Executive Class posts, Ugandans held only 102 posts (25 per cent); 106 posts were vacant. The administrators, professional cadres, and middle grades of the executive class were also in short supply. Of the 1,250 established posts 'in the super-scales and A-scale as at 1 December 1962, only 269 were filled by Ugandans, while there were no less than 265 vacancies some of which were filled by temporary staff'. Uganda 'had no Ugandan chartered accountant, solicitor, architect, electrical or mechanical engineer or pathologist, while there was only one geologist, one veterinary officer, one entomologist and two dentists…'.

Today, Uganda's Weberian credentials have waned further. While recruitment into the public service is done by the Uganda Public Service Commission, which is formerly a meritocratic institution, the practice is different. Meritocratic recruitment has been overshadowed by the politics of *who knows whom* (Kiiza, 2000). Patrimony, rather than academic merit, is the basis for public sector recruitment and promotion (Kiiza, 2000). Consequently, the officers charged with the task of national economic governance are not necessarily the 'best and brightest'. This appears to have gotten worse under the World Bank sponsored decentralization programme, under which the powers of central state agencies have been devolved to local governments. Second, retrenchment in the name of 'right-sizing' seems to have incapacitated public service delivery and national development. Public servants have been retrenched from 3,20,000 in 1993 to 1,50,000 in 2000. Third, retrenchment has triggered 'insecurity of tenure' resulting in heightened corruption as employees seek to 'grab' as much as they can before they lose their jobs.

But that is not all. Uganda's bureaucrats are underpaid and demoralized. According to Gerald Sendaula, Uganda's 'mean salary levels for public servants are only 40 per cent of private sector salaries for equivalent jobs, while for some key professionals – such as accountants, economists and engineers – public sector salary levels are only a third of market levels'

(Sendaula, 2000: 37–8). This constrains government's capacity to attract, retain and utilize the most capable skills. Uganda's public servants have low motivation to work, and 'the incentive to moonlight or engage in corruption in order to supplement [their meagre] wages is high' (Sendaula, 2000: 37–8). More importantly, Uganda's economic bureaucrats are religiously committed to economic liberalism. Free-market economics is seen to be the only avenue of governing the economy. Thus, in comparison with Mauritius and Botswana, Uganda's state bureaucrats have no 'autonomy' (cf. Evans, 1995). They are captured by economic internationalism, thanks to the dominant ideology of the IMF/World Bank fraternity.

10.   Conclusion

This chapter has attempted to examine the association between developmental nationalism, institution building and economic performance in Mauritius, Botswana, and Uganda. Two conclusions emerge.

First, the Mauritius-Botswana-Uganda differences are associated with differences in commitment to developmental nationalism and the Weberianness of state institutions. This is not to suggest that no other factors contributed to differences in economic performance. Mauritius and Botswana, as already noted, have had stable regimes while Uganda has been bedevilled with conflicts and unstable regimes. Coalition-building and rotation of high offices among a few elites in Mauritius and Botswana have also contributed to policy continuity and development. However, these 'confounding' variables have influenced, not determined the Mauritius-Botswana-Uganda differences in economic performance. The key determinants of cross-national variations, it appears, were the presence of developmental nationalism and Weberian institutions in Mauritius and Botswana, and their absence in Uganda.

The second conclusion modifies the first. While developmental nationalism is strongly associated with growth, it cannot deliver durable developmental dividends unless it is institutionalized in and through Weberian bureaucracies. Mauritius and, to a lesser extent, Botswana illustrate the significance of institutionalizing and deepening developmentalism. The Ugandan case, by contrast, shows the price (in a developmental sense) of replacing post-independence developmental nationalism with economic liberalism. It also underscores the cost (in terms of lost opportunities) of driving a meritocratic civil service and developmentalist institutions (such as Uganda Development Corporation) to their deathbed. To other developing countries, Uganda seems to be shouting: *Don't Follow Me! I Know Not Where I'm Heading!*[2]

Three critical lessons emerge. First, sub-Saharan African countries that have stifled their post-independence developmentalism and embraced economic liberalism need to rethink their preferences. Economic liberalism is not necessarily a wrong ideology. It is simply inappropriate for sub-Saharan Africa at the current stage of development. This underscores a more profound lesson for developing countries. Impeccable evidence (e.g., Chang, 2002: 1–68) shows that the now developed countries (NDCs) used nationalistic cum mercantilist policies (such as infant industry protection) when they were developing. Today, the gospel according to the NDCs reads: *Do as We Say, Not as We Did to Advance!* Developing countries must reject this gospel. For one thing, the 'good' economics for the NDCs may be 'bad' for developing countries; and the 'good' institutions (or policies) of the NDCs are not necessarily 'good enough' for developing countries.

The second lesson is really a warning. Developing countries (such as Uganda) that have implemented orthodox institutional reforms such as the 'hollowing-out' of public bureaucracies (via privatization, retrenchment, and contracting out) need to know that building Weberian institutions is a difficult and tedious process. Destroying them (in the name of 'right-sizing') is easier. Rather than rushing to attack their bureaucracies for being 'too bureaucratic', developing countries should learn that their fundamental institutional problem is one of too little, not too much Weberian bureaucracy. The way forward, it appears, is to build and/or deepen the Weberianness of public institutions through meritocratic recruitment and promotion; offering predictable, rewarding and long-term careers; and reconstituting former developmentalist agencies (such as UDC) into key organs of national development.

The third lesson is simpler. Replacing the spoils system of administration with a meritocratic, professional system of administration not only rewards state officials with job security. It actually boosts their morale, increases their commitment to official work and expands prospects of growth, as the cases of Mauritius and Botswana illustrate. Thus, sensible developing countries must embark on the difficult but rewarding task of replacing the spoils system with a Weberian system of administration. The challenge is gigantic but not impossible.

Notes

1. I acknowledge, with thanks, the comments received from Ha-Joon Chang, Howard Stein, John Toye, and other participants at the UNU-WIDER workshop of 18–19 April 2005 in Helsinki. Unfortunately, but perhaps inevitably, I was unable to adopt all the suggestions made. Errors and omissions, if any, are mine.
2. An important issue that calls for detailed future research is the paradox of weak institutions but 'robust' growth in Uganda. I call this a paradox because it challenges the theory of developmentalist institutions, which predicts that weak institutions will result in weak economic performance. In order to explain the Ugandan paradox, we need to understand in detail the quality of growth, the sources of growth, and whether or not the Ugandan economy has been or is likely, in the foreseeable future, to be transformed into a higher value-added industrial and information economy comparable to Mauritius.

References

Acemoglu, D., Johnson, S. and Robinson, J. 2001. 'Reversal of Fortune: Geography and Institutions in the Making of the Modern World Income Distribution', NBER Working Paper 8460.

Acemoglu, D., Johnson, S. and Robinson, J. 2003. 'An African Success Story: Botswana', in D. Rodrik (ed.), *In Search of Prosperity: Analytic Narratives on Economic Growth*. Princeton, NJ: Princeton University Press.

Alladin, I. 1993. *Economic Miracle in the Indian Ocean*. Rose Hill, Mauritius: 100–102.

Bardhan, P. 2005. *Scarcity, Conflicts and Cooperation: Essays in the Political and Institutional Economics of Development*. Cambridge MA: MIT Press.

Bates, R. 1989. *Beyond the Miracle of the Market: The Political Economy of Agrarian Development in Kenya*. Cambridge: Cambridge University Press.

Beaulier, S. (forthcoming) 'Explaining Botswana's Success: The Critical Role of Postcolonial Policy', *Cato Journal*.

Cameron, R. 1989. *A Concise Economic History of the World*. New York: Oxford University Press.

Carol, W. and Carol, T. 1997. 'State and Ethnicity in Botswana and Mauritius: A Democratic Route to Development?' *Journal of Development Studies*, 33(4): 464–86.

Chang, H-J. 2002. *Kicking Away the Ladder: Development Strategies in Historical Perspective*. London: Anthem Press.

Cole, C. W. 1936 [1964]. *Colbert and a Century of French Mercantilism*. London: Frank Cass. Vol. II.

Coleman, D. (ed.). 1969. *Revisions in Mercantilism*. London: Methuen.

Dale, R. 1995. *Botswana's Search for Autonomy in Southern Africa*. Westport CT: Greenwood Press.

Diamond, J. 1997: *Guns, Germs, and Steel: The Fates of Human Societies*. New York: W.W. Norton.

Dobb, M. 1946. *Studies in the Development of Capitalism*. London: Routledge.

Evans, P. 1995. *Embedded Autonomy: States and Industrial Transformation*. Princeton NJ: Princeton University Press.

Evans, P. and Rauch, J. 2005. *Bureaucracy and Growth: A Cross-National Analysis of the Effects of 'Weberian' State Structures on Economic Growth*. Unpublished.

Frieden, J. and Lake, D. 1987. *International Political Economy: Perspectives on Global Power and Wealth*. New York: St Martin's Press.

Goldsmith, A. A. 2005. 'Good Governance and Economic Reform: What Comes First?' Paper for the 27th Association for Public Policy Analysis and Management (APPAM) Conference, 3–5 November, Washington DC.

Good, K. 1992. 'Interpreting the Exceptionality of Botswana', *Journal of Modern African Studies*, 30(1): 69–95.

Grindle, M. S. 2004. 'Good Enough Governance: Poverty Reduction and Reform in Developing Countries', *Governance* 17 (October): 525–48.

Gann, L. and Duignan, P. 1967. *The Burden of Empire*. Stanford, CA: Hoover Institution Press.

Hall, R. and Jones, C. 1999. Why Do Some Countries Produce More Output per Worker than Others? *Quarterly Journal of Economics*, 114(1): 83–116.

Harvey, C. 1992. 'Botswana: Is the Economic Miracle Over?' *Journal of African Economies*, November, 1(3): 335–68.

Hope, K. 1998. 'Development Policy and Economic Performance in Botswana: Lessons for the Transition Economies in Sub-Saharan Africa' *Journal of International Development*, 10(4): 539–54.

Jefferis, K. and Kelly, T. 1999. 'Botswana: Poverty amid Plenty' *Oxford Development Studies*, 27(2): 221–31.

Jutting, J. 2003. 'Institutions and Development: A Critical Review'. OECD Development Center Technical Paper 210.

Kasper, W. and Streit, M. 1998. *Institutional Economics*. Cheltenham: Edward Eldgar.

Kiiza, J. 2000. 'Market-Oriented Public Management in Uganda: Benchmarking International Best Practice?' *Ufahamu*. XXVIII(1): 94–124.

Knack, S. and Keefer, P. 1995. 'Institutions and Economic Performance: Cross Country Tests Using Alternative Institutional Measures', *Economics and Politics*, 7: 207–27.

Lange, M. 2003. 'Embedding the Colonial State. A Comparative-Historical Analysis of State Building and Broad-Based Development in Mauritius', *Social Science History*, 27: 397–423.

List, F. 1885. *National System of Political Economy*. London: Longmans. Translated by Samson S. Lloyd, MP.

Mamdani, M. 1996. *Citizen and Subject: Contemporary Africa and the Legacy of Late Colonialism*. Princeton NJ: Princeton University Press.

Maundeni, Z. 2001. 'State Culture and Development in Botswana and Zimbabwe' *Journal of Modern African Studies*, 40(1): 105–132.

Meade, J. M. 1961/1968. *The Economic and Social Structure of Mauritius*. London.

Meisenhelder, T. 1994. 'Bonanza and Dependency in Botswana', *Studies in Comparative Economic Development*, 29: 38–49.

Meisenhelder, T. 1997. 'The Developmental State in Mauritius', *Journal of Modern African Studies*, 35(2): 279–97.

North, D. 1990. *Institutions, Institutional Change, and Economic Performance*. New York: Cambridge University Press.

Qian. Y. 2001. 'How Reform Worked in China', *Working Paper*, Berkeley: University of California.

Rauch, J. and Evans, P. 1999. 'Bureaucratic Structures and Bureaucratic Performance in Less Developed Countries'. University of California, San Diego Discussion Paper 99–06.

Sachs, J. 2001. 'Tropical Underdevelopment', NBER Working Paper 8119.

Samatar, A. I. 1999. *An African Miracle: State, Class Leadership and Colonial Legacy in Botswana Development*. Heinemann: Portsmouth, NH.

Sendaula, G. 2000. 'The Ugandan Reform Experience', *Reform and Growth in Africa*, Paris: OECD, pp. 33–38.

Smith, A. 1776 [1937] *An Inquiry into the Nature and Causes of the Wealth of Nations.* Edited by Cannan. New York: Modern Library.

Tregenna, F. 2003. 'Explaining and Evaluating the Botswana Growth Experience', Manuscript.

UBOS (Uganda Bureau of Statistics) 2005: *Uganda Poverty Mapping,* Government Printery: Kampala.

Uganda. 1988. *Background to the Budget, 1988/1999.* Kampala: Uganda.

Uganda. 2005. *Background to the Budget, 2005/2006.* Kampala: Uganda.

van Arkadie, B. 1990. 'The Role of Institutions in Development', in World Bank, *Proceedings of the World Bank Annual Conference on Development Economics, 1989.* Washington, DC. World Bank.

von Schmoller, G. 1896. *The Mercantilist System and Its Historical Significance.* New York: Macmillan.

Weber, M. 1968. *Economy and Society.* Edited by Guenter Roth and Claus Wittich. New York: Bedminster Press.

Weber, M. 1999. *Botswana: A Case Study of Economic Policy Prudence and Growth.* Oxford: Oxford University Press for the World Bank.

Weber, M. 2001. *World Development Report 2002: Building Institutions for Markets.* Oxford: Oxford University Press for the World Bank.

INDEX